JEAN COCTEAU and ANDRÉ GIDE

An Abrasive Friendship

"At Hyères, at the Noailleses', where I find Marc, together with Cocteau and Auric." (Gide's *Journal* entry for January 3, 1930.) Left to right: Jean Cocteau, André Gide, Vicomte Charles de Noailles, Vicomtesse Marie-Laure de Noailles, Georges Auric. Photo Marc Allégret.

JEAN COCTEAU
and ANDRÉ GIDE

An Abrasive Friendship

Arthur King Peters

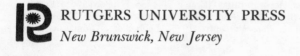

RUTGERS UNIVERSITY PRESS
New Brunswick, New Jersey

Library of Congress Cataloging in Publication Data

Peters, Arthur King, 1919–
  Jean Cocteau and André Gide: an abrasive friendship.

  "The entire known correspondence between the two men is contained in this book, in both French and English."
  Includes bibliographical references.
  1. Cocteau, Jean, 1889–1963. 2. Gide, André Paul Guillaume, 1869–1951. I. Cocteau, Jean, 1889–1963.
  II. Gide, André Paul Guillaume, 1869–1951.
  III. Title.
  PQ2605.015Z77   848'.9'1209 [B]   73–10002
  ISBN 0-8135-0709-X

Permission to reprint has been kindly granted by the following: George Braziller, Inc.: Claude Mauriac, *Conversations with André Gide* (1965). Cassell and Company, Ltd.: André Gide, *The Counterfeiters* (trans. Dorothy Bussy) (1950). Editions Gallimard: Jean Cocteau, *Maalesh* (1949), *Poésie critique* (1959, 1960). André Gide, *Correspondance André Gide et Roger Martin du Gard* (1968), *Les Faux-Monnayeurs* (1925), *Journal 1889–1939* (1948), *Journal 1939–1949* (1954), *Si le grain ne meurt* (1955). André Gide, ed., *Tableau de la littérature française* (1939). Jean Schlumberger, *Œuvres* (1958, 1959). Editions Bernard Grasset: Jean Cocteau, *Journal d'un inconnu* (1953), *Portraits-Souvenir* (1935). Claude Mauriac, *Une Amitié contrariée* (1970). Humanities Press: Jean Cocteau, *Maalesh* (1956). Alfred A. Knopf, Inc.: André Gide, *The Counterfeiters* (trans. Dorothy Bussy) (Copyright 1927, renewed 1955), *The Journals of André Gide* (trans. Justin O'Brien) (Copyright 1947–1951). Editions Albin Michel: Claude Mauriac, *Conversations avec André Gide* (1951). Adrienne Monnier, *Rue de l'Odéon* (1960). Peter Owen, Ltd.: Jean Cocteau, *Maalesh*. Librairie Plon: Jean Cocteau, *Le Cordon ombilical* (1962). *Correspondance Marcel Proust et Jacques Rivière 1914–1922* (1955). Random House: André Gide, *If it die* (trans. Dorothy Bussy) (Copyright 1935, renewed 1963). Editions Stock: Jean Cocteau, *Le Grand Ecart* (1923), *Lettre à Jacques Maritain* (1926), *Opium* (1930), *Le Potomak* (1924), *Le Rappel à l'ordre* (1926). Léon Pierre-Quint, *André Gide* (1952).

To My Wife
Sarah Jebb

Contents

Acknowledgments

Like the protagonist of ancient myth, an American scholar engaged for the first time in research outside his own country leaves his familiar world on a quest often marked by hazards, drudgery, and disappointments. With good fortune, however, he encounters along the way wise and benevolent strangers who guide him safely to his goal. As one who has made such a journey of initiation, I wish to thank the many people whose kind help made this book possible.

Without the enthusiasm and encouragement of the late Professor Justin O'Brien, the book would not have been undertaken; without the support of Professor Leon S. Roudiez, it might never have been completed.

The path between its start and finish is crowded with friendly creditors: Professor Auguste Anglès, Professor Frederick Brown, André Fraigneau, the late Professor Jean-Jacques Kihm, Professor Claude Martin, Francis Steegmuller, and Roger Stéphane, who freely discussed with me their own recent works concerning André Gide or Jean Cocteau; François Chapon, Conservateur Adjoint of the Bibliothèque Littéraire Jacques Doucet, whose skill and experience solved many manuscript mysteries, and his staff, Mlle Jasinski, Mme Prévot, and Mlle Zacchi, whose patience was unfailing through a long winter of Paris discontent before the riots of May 1968; the staffs of the Bibliothèque Nationale, the Columbia University Library, the Cinémathèque Française, the ORTF, and the Maison Culturelle d'Amiens; Jacques Naville of the Comité Gide, and Pierre Chanel, Conservateur of the Musée de Lunéville, who is now classifying the Archives Cocteau at Milly-la-Forêt.

Many friends of either Gide or Cocteau helped to situate the two great authors in the context of their times and to convey to me their spirit as individuals: the late François Mauriac, Nobel *lauréat*, Georges Auric, Mme Dominique Aury, Jean Dauven, the late Dominique Drouin, Pierre Georgel, Jean Marais, the late Jean Paulhan, and Monroe Wheeler.

A special debt is owed to those who so generously opened to me their homes, personal recollections, and collections of unpublished documents: Mme Philippe Gastambide, whose restoration of Cuverville has preserved Gide's former home as an architectural document of the first importance for students of Gide, M. and Mme François Corre, M. and Mme Marcel Jouhandeau, M. and Mme Georges Mévil-Blanche, Mme Jacques Rivière, and Mme Alec Weisweiller.

The invaluable contributions made to this study by Marc Allégret, Jean Denoël, and Claude Mauriac, each a friend of both André Gide and Jean Cocteau, deserve particular mention and appreciation.

Last, but far from least, I wish to thank Mme Catherine Gide and Edouard Dermit for their gracious permission to reproduce the Gide and Cocteau materials and to translate them into English. Their sympathy for the project, the access they generously granted to personal archives, and their warm hospitality made research a delight. It is hoped that this work may justify their confidence and express a small measure of my profound gratitude.

In the preparation of the final manuscript I wish to record my special gratitude to Mrs. Ursula Schneider Hazarian, whose hands, though invisible, were present at every stage of this work from beginning to end.

In presenting the letters between André Gide and Jean Cocteau an effort has been made to remain faithful to the text of the originals, which were often written rapidly, under stress, and dispatched uncorrected. This applies especially to Cocteau's letters, which retain a special flavor and spontaneity due in part to his unorthodox punctuation and paragraphing, occasional misspelling, endless postscripts, and marginal notes. Such irregularities have generally been clarified only where it seemed necessary. The stars and hearts that were usually part of his signature, and the cartoons that illustrated many of his letters, have been omitted from the printed texts; however, facsimiles of a few of the letters appear in the body of the book and in the Appendices. Letters between Cocteau and Gide that are not presented in the text, or only in part, will be found in the Appendices. Thus the entire known correspondence between the two men is contained in this book, in both French and English.

In view of the frequently elliptical and fragmented nature of the Cocteau-Gide correspondence, and mindful of the warning "Traduire, trahir!", a literary translation has been eschewed in favor of a more direct rendering. Except where otherwise indicated, the translations of French texts into English are my own.

A. K. P.

Foreword

Jean Cocteau felt that to be beautiful a work of art must have a moral end. André Gide believed that an act was not moral unless it was also beautiful. The two viewpoints, which suggest characteristic differences between the two authors in their approach to similar concerns, are a justification of Cocteau's statement about Gide: "Nos chiffres, si différents, arrivent à produire le même total."

Far apart in spirit and form as their work often appeared, these two major figures of the first half of the twentieth century had many qualities in common. As disturbers of the status quo, they agreed that art was an effective form of action, and were united on the side of individual man in his collisions with society. Both authors appealed to youth as their audience and actively sought recognition as *chefs de file*. By their audacious work and life style each provoked storms of controversy between partisan admirers and critics. Running counter to an age that favors specialization even in art. both worked with protean variety in a wide range of literary genres. They excelled, however, in different forms.

As men, Gide and Cocteau each encountered the problem of homosexuality and found a similar solution to that problem in their careers as artists. To both writers their art provided a catharsis, a return to innocence, and a discipline vital to the achievement of an inner equilibrium. The creative act delivered them from an imbalance which resisted the therapy of escape that each tried in various forms: travel, erotic encounters, flirtation with religious conversion, and, in Cocteau's case, opium.

The author of the *Journal* wished to overflow his era; the producer of *Le Sang d'un poète* constantly sought to precede his times. Each from his particular vantage point expressed differing aspects of his epoch. Gide's involvement with social problems and Cocteau's concern for beauty in all its forms contributed significantly to the part literature has played in shaping the ethical and esthetic transformations taking place about us.

To trace the history of the relationship between two such important innovators, who were sometimes friends and always rivals, is to establish the contours of an abrasive friendship whose breadth and depth have not previously been charted. In the process some of the mist that has gathered around Gide and Cocteau in recent years may be dispelled and their true outlines more clearly revealed.

Jean Cocteau and André Gide: *écrivains à part, hommes à part.* It is not surprising therefore that they shared an *amitié à part,* one whose salient feature was rivalry. Although not intimate friends (their correspondence always used the formal "vous"), they maintained contact for nearly forty years through a variety of personal and professional channels. The line of their friendship during that period followed the endless up and down pattern of a sine curve. This ambivalence, which ranged between attraction and repulsion, admiration and disapproval, envy and disdain on both sides, can be traced to Gide's twenty-year seniority over Cocteau, their competitive situation as artists, and their condition as homosexuals of a different order. There is good reason to believe that each author suffered from an inferiority complex about the other: that Gide regretted his own lack of the social ease, the light touch, the wit and imagination he recognized in Jean Cocteau, and that the latter envied Gide his power as a founder of the *NRF* empire and his prestige as an intellectual whose words carried impressive weight throughout the world.

The relationship between them was initiated and largely kept alive by Cocteau, a natural circumstance in view of their relative ages and standing as writers at the time they first met. It was Cocteau who wrote the first and last letters in their extensive correspondence, and his known letters to Gide are three times the number Gide addressed to him. Although this typical imbalance in their relationship is inevitably reflected in the present book, where Cocteau's side seems to outweigh that of Gide, this does not in fact diminish Gide's importance in the relationship.

André Gide's impact on the development of the younger poet was considerable, far more than Cocteau's influence on Gide, and it will be observed that at critical junctures in Cocteau's career, especially in the early years, Gide's intervention was a genuine force for change and growth. Like a stone caught up by the roots of a sapling and forever imbedded

in the heart of the mature tree, a residual presence of André Gide remains at the core of Jean Cocteau's work: his example.

The daring and the humanism in the work of both authors, as well as Cocteau's compulsion to bridge his differences with a lifetime rival who had been an early master, might well have prompted Cocteau to acknowledge the fundamental convergence of their points of view by paraphrasing Gide's famous statement: "Les extrêmes se touchent."

Arthur King Peters

Bronxville, New York
January 1973

JEAN COCTEAU
and ANDRÉ GIDE

An Abrasive Friendship

CHAPTER ONE

Beginnings

"Je naquis le 22 novembre 1869," André Gide writes in his autobiographical *Si le grain ne meurt,* a work whose urgent confessional aspect is quickly apparent.

Gide's first page takes the reader straight into the family apartment on the rue de Médicis in Paris, where, under a large table covered with a low hanging drapery, the child André and the concierge's son are at play. "L'un près de l'autre, mais non l'un avec l'autre pourtant, nous avions ce que j'ai su plus tard qu'on appelait 'de mauvaises habitudes.'"[1] ("One next to the other, but not one with the other, however, we engaged in what I later learned were called 'bad habits.'") As though anxious to paint his childhood character in the worst possible light, Gide continues with a catechism of self-incrimination. "À cet âge innocent où l'on voudrait que tout l'âme ne soit que transparence, tendresse et pureté, je ne revois en moi qu'ombre, laideur, sournoiserie."[2] ("At that innocent age when one would wish for all the soul to be only transparency, tenderness, and purity, I recall in myself only darkness, ugliness, and slyness.")

Gide's *Si le grain ne meurt* and other recollections of his beginnings in *Et nunc manet in te* or the *Journal,* and Cocteau's *Portraits-Souvenir* and *La Difficulté d'être,* provide many keys to understanding the two artists in their maturity. Yet in considering their testimony one must take into account that both authors had a propensity for personal mythmaking, for inventing, and for predetermining the reader's reactions. They present

only carefully selected scenes from their formative years, with a weather eye to the judgments of posterity. Despite the excellent psychobiography of André Gide by Jean Delay, much work remains to be done before scholars will know the truth, although perhaps never the whole truth, about Gide's crucial early years. The same holds true for Cocteau.[3] There can be no doubt, however, in spite of this caveat, that the paths of their childhoods took many of the same twists and turns over difficult terrain.

In Gide's case, beyond the mischievousness, the experimentation, and even the cruelty common to the behavior of most young boys, certain incidents in his childhood emerge in retrospect as clues to a disturbing temperament. Most are too familiar to students of Gide's work to need repetition here. Gide himself describes them in historical terms, and Jean Delay analyzes them in psychological terms as early signs of the instability, insecurity, and inadequacy to which Gide's later role as a social disturber can be traced.[4] The adult life of André Gide richly illustrates the maxim that the child is father to the man, and from the disturbing portrait Gide paints of himself as a child it is not surprising that in manhood he would affirm: "Inquiéter, tel est mon rôle." [5]

The early nervous instability and anxiety, the lack of physical stamina, the illness fancied and real, the fitful education, and perhaps most important of all the premature loss of his father, represent only a few of the critical factors of heredity and environment that Gide and Cocteau experienced in common. Many of the views Jean Delay expresses about the effect of such factors on Gide's development as man and artist would also be appropriate to the author of *Les Enfants terribles*.[6]

Gide's social and religious heritage was essentially bourgeois and Protestant. The family on the side of his mother, Juliette Rondeaux, had long been established in the Rouen area of Normandy, and his father, Paul Gide, came from the village of Uzès in Languedoc. Although André was born and brought up largely in Paris, his Protestant and provincial family origins were to become a barrier between him and the Catholic, Parisian Cocteau.

Paul Gide, a professor of law at the University of Paris, died when André was only eleven, and except for a photograph of his father Gide says he would have remembered him only by his great gentleness. Predictably, the widowed Juliette Gide

turned all attention to her only child. "Je me sentis soudain," wrote Gide, "tout enveloppé par cet amour, qui désormais se refermait sur moi." [7] ("I suddenly felt myself," wrote Gide, "all enveloped by that love, which from then on closed itself around me.") Gide's loss of his father, his envelopment by a strongly protective mother, and his subsequent exposure to the predominantly feminine influences that surrounded him at home, of mother, aunts, and girl cousins, prefigure a pattern that was to repeat itself with Jean Cocteau. If the homosexual tendency happens to preexist in a boy's character, this sport bud sometimes flowers in disjointed family environments of the kind that Gide and Cocteau faced as they entered the difficult stage of adolescence.

His father's death in 1880 marked the end of André Gide's "first childhood." It also perhaps marked the beginning of Gide's coming to terms with himself: an awareness of his differentness. Seated one day at table alone with his mother, the boy suddenly burst into tears, flung himself into her arms, and sobbed in desperation: "Je ne suis pas pareil aux autres! Je ne suis pas pareil aux autres!" [8]

André Gide's experiences at the Ecole Alsacienne, where he had been admitted when he was eight, had no doubt confirmed his inner feelings of insecurity and accelerated his recognition of his anomaly. He had not performed well as a student the first year, although he became a "fort en thème" a few years later (and so, unwittingly laid the foundation of an intellectual barrier between himself and Jean Cocteau, who never overcame his sensitivity at being the "cancre de la classe"). Gide had also been discharged for three months for his "mauvaises habitudes," in which his teacher easily surprised him since Gide, in his naïveté, made little effort to conceal his behavior.

Ce matin-là, sur mon banc, . . . je faisais alterner le plaisir avec mes pralines. Tout à coup, je m'entendis interpeller:
— Gide! Il me semble que vous êtes bien rouge? Venez donc me dire deux mots.
Le sang me monta au visage plus encore, tandis que je gravissais les quatres marches de la chaire, et que mes camarades ricanaient.
Je ne cherchai pas à nier. À la première question que M. Vedel me posa, à voix basse, penché vers moi, je fis de la tête un signe d'acquiescement: puis je regagnai mon banc plus mort que vif.[9]

(That particular morning, on my bench . . . I alternated pleasure with my pralines. All at once I heard myself being summoned:

"Gide! It seems to me you are quite red? Come here and have a word with me."

The blood rushed to my face even more, as I climbed the four steps to the rostrum, and as my comrades snickered.

I didn't try to deny it. At the first question M. Vedel put to me, in a low voice, leaning toward me, I nodded my head as a sign of acquiescence and returned to my seat more dead than alive.)

Those early school years were filled with terror for André at the hands of his classmates. He took long detours on the way home to avoid the enemies who lay in wait for him after class: "Certains jours je rentrais dans un état pitoyable, les vêtements déchirés, pleins de boue, saignant du nez, claquant des dents, hagard." [10] ("Certain days I came home in a pitiful state, my clothes torn, covered with mud, nose bleeding, teeth chattering, haggard.") As a schoolboy, Gide had his share of scrapes and beatings, of victories and defeats, but owing to his sensitivity they perhaps went deeper with him than with other boys. One in particular left an indelible impression. It involved Gomez, the class bully who corresponded in type to Cocteau's Dargelos. While other boys pinned Gide's arms, Gomez, in a classic act of boy's inhumanity to boy, took a dead cat from the gutter and scrubbed Gide's face with it.

When Gide was only nine years old he attended his first costume ball at the Gymnase Pascaud. The event is noteworthy in several respects: it shows even at this age Gide's penchant for role-playing, for camouflaging himself, and for trying on colorful personalities that were not altogether his own. This was the very trait for which he was strongly to criticize Jean Cocteau at the time of *Le Coq et l'Arlequin*. "L'idée de devoir me déguiser me mit la tête à l'envers," Gide records in *Si le grain ne meurt,* and he explains this delirium as "le plaisir plutôt d'être en couleur, d'être brillant, d'être baroque, de jouer à paraître qui l'on n'est pas..." ("The idea of having to disguise myself made my head whirl . . . the pleasure rather of being in color, of being brilliant, of being baroque, of playing at appearing to be a person one is not...") Gide's mother sent her son to the ball dressed as a pastry cook, all in white with a wooden spoon tucked in his belt, and feeling as insipid as a pocket handkerchief. At the ball, where he was dismayed

to find twenty other pastry chefs, Gide's eye fell on a boy with the costume Gide coveted and the manners to match.

Je tombai amoureux, oui, positivement amoureux, d'un garçonnet un peu plus âgé que moi, qui devait me laisser un souvenir ébloui de sa sveltesse, de sa grâce et de sa volubilité. Il était costumé en diablotin, ou en clown, c'est à dire qu'un maillot noir pailleté d'acier moulait exactement son corps gracile. Tandis qu'on se pressait pour le voir, lui sautait, cabriolait, faisait mille tours, comme ivre de succès et de joie; il avait l'air d'un sylphe; je ne pouvais déprendre de lui mes regards. J'eusse voulu attirer les siens, et tout à la fois je le craignais, à cause de mon accoutrement ridicule; je me sentais laid, misérable.[11]

(I fell in love, yes, positively in love, with a young boy a little older than I, who was to leave with me a dazzled memory of his slimness, his grace, and his volubility. He wore the costume of a little devil, or clown, that is to say, black tights spangled with steel sequins exactly molded his slender body. While everyone crowded to see him, he leaped, capered, did a thousand twirls, as though drunk with success and joy; he looked like a sylph; I couldn't take my eyes off him. I would like to have attracted his own, and at the same time I feared him because of my ridiculous getup; I felt ugly, miserable.)

The ambivalence of Gide's reactions is significant in this situation: his attraction to the *diablotin* and his concurrent fear of the glittering child. His decision to leave the ball shortly afterward, with death in his heart, may be seen as foreshadowing Gide's lifelong uneasiness in close proximity to people he felt cut a more brilliant figure than he. Gide's description of this infatuation, one that intensified his painful feelings of inadequacy, could almost have been written about his ambivalent attitude toward another charming young *diablotin*, Jean Cocteau, who whirled into Gide's life many years later arousing similar responses of alternating attraction and reticence, in whose volatile presence Gide confessed he felt heavy and morose. In the back of Gide's mind during his attack on Cocteau in the *Coq et l'Arlequin* episode of 1919 there may well have lingered a residual traumatic image of that capering, boyish harlequin in a sequined *maillot* at the Gymnase Pascaud.

School became so painful an experience for Gide that despite his basically sturdy constitution he developed a nervous tic which, aided by his imagination, assumed alarming proportions. What had begun as a slight dizzy spell during his convalescence from smallpox developed into a studied repertory

of twitches, spasms, and St. Vitus' dance-like gyrations that Gide displayed to suit his fancy. "Ces mouvements que je faisais, s'ils étaient conscients, n'étaient qu'à peu près volontaires. C'est-à-dire que, tout au plus, j'aurais pu les retenir un peu." [12] ("These movements I made, if they were conscious, were only somewhat voluntary. That is to say that, at the very most, I could have checked them a little bit.") A medical consultation, bath treatments at the mineral spas of Lamalou and Gérardmer, and perhaps the bored indifference with which his uncle viewed one of his most dramatic spasms, finally cured Gide of this problem. Once back in the Ecole Alsacienne, however, he developed migraine headaches, which bothered him until the age of twenty, and insomnia, which plagued him for the rest of his life.

Adolescence also brought with it the first pangs of love. Although he was reserved with boys during his childhood, Gide was very much at ease with girls. His cousin Madeleine Rondeaux inspired in him the ardent desire to perfect and discipline his tastes and thoughts in order to be more worthy of her. Madeleine's goodness gave a new and uplifting orientation to Gide's life even then, and her gentle regard for him seemed to Gide a mysterious portent of happiness to come. This portent was matched unexpectedly by another in 1884, when Gide was fifteen. On New Year's Day, as he walked home, a golden bird alighted on the young man's cap. Gide naturally enough took this to be a sign of divine favor and happily brought the canary home to show his mother. Astonishing as this event was, when it was repeated a few days later with a second canary Gide was more convinced than ever of his predestination, of a benevolent force at work in his life.

Ill health forced Gide to withdraw from the Ecole Alsacienne, and his education was carried on intermittently by tutors until 1887 when he was readmitted. As though stirred from a deep sleep, Gide's intellect was then awakened by his discovery of Greek literature. Surprisingly he found that his religious instruction, which was under way at the same period, did not seem to conflict with the pagan Greek influence. Gide read the Bible avidly in tandem with the *Iliad,* and rejoiced in the harmonious blend of religion and art. It was only much later, however, that the New Testament in his pocket was to be replaced by a thumb-worn copy of Virgil. Gide's religious fervor became, for the moment, a serious part of his daily regimen. He

slept on boards, roused himself in the night to kneel in prayer, arose at dawn to plunge into an icy bath, and interspersed his studies with prayers every hour. "Il me semblait alors atteindre à l'extrême sommet du bonheur." [13]

In his last year at the Ecole Alsacienne, stimulated by his friendship with Pierre Louÿs, Gide had already begun to write poetry, to keep a journal, and to be driven by the desire to write a book that would bring into focus all his inner questions, all his problems, and most of all his love for his cousin Madeleine. *Les Cahiers d'André Walter,* his first book, was already taking form. When it appeared in print, Gide was abashed to find that it did not win the heart of Madeleine as he had hoped.

He then entered on a confused phase of his life, with Schopenhauer as his primary philosophical influence, and Mallarmé, to whom he had been introduced by Louÿs, as his social and literary focal point. This disturbed period of Gide's life did not end until he went to North Africa with his friend Paul Laurens in 1893. In Tunis, chafing under the constraints of their bourgeois religious and moral precepts, the two young men vowed to abandon their virginity in favor of a more healthy fulfillment. Gide had already mentally divorced his sacred love for Madeleine from the profane sort he experienced with the young Ouled girl Meriem, and with the Arab boys Ali and Athman. In Africa he achieved a pagan resurrection which he felt was closer to Christian intentions than the religious dogma to which he had been trained. His puritan conscience had been assuaged by the intellectual dissociation of love and desire, of spirit and flesh. Gide discovered an important part of himself in North Africa: the violence of his pederasty and an ethic to suit it: "Ose devenir ce que tu es." He transmuted both into art and brought back with him to France some of the themes for *Les Nourritures terrestres,* which appeared two years later.

Gide's self-abandonment and self-discovery in Tunis closely preceded a second liberation of his conscience which came with his mother's death in 1895. All his life Gide had felt the pressure of her inflexible ethics: "Elle avait une façon de m'aimer qui parfois m'eût fait la haïr." [14] ("She had a way of loving me that sometimes made me hate her.") After Africa, her constraint had become unbearable, and it is not surprising to hear Gide's avowal that the moment her heart stopped

beating "je sentis s'abîmer tout mon être dans un gouffre d'amour, de détresse et *de liberté*."[15] ("I felt all my being swallowed up in an abyss of love, of distress, and of *freedom*.")

It was shortly after Mme Gide's death that Madeleine, who had earlier refused him, agreed to become André Gide's wife, and they were married in October 1895 at Cuverville. Gide's *mariage blanc*, his platonic attitude toward Madeleine, who in a sense succeeded his mother, may have reflected in part the sexual taboos associated with the mother image, and also the innate fear of the homosexual for *la femme castratrice*. It is difficult to know which of the two forces, Madeleine's extraordinary influence, or his anomaly, exercised the greater effect on his art. Gide later told his friend Jean Schlumberger: "Ce qu'on ne comprendra jamais assez, c'est à quel point Madeleine est au centre, à quel point elle est l'explication de tout ce que j'ai écrit. . . ."[16] ("What people will never understand clearly enough is how much Madeleine is at the center, how much she is the explanation for all I have written. . . .")

With his marriage, the mold of Gide's life was now basically formed: he had learned who he was and where he was going. His fundamental moral, religious, esthetic, and social doctrines were already in bud and to blossom awaited only external developments in his life. The fatal opening moves of the game, from which all subsequent plays must follow, had now been made; and Gide's life began to gather momentum with the inevitability of Greek tragedy.

His literary career unfolded with a series of important critical essays, journals, and plays which identified Gide as a force to be reckoned with even if they did not immediately win a broad public and critical following. In 1908, with a group of friends, he founded the *Nouvelle Revue Française*, which, with its publishing and theatrical adjuncts, became the center of French critical and literary power in the twentieth century. This mantle of authority André Gide feigned to wear as loosely as his famous cape. It nevertheless dazzled and attracted the young writers reared on *Les Nourritures terrestres* who, along with François Mauriac and Roger Martin du Gard, entered the literary arena just after the turn of the century. Eager for a place in the vanguard of this second generation was the young poet Jean Cocteau.

"Je suis né le 5 juillet 1889, place Sully, à Maisons-Laffitte (Seine-et-Oise)," Cocteau wrote in his collection of auto-

biographical essays *La Difficulté d'être*.[17] Clément Eugène Jean Maurice Cocteau, according to his grandmother Lecomte, "poussait un joli cri, d'une voix sonore et forte" in the small hours of the morning.[18] He was born just outside Paris in the summer home of his mother's parents.

Before the turn of the century Maisons-Laffitte was a charming suburb of gardens and well-tended lawns surrounding the villas of the wealthy Parisian families who vacationed there. The pursuits of idleness and prosperity gave it the atmosphere of gaiety and leisure from which the Belle Epoque drew its name. Elegant ladies strolled in the parks airing their pet rabbits on the leash. Max Lebaudy, the sugar king, had his gleaming carriages washed down in champagne. And on weekends the Place Sully became an Impressionist painting filled with light and color as the *gratin* of Paris came to see and be seen at the races.

Jean Cocteau's maternal grandfather, Eugène Lecomte, was a wealthy Catholic stockbroker whose family, like André Gide's, belonged to the bourgeoisie of the Second Empire. The Cocteau family shared his town house in Paris in winter. It was there, at 45 rue La Bruyère, that Jean Cocteau, with his parents Georges and Eugénie Cocteau, and his brother and sister, spent most of his childhood. His brother Paul, eight years older than he, and his sister Marthe, twelve years older, were too far ahead of Jean in years to be close companions. It was Marianne Lecomte, a girl cousin two years his senior, who was young Jean's confidante and playmate for many years both in Paris and at Maisons-Laffitte. With her, Cocteau would explore the "potager des découvertes" at his Uncle André's house across the Place Sully, or go off into the leafy seclusion of the Saint-Germain forest to smoke pipes carved from horse chestnuts. Cocteau's early initiation into some of the mysteries of adult life came about through Marianne. One day, hidden in the old carriage that took the family to church, she confided to him:

> Ecoute, je sais tout. Il y a des grandes personnes qui se couchent en plein jour. On les appelle, les hommes: des lapins, les femmes: des cocottes. Oncle André est un lapin. Si tu le répètes je te tuerai à coups de bêche.[19]

> (Listen, I know everything. There are grownups who go to bed in broad daylight. The men are called rabbits, the women chickens. Uncle André is a rabbit. If you repeat a word I'll beat you to death with a spade.)

"Mon enfance a été celle de tous les enfants," Cocteau recalled toward the end of his life.[20] But there were traumatic differences. Jean Cocteau was not quite nine years old when his father, Georges Cocteau, a man of gentle disposition and a lawyer, committed suicide, "dans des circonstances qui feraient que personne ne se suiciderait plus maintenant"[21] ("under circumstances that would not drive anyone to suicide these days"). In his journal of a disintoxication, *Opium*, Cocteau affirms that several times a week for thirteen years he dreamed that his father had changed into a parrot at the Pré-Catalan. "Je savais que ma mère savait et ne savait pas que je savais, et je devinais qu'elle cherchait lequel de ces oiseaux mon père était devenu, et pourquoi il l'était devenu. Je me réveillais en larmes à cause de sa figure qui essayait de sourire."[22] ("I knew that my mother knew, and didn't know that I knew, and I guessed that she was trying to find out which of these birds my father had become, and why he had become that one. I awoke in tears because of her face, which was trying to smile.") The dream stopped, Cocteau says, in 1912. This apparently was the year he met André Gide.

The three dominant personalities in Jean Cocteau's life during those tender years were feminine: a loving and protective mother whom the boy adored, his cousin Marianne Lecomte, and his German nurse Fräulein Joséphine Ebel ("Jéphine," as Cocteau called her). It was in their company that Jean first crossed the thresholds of those twin magic worlds which came to be so important to him: the circus and the theater.

The Nouveau-Cirque in the Faubourg Saint-Honoré, with all its odors, sights, and sounds, the acrobats, and the clowns Footit and Chocolat, was to be a seedbed for many motifs in Cocteau's later works, such as *David* and *Parade*. His adult interest in the transvestite trapeze artist Barbette and the Negro boxing champion Al Brown can be traced to those childhood delights.

The crimson and gold of the theater, the lights and crowds, "Premiers spectacles! Premiers vertiges!"[23] dazzled Jean Cocteau at the age of six when, led to his Thursday seat in the Châtelet theater by an attendant with a pink bow and a gray mustache, he first saw *Le Tour du monde* and *La Biche au bois*.[24] Even then, his alert eye noticed that the painted canvas curtain did not quite touch the boards, and that in the slit of light one caught a glimpse of another world glowing with feverish ac-

tivity.[25] As small boys, he and his friend René Rocher tirelessly painted empty cartons from the Old England department store, fashioning model theaters in the courtyard of the Lecomte home.[26] Part of Cocteau's genius in his mature stage and film works lay in his ability to transmit something of the charming naïveté with which, as a child, he confronted the make-believe world of the theater. It was this purity of vision that enabled Cocteau to see the theater not only as a metaphor of the real world, but in a way as more real than the real world.

"J'étais d'une famille éprise de musique, de peinture et où les lettres jouaient peu ou mal" ("I came from a family captivated by music, by painting, in which letters counted for little or nothing"), Cocteau wrote later in life,[27] calling to mind his grandfather Lecomte's collection of paintings, the old gentleman's Stradivarius in its velvet case, and the Wagner concerts they attended together at the Conservatory. Although the emphasis on painting and music in his environment stimulated Cocteau's eye and ear from an early age, it diminished the importance of reading, and this lack soon showed in his school performance. In 1900 he entered the sixth form at the Petit Condorcet school in Paris, where the reports of his teachers testified to his intelligence, short attention span, restlessness, and unevenness as a student. Although he succeeded in winning prizes in German, drawing, and gymnastics, Cocteau always considered himself the class dunce. The cruelty and crudity of his peers' behavior at school had a harsh effect on Cocteau, as they had had on Gide. He never forgot the torture of being first bound and then tossed in the air by the older boys and caught in a baggage net.[28] Cocteau was both shocked and fascinated by the open sexuality of his schoolmates. His description of art class (*Le Livre blanc*) reproduces a scene almost identical with that described by Gide in *Si le grain ne meurt,* both involving a classroom humiliation.

It was not the Petit Condorcet that left the deepest imprint on Cocteau's formation from eleven to fifteen, but a classmate, "l'élève Dargelos," and the Cité Monthiers, an enclosed court through which Jean passed on his way to school. The Cité Monthiers became the set and Dargelos the principal actor in the snowball fight Cocteau later described in *Les Enfants terribles* and *Le Sang d'un poète.* Dargelos, whose name recurs throughout Cocteau's later works, embodies a number of motifs and themes which distinguish Cocteau's art: the snow-

ball, the marble fist, the Orphic profile, "angélisme," "la conjugaison des forces viriles," and "le sexe surnaturel de la beauté." Dargelos may properly be viewed as a precursor to Raymond Radiguet, Jean Desbordes, Marcel Khill, Jean Marais, and other young men to whom Cocteau was attracted.[29]

By 1904 young Cocteau had entered the Lycée Condorcet. Since visiting the Palais de Glace and the Looping the Loop with his friends often proved more appealing than his classes, at Easter time he was urged to drop out of school. There followed a brief stay at the École Fénelon before his distraught family sent him to tutor at Val André in Brittany. This pension was conducted by Hermann Dietz, who had been André Gide's teacher many years before at the Ecole Alsacienne, and who inspired the character of M. Berlin in Cocteau's *Le Grand Ecart* of 1922. Both Gide and Cocteau remembered Dietz with affection. Gide, in *Si le grain ne meurt*, wrote: "Dietz était devant sa classe comme un organiste devant un clavier; ce maestro tirait de nous à son gré, les sons les plus inattendus, les moins espérés par nous-mêmes. Parfois on eût dit qu'il s'en divertissait un peu trop, comme il advient aux virtuoses. Mais que ses cours étaient amusants! J'en sortai surnourri, gonflé. Et combien j'aimais sa voix chaude! et cette affectation d'indolence qui le couchait à demi dans le fauteuil de sa chaire, de travers, une jambe passée sur un bras du fauteuil, le genou à la hauteur du nez..."[30] ("Dietz before his class was like an organist before the keyboard; this maestro drew from us at his pleasure sounds that were the most unexpected, the least hoped for by ourselves. Sometimes it might be said that he diverted himself a little too much, as happens with virtuosi. But how amusing his courses were! I came away overfed, swollen. And how I loved his warm voice! And that affectation of indolence which had him half lying down in the chair of his rostrum, askew, one leg over the arm of the chair, the knee at nose level...")

Jean Cocteau also describes Dietz in his *Portraits-Souvenir*. "Je décrirais mal après André Gide, ce maître qui nous étonnait par le contraste de son protestantisme et de ses poses d'odalisque. Il s'étalait, se coulait, se nouait, se dénouait, envoyait un bras de-ci, une jambe de-là, nous observant pardessus des binocles, secoué de rires ironiques."[31] ("After André Gide, I would be poor at describing this master, who astonished us by the contrast between his Protestantism and his odalisque-like poses. He sprawled, slipped, knotted himself up, un-

knotted, sent an arm from here, a leg from there, watching us over his pince-nez, shaken by ironic laughter.")

Furious at having to study in the summer, and fearful of the imagined restrictions of Val André, Cocteau ran off to Marseilles. Here he took the name Jean Bourgoin and lived in the Old City, into which even the police were reluctant to venture.[32] It was probably in Marseilles that Cocteau first tried opium, an experiment that became a lifelong habit, if an intermittent one. The escapade lasted only a month or two, but it went deep with Cocteau: "Ah! ça m'a affranchi," he proclaimed even sixty years afterward; and he later drew on his Marseilles adventures in such works as *Le Fantôme de Marseille*.

Cocteau's studies with M. and Mme Dietz at Val André and in Paris from 1906 to 1907 proved to be far more inspiring than he anticipated,[33] but they were not enough to assure his passing the *baccalauréat* examinations. After he had made three fruitless attempts, Cocteau's formal education came to an end in 1907.

The summer of that year was an emotional as well as an educational turning point in Cocteau's life. At a moment when a father would have filled a great need, Cocteau encountered "un sphinx à la porte qui passe de l'enfance à l'adolescence."[34] At eighteen, the fatherless Jean Cocteau was still torn by inner struggles, as two letters to his mother at that time reveal:

Je me raidis sans cesse contre ma chienne de nature que j'ai pourtant dompté sur bien des points mais qui se révolte encore parfois. Dans quelques jours je pense avoir sur elle une victoire définitive et j'ai honte de me sentir brute devant l'exquise paternité de notre cher "Patron."[35]

(I stiffen myself constantly against my bitch of a nature, which I have dominated in many respects but which still rebels sometimes. In a few days I expect to win a definitive victory over it, and I am ashamed to feel myself brutish before the exquisite paternity of our dear "Master.")

The second letter elaborates on the theme of the first, and hints at the maturing homosexual instincts of which Cocteau had already become aware years before in his infatuation with Dargelos:

Tu vois que je me mets en garde contre les tentations de mon caractère que vous direz faible — et que je dis aimant — Tu ne peux pas t'imaginer ce que la vie me serait sans affections —[36]

(You see that I am putting myself on guard against the temptations of my character which you will call weak—and which I call loving— You can't imagine what life would be like to me without attachments—)

In *Le Livre blanc* Cocteau also describes several childhood episodes which he later identified as homosexual in nature: his fainting at the sight of a naked farm boy on a horse; his fascination with three naked gypsy boys in a tree; his erotic experiments with Gustave, a young servant.[37]

Jean Cocteau's psychophysical development through adolescence was characterized in part by a highstrung, difficult temperament on one hand, and an agile but frail physique on the other. Like many young children intent on having their way or attracting attention, he was not above threatening his mother with tantrums or even convulsions as occasion demanded. One of his childhood games was "la petite mort," a punishment that Cocteau invited by deliberately bad behavior, and which consisted of his being hauled upstairs enclosed in a sack slung over the shoulder of his grandfather's manservant. As an adult, Cocteau continued to experience the titillating anxiety and apprehension he associated with his childish "crise de petite mort," but in maturity they followed disappointing love affairs. "Je traverse une autre crise de 'petite mort.' Ces phénomènes de nymphes fatiguent et rendent triste," he wrote to Gide from Rome in 1917.[38] ("I am going through another crisis of 'little death.' These nymph phenomena are tiring and sadden one.")

Even before he had left the classes of M. Dietz, Cocteau's life had taken a worldly turn through various encounters with women. His contact with commercial love in the bordellos of the rue de Provence revolted him, and other affairs were unsatisfactory. He was, however, both attractive to women and attracted by them in varying degrees, and this bisexual orientation continued throughout his life. His relationship with the actor Edouard de Max in 1908 and his affair in 1909 with Madeleine Carlier define the sexual polarity that was to be Cocteau's norm from then on.

De Max's presentation of Cocteau's poetry at the Théâtre Femina in 1908 opened the doors of the Parisian salons to Jean Cocteau. In the next few years, giddy with the acclaim of his precocious success, he fell under one influence after an-

other: Edmond Rostand, Catulle Mendès, Anna de Noailles, and Serge Diaghilev. His professional career at first benefited by this *mondain* popularity since it focused attention on his work. In quick succession he published two volumes of poetry, *La Lampe d'Aladin* (1908) and *Le Prince frivole* (1910). In between he founded *Schéhérazade*, an elegant journal consecrated to poetry. In 1911 he was commissioned by Diaghilev to draw posters for *Spectre de la rose;* and that same year Cocteau and his friend Reynaldo Hahn collaborated on a ballet called *Le Dieu bleu*, which was presented by the Ballets Russes on May 13, 1912. Cocteau returned from a journey to Algeria with Lucien Daudet just in time for the première. It was on this trip to North Africa, where he followed closely in Gide's footsteps, that Cocteau buried himself in Gide's writing. On his return to France he at once wrote Gide, on April 20, 1912. The evidence indicates it was later that summer that the budding poet and the established author, old enough to be his father, met for the first time.

Even across a generation gap of twenty years and despite differences in regional and religious origins, the fatherless Cocteau was drawn to the childless André Gide. There were, however, parallels in their social and educational background; and the dedication of both men to literature promised to be a powerful bond between them. The anomaly common to the two men promised to be another. Yet Cocteau was to find almost at once that it was the differences between them that seemed to attract the two men, whereas their similarities pushed them apart.[39] He had embarked with Gide on an abrasive friendship that would not run its course until Gide's death nearly forty years later.

"La Danse de Sophocle"

Georges Mévil-Blanche, nephew of the painter Jacques-Emile Blanche, remembers as a small boy the regular summer visits Jean Cocteau made to the Blanche home at Offranville in the years just before the outbreak of World War I. Mme Blanche and Cocteau's mother were friends, and Jean Cocteau often spent a few weeks of July or August with the Blanche family in Normandy. There Cocteau and Princess Marie Murat, a friend of Blanche's and a contemporary of Gide's, would go off together to the La Caille market in Dieppe to buy colorful fishermen's clothes. Once Cocteau bought a new jacket and immediately traded it to a fisherman for an old and "authentic" one. At the market they also bought bags of *pétards,* the little grenades bicyclists threw to discourage dogs that pursued them.

Cocteau's letters to Jacques-Emile Blanche at this period of his life indicate that some of his most carefree days were spent at Offranville. Here on long summer evenings Cocteau used to amuse and alarm the children in the Blanche household with his sketches of Mme Mühlfeld, widow of the literary critic Lucien Mühlfeld, Blanche himself, and the early Eugènes cartoons that were to become familiar in *Le Potomak.* Blanche partially filled the void left by Cocteau's father; and, no doubt at the prompting of the anxious Mme Cocteau, he gave paternal counsel to the young man, for years receiving his confidences in return.[1]

In July of 1912 Jean Cocteau had just celebrated his twenty-

third birthday. He and Lucien Daudet had recently returned from their extended trip to Algiers which had paralleled that of Gide and Henri Ghéon. August found him enjoying the leisurely delights of a Norman summer at the Blanches'. A full-length portrait of the young poet standing in the garden was painted by Blanche at the time, and the slender silhouette and angular features that Cocteau was to retain all his life are clearly defined.[2] In this ambiguous painting, however, the profile is dominated by the sharp fox-like nose which projects far out over a petulant down-sloping mouth. The delicate chin line angles back and up to an ear which barely escapes the pointed contour of a faun's. Yet three of Jean Cocteau's most striking features are suppressed in Blanche's portrait. The wiry hair that displeased Cocteau (as did his overlapping teeth) is concealed beneath a soft hat whose brim shades the upper face. The extraordinary large eyes are closed to near slits against the sun's glare. And the articulate, bony fingers, which seem to extend straight from the wrist, are muffled beneath Cocteau's sleeves. Curiously limp, the arms hang straight and close to the body, and the right hand idly holds a thin stick. The chrysalis of a loose-fitting jacket, slacks, and pointed shoes completes a portrait remarkable, not for having stopped a dashing young poet in midflight, but for seeming to depict a young man at odds with himself, paralyzed by boredom, wondering what to do next, whose spirit is already restlessly exploring beyond the quiet confines of this Norman garden. The portrait projects an image of the young Cocteau much like that of the self-portrait Cocteau was to offer later in *Le Grand Ecart* under the guise of Jacques Forestier:

N'ayant pas l'apparence qu'il eut souhaitée, ne répondant pas au type idéal qu'il se formait d'un jeune homme, Jacques n'essayait plus de rejoindre ce type dont il se trouvait trop loin. Il enrichissait faiblesses, tics et ridicules jusqu'à les sortir de la gêne. Il les portait, volontiers, au premier plan.

À cultiver une terre ingrate, à forcer, à embellir de mauvaises herbes, il avait pris quelque chose de dur qui ne s'accordait guère avec sa douceur.

Ainsi, de mince qu'il était, s'était-il fait maigre; de nerveux, écorché vif. Coiffant difficilement une chevelure . . . plantée en tous sens, il la portait hirsute.[3]

(Not having the appearance he would have wished, not corresponding to the notion he himself had formed of the ideal type of young

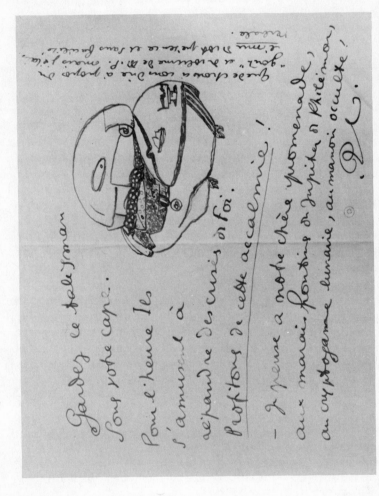

Gardez ce taliman
Sous votre cape.
Pour l'heure les
s'amuse à
répandre des cris à foi.
Profitons de cette accalmie!

— Je pense à notre chère promenade
aux marais. Pontins et Jupiter et Philémon,
au cryptogame lunaire, au manoir occulte,

J. C.

Quelle chose sombre à penser,
"gris" à la lueur de M. P. amour, je le
tiens j'irai je te le et sans fautes!
veale.

Note from Cocteau to Gide with an Eugène of the Mortimer-Ménard type, Cocteau's image of the pompous, overfed, complacent bourgeois in *Le Potomak*. Written in November 1913(?).

man, Jacques no longer tried to conform to this type from which he
found himself too far removed. He enriched weaknesses, tics, and
little absurdities to a point just this side of embarrassment. He
brought them, purposely, into the foreground.

Through cultivating an uncompromising soil, through forcing, im-
proving the looks of the weeds, he had taken on a hardness that did
not go well with his gentleness.

So, from being slender he made himself skinny; from highstrung
to flayed to the quick. Grooming with difficulty a head of hair . . .
that grew every which way, he wore it shaggy.)

In Blanche's portrait of Jean Cocteau at twenty-three there
are of course no signs as yet of the marks life would later leave
on him. There is only a suggestion of the slightly drooping
right shoulder, caused by a mild spinal curvature, which
Cocteau usually tried to conceal by placing his hand on his
right hip, by standing in a doorway with his right arm up-
raised, or by leaning on some object in order to lift the shoulder
line. Opium, although he had smoked it off and on since his
boyhood escapade in Marseilles in 1906, had not yet given his
eyes the bulging, fishy cast that Cecil Beaton would comment
on later. Nor was the light gray ring around the irises of both
eyes to appear until after his typhoid attack in 1931. Cocteau's
features were still smooth and boyish, without the wrinkles of
age that repeated plastic surgery toward the end of his life
could not obliterate.

Blanche's portrait could not, of course, convey the remarkable voice that Cocteau possessed even then. High but
pleasantly pitched, it had a dry metallic ring and a range well
suited to a theatrical personality. Cocteau was already a clever
mimic and frequently amused Blanche's household by his imitations of the speech and gestures of Gide and Charles du Bos
arguing with each other.[4] His own speech was rapid, graphic,
and filled with the laughter he enjoyed provoking in others.

This, then, was the aspect of the young Jean Cocteau whom
Gide met, probably for the first time, at Offranville in the
summer of 1912. André Gide was approaching his forty-
third birthday. Already an established author, Gide had to his
credit an impressive list of more than thirty published titles
in many genres. He was also the power to be reckoned with in
the influential *NRF*. Twenty years Cocteau's senior, Gide
looked even older because of the early baldness that emphasized the handsomely modeled arc of cranium and forehead.

His brown eyes were set close up under the heavy brows that divided upper and lower face. Wide-set cheek bones and a square jaw and chin were echoed in the blunt peasant hands. Gide's expression in repose was mask-like, even wooden, but in conversation it became animated and intense. Although the deep vertical seams that creased his cheeks in later years had not yet appeared, he already had the faintly Mongolian, monkish cast to his features that grew more pronounced with age. Cocteau teasingly called it a "tête d'éléphant ironique-apostolique,"[5] but he also spoke of Gide's "visage secret, noble et *pur*."[6]

When Gide spoke his carefully chosen words, it was often through clenched teeth with the syllables separated and stretched out for emphasis and nuance. Cocteau, for whom the voice told much about the person, later described Gide's manner and speech in these terms:

Il était gai, vif, rapide, et s'amusait d'une foule de petites choses qui nourrissent les dialogues. Il adorait le verbe. Il prononçait les mots avec manie, ciselant consonnes et voyelles. Il semblait les tirer de très loin.[7]

(He was gay, keen, quick, and amused himself with a swarm of little things that nourish dialogues. He adored speech. He was finicky in his pronunciation of words, chiseling consonants and vowels. He seemed to draw them out from far away.)

Cocteau commented further on the musical, sinuous quality of Gide's voice in his posthumous *hommage* to his "vieux maître."

[La voix] de Gide montait, descendait, glissait, s'amincissait, s'enflait, musicale et tortueuse. Il savait y mettre en relief quelque terme, sur lequel, comme un peintre, il appuyait la touche blanche de l'éclairage, le point que les portraitistes chinois font payer si cher, lorsqu'ils le placent, le dernier jour de pose, dans l'œil du modèle.

Parfois, il semblait que les mots fussent halés par lui des profondeurs d'une citerne.[8]

(Gide's [voice] rose, fell, glided, thinned out, swelled, musical and tortuous. He knew how to point up an expression, to which, like a painter, he applied the highlight, the spot the Chinese portraitists charge so much for when they place it, the last day of the pose, in the model's eye.

Sometimes it seemed that he hauled the words up from the depths of a cistern.)

Gide at forty-three did not affect the dandified style of dress then popular with young men of Cocteau's age (although collar, tie, and jacket were de rigueur for him even when he played tennis with his friend Jacques Copeau). Instead he favored loose-fitting suits and his famous cape and slouch hat, about which his friend Jacques-Emile Blanche used to comment sarcastically to Cocteau. Such was the general appearance of André Gide when Jean Cocteau first met him.

Among the evidence for placing their first meeting in the summer of 1912 is a letter to Jacques-Emile Blanche from Cocteau which can be dated in July of 1912. This letter refers to an invitation Cocteau received from Blanche for the tenth of either July or August, and to a forthcoming meeting with Gide:

Cher Monsieur et grand ami

Je pense que tout s'organiserait fort bien pour le 10 par ex. ou n'importe quelle date commode dans ces parages — après une correspondance émue, un regret de n'avoir pas mon livre et une "joie" de l'avoir — Gide garde un silence qui me fait craindre sa rencontre. Quel dommage — Je le devine hélas balançant entre Ghéon et Schlumberger une molle tête d'éléphant ironique-apostolique. La Princesse Marie saute vers le Caucase rebondit chez les Croissets avec une étonnante robe boîte à feu assez pratique du reste pour les loisirs du voyage — Respects et affections

Jean C.[9]

(Dear Sir and great friend,

I think everything would work out very well for the 10th, for example, or any convenient date thereabouts— After a moving correspondence, a regret at not having my book, and a "joy" at having it—Gide is keeping a silence which makes me fear meeting him. What a shame—I can visualize him, alas, wavering between Ghéon and Schlumberger, a languid elephant's head, ironic-apostolic. Princess Marie hops toward the Caucasus, bounds back to the Croissets with a stunning "boîte à feu" gown, practical enough at any rate for the leisures of travel— Respects and affection,

Jean C.)

This important letter fills in certain gaps in the early correspondence between Gide and Cocteau.

The first letter on record between the two authors was dated April 20, 1912, from Cocteau to Gide. This was a typically flowery letter from an ambitious young poet to an older writer whom he admired, and, fitting form to content, Cocteau wrote it in the ornate script he had learned from Anna de Noailles's example.

10, Rue d' Anjou
20 Avril 1912

Monsieur:
Vous allez lire une lettre bien émue. J'arrive d'Alger si laide et si captivante où j'avais emporté votre œuvre entière. (J'excepte André Walter, difficile à cause des possesseurs prudents et "Amyntas" que mon libraire me procure au retour comme un baume à la molle plaie orientale.)

L'enthousiasme est, il me semble, une des plus hautes formes de l'orgueil. Plus il est fort, plus il prouve le prix instinctif que nous attachons à notre jugement. De là ma gêne. Car il m'est encore impossible (bientôt peut-être) d'alléguer cet orgueil sans lequel mon élan n'aurait la valeur que d'un élan anonyme. C'est donc, en quelque sorte, une lettre "à lire plus tard" que me dicte ce double voyage de bateaux et de volumes.

Une enfance hâtive et fiévreuse, la rencontre de guides néfastes, en somme un terrible détour avec une manière de gêne causée par la bonne impulsion atavique, voilà ce qui me pousse tout à coup en face de votre visage secret, noble et *pur*. Vous rencontrez un Nathaniel [*sic*] qui se trouve être "enfant prodigue de naissance," mais votre lampe si elle éclaire les marches d'un perron et la grille d'une route est un tendre signal *d'appel*. Je vous offre une reconnaissance profonde. Vous m'avez appris comment il fallait se répandre sans être épars. N'est ce pas le Sésame du trésor?

Jean Cocteau [10]

10 rue d'Anjou
April 20, 1912

(Dear Sir,
   You are going to read a highly emotional letter. I have just arrived from Algiers, that ugly and captivating city, to which I had taken your complete works. (Except for *André Walter*, difficult to borrow because of its prudent owners, and *Amyntas*, which my book dealer has just procured for me on my return to serve as a balm for the soft Oriental wound.)

Enthusiasm, it seems to me, is one of the highest forms of pride. The stronger it is, the more it proves what instinctive price we set on our judgment. Hence my embarrassment. For I still find it impossible (soon perhaps) to admit this vanity without which my enthusiasm

would only have the value of an anonymous judgment. This is then, to some extent, a letter "to be read later" which has been dictated to me by this double journey of ships and books.

A hasty and feverish childhood, an encounter with baneful guides, in sum a terrible detour, with a kind of uneasiness due to a good atavistic impulse, this is what thrusts me suddenly before your inscrutable, noble, and *pure* face. You meet in me a Nathaniel who happens to be "a born prodigal son," but if your lamp lights a flight of steps or a fence along the road, it is also a gentle, *beckoning* signal. I offer you a deep gratitude. You have taught me how to expand without spreading myself thin. Isn't that the "Open Sesame" to the treasure?

Jean Cocteau)

There is no record that Gide replied to this letter. Cocteau followed up shortly afterward by sending Gide a copy of his latest book of poems, *La Danse de Sophocle*. Having apparently received no acknowledgment from Gide, Cocteau investigated what had gone wrong and sent the following telegram to Gide:

Maisons-Laffitte
4 Juillet 1912

Stupide histoire service mercure prouve livres égarés. Avez vous la Danse de Sophocle — tiens à vous plus que tous. Cœur ému.

Jean Cocteau [11]

Maisons-Laffitte
July 4, 1912

(What a nuisance. Messenger service no good. Books lost. Have you got *La Danse de Sophocle?* More fond of you than anyone. Tender heart.

Jean Cocteau)

Cocteau's letter of July 1912 to Blanche indicates that Gide subsequently advised Cocteau his book had not been received and that he would be glad to have a copy. Cocteau evidently then dispatched a second copy of the volume to Gide. After waiting anxiously for a favorable comment, Cocteau wrote Gide:

Samedi

Vous détestez donc ce livre jusqu'au silence? Cependant un blâme lumineux remplace bien une louange et la franchise de ceux qu'on admire dissipe des malaises intolérables.

Votre
Jean Cocteau [12]

Saturday
(Do you hate the book so much that you remain silent? Yet, enlightened criticism easily takes the place of praise, and the candor of those we admire dispels intolerable anxiety.

Your
Jean Cocteau)

This time Gide replied to Cocteau by a letter dated August 6, 1912, of which only part remains available:

Cher jeune et amical Cocteau
Si je les avais trouvés mauvais vos vers (Danse de Sophocle) vous le sauriez déjà et je vous aurais mal pardonné la grosse déception qu'ils m'auraient causée. . . .
. . . Vous êtes prodigieusement, périlleusement bien doué. De toute ma morosité je souris à votre jeunesse. Quel jugement saurai-je porter sur vos poèmes? Et comment critiquer la danse lorsque le danseur est charmant. . . .[13]

(Dear young and friendly Cocteau,
If I had found them bad, your verses (*Danse de Sophocle*), you would already know it, and I would have hardly forgiven you for the heavy disappointment they would have been to me. . . .
. . . You are prodigiously, perilously gifted. With all my moroseness I smile at your youthfulness. What judgment am I able to make of your poems? And how can one criticize the dance when the dancer is charming. . . .)

Since this fragment contains no specific criticism of *La Danse de Sophocle*, Gide's reply appears complimentary in tone. The reason behind this polite evasiveness may have been that he had not yet read Cocteau's poems. Gide's private library does contain two copies of *La Danse de Sophocle*, very likely the first and second copies sent him by Cocteau, both of which are inscribed to Gide in Cocteau's handwriting. Both copies, however, remain uncut.
One copy carries this inscription on the flyleaf:

"Si, si, là bas où je t'aurais rejoint, tu m'aurais reconnu pour ton frère; même il me semble encore que c'est pour te retrouver que je pars —."
À André Gide

Jean Cocteau.[14]

("Yes, yes, out there where I would have rejoined you, you would have recognized me for your brother; it even seems to me, moreover, that it is to meet you that I leave—"
To André Gide

Jean Cocteau)

The second copy of *La Danse de Sophocle* in Gide's library bears this inscription written broadside by Cocteau on the title page:

Συγχὶωμαλ!———
Συμπασχω!———
— Jean Cocteau à André Gide et à la mémoire d'André Walter ——
1912.[15]

(I make use of along with!
I feel sympathy with!
—Jean Cocteau to André Gide and to the memory of André Walter——1912.)

Three elements stand out in the fragment of Gide's letter of August 6, 1912: "Vous êtes prodigieusement, périlleusement bien doué," "je souris à votre jeunesse," and "le danseur est charmant." These same elements were to appear again in Henri Ghéon's review of Cocteau's book in the *NRF*. Somewhere in Gide's letter, however, there were undoubtedly some less favorable comments, including an allusion to the influence of the Countess Anna de Noailles on the poetry of her young friend Cocteau. The presence of such critical comments by Gide is supported by the details of the following apologetic letter Cocteau wrote to Gide:

Maisons-Laffitte (S et O)
Tristesse retrospective à ressentir votre étonnement! Un bref commentaire s'impose. Bien que cette danse piétine déjà loin sur la route où l'on se "course" et qu'il faille pour la "mal voir" l'effort que je me retourne, bien que des influences puériles l'imprègnent et que tels bonds me remplissent de malaise, elle représente malgré tout une phase de ma courbe et je ne possède ni le droit, ni le moyen d'en renier le désordre. — D'autre part il faut un instinct rigoureux et sans doute infaillible pour m'affirmer que des pages de cette facile inquiétude répondront à la fiévreuse angoisse d'André Walter — Peut-être un "même acharnement" à mettre les pédales alors que les virtuoses en évitent la molle fourberie. (Immoraliste, Porte Etroite, etc....) J'ajoute que mon sang ne reflète pas *"une rose crétoise"* comme le

sang d'une amie à nous, mais bien "un géranium de Seine et Oise" ce qui respecte la rime opulente mais retire de la température. Je n'ose relire, pardon du style je suis bien fatigué!

Votre Nathanaël

Jean Cocteau

P.S. Croyez vous que j'ignore l'erreur de ce jeune barbare ivre d'érudition récente et de musées découverts? — Mais l'attitude admirative et affectueuse oblige à certaines schématisations qu'il est difficile d'épanouir sans paraître lâche même lorsque la cause s'en avère minime. — "Les Russes" m'importe peu. J'aime leur Vestris parce qu'il s'apparente à Ménalque et à l'aéroplane, pour ce qu'il rappelle et propose. Je vous livre le reste. —

Mon hamac appareille loin des dangers slaves ou hellènes, car je ne sais pas sî Sophocle s'évertue dans une Athènes pavoisée ou bien entre des façades hermétiques derrière lesquelles tout le monde avale comme hostie en cloître le pain à cacheter de Mlle. Silve-Mirepoix.

Encore pardon de l'incohérence. Fatigue atroce.

JC [16]

Maisons-Laffitte (S et O)

(Looking back in sorrow to feel your astonishment! A word of explanation is in order. Though this dance [*Danse de Sophocle*] marks time a goodly distance along the path where we "race" and to "see it as bad" I must make an effort to turn around, though it is permeated by childish influences and such leaps fill me with discomfort, it nevertheless represents one phase of my curve, and I have neither the right nor the means to deny its disorder. On the other hand, a rigorous and no doubt unerring instinct is needed to prove to me that certain pages of this easy uneasiness do respond to the fevered anguish of *André Walter*. Perhaps a same eagerness to apply the pedals when virtuosi avoid such soft cheating. (*Immoraliste, Porte étroite*, etc....) May I add that my blood does not reflect "une rose crétoise," as does the blood of a lady whom we both know [Anna de Noailles], but rather "un géranium de Seine-et-Oise" which respects opulent rhyme but benefits from the temperature. I dare not reread this; forgive the style. I am so tired.

Your Nathaniel,

Jean Cocteau

P.S. Do you think I am unaware of the ignorance of this young barbarian who is intoxicated with fresh learning and by newly discovered museums? But an admiring and affectionate attitude forces me to adopt certain diagrammatic processes which are difficult to develop without seeming cowardly even if the reason proves trivial. "Les Russes" don't mean much to me. I like their Vestris because he has something in common with both Ménalque and the airplane, both because of what he recalls and because of what he proposes. I leave the rest to you.

My sailor's hammock sets sail far from Slavic or Hellenic perils, since I do not know whether Sophocles is exerting himself to the utmost in a decked-out Athens or amid hermetic façades behind which everyone swallows Mlle Silve-Mirepoix's sealing wafer as if it were the Host in a cloister.

Again, forgive this incoherence. Terrible fatigue.

JC)

After receiving Gide's letter of August 6, Cocteau wrote a postcard to his mother:

Offranville
13 Août 1912

Pluie et désastre autour d'une bonne maison pleine de cœurs et de jeux — Pas lu le moindre Comoedia donc pas le moindre P. Envoie une dépêche préventive —

Nous avons ici Miss [Edith] Whorton [*sic*], l'auteur, tu sais, des "Heureux de la vie" [*Chez les heureux de ce monde*]... Elle goûte les choses avec tact et semble érudite à la maniére anglaise, avec abondance et nationalisme. Le soir je fais la lecture: Outre Tombe ou bien des poèmes de la Comtesse — c'est te dire que je nage dans ce qui représente à beaucoup le fièvre et à moi le repos total.

Cœur.

Jean.

Offranville
August 13, 1912

(Rain and disaster around a good house full of hearts and games — Haven't read the least *Comoedia* hence not the least P. Send a preventive telegram —

We have here Miss [Edith] Whorton [Wharton], the author, you know, of *Heureux de la vie* [*The House of Mirth*]... She tastes things with tact and seems learned in the English manner, with abundance and nationalism. In the evening I read *Outre-Tombe* or else poems by the Countess — this is to tell you that I am swimming in what to many represents fever and to me total rest.

Heart.

Jean)

On the face of the postcard Cocteau continued his note:

Les fleurs ici poussent comme des soupirs et des cris du sol. Ce n'est pas la terre, terre à terre de maisons, qui rechigne à ce romantisme. Décidément notre famille R. est charmante, compréhensive, enthousiaste (voire drôle) et ouverte aux belles audaces. J'ai reçu enfin une lettre de Gide protestante et affectueuse, telle que la désirait ma curiosité admirative.[17]

(The flowers here emit something like sighs and cries from the soil. It is not the earth, hard as cement, which looks sour at this romanticism. Decidedly our R. family is charming, intelligent, enthusiastic (even funny), and open to beautiful audacities. I have at last received a letter from Gide, protesting and affectionate, the way my admiring curiosity wanted it.)

Gide's long-awaited letter was the first, but informal, reaction Cocteau received from the *NRF* group. Official notice came later from Henri Ghéon. Cocteau had also sent a copy of *La Danse de Sophocle* to Ghéon with the following inscription:

À Monsieur Ghéon en souvenir de la chère Algérie dont ses poèmes me furent Baedecker.

Jean Cocteau.[18]

(To Monsieur Ghéon in memory of the dear Algeria for which his poems were my Baedeker.

Jean Cocteau)

Ghéon was a physician who had become engrossed in the literary life of Paris and who, like Gide, was important to Cocteau at the time because of his position as critic for the *NRF*. Ghéon was then a close friend of Gide's and a practicing homosexual. He is reported to have abandoned the homosexual way of life after his conversion to Catholicism in 1916.[19] His association with Jacques Copeau at the *NRF*, and later at the Théâtre du Vieux-Colombier, was also undoubtedly noted by Cocteau for future reference.

In the September-October 1912 issue of the *NRF* Ghéon wrote a four-page review of *La Danse de Sophocle*. As the first review of a work by Cocteau to appear in the *NRF*, it marked an important milestone in the young poet's career.

Welcome though the review was in terms of recognition that could enhance his reputation, Cocteau was crestfallen to find that Ghéon's critical comments focused attention on the deficiencies not only in the volume under review but in Cocteau's literary character as a whole. Ghéon saw Cocteau as a poet whose image had been fabricated by "les chroniqueurs mondains, les journaux de théâtre, tous les dispensateurs de gloire immédiate" ("fashionable reporters, theater papers, all the dispensers of instant glory"), as a trumped-up reincarnation of "l'enfant de génie" after the manner of Alfred de Musset. Pointing with distaste to Cocteau's earlier book of verse

Le Prince frivole, Ghéon declared that Cocteau had not yet purged himself of his frivolous approach to poetry in writing *La Danse de Sophocle*. In a comment strongly reminiscent of Gide's letter of August 6 to Cocteau, Ghéon remarked: "sa jeunesse . . . est extrême. M. Jean Cocteau me paraît extra-ordinairement doué" ("his youthfulness . . . is extreme. M. Jean Cocteau seems to me extraordinarily gifted").

He went on to raise the question of Cocteau's originality: "Mais pour bien discerner, d'entre ses dons, lesquels sont authentiques, lesquels d'emprunt, il faudrait déployer la plus patiente analyse. Il trouve et il retrouve." ("But to determine which of his gifts are authentic, which ones borrowed, would require the most patient analysis. He invents, and he re-invents.") Among the writers who had influenced Cocteau, Ghéon mentioned Baudelaire, Emmanuel Signoret, the Pindaric poet who died at twenty-eight, and the Countess Anna de Noailles. Although Ghéon paid tribute to Cocteau's ability to think in images and to his virtuosity with parnassian and neoclassic verse, he asserted that even Cocteau's most successful strophes lack "l'homogénéité morale nécessaire." Cocteau's originality, for Ghéon, lay in his bold new use of words, "qui fait que tous . . . prennent dans le vers un éclat, une patine, un relief qui les tirent du domaine de la con-versation commune" ("which results in all of them . . . taking on in the verse a brilliance, a patina, a relief, which lift them out of the realm of ordinary conversation").

On September 5, 1912, in response to Ghéon's review, Cocteau wrote Ghéon a letter, the extreme brevity of which was a measure of his disappointment:

Cher Monsieur
Par Chevassu: Non — mais par vous c'est autre chose et l'intel-ligence perspicace en blâme touche d'avantage que l'encensoir my-ope. À bientôt j'espère.
Jean Cocteau.

P.S. Nul sot orgueil de titre — Sophocle dansant plus ou moins en mesure mais sous un somptueux soleil ne savait pas s'il serait "So-phocle" ou Bernstein — ni même Vestris ou Mr. de Fouquières!!!!!! [20]

(Dear Sir:
By Chevassu: No—but by you that's something else, and intel-ligence shrewd in censure reaches further than myopic flattery. I hope to see you soon.
Jean Cocteau.

P.S. No foolish pride of title—Sophocles dancing more or less in time but beneath a sumptuous sun didn't know if he'd be "Sophocles" or Bernstein—or even Vestris or Mr. de Fouquières!!!!!!)

At about the same time Cocteau wrote Jacques-Emile Blanche a similar letter:

L'article de Ghéon très "écho de lettre Androgyde" m'amuse et m'enseigne — mais il oublie les privilèges de la jeunesse et semble ignorer que Sophocle dansant ne savait pas s'il serait plus tard "Sophocle" ou Bernstein. — voire Vestris ou Mr. de Fouquières. . . .[21]

(The Ghéon article, very "echo of Androgyde letter," amuses and instructs me—but he forgets the privileges of the young and seems not to know that Sophocles dancing didn't know if later on he would be "Sophocles" or Bernstein—even Vestris or Mr. de Fouquières. . . .)

Although with Ghéon's review Cocteau had achieved a certain recognition by the influential *NRF*, it was the sort of critical recognition that could blight a budding career. Cocteau, however, was quick to learn from his errors; and the Ghéon analysis no doubt instructed more than it amused him. Also, coming as it did after Gide's letter of August 6, it was somewhat anticlimactic to Cocteau.

In later years Cocteau referred more than once to the salutary effect Ghéon had had on his writing. In 1914 he called on his two critical friends, Henri Ghéon and André Gide, for help in his campaign to persuade Jacques Copeau to produce the Cocteau-Stravinsky ballet *David*.[22]

Ghéon's criticism drew fire from Marcel Proust, who was then on friendly terms with Cocteau, and who complained to Jean-Louis Vaudoyer of Ghéon's evaluation of Cocteau as a mere "boulevard" writer.[23] Yet Ghéon's appraisal of Cocteau as gifted but imitative and not yet serious enough was shared by Georges Duhamel, who wrote of *La Danse de Sophocle* in the *Mercure de France* for July 16, 1912:

Si je cherchais à résumer en une formule critique aussi brève que possible l'impression que me procure la lecture du livre de M. Jean Cocteau, je dirais: détestable talent. . . . M. Jean Cocteau sait aussi bien que moi quels sont les gens qu'il imite et quels ceux qu'il ne veut pas imiter. . . . Si j'avais les moyens poétiques de M. Cocteau, son élégance et sa facilité, je mettrais mon point d'honneur à me défaire de toute cette pacotille. J'écrirais alors un beau livre austère, nu,

dépouillé de toute préciosité, de toute mignardise, de tout faux esprit, et je ferais tant et si bien que mes propres amis ne me reconnaîtraient plus.

(If I tried to sum up in as brief a critical formula as possible the impression I receive from reading M. Jean Cocteau's book, I would say: detestable talent. . . . M. Jean Cocteau knows as well as I which people he imitates and which ones he doesn't wish to imitate. . . . If I had the poetic means of M. Cocteau, his elegance and his facility, I would make it my point of honor to rid myself of all that shoddy stuff. Then I would write a beautiful book, austere, naked, stripped of all preciosity, of all affectation, of all false wit, and I would work to such good purpose that my own friends wouldn't recognize me any more.)

These opinions, which have by now become critical clichés applied to Jean Cocteau's work, were not without their effect on him at the moment. The year 1912 was a time for self-appraisal by Cocteau, triggered in part by Ghéon's review and Gide's letter; and subsequent events proved it to be a turning point in his career. *La Danse de Sophocle* was later deleted from the official bibliography of his works by Cocteau's own decision, together with his two earlier volumes of poetry, *La Lampe d'Aladin* (1908) and *Le Prince frivole* (1910), as products of his "enfance hâtive et fiévreuse, la rencontre de guides néfastes."

CHAPTER THREE

"Le Coq et l'Arlequin"

Gide's criticism of *La Danse de Sophocle* was accepted by Cocteau as a "douche écossaise": unpleasant but salutary in its effect. A few years later, however, when Gide wrote Cocteau a seemingly unprovoked open letter that overstepped criticism into reprimand, Cocteau reacted explosively with an open reply of his own that in turn drew an angry rebuttal from Gide. This exchange of open letters became a focal point in their deteriorating relations.

The episode was set off by Cocteau's *Le Coq et l'Arlequin*, a work the author classified as an urgent alarm, "cet ouvrage écrit sur deux notes, comme l'appel de la pompe à feu" [1] ("that work written on two notes, like the siren of a fire engine"). The developments that followed its publication were to mark Cocteau, and to a lesser extent Gide, for life. Time and again in later years Cocteau was to hark back obsessively to the controversy prompted by Gide's reaction to *Le Coq et l'Arlequin*. Other important literary figures, including Marcel Proust, Anna de Noailles, Max Jacob, Jacques-Emile Blanche, and Jacques Rivière, were drawn into it.

It is now apparent that the events of the controversy reveal central aspects of the personal rivalry between Cocteau and Gide, their temperaments, their modus operandi in literary politics, and their epistolary and polemical skill. On a broader scale, the skirmish in the wake of *Le Coq et l'Arlequin* was a symptom of the eclectic nature of the times; a phase of the conflict in postwar Paris between the relatively

austere literary establishment represented by the dedicated professional members of the *NRF* and the young writers, who were often suspected of being frivolous, *mondain,* and ultra-modern as they struggled to find their place in French letters.

On March 19, 1918, Cocteau signed his preface to the little volume entitled *Le Coq et l'Arlequin.* This was a manifesto extolling the new music of Les Six [2] as opposed to the romantic, picturesque compositions of Wagner, Debussy, and Ravel. To the annoyance of Cocteau's friend Igor Stravinsky, the book was dedicated to Georges Auric. It was published by Cocteau's own publishing enterprise, Editions de la Sirène, which he had founded in 1918 with the Swiss poet Blaise Cendrars and Paul Lafitte. A large part of *Le Coq et l'Arlequin* took the form of aphorisms on music and art, reflecting the epigrammatic wit in which Cocteau had been schooled in the Paris salons.

Marcel Proust was among those of Cocteau's contemporaries who admired the lapidary and penetrating style of the book. On February 11, 1919, he wrote his young friend:

Mon cher Jean,
Je lis, je relis le Coq et l'Arlequin avec émerveillement. Il n'y a pas une pensée qui ne soit profonde, ni une expression d'un bonheur incroyable. On croit vous entendre quand on lit La source désapprouve presque toujours l'itinéraire du fleuve. . . .
J'envie vos formules saisissantes. . . .
Mille tendresses de votre
Marcel [3]

(My dear Jean,
I read, I reread *Le Coq et l'Arlequin* with wonder. There isn't one thought that is not profound, nor one expression not unbelievably felicitous. One can almost hear you when one reads: The spring almost always disapproves of the river's course. . . .
I envy your striking formulas. . . .
A thousand caresses from your
Marcel)

Cocteau's book emphasized the shifting values in the arts in the immediate postwar period. It also reflected the attitudes, and more than once the specific statements, of his friends at the time, among whom were Auric, Picasso, Anna de Noailles, Max Jacob, Modigliani, Charles Péguy, Guillaume Apollinaire, Erik Satie, and Jacques-Emile Blanche. Cocteau has often been

reproached, perhaps excessively, for passing off the brilliance of others as his own. In this instance any desire for self-aggrandizement the young poet may have had seems to have been subordinated to the polemicist's need to capture public attention and to use all available ammunition regardless of origin. Where Cocteau's sources were painters, musicians, and salon conversationalists rather than professional writers, they were probably more often than not pleased to have Cocteau record their ideas in permanent, written form, with wider circulation than they could themselves accomplish. Where Cocteau borrowed from other writers without acknowledgement, however, he was more vulnerable to criticism.

One such source was André Gide, who first read *Le Coq et l'Arlequin* early in 1919, very likely during a brief visit at the Offranville home of his friend Jacques-Emile Blanche, who had the proofs at the time. Gide was quick to note a phrase that Cocteau had taken from his own conversation and used without permission and without credit to Gide. Annoyed at this trespass, Gide telephoned to Cocteau's close friend Countess Anna de Noailles and asked her to intercede for him with Cocteau. On February 7, 1919, Anna de Noailles wrote Gide:

Dois-je vous dire, cher Monsieur, la surprise et la tristesse que j'ai eues hier soir, en apprenant par des tiers que notre premier entretien par téléphone au sujet du *Coq et l'Arlequin, dont j'ignorais l'existence* et dont *vous teniez* les feuillets chez Blanche, a été inexactement rapporté à Cocteau, qui pense que *c'est moi* qui vous ai averti de la phrase inamicale, alors que c'est vous qui, étonné et chagriné, m'en faisiez part! J'ai cru vous être utile en réclamant le plus affectueusement du monde à Cocteau ce que vous sembliez désirer, mais pour ma part, je ne me suis étonnée de cet incident que par une loyale passion d'esprit qui m'est habituelle, et parce que je croyais que, la rectification obtenue (dont, pour ménager votre affection pour Cocteau, j'avais assumé l'amicale exigence), rien de nos entretiens réitérés et confidentiels ne serait rapporté a l'intéressé.

Cocteau a été très bien en tout cela; c'est un vieil ami pour moi, et j'aurais été peinée qu'il eût gravement tort. Il vous est extrêmement attaché. Notre explication a été parfaite, et implique que nous ne parlerons plus de cela. Je vous supplie donc, cher Monsieur, de ne pas faire allusion à cette joute pour l'exactitude, que lui et moi eûmes ensemble, qui est terminée et dont la continuation serait vaine et irritante: mon jeune vieil ami a été sincère dans ses explications, j'en ai été touchée, l'incident n'existe plus. Permettez, cher Monsieur, à la raison qui souvent me sert, de vous assurer que rien n'est plus

utile et prudent que d'établir entre des amis communs et qui nous sont très chers ces légères et solides murailles de papier que les Japonais — gens merveilleux — emploient pour former leurs demeures. Il est entendu, formellement, avec Jean que jamais plus nous ne parlerons de rien de tout cela.[4]

(Need I tell you, dear Sir, the surprise and sorrow I felt yesterday evening on hearing from a third person that our first telephone conversation about *Le Coq et l'Arlequin, which I didn't know existed* and of which *you had* the pages at Blanche's, has been inaccurately reported to Cocteau, who thinks *it is I* who told you about the unfriendly sentence, whereas it is you who, shocked and chagrined, told me about it! I thought I was helping you by demanding from Cocteau, in the most affectionate way in the world, what you seemed to want; but for my part I am only surprised at that incident because of a straightforward turn of mind that is usual with me, and because I believed that once the correction was obtained (which, to save your affection for Cocteau, I had taken it on myself to exact in a friendly way), nothing of our repeated and confidential conversations would be reported to the interested party.

Cocteau has been very good about all this; he is an old friend of mine, and I would have been hurt if he had been seriously in the wrong. He is extremely attached to you. Our accounting was perfect, and implies that we will not speak of this any further. I beg you, therefore, dear Sir, not to make allusion to this joust for exactitude that he and I had together, which is finished, and the continuation of which would be useless and irritating. My young old friend has been sincere in his explanations, I have been touched by them, the incident is closed. Permit, dear Sir, with the reason which often serves me, to assure you that nothing is more useful and prudent than to establish between common friends, who are very dear to us, those light and solid walls of paper that the Japanese — wonderful people — use to build their dwellings. It is understood, formally, with Jean, that never again will we say anything about all this.)

From this letter it is clear that Gide spoke to Anna de Noailles more than once about Cocteau's borrowing in *Le Coq et l'Arlequin,* and that he asked the Countess to suggest to Cocteau the insertion of a *papillon* or acknowledgement slip in the text designating Gide as the source of the quotation. Why Gide decided to use Anna de Noailles as his emissary instead of approaching Cocteau directly is a matter for speculation. It is possible that Gide already had conceived the idea of an open letter to Cocteau to appear shortly in the *NRF,* and wished to avoid either a premature direct confrontation with

Cocteau or any action that might make later developments appear personally motivated.

In any event, Gide replied in haste to Anna de Noailles's letter as follows:

Croyez que je m'affecte bien davantage des lignes de votre lettre au sujet du différend de l'Arlequin. L'idée d'avoir pu vous désobliger, vous déplaire, m'a tourmenté toute la nuit. Si j'avais rien dit qui pût se retourner contre vous, j'en resterais inconsolable. Mais non: la personne à qui, pressé de questions, j'ai pourtant dû parler savait être seule en possession du petit volume — et que vous ne le connaissiez pas encore. La confusion vient évidemment de ceci, que je n'ai été entrainé à vous parler de la phrase de *l'Arlequin* qu'après que vous m'aviez signalé certaines imitations du *Cap*.

J'ai revu Jean la veille de mon départ; si exquises qu'aient eté son explication et la réparation qu'il me propose, elles ne me paraîtraient point parfaites si elles laissaient subsister le moindre nuage entre vous et moi. . . .[5]

(Be assured that I am much more concerned over what you say in your letter about the Arlequin dispute. The idea that I could have offended you, displeased you, tormented me all night. If I had said anything that might turn round against you I should be unconsolable. But no: the person to whom, pressed with questions, I had to speak, however, knew he was the only one in possession of the little volume — and that you were not yet familiar with it. The confusion evidently comes from this, that I was only led to speak to you about the *Arlequin* sentence after you had pointed out to me certain imitations in the *Cap* [*de Bonne-Espérance*].

I saw Jean again the evening before my departure; however exquisite his explanation and the reparation he proposes to me, they would not seem perfect to me if they left the slightest cloud between you and me. . . .)

Before the next month was out, Cocteau had arranged for the insertion of a *papillon* between pages 18 and 19 in *Le Coq et l'Arlequin*, and sought to placate Gide further by sending him a copy of the corrected book, inscribed:

à André Gide "Le Piano et le papillon"
LE COQ ET L'ARLEQUIN
son ami, de tout cœur
Mars 1919,
Jean Cocteau [6]

(To André Gide "The Piano and the butterfly"
LE COQ ET L'ARLEQUIN
his friend, with all affection
March 1919
Jean Cocteau)

Paragraph 6, page 18 of *Le Coq et l'Arlequin* reads: "Presque tous les idiomes ont des pédales, mais la langue française est un piano sans pédales." ("Nearly all languages have pedals, but the French language is a piano without pedals.") Cocteau's *papillon* reads: "Un oubli de guillemets m'enrichissant d'une phrase dite par André Gide: 'La langue française est un piano sans pédales,' je me fais un scrupule de signaler au lecteur cette interpolation involontaire." [7] ("Forgetting a set of quotation marks having enriched me by a sentence spoken by André Gide: 'The French language is a piano without pedals,' I make it a scrupulous point to inform the reader of this involuntary interpolation.")

Having thus done public penance for his sin, Cocteau turned on his old friend Jacques-Emile Blanche, in all probability the "third person" mentioned in Anna de Noailles's letter to Gide, and bitterly attacked him for his duplicity:

Mars 1919

Mon cher Blanche,

Comme je déteste le vague, je tiens à vous faire savoir la raison pour laquelle vous ne recevez pas le Coq et l'Arlequin avec mes services. Après m'avoir dit à moi que ce petit livre était un "chef d'œuvre" vous avez dit a tous (au charmant Gaspard Michel entre autres) que c'était un ramassis de choses prises à droite et à gauche. N'ayant l'habitude que de donner, je vous laisse donc l'exemplaire incomplet que vous avez cru bon de soumettre et de commenter malgré prière instante.

Cette petite bassesse s'ajoute à quelques mensonges gratuits pour lesquels je ne peux que vous plaindre.

Jean Cocteau [8]

March 1919

(My dear Blanche,

Since I detest vagueness, I am determined to let you know the reason why you are not receiving *Le Coq et l'Arlequin* through my offices. After having told me personally that this little book was a "master-piece" you told everyone else (the charming Gaspard Michel among

others) that it was a scratch collection of things taken from all quarters. Only having the habit of giving, I therefore leave with you the incomplete copy that you have seen fit to exhibit and to comment on despite my urgent request to the contrary.

This contemptible little action is added to several gratuitous lies for which I can only pity you.

Jean Cocteau)

Blanche, upset by Cocteau's attack, retaliated by writing a letter to Gide in which he spoke unkindly of Cocteau and of *Le Coq et l'Arlequin*. Blanche was careful not to use any names in his letter, a prudent gesture in case Gide showed the letter to a third person:

Cher ami

Comme vous n'êtes pas venu, je vous confie ce document. Malgré ma patience avec ce petit être dont je subis les impertinences depuis des ans, je ne puis hélas! tolérer une minute de plus le ton que prend vis à vis de moi un si redoutable malade. Vous aurez peut-être la bonté de lui faire savoir que dès qu'il sera relié, ce petit volume dont j'avais, vous vous le rappelez, été ravi — lui sera rendu, comme une précieuse curiosité bibliographique. J'ajoute seulement qu'il n'a jamais *prié avec insistance,* mais téléphoné au matin pour que je lui tendisse cet exemplaire qu'il m'avait confié à fin que j'en parlasse dans la R[evue] de P[aris], et qu'il renvoyait, disait-il à l'imprimeur. J'ai su, ensuite, que c'était à dessein de supprimer quelques formules, ou pour les rendre à leurs propriétaires. Qu'il ne craigne rien, cette rareté pour bibliophiles n'appartiendra qu'à l'auteur.

T. à v.
J.[9]

(Dear friend,

As you did not come, I am committing this document to your care. In spite of my patience with this little creature whose impertinences I have put up with for years, I cannot, alas! tolerate one minute longer the tone of such a dangerous sick man towards me. Perhaps you will be good enough to let him know that as soon as it is bound, this little volume, which as you know delighted me, will be given back to him, as a precious bibliographic curiosity. I add only that he never *asked insistently,* but telephoned in the morning that I should hand over this copy which he had entrusted to me so that I might speak of it in the *Revue de Paris,* and which he was sending back, he said, to the printer. I learned later that it was with a view to suppressing several phrases, or to return them to their owners. He need not fear anything, this rarity for bibliophiles will only belong to its author.

Yours very truly,
J.)

It was characteristic of Cocteau that he was unable to nurse a grudge, and he soon wrote Blanche a second letter repairing the bonds of friendship between them:

Mon cher J.E.

Je n'ai pas lu votre lettre. Je redoute qu'elle m'empêche d'agir selon mon cœur.

Et d'abord je disculpe Gaspard Michel – il me prévenait de la phrase Gide "sans avoir l'air" ignorant la présence d'un papillon explicatif. Pensant qu'il connaissait ce papillon – j'ai cru qu'il insinuait d'autres interprétations signalées par vous et comme on peut tout me reprocher sauf de "prendre" j'ai eu un reflexe excusable. Ce malentendu s'ajoutait à mille ragots féroces d'amis spirituels.

Enfin, après expérience – je vous aime plus que la sécurité et je vous embrasse, si

vous voulez bien.

Jean [10]

(My dear J.E.,

I have not read your letter. I fear it might keep me from acting as my heart dictates.

And first of all I exonerate Gaspard Michel – he warned me of Gide's phrase "without seeming to," not knowing of the presence of an acknowledgement slip. Thinking that he did know of this slip – I thought he was insinuating other interpretations pointed out by you, and since I can be reproached for everything except "taking" I had a forgivable reaction. This misunderstanding added on to a thousand bits of savage gossip by witty friends.

Finally, after experience – I love you more than peace of mind, and I embrace you, if

you are willing,

Jean)

Although complete dated records are not available for the entire period, the probable sequence of subsequent events can be reconstructed from later correspondence between Gide, Cocteau, and Jacques Rivière. Rivière, a young protégé of Gide's, was now editor of the *NRF* and no admirer of Cocteau's. By mid-April of 1919, Gide had advised Rivière of his plan to write an open letter to Jean Cocteau, and on May 5, Rivière approved the draft of the open letter, suggesting it as a lead article in the first postwar issue of the *NRF*.

Gide's decision to publish his open letter to Cocteau touched off a round robin of correspondence, telephone calls, and personal confrontations during the month of May, 1919, between Gide, Cocteau, and Jacques Rivière.

The exchange of open letters between Gide and Cocteau consisted of a first letter by Gide in the *NRF*, a reply by Cocteau in the *Ecrits Nouveaux*, and a second letter by Gide in the *Ecrits Nouveaux*. The version of the chronology of events given by Cocteau in his open reply, and the version given by Gide in his second open letter, vary in detail but not in substance. It is probable that neither account is entirely accurate or objective. The facts now known about the episode support the following summary of events in early May and June of 1919:

Early May 1919—Gide told Cocteau verbally of his intention to have an open letter published in the *NRF*.
Saturday [May 3]—Cocteau wrote Gide asking to see Gide's open letter before it was printed.

Samedi

Mon cher Gide
  Vous êtes à Paris — je voudrais vous voir — il est *indispensable* pour la sauvegarde de notre amitié — que je lise votre lettre ouverte avant que N.R.F. l'imprime. Jacques Rivière était à ma séance lecture du Cap. Son attitude vous aurait fait plaisir puisque vous songiez à nous réunir de longue date. Sa figure toute jeune, presque de collégien m'a surpris beaucoup. Téléphonez ou faites téléphoner un matin.
  Dites à notre Marc que je pense souvent à lui.
Je vous embrasse
Jean Cocteau

  P.S. Publiez vous l'Eubage de Cendrars? — Si oui — je vous félicite — c'est une de ses très bonnes choses.[11]

Saturday

(My dear Gide,
  You are in Paris—I want to see you. It is *essential* for the preservation of our friendship that I read your open letter before it is printed by the *NRF*. Jacques Rivière was at my reading of the *Cap* [*de Bonne-Espérance*]. His attitude would have pleased you since you had meant for a long time to have us meet. His very young face, almost that of a schoolboy, surprised me greatly. Give me a ring or have someone call me some morning.
  Tell our Marc [Allégret] I often think of him.
Affectionately,
Jean Cocteau

  P.S. Are you publishing Cendrars's *Eubage*? If so, I congratulate you—it's one of his really good things.)

May 5 — Gide showed Cocteau a draft of the letter at his Villa Montmorency in Auteuil. Cocteau, greatly upset, protested the language and intent of the letter, and asked Gide to modify it.

May 5 — Gide, disturbed by Cocteau's reaction, read his open letter that afternoon to Charles Du Bos, Gaston Gallimard, and Jacques Rivière.

May 5 — Rivière wrote Gide urging him to publish his open letter to Cocteau without alterations:

Paris, le 5 mai 1919

Mon cher André

Décidément, tout bien réfléchi, il faut que tu publies ta lettre à Cocteau telle quelle. Elle m'a paru ce soir plus excellente, et plus utile encore, que la première fois. Elle formera un des meilleurs morceaux de notre premier numéro.

Comme je t'ai dit, je vais voir Cocteau Jeudi. Je tâcherai de lui faire entendre raison et de lui expliquer l'impression que fait ta lettre sur un *neutre* (je me donnerai un peu hypocritement hélas! mais il le faut, pour tel).

Je t'assure

Bien à toi
J.R.[12]

Paris, May 5, 1919

(My dear André,

Decidedly, everything carefully considered, you must publish your letter to Cocteau as is. It seemed to me this evening more excellent and more useful still than the first time. It will make one of the best pieces of our first issue.

As I told you, I am going to see Cocteau Thursday. I will try to make him listen to reason and to explain to him the impression your letter makes on a *neutral party* (I will present myself a bit hypocritically as such, alas! but it is necessary).

I assure you,

Yours truly,
J.R.)

May 6 — Convinced by his colleagues that his letter was acceptable, Gide sent Cocteau a friendly but firm *pneumatique* advising that he felt obliged to publish the open letter, but mentioning several minor changes in wording:

Mardi matin le 6

Mon cher Jean

Je n'en sors pas. Plus je relis ma lettre et la retourne — plus je me persuade qu'elle est telle qu'elle doit être, et pas inamicale du tout.

J'ai néanmoins rajouté 3 lignes au sujet du Cap en tête de la lettre et changé le mot "étourdissant" qui vous offusquait — encore que je ne puisse comprendre ce que vous y trouvez de blessant. L'expérience que je viens de faire en la lisant à Gallimard, Rivière et Du Bos (dont vous connaissez la délicatesse), rencontré par hasard ce soir à la Revue, achève de m'en convaincre. Vous savez bien que s'ils avaient pu y voir quelque dureté ou "méchanceté" comme vous disiez, ils m'en auraient averti — car c'est à ce sujet que je les consultais. (Et il ne s'agit plus de *mes* sentiments que vous connaissez et donc, à nouveau, j'espère avoir su vous convaincre — mais de l'impression produite sur un lecteur non averti.) Près de vous je ne connais plus qu'une chose: mon désir de ne pas vous peiner. Mais tout de même il y a plus important que cela, et l'amitié se nourrit mal de réticences.

Toutes les atténuations et précautions oratoires que je pourrais apporter à ma lettre ne réussiraient qu'à lui enlever son ton de franchise où précisément se marque ma cordialité. Ce que je vous dis dans cette lettre et que je *dois* vous dire, et dire en public — je vous dois de le *dire* et non de l'insinuer. Je comprends que mon jugement vous gêne, mais vous savez bien qu'il vous gênerait moins s'il était moins exact — et que par conséquent cette gêne même est salutaire.

Il me serait certes plus agréable de vous adresser des louanges; mais je ne puis donner mon amitié que sincère.

À bientôt et aussi affec.[tueusement] que devant.

Votre
A.G.[13]

Tuesday morning, the 6th

(My dear Jean,

I see no way out. The more I reread my letter and turn it over in my mind, the more I am satisfied that it is as it must be, and is not at all unfriendly. Nevertheless I have added several lines at the beginning about the *Cap* [*de Bonne-Espérance*] and changed the word "astounding," which offended you, even though I can't understand what you found so wounding about it. The experiment I have just conducted by reading it to Gallimard, Rivière, and Du Bos (whose delicacy is familiar to you), whom I met by chance this evening at the *Revue*, finally convinces me. You well know that if they had been able to see in the letter any harshness or "maliciousness," as you said, they would have told me—because it was on this aspect that I asked their opinion. (And it is no longer a question of *my own* feelings, which you already know and respecting which, again, I hope I have been able to convince you, but of the impression created on an uninformed reader.) When near you, I feel only one thing: my wish not to hurt you. But just the same there is something more important than that, and friendship is ill nourished on reticence.

All the qualifications and oratorical precautions that I could muster in my letter would only succeed in robbing it of the very tone

of candor that testifies to my cordiality. What I say to you in this letter, and what I *must* say to you and say publicly, I owe it to you to *say* and not to insinuate. I understand that my judgment annoys you, but you also know that it would bother you less if it were not so accurate—and that consequently the annoyance itself is salutary.

It would of course be more pleasant for me to send you praise, but I can give my friendship only if it is sincere.

See you soon and as affectionately as before.

> Your
> A.G.)

May 6—The same day Cocteau replied with a brief note written in the tone of someone accepting a challenge to a duel, and going on record with Gide that he wanted the right to reply, presumably also by open letter in the *NRF*:

Mon cher Gide, le 6 Mai 1919

Vous aviez à choisir entre le public et moi — Vous avez choisi; mais, ma mère étant malade, je ne peux pas attacher à votre "*controverse*" l'importance qu'elle mérite.

Je réclame simplement le "droit de réponse."

> Jean Cocteau

P.S. Mille grâces pour votre petit "renvoi."[14]

(My dear Gide, May 6, 1919

You had to make a choice between the public and me—you have chosen; but since my mother is ill I cannot attach to your "*controversy*" the importance it deserves.

I simply claim the "right to reply."

> Jean Cocteau

P.S. A thousand thanks for your little "postscript.")

May 6—Having now received Rivière's letter of May 5 urging him to publish the open letter in its original form, Gide dispatched a reply to Rivière approving of his plan to see Cocteau Thursday [May 8] in an effort to persuade the outraged poet to accept the open letter in the friendly spirit in which it was written and published:

Cher Jacques Mardi — 6 mai 1919

Je trouve ta lettre en rentrant de la poste où je viens de jeter un pneu pour Cocteau; lui disant que malgré mon chagrin de devoir le peiner, je ne pouvais trouver rien à changer à ma "lettre ouverte" et que... (je t'enverrai copie de ce pneu demain quand ma secrétaire me rapportera une dactylographie double du brouillon). Je crois

cette nouvelle lettre (fermée) aussi ferme de ton que la première (et malgré cela très amicale de ton).

Mais il sera très bon que tu le vois jeudi et lui parle dans le sens que tu dis. Je voudrais faire ce tour de force de lui faire accepter *amicalement* cette critique — qu'il est parfaitement sincère de dire que j'écrivais amicalement.

Ton
A.G.[15]

Tuesday, May 6, 1919

(Dear Jacques,

I find your letter on returning from the post office where I just dropped off a *pneu* to Cocteau, telling him that despite my chagrin at having to hurt his feelings I could find nothing to change in my "open letter" and that... (I'll send you a copy of this *pneu* tomorrow when my secretary brings me a typed copy of the draft). I think this new letter (which ends the discussion) is as firm in tone as the first (and in spite of that very friendly in tone.)

But it will be very good that you see him Thursday and talk to him in the way you mention. I would like to accomplish this feat of strength: to make him accept this criticism in a friendly way — which it is perfectly sincere to say I wrote in a friendly way.

Your
A.G.)

May 11 — Gide wrote Jacques Rivière directing additional minor revisions in his open letter.

Dimanche

Mon cher Jacques

Je te prie d'apporter à ma lettre à Cocteau cette légère modification. . . .

Autrement dit, il faut qu'on lise: "Ce n'est point que je ne reconnaisse, et depuis longtemps, la justesse de vos maximes, mais certaines etc." Corrections très importantes, qui d'autre part supprime la "forme un peu étourdissante" qui offusquait l'auteur.

G.[16]

Sunday

(My dear Jacques,

I beg you to make this slight change in my letter to Cocteau. . . .

In other words, it should read: "It is not at all that I do not recognize, and for a long time past, the aptness of your maxims, but certain ones etc." Very important corrections, which, on the other hand, suppress the "rather astounding form" that offended the author.

G.)

May 16 — Rivière replied to Gide that the changes would be made as directed.[17]

Late May — Rivière and Cocteau met at the *NRF* offices, 35–37

P.S. J'ai lu cette réponse à notre ami A[ndré] L[hote] qui l'approuve sans restrictions.[21]

(My dear Rivière,

(Forgive me this familiarity, which shows my keen pleasure in knowing you and in the prospect of seeing you again.)

Here is my reply to Gide. In sending it to you I prove how much it works above intimate relationships. I like Gide. I admire his notes on Germany and besides am going to say so publicly in an article. But his letter displeases me. In addition to finding it unbecoming I do not grant him that air of necessity which makes an unfriendly gesture excusable (my attitude toward Igor Stravinsky for example). The only things his letter can reach are outside me and so precious, so delicate, that I must defend them with a little fencing and much firmness. How stupid I am. You understand the situation before one even speaks!

Your faithful
Jean Cocteau

P.S. I read this reply to our friend André Lhote, who approves of it unqualifiedly.)

June 11 — Following a noontime discussion with Gide of Cocteau's open letter, which Gide was then agreeable to printing in the *NRF*, Rivière wrote Gide a long letter not only urging him to reconsider his plan to publish Cocteau's reply but declaring that he, Rivière, as Editor of the *NRF* would print the reply only if Gide absolutely forced him to do so. Rivière considered it defamatory and offered to write Cocteau an appeal to reason.

Paris le 11 juin 1919 —
Mercredi soir

Mon cher André,

Comme je disais ce soir à Gaston, que tu consentais à la publication de la lettre de Cocteau, il m'a demandé à la relire. Je l'ai relue par dessus son épaule. L'avis de Gaston a été immédiat et sans hésitation: "Impubliable!" s'est-il ecrié. Et je t'avoue que, parallèlement, l'impression que ta trop prompte acceptation m'avait empêché à midi de te formuler, s'est reformée en moi, — l'impression d'une chose impertinente et déplacée, d'une chose à laquelle nous n'avons aucune raison sérieuse d'ouvrir nos pages. Soyons sincères: seul l'énorme "culot" du Monsieur nous a l'un et l'autre intimidés. (C'est toujours par ce "culot" qu'il réussit partout.) Tout réfléchi, rien ne l'autorise à répondre à ta lettre si pesée, si mesurée par cette pétarade de perfidies sans véritable valeur psychologique.

Si tu veux, je me charge de lui écrire une lettre où je lui expliquerai que tu me demandais de laisser paraître sa réponse, mais que j'ai refusé, la trouvant trop personnelle et portant le débat sur un terrain où il n'a rien à dire. Car enfin réfléchis qu'au lieu de répondre à aucune des critiques que tu lui as adressées, il te jette à la tête toutes les méchancetés qu'il peut trouver, sans lien, sans autre prétention que de mordre. Ce n'est pas de la polémique telle que nous sommes disposés à l'accepter à la revue, je crois.

Je te renvoie la lettre pour que tu puisses encore méditer dessus. Mais je t'avoue dès maintenant que je ne la publierai que tout à fait contraint et forcé.

Excellente conversation avec Ghéon qui retire sa lettre et se contentera d'indiquer légèrement sa position en tête d'une note sur Pierre Gilbert. Tout va bien.

Toujours ton
J.R.

Ne manque pas de me renvoyer la lettre au même temps que tu m'aviseras de ta décision définitive.[22]

Paris, June 11, 1919 —
Wednesday evening

(My dear André,

As I told Gaston this evening that you consented to the publication of the letter from Cocteau, he asked to reread it. I read it again over his shoulder. The advice of Gaston was immediate and unhesitating: "Unpublishable!" he exclaimed. And I admit that, similarly, the impression that your over-prompt acceptance had prevented me from formulating to you at noon took shape again in my mind—the impression of a thing both impertinent and uncalled for, of a thing to which we have no serious reason to open our pages. Let's be honest: only the enormous "nerve" of the Gentleman has intimidated us both. (It's always by this "nerve" that he succeeds everywhere.) Everything considered, nothing justifies him in answering your letter, which was so carefully weighed and measured, by that outburst of treacheries which have no real psychological value.

If you wish, I take it on myself to write him a letter in which I'll explain to him that you asked me to let his reply appear, but that I refused, on the grounds that it was personal and carried the debate onto ground where it has no meaning. For consider, after all, that instead of answering any of the criticisms that you directed to him, he flings at your head all the spiteful things he can find, without restraint, without any aim but to bite. This is not the sort of polemics we are ready to accept at the review, I believe.

I am sending the letter back so you can meditate further on it. But I declare to you as of now that I will publish it only if absolutely constrained and compelled to.

Excellent conversation with Ghéon, who withdraws his letter and will be satisfied to indicate lightly his position at the head of a note on Pierre Gilbert. All is going well.

Always your

J.R.

[P.S.] Don't fail to send the letter back to me at the same time you let me know of your final decision.)

June 14—Rivière wrote a lengthy letter to Cocteau emphasizing the personal and vindictive tone of Cocteau's open reply and inviting him to withdraw it.

Mon cher Cocteau,

Nous sommes loin de compte. Quand vous êtes venu me voir à la fin du mois dernier, encore sous le coup de la lettre que Gide venait de vous lire, vous m'avez assuré qu'elle ne vous chagrinait que dans la mesure où elle méconnaissait l'esthétique dont vous vous êtes fait le défenseur et les tendances nouvelles auxquelles obéissent vos amis. Encore aujourd'hui vous m'écrivez: "Les seules choses que puisse atteindre la lettre de Gide sont en dehors de moi." Votre grief est donc uniquement que Gide vous ignore, comprend mal ce que vous faites, ce que vous voulez faire, vous et vos amis.

C'est ainsi tout au moins que j'ai entendu la chose et c'est pour vous permettre de vous expliquer sur la doctrine que vous accusiez Gide de traiter par le dédain, que je vous ai fait entrevoir la possibilité d'accueillir une réponse de vous dans la N.R.F. Je me suis même déclaré enchanté, je m'en souviens bien, à l'idée de voir s'ouvrir dans nos pages une discussion sur un point que je considérais et que je considère toujours comme d'un intérêt palpitant pour tous nos lecteurs.

Mais voici qu'aujourd'hui vous me demandez d'insérer une réponse qui est, ou se veut, à tel point du tac au tac que, loin d'élargir le débat, elle le rétrécit de façon inacceptable. Pour défendre votre ruche, vous foncez en aveugle et ne cherchez qu'à piquer votre adversaire le plus sensiblement possible. Vous cherchez son amour-propre, et non pas sa raison. Vous ne voulez pas le convertir; le paralyser seulement. Même s'il y avait, dans ce qu'il vous a écrit, quelque chose de dur — et je persiste à ne pas le voir — rien du moins ne dépassait le plan littéraire, ne touchait à la vie privée. Votre impétuosité vous fait franchir ces bornes.

Gide très généreusement voulait que je laisse paraître votre lettre. Vous comprendrez certainement, à la reflexion, que je ne peux absolument pas obéir à son désir. Outre que je lui garde trop de respect pour le laisser houspiller ainsi sous mon autorité, nos lecteurs ne comprendraient pas que nous prétendions les intéresser à une querelle personnelle.

Et laissez-moi vous dire, mon cher Cocteau, que je ne crois pas vous rendre un si mauvais service en vous invitant à retirer votre lettre. Elle ne vous ferait pas d'amis. Et c'est en grande partie parce que je désire conserver avec vous des relations cordiales que je l'arrête au passage.

Je vous envoie ma meilleure sympathie.

Jacques Rivière [23]

(My dear Cocteau,

We are sadly out in our reckoning. When you came to see me at the end of last month, still under the shock of the letter Gide had just read to you, you assured me that it vexed you only to the extent that it failed to recognize the esthetic of which you have made yourself the defender, and the new trends that your friends are following. Even today you write me: "The only things that Gide's letter can reach are outside me." Your complaint then is simply that Gide does not know you, understands badly what you are doing, what you wish to do, you and your friends.

At least this is how I have understood the matter, and it was in order to permit you to explain yourself on the doctrine that you accused Gide of treating with disdain that I indicated to you the possibility of welcoming a response from you in the *NRF*. I even declared myself delighted, I remember clearly, at the idea of seeing unfold in our pages a discussion on a point which I considered, and which I still consider, to be of pressing interest to all our readers.

But today, here you are asking me to put in a reply which is, or which means to be, tit for tat to such a degree that far from enlarging the debate it narrows it in an unacceptable manner. To defend your hive you lash out like a blind man and only try to sting your adversary as painfully as possible. You aim at his vanity and not at his reason. You don't want to convert him, only to paralyze him. Even if there had been, in what he wrote you, something hard—and I still do not see it—at least nothing went beyond the literary area, or touched on private life. Your impetuosity makes you overstep these boundaries.

Gide very generously wanted me to let your letter appear. You will surely understand, upon reflecting, that I absolutely cannot obey his wish. Besides my having too much respect for him to allow him to be mauled in this way under my authority, our readers would not understand why we took it upon ourselves to interest them in a personal quarrel.

And let me tell you, my dear Cocteau, that I do not feel I am doing you too much of a disservice by inviting you to withdraw your letter. It would not win you any friends. And it is in large part because I wish to maintain cordial relations with you that I stop it in passage.

I send you my best regards.

Jacques Rivière)

June [15–16]—Cocteau replied to Rivière. Although he claimed that he had not yet seen Rivière's letter, Cocteau said its contents were communicated to him by André Lhote, who had been alternately hearing both sides of the problem from Cocteau and Rivière. Cocteau insisted that his reply be printed in the July 1 issue of the *NRF*.

Mon cher Rivière,
   Je n'ai pas encore votre lettre mais Lhote m'en téléphone à peu près le contenu. J'ai *beaucoup* réfléchi à cette réponse et je ne la donne qu'aprés de nombreuses coupures. Elle doit paraître dans les limites de la lettre de Gide et surtout ne rien avoir d'un manifeste. Cette lettre trouve sa place dans l'œuvre que je voudrais accomplir — Elle est importante à l'interligne. Du reste cette question "d'importance" est en dehors du droit (amical) de réponse — Où je n'invoque aucun autre droit ridicule. Me demander d'étendre un passage serait demander au peintre de mettre plus de rouge ou de rompre l'équilibre du dessein. Des "semailles" ne peuvent se définir. Il faut une atmosphère de grouillement qui se trouve dans ma lettre — et l'ébauche d'une attitude. Sinon: article.
   Dans l'intérêt de Gide et dans le mien je vous demande en grâce de publier ma réponse ainsi faite dans le numéro du 1ᵉʳ Juillet. Ce serait si désagréable de m'obliger à une publication qui donnerait à Gide l'air d'avoir refusé une réponse légitime.
   Du reste, je n'envisage pas une véritable difficulté, venant de vous, pour une chose si simple.

Votre fidèle
Jean Cocteau [24]

(My dear Rivière,
   I do not yet have your letter, but Lhote has telephoned me its general contents. I have reflected *a long time* on this reply, and I submit it only after much pruning. It must seem within the limits of Gide's letter and above all be nothing like a manifesto. This letter finds its place in the work I would like to accomplish—it is important "between the lines." Anyway, this question of "importance" is outside the (friendly) right to reply— In which I do not invoke any other ridiculous right. To ask me to dilute a passage would be asking the artist to add more red or to disturb the equilibrium of his design. Seedtimes cannot be defined. There must be an atmosphere of rumbling, which is found in my letter—and the rough outline of an attitude. If not: article.
   In Gide's interest and in mine I entreat you to publish my reply, as it stands, in the issue of July 1st. It would be so disagreeable to force me into a publication that would make Gide seem to have refused a legitimate response.

In any event, I do not foresee a real problem, coming from you, for such a simple thing.

Your faithful
Jean Cocteau

June 15 — Cocteau was now doubly hurt, not only by the harshness of Gide's open letter but by the apparent refusal of the *NRF* to grant him the courtesy of a reply — a reply to which he felt legally entitled on a quid pro quo basis according to French law and custom. Gide was willing to publish Cocteau's reply, but Rivière and Gallimard were adamant in their opposition. Cocteau therefore wrote again to Gide, this time asking that his reply be published in the *NRF*, and offering to delete certain passages if Rivière insisted. Cocteau also pointed out to his adversary that he had had his reply approved by *five* disinterested friends; Gide's letter had been approved by only three:

Mon cher Gide,
   J'ai de Rivière une étrange lettre. Il désirait une certaine réponse et il s'étonne d'en recevoir une autre. Il "refuse" ce qui ne se refuse pas: une *réponse* ouverte à une lettre ouverte. Il voudrait un *article* en réponse à une *lettre*. Je sais que vous n'êtes pour rien dans cet acte inadmissible, mais je suis obligé de vous en rendre responsable. On ne se bat pas en duel dans un costume blindé. Je compte sur vous pour exiger que cette réponse paraisse en même place que votre lettre.

Votre ami.
Jean Cocteau

   J'ai, à votre exemple, lu ma réponse à 5 amis désintéressés qui l'approuvent — mais je suis prêt si Rivière le désire à supprimer certains passages — car pour nous deux il *faut* que la réponse paraisse.[25]

(My dear Gide,
   I have a strange letter from Rivière. He *wished* a certain reply and wonders why he receives a different one. He "refuses" what is never refused: an open *reply* to an open letter. He wanted an *article* in answer to a *letter*. I know you have nothing to do with this inadmissible action, but I am obliged to make you responsible. One does not fight a duel clad in armor. I count on you to demand that my reply be published in the same place as your letter.

Your friend,
Jean Cocteau

   [P.S.] Following your example, I read my reply to five disinterested friends who approved it — but I am ready to suppress certain

passages if Rivière wishes—because for both our sakes the reply *must* be published.)

June 15—In a conversation with Rivière, Cocteau agreed to resubmit his reply to Gide's open letter the following day, with purely personal comments deleted.

June 16—Cocteau, after a change of heart, told Rivière that his reply had to be published in the *NRF* without deletions. Failing this, Cocteau threatened legal action against the review to force publication of his response. Rivière replied: "Go ahead," and the two men shook hands.

June 17—Jacques Rivière's wife, Isabelle, wrote Gide at her husband's request:

M.   A. Gide à
Cuverville par Criquetôt l'Esneval

Cher ami,

Jacques, extrêmement fatigué, me charge de vous mettre au courant de l'affaire Cocteau.

Il avait été entendu Dimanche, après une très longue discussion, que Cocteau rapporterait le lendemain à Jacques sa lettre, débarrassée de tout ce qui était attaque purement personnelle.

Le lendemain – hier – Cocteau disait à Jacques: "Cette lettre doit paraître telle quelle ou pas du tout. Puisque vous refusez de la prendre, j'userai du droit que me donne la loi de répondre malgré vous. Je suis absolument désolé, mais je vais vous envoyer un huissier. – Faites, lui a répondu Jacques."

Et ils se sont quittés en serrant la main.

Jacques attend l'huissier. Que pensez-vous de cette absurde comédie? Autre chose: Jacques est désolé que vous ne lui donniez pas le papier sur les "déséquilibrés." D'autant plus qu'étant donnée l'affaire Cocteau il serait peut-être plus prudent d'ajourner le "Carnet d'un cubiste."

Et Jacques réclame vos épreuves le plus vite possible. Mes bien affectueuses pensées pour Madame Gide et vous.

Isabelle

Reçu ta lettre et le manuscrit Montherlant. Merci.[26]

(M.   A. Gide at Cuverville
by Criquetôt l'Esneval

Dear friend,

Jacques, extremely tired, asks me to bring you up to date on the Cocteau matter.

It had been understood Sunday, after a very long discussion, that

the next day Cocteau would bring his letter back to Jacques with everything removed that was a purely personal attack.

The following day—yesterday—Cocteau said to Jacques: "This letter must appear as is or not at all. Since you refuse to accept it, I will avail myself of the right the law gives me to answer in spite of you. I am terribly sorry, but I am going to send you a process-server." "Go ahead," Jacques replied. And they parted after shaking hands.

Jacques is waiting for the process-server. What do you think of this absurd comedy? Another thing: Jacques is sorry that you didn't give him the paper on "unbalanced" people. Especially since in view of the Cocteau matter it would perhaps be more prudent to postpone the "Notebook of a Cubist."

And Jacques requires your proofs back as quickly as possible. My affectionate wishes to Madame Gide and to you.

Isabelle

[P.S.] Received your letter and the Montherlant manuscript. Thanks.)

June 19—Cocteau sent Gide a copy of his new book *Le Potomak* inscribed: "À Gide au dessus de la mêlée, Jean Cocteau." The inscription was embellished by a drawing of one of Cocteau's ferocious Eugène figures with saw-like teeth.[27]

June 20—Cocteau sent a process-server to Gaston Gallimard at the *NRF* to present a formal demand for insertion of his reply in the July issue.

June [21]—Cocteau wrote a friendly letter to Rivière, expressing the hope that the *NRF* editor would find as much amusement in reading the text of the official summons as Cocteau had had in writing it.

June [23]—Cocteau sent a copy of *Le Potomak* to Rivière with an effusive incription.

June 25—Rivière wrote Gide reporting that the *NRF* was awaiting further legal developments, and that three years might elapse before the *NRF* was legally obliged to print Cocteau's reply:

Paris, le 25 juin 1919

Mon cher André,

J'ai voulu économiser le plus possible de lettres, ces jours derniers, pour me reposer l'esprit. De là ma lenteur à te répondre. Mais la lettre d'Isabelle t'aura fait prendre patience, j'espère.

Cocteau a envoyé son "exploit" à Gaston, (comme gérant) et il l'a fait suivre d'une lettre très aimable, où il m'exprimait son espoir que le texte m'en amuserait autant qu'il l'avait amusé à composer. Deux

jours après, le *Potomak* m'arrivait avec une dédicace pleine d'effusion.

En attendant nous ne bougeons pas. Nous avons remis l'exploit à l'homme d'affaires de la revue qui nous a conseillé de ne pas broncher et d'attendre une assignation. Il parait que ça peut durer trois ans avant que nous ne soyons condamnés légalement à l'insertion. . . .[28]

Paris
June 25, 1919

(My dear André,

I wanted to economize as much as possible on letters these last few days to give my mind a rest. That's why I am slow to answer you. But Isabelle's letter will have given you patience I hope.

Cocteau has sent his "summons" to Gaston (as manager), and he followed it by a very friendly letter in which he told me of his hope that the text would amuse me as much as it had amused him to compose it. Two days later the *Potomak* reached me with a dedication full of effusion.

Meanwhile we are not budging. We turned the summons over to the review's business manager, who advised us not to waver and to wait for a subpoena. It seems this can go on for three years before we may be legally ordered to make the insertion. . . .)

June 26—Gide complimented Cocteau on his recent letter to Marc Allégret and looked forward with pleasure to seeing him Tuesday.[29] This is a surprising letter in view of the fact that Gide had presumably already seen Cocteau's vindictive reply (sent on June 7 to Rivière) to Gide's open letter. Perhaps Gide still felt he could reason with Cocteau and get him to withdraw his reply. Cocteau may also have felt he could still prevail on Gide to print his reply in the *NRF*. Both expectations proved groundless, as subsequent developments showed.

July—Cocteau's open reply to Gide appeared in the June-July 1919 issue of *Ecrits Nouveaux:*

RÉPONSE À ANDRÉ GIDE

Gide me dit un jour: "Je viens de vous écrire une lettre à propos du COQ ET L'ARLEQUIN. Comme je n'ose vous l'envoyer, je vais la publier dans la *Nouvelle Revue Française.*" Rien de plus Gide. Je souris et j'approuvai cette pudeur étrange, me réservant toutefois de répondre en même place, si je l'estimais utile. "Je l'espère bien," s'écria Gide, "ce qui donne de l'intérêt à une rubrique de Lettres Ouvertes, c'est justement qu'elle excite, qu'elle est vivante, qu'elle comporte des réponses."

* * *

Un matin, Gide me montra sa lettre. On l'a lue dans le numéro du 1ᵉʳ juin de la *Nouvelle Revue Française*. Elle était alors un peu autre. Au lieu de me tendre un morceau de sucre (de restrictions) avant la drogue, il me le tendait après.

Cette lecture se passait à Auteuil.

Gide s'y est fait construire une maison symbolique. Les fenêtres ne regardent pas en face. À l'intérieur, des couloirs, des escaliers s'entrecroisent, *se contredisent*.

Serait-ce un état d'âme de Dostoïewski ou le véritable chalet NORMAND?

Gide, se rendant compte du ridicule d'envoyer, ouverte, à un ami, sans que personne le demande, une lettre pareille, m'avait laissé seul avec les feuillets de machine à écrire.

Enfin, il rentra. Du premier coup d'œil, il m'était apparu que sa lettre n'avait pas cet air de nécessité qui excuse tout: trop courte ou trop longue, trop venimeuse ou trop sirupeuse, sans le moindre intérêt général.

Je répugne à y chercher la manœuvre que certains y virent. Je ne trouve qu'une incompréhension fort excusable chez un écrivain mal renseigné sur le travail des jeunes compositeurs.

Mes reproches étonnèrent Gide. Il croyait m'avoir souvent dit ce que contenait sa lettre.

Outre que c'est inexact et qu'il "n'osait me parler du livre" sauf pour m'en réclamer une phrase et me remercier passionnément de la lui rendre, Gide, s'il se sent ours en ma présence, porte tant de miel à ses pattes que je distingue peu les griffes.

Non, la vérité me frappait pour la première fois.

Mon livre vise Arlequin. Et voici que sous les losanges et le loup, je reconnaissais un regard, une démarche. Arlequin répondait à mon livre une lettre aigre-douce et me retournait mes propres griefs avec agilité.

Cette lettre, disait-il, prenant la voix de Cassandre: "Je la dois au public" (! ?) Ou bien encore: "La véritable amitié ne se nourrit pas de réticences."

Je n'avais donc pas à essayer de convaincre. J'étais puni d'une paresse qui nous cache trop souvent les mésententes profondes.

Le surlendemain, Jacques Rivière me demanda un rendez-vous. J'allai le voir à la Revue et nous eûmes un long entretien. Rivière croyait devoir me convaincre que la lettre de Gide n'était pas inamicale.

Je l'arrêtai, portant tout de suite la dispute plus haut. La lettre de Gide devenait pour moi une occasion de marquer certaines distances.

Rivière se déclara enchanté à l'idée d'une discussion "sur un point qu'il considère comme d'un intérêt palpitant pour ses lecteurs."

J'emportai de cette rencontre une sympathie qui sort intacte de nos entêtements mutuels.

Je déjeunai avec Gide et lui annonçai que j'écrivais ma réponse. "Les seules choses, dis-je, que votre lettre puisse atteindre sont en dehors de moi, et si chères, si délicates, que je dois les défendre avec un peu d'escrime et beaucoup de fermeté."

Gide se félicita encore d'une forme de duel *réinstituant* s'écriait-il, *une chevalerie littéraire.*

J'envoyai donc ma réponse. J'évitais l'article, le manifeste. Je voulais répondre à une lettre par une lettre.

Rivière m'écrivit que cette lettre était trop une lettre, qu'elle rétrécissait le débat au lieu de l'élargir et, oubliant que Gide s'en prenait à ma nature même, m'accusa de "franchir les bornes du plan littéraire." Bref, il refusait d'insérer.

Ici je m'étonne. Une réponse ne se refuse pas, ne se discute pas. Si on contrôle le moindre texte d'une revue, on n'y laisse rien publier qui entraîne une réponse hasardeuse. Un groupe *fermé* n'accueille pas de lettres *ouvertes.*

Gide "très généreusement voulait que je laisse paraître votre lettre," ajoute Rivière. "Généreusement" n'est pas de mise. Le droit de réponse est un droit légal.

Je respecte les scrupules de Rivière. Je n'avais qu'un moyen de le couvrir vis-à-vis de Gide et d'éviter à Gide une fausse attitude. Je l'employai.

Toutefois je m'appliquai à rendre mon EXPLOIT le moins grave possible. J'eusse voulu amuser Gaston Gallimard en le lui faisant lire par un comédien du Théâtre-Français.[30]

Dans ce texte, selon le mot d'un ami, la cuiller tient debout.

LETTRE À ANDRÉ GIDE

Destinée au numéro du 1er juillet de *La Nouvelle Revue Française*

Mon cher Gide,

Vous connaissez la baraque foraine où le bon tireur déclenche un mécanisme. Une trappe s'ouvre et une silhouette se montre. Je sentais bien que mon petit livre avait fait mouche et qu'une silhouette allait paraître, mais je ne songeais pas à la vôtre.

Le premier mouvement de surprise passé, je m'approche et je cherche à démêler pourquoi c'est vous que mon "livre dans le mille" a fait sortir.

Vous avez, Gide, tout un système de mystères, de réserves, d'imparfaits du subjonctif, d'alibis et d'imbroglios.

La nécessité de publier ces lignes ailleurs que dans la Revue où Gide m'a interpellé, m'autorise à rétablir ici un paragraphe

d'ordre critique et à en supprimer un autre d'ordre plus personnel.

C'est mon tour, si j'y pense, de m'avouer ours aux pattes lourdes et de suivre, dans l'arbre, vos cache-cache d'écureuil.

Gide aime-t-il X...? Admire-t-il Y...? On l'interroge. Il renifle, se penche, hausse les épaules. Son genou dit que oui, son coude que non. Et n'ai-je pas, le premier, mis cette attitude sur le compte de votre sensibilité? Elle vous empêche de hasarder vos préférences fragiles dans les dialectiques sans restrictions.

J'admets donc ce système et ces tours de cartes. J'eusse trouvé inamical un pressant besoin de dire en public combien ils m'incommodent.

Je ne compte pas entreprendre ici l'éloge de LE COQ ET L'ARLEQUIN. Il a été lu, relu et approuvé en épreuves par le groupe des jeunes musiciens. Il les exprime. C'est un manuel de poche où je ne parle de moi qu'à cause de PARADE, et de PARADE qu'à titre d'exemple et aussi comme du SACRE pour fixer des points d'histoire.

Vous vous êtes récemment approché de nos semailles avec un intérêt louable chez un homme qui récolte.

Vous ne regardiez pas certaines audaces. Vous les regardez. Mais vous regardez *du dehors*.

Vous vous êtes même rendu acquéreur d'une toile de Georges Braque. Lorsque je vous demandai ce qu'elle représentait, si c'était sa "grappe de raisin," vous me répondites avec impatience que vous ne saviez pas, et que, du reste, cela vous était égal. Or, tout est là. Car si Braque ne partait pas d'une base solide, s'il n'emmenait pas une grappe, en libre logicien, où bon lui semble, vous ne goûteriez pas cette toile légère. Le raisin d'Apelle était un "trompe-l'œil d'oiseaux," le raisin de Braque est un "trompe-l'esprit d'hommes," non un décor.

Ce qui vous attire, c'est un décor, un tumulte, une marche sur les mains, qui sont l'écume du mouvement moderne.

Dans toute révolution, il existe une période aiguë de sauvagerie, une "terreur," où l'influence exotique se présente sous forme de bariolages (Michelet cite des anecdotes cannibales). Un instinct de réagir contre ces excès décide l'ordre nouveau. C'EST CET ORDRE QUI IMPORTE.

Vous vous êtes approché d'un *spectacle*. Si vous étiez à *l'intérieur*, vous vous rendriez compte qu'il était urgent et brave de mettre de l'ordre, de passer outre le blâme des agents provocateurs, des surenchères, d'un état d'esprit nègre qui consiste à déifier la machine.

Après ce coup d'œil moins superficiel, vous ressentiriez la gêne d'encourir certaines approbations.

Vous reprochez aussi, tacitement, au COQ d'être en désaccord avec le CAP DE BONNE-ESPÉRANCE. C'est possible. Un écrivain doit-il camoufler ses fautes en méthode? Nous ne l'admettons plus. Le COQ a été écrit après le CAP. Je n'ai pas pensé au CAP en écrivant le

Coq. Si le Coq et l'Arlequin corrige certains passages du Cap de Bonne-Espérance, il a raison parce qu'il arrive après. Je m'estimerais peu si j'avais renoncé à écrire l'un parce qu'il pourrait fournir une arme contre l'autre.

Du reste, mon cher Gide, l'incertitude n'est-elle pas le charme de vos œuvres et de votre style? On pense à une belle baigneuse qui n'ose se jeter à l'eau et qui se mouille les seins en poussant de petits cris.

Il y a en vous du pasteur et de la bacchante. Il arrive que ce mélange déconcerte à force qu'on le sente concerté. Ce n'est point que je ne reconnaisse la grâce de vos ivresses prudentes, mais certaines d'entre elles me semblent bien moins en rapport avec celui que vous êtes qu'avec celui que vous voudriez qu'on vous crût.

Pour le reproche de sauter des marches, je montais depuis l'enfance un escalier absurde. Vous êtes de ceux m'ayant fait voir qu'il en existait un autre. Bondir de celui-ci sur celui-là, au risque de se rompre le cou, n'est pas ce que j'appelle: sauter des marches. Ensuite, il ne faut pas confondre "sauter des marches" avec monter marche à marche un escalier où la lumière n'éclaire les marches que par intervalles.

Bien des nuances, mon cher Gide, que vous négligez et qui comptent lorsqu'on entame une controverse si impérieuse qu'elle dépasse les scrupules du cœur.

Dans le Coq et l'Arlequin, j'avais, sans m'en rendre compte, emprunté une phrase à votre conversation et vous la restituai, sur votre prière instante, par l'entremise d'un *papillon.* Ce papillon était une preuve de mon amitié. Ne voyez pas autre chose dans cette réponse qu'un papillon aux ailes un peu plus lourdes.

Jean COCTEAU

P.S. — Je ne vais pas ratiociner sur Parade, notre grand jouet mécanique. Vous suivez une mode qui était d'en dire du mal sans l'avoir vu. Ce spectacle proposait, comme tout spectacle, des perspectives de mystère, mais ne cherchait pas le moins du monde à les mettre en valeur au détriment du plaisir des yeux.

Mon droit était formel.

La *Nouvelle Revue Française* passe outre et m'oblige à poursuivre sur un terrain désagréable. Je le regrette, car je suis forcé de rendre Gide seul responsable.

Je sais fort bien que Gide se réfugiera derrière la phrase où "généreusement" sonne si faux, mais il suffisait qu'il insiste. Il devait exiger que ma réponse paraisse.

Gide parle de duel. Il vient de se battre dans un costume blindé.

Pourquoi voulez-vous que je m'en prenne aux amis qui lui jouèrent cette farce par sollicitude, ou même au fabriquant de blindages? Je constate. Je lève le pouce. Les témoins s'approchent. On découvre la cotte de maille, et chacun rentre chez soi.

Jean COCTEAU.[31]

(REPLY TO ANDRÉ GIDE

Gide said to me one day: "I have just written you a letter about *Le Coq et l'Arlequin*. Since I dare not send it to you I am going to print it in the *Nouvelle Revue Française*." Typical of Gide. I smiled and consented to that curious modesty, at the same time reserving my right to reply in the same place if I judged it advisable. "I very much hope so," cried Gide, "that's exactly what makes a column of Open Letters interesting: it stimulates, it is alive, it provokes responses."

*   *   *

One morning Gide showed me his letter. Everyone read it in the June 1st issue of the *Nouvelle Revue Française*. It was then quite a different letter. Instead of offering me a lump of sugar (of restrictions) before the medicine, he gave it to me afterward.

That reading took place at Auteuil.

There Gide had built a symbolic house. The windows do not face the street. Inside, hallways and staircases intersect, *contradict each other*.

Would this represent a mood of Dostoevsky or the genuine NORMAN chalet?

Gide, realizing the absurdity of sending such a letter, open, to a friend, without anyone having asked for it, had left me alone with the typed sheets of paper.

Finally he reappeared. From the first glance I had seen that the letter did not have that air of necessity which excuses everything: too short or too long, too venomous or too syrupy, without the slightest general interest.

I shrink from finding in the letter the intrigue that some people see in it. I only find a lack of comprehension altogether understandable in an author who is poorly informed about the work of young writers.

My protests astonished Gide. He believed he had often told me what was in his letter.

Aside from being inaccurate and saying that he "dared not speak to me about the book," except to reclaim one of its sentences from me and to thank me fervently for giving it back to him, Gide, if he does feel like a bear in my presence, has so much honey on his paws that I scarcely notice the claws.

No, the truth struck me for the first time.

My book aims at Harlequin. And here beneath the lozenges and the magnifying glass I recognized a gaze, a gait. Harlequin answered my book with a bitter-sweet letter and cleverly turned my own complaints back on me.

"This letter," said he, adopting Cassandra's voice: "I owe to the public" (!?). And again: "True friendship is ill-nourished on reticence."

I had no need therefore to try and persuade. I was paying the penalty for a laziness that too often conceals deep misunderstandings from us.

Two days later Jacques Rivière asked to meet with me. I went to see him at the *Revue* and we had a long interview. Rivière felt he must convince me that Gide's letter was not unfriendly.

I interrupted him, carrying the dispute at once to a higher level. Gide's letter became for me the opportunity to establish certain distances.

Rivière declared he was delighted by the idea of a discussion "on a point he considered to be of thrilling interest for his readers."

From that meeting I carried away a sympathy which emerges intact from our mutual obstinacy.

I lunched with Gide and advised him that I was writing my reply. "The only things," I said, "that your letter could reach are outside me and are so precious, so delicate, that I must defend them with a bit of fencing and a great deal of firmness."

Gide still congratulated himself on a kind of duel that *reinstated*, he cried, *a literary chivalry*.

So I sent in my reply. I avoided making it an article, a manifesto. I wanted to reply to a letter with a letter.

Rivière wrote me that my letter was too much a letter, that it narrowed the debate instead of enlarging it, and, forgetting that Gide had even attacked my character, accused me of "exceeding the limits of the literary frame of reference." In short, he refused to print my letter.

At this point I am astonished. A reply is not to be refused, it is beyond questioning. If every word in a magazine is censored, nothing that elicits a dangerous response is allowed to be published. A *closed* group doesn't welcome *open* letters.

Gide "very generously wanted me to let your letter appear," Rivière added. "Generously" is out of place. The right to reply is a legal right.

I respect Rivière's scruples. I only had one means of shielding him from Gide and of avoiding a false posture toward Gide. I used it.

I made an effort, however, to present my EXPLOIT with the least possible gravity. I wanted to amuse Gaston Gallimard by having it read to him by an actor from the Comédie-Française.

In this text, as a friend says, the spoon stands on end.

LETTER TO ANDRÉ GIDE

Intended for the July 1st issue of *La Nouvelle Revue Française*

My dear Gide,

You're familiar with the booths at fairs where the crack shot trips a mechanism. A trapdoor opens and a target suddenly appears. I felt quite sure my little book had hit the bull's eye and that a silhouette was going to appear, but I didn't dream it would be yours.

When the first wave of surprise had passed, I went up close to try to figure out why it was you my "one book in a thousand" had unearthed.

You have, Gide, a complete system of mysteries, of reserves, of imperfect subjunctives, of alibis, and of entanglements.

> The necessity of publishing these lines somewhere else than in the Revue where Gide has challenged me, authorizes me to restore here a paragraph of a critical order and to suppress another of a more personal nature.

It is my turn, if I think about it, to acknowledge myself to be a heavy-footed bear and to follow your squirrel's hide-and-seek in the tree.

Does Gide like X...? Does he admire Y...? Someone asks him. He sniffs, hunches over, shrugs his shoulders. His knee says yes, his elbow says no. And wasn't I the first one to attribute this attitude to your compassion? It prevents you from venturing your fragile preferences without reservations in argument.

Therefore I accept this system and these card tricks. I would have considered as unfriendly an urgent need to say publicly how greatly they upset me.

I do not expect to take up the cudgel here for *Le Coq et l'Arlequin*. It was read, reread and approved before publication by the group of young musicians. It expresses them. It is a pocket textbook in which I speak of myself only because of *Parade*, and of *Parade* only by way of example and also as I do of *Sacre* [*du Printemps*]: to mark points in history.

You recently approached our sowing with an interest that is praiseworthy in a man who is gathering his sheaves.

You had not been watching certain audacities. Now you do. But you watch them *from the outside*.

You even acquired a painting by Georges Braque. When I asked you what it represented, whether it was his "bunch of grapes," you answered impatiently that you didn't know and that anyway it was all the same to you. However, that's the whole point. Because if Braque had not started from a solid base, if he had not, as a free

logician, developed a bunch of grapes as he saw fit, you would not relish that airy canvas. Apelles' grape was a "trompe l'œil for birds," Braque's grape is a "trompe l'esprit for men," not a decoration.

What attracts you is a decoration, an uproar, a walking on hands, which are the froth of the modern movement.

In all revolution there is a sharp period of savagery, a "terror," where exotic influence shows up in the form of motley ideas (Michelet cites cannibal stories). An instinct to react against these excesses determines the new order. IT IS THIS ORDER THAT COUNTS.

You approached a *play*. If you had been on *the inside* you would have recognized that it was urgent and courageous to go beyond the censure of *agents provocateurs*, of higher bidders, to bring some order to a primitive state of mind that consists of deifying the machine.

After this less superficial glance you would have felt the discomfort of incurring certain approvals.

You also tacitly reproach the *Coq* for being out of tune with the *Cap de Bonne-Espérance*. That's possible. Must a writer camouflage his errors of method? We don't permit it any longer. The *Coq* was written after the *Cap*. I didn't think about the *Cap* when writing the *Coq*. If the *Coq et l'Arlequin* corrects certain passages of the *Cap de Bonne-Espérance*, it has reason to since it happened afterward. I would have little regard for myself if I had refused to write one because it might provide a weapon against the other.

Besides, my dear Gide, isn't uncertainty the charm of your work and style? One is reminded of a beautiful woman bather who dares not throw herself into the water and who sprinkles her bosom while uttering little shrieks.

There is in you something of the pastor and of the bacchante. It happens that this mixture disconcerts through one's sensing it to be concerted. It is not at all that I do not recognize the charm of your prudent raptures, but some of them seem to me much less in harmony with the person you are than with the person you would have us believe you to be.

As for your reproach about my skipping stairs, ever since childhood I have been climbing an absurd staircase. You are one of those who made me see that another existed. To leap from the former to the latter, at the risk of breaking my neck, is not what I call skipping stairs. Furthermore, you must not confuse "skipping stairs" with climbing one by one a staircase where the steps are only lighted here and there.

There are many nuances, my dear Gide, which you disregard and which are important when you undertake a controversy so imperious that it transcends the scruples of the heart.

In the *Coq et l'Arlequin* I had, without being aware of it, borrowed a phrase from your conversation and I gave it back to you promptly

at your insistence by means of an *acknowledgement slip*. That *papillon* was a proof of my friendship. You should not see anything else in this reply than a butterfly with somewhat heavier wings.

Jean COCTEAU

P.S. I am not going to talk endlessly about *Parade*, our big clock-work toy. You are following a fashion which was to speak ill of it without having seen it. This play, like all plays, offered some perspectives of mystery, but didn't in the least try to emphasize them to the detriment of the eye's pleasure.

My right was categorical.

The *Nouvelle Revue Française* disregards it and obliges me to pursue the matter onto disagreeable ground. I regret it because I am forced to hold Gide alone responsible.

I know very well that Gide will take refuge behind the sentence in which "generously" sounds so false, but it was enough that he insist. He should have insisted that my reply appear.

Gide speaks of a duel. He has just been fighting in armor.

Why do you wish me to blame the friends who played this prank on him out of concern, or even the armorer? I note. I raise my thumb. The witnesses approach. The coat of mail is discovered, and everyone goes home.

Jean COCTEAU)

July 8 — Cocteau wrote Gide a letter explaining that the *NRF* refusal to publish his reply had obliged him to make other arrangements. Cocteau disclaimed having asked Mme Mühlfeld, a common friend, to intercede for him with Gide:

8 Juillet 1919

Mon cher Gide,

L'attitude de la N.R.F. m'a obligé à prendre des décisions qui rendaient une rencontre entre nous gênante, jusqu'à nouvel ordre. Croyez bien que ce n'est pas moi qui ai prié Madame Mühlfeld de vous voir et que j'ignorais les convives (sauf Florent et Fargue) — Je ne voudrais pour rien au monde avoir l'air d'une girouette.

Je vous avoue que j'emporte de ce déjeuner une sorte de mélancolie au cœur. Mais ces mêmes raisons que vous invoquiez dans une de vos lettres m'obligent à vaincre une faiblesse sentimentale.

Jean Cocteau [32]

July 8, 1919

(My dear Gide,

The *NRF*'s attitude forced me to take decisions that made a meeting between us disturbing until further notice. Please believe that it was not I who asked Mme Mühlfeld to see you and that I didn't even know

the guests (except Florent and Fargue)—I wouldn't for anything in the world want to look like a weathervane.

I must confess to you that I carry away from that luncheon a sort of melancholy of the heart. But those same reasons that you invoked in one of your letters oblige me to master a sentimental weakness.

Jean Cocteau)

July 9—Gide and Cocteau met, probably by accident, at the *NRF* offices.

July 11—Gide, brooding over Cocteau's stricken look during their encounter two days before, wrote Cocteau a long letter calculated to soothe Cocteau's feelings. Gide explained again that the *NRF* refusal to print Cocteau's reply was counter to his own wishes. He then revived at length the issue of Cocteau's plagiarism in *Le Coq et l'Arlequin,* a gesture that could only rub salt in the wound since Cocteau had long ago publicly humbled himself by having an acknowledgement slip crediting Gide inserted in the volume.

11 juillet 19

Mon cher Jean

Puisque vous estimez qu'il faut toujours répondre, sans doute attendez-vous un mot de moi en retour de votre lettre — que je ne comprendrais pas bien si je ne me souvenais de votre visage d'avant-hier, si contracté, si douloureux, que j'éprouvais de mon côté, bien vive, cette "mélancolie du cœur" dont vous parlez.

Je voudrais du moins qu'il n'y eût pas de malentendus entre nous: Vous aurez su, je pense, que le refus d'insérer votre lettre ne venait pas de moi. Rivière, se refusa à y voir proprement une réponse et me déclara qu'il considérait la lettre comme impubliable. "Au lieu de *répondre* à aucune des critiques que tu lui adresses dans ta lettre si pesée, si mesurée, m'écrivait-il (j'étais à Cuverville) il te jette à la tête toutes les méchancetés qu'il peut trouver, sans lien, sans autre intention que de te mordre." — Je suis né pour être mordu; néanmoins j'acquiesçai aux arguments de Rivière qui me parurent justes.

Le point sur lequel je voudrais revenir est celui-ci: vous semblez avoir fort mal compris le sentiment qui m'a fait vous demander ce que vous appelez "le papillon" — que j'appelerai plus exactement "le paratonnerre." Vous savez pourtant fort bien que cette phrase de moi n'était pas la seule dans votre petit livre, empruntée par vous, consciemment ou inconsciemment (peu m'importe). Vous même m'aviez avisé qu'on vous en avait signalé une autre — et s'il vous avait fallu faire des papillons pour tous les "emprunts" de votre Coq, ces papillons eussent rappelé ceux dont parle Darwin dans le récit de

son voyage, "si nombreux qu'ils suffisent à modifier le paysage." Je vous ai proposé celui-ci pour *sauvegarder* le reste; vous auriez pu, ce me semble, m'en savoir gré. — Et pouvais-je indiquer cette appropriation du bien d'autrui avec plus de modération, plus de courtoisie que je n'ai fait dans ma "lettre ouverte"? Je ne crois pas.

Ne m'étant jamais mépris sur vous, je n'ai pas à modifier mes sentiments à votre égard; votre attitude ne m'apporte pas grande surprise et je reste (il ne tient qu'à vous de l'éprouver) aussi affectueusement qu'auparavant.

André Gide

P.Sc. J'ai voulu demander à Rivière l'autorisation de cette citation de sa lettre. De là le retard de celle-ci.[33]

July 11, 1919

(My dear Jean,

Since you think that one must always reply, you no doubt await word from me in answer to your letter—which I would not understand very well if I didn't remember your face of the day before yesterday, so drawn, so sorrowful, that I too felt most keenly that "sadness of the heart" of which you speak.

I would at least like not to have any misunderstandings between us. You know, I think, that the refusal to insert your letter was not my doing. Rivière refused to see it as a proper "reply" and declared to me that he considered the letter unpublishable. "Instead of *answering* any of the criticisms contained in your letter, so carefully weighed and measured," he wrote me (I was in Cuverville), "he flings at your head all the spiteful things he can think of, without any connection, with no other intention than to bite you."—I was born to be bitten: nevertheless, I acquiesced in Rivière's arguments, which seemed just to me.

The point to which I would like to return is this: you seem to have very badly misunderstood the feeling that prompted me to ask you for what you call "the butterfly"—and which I call more accurately "the lightning rod." You know very well, however, that this sentence of mine was not the only one in your little book that you borrowed either knowingly or unknowingly (it makes little difference to me). You yourself had let me know that another one had been pointed out to you—and if you had had to make butterflies for all the "borrowing" in your *Coq*, those butterflies would have recalled the ones Darwin speaks of in the account of his voyage: "so numerous they are enough to change the landscape." I proposed this one to you in order to keep the others safe; you might, it seems to me, have been grateful to me for this. And could I have indicated this appropriation of others' property with more restraint or courtesy than I did in my "open letter"? I believe not.

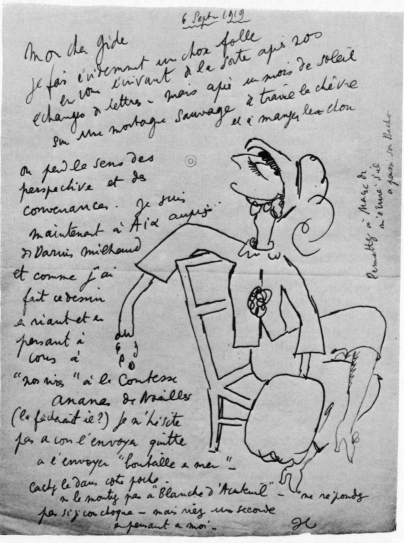

Letter from Cocteau to Gide of September 6, 1919, with a caricature of their mutual friend Comtesse Anna de Noailles. Photo J. M. Schlemmer.

Since I have never been mistaken on your account, I need not modify my feelings about you. Your attitude does not greatly surprise me, and I remain (it is only up to you to find out) as affectionately yours as before.

André Gide

P.S. I wanted to ask Rivière's permission to quote from his letter. Hence the delay in my own.)

Despite the mild tone of this letter, Gide had already drafted his second open letter attacking Cocteau. Here he adopted the same personal and vindictive manner that he and Rivière had previously deplored in Cocteau.

July 12 — Rivière wrote Gide suggesting that he tone down the language of his second open letter to Cocteau.

Paris, le 12 Juillet 1919

M.   A. Gide
Auteuil

Mon cher André,
Je t'envoie ci-joint la copie demandée de ta lettre à Cocteau. En relisant celle-ci, je me suis demandé si par hasard tu ne retirerais pas la "pétarade de perfidies" qui, seule, dépasse notablement le ton de la lettre que j'ai écrite directement à Cocteau, et qui pourrait aggraver son hostilité contre moi. J'ai quelques scrupules à te faire recopier toute la lettre pour cette seule suppression. Tu feras comme tu voudras.

Ton ami,
Jacques Rivière

Tu pourrais mettre quelque chose comme: "Ce que vous appeliez "réponse" Rivière se refusait à y voir autre chose qu'une agression personnelle."
La seconde phrase que tu cites de moi suffirait, je crois, à te dégager. Je joins aussi la phrase que tu m'avais remise pour servir de "chapeau" pour le cas où tu voudrais la lui montrer.[34]

Paris, July 12, 1919

(M.   A. Gide
Auteuil

My dear André,
I send you herewith the copy of your letter to Cocteau that you asked for. In reading this over again, I wondered if by chance you wouldn't take out the "outburst of perfidies," which is the only part that notably exceeds the tone of the letter I wrote directly to Cocteau, and which might aggravate his hostility towards me. I feel badly

about making you recopy the whole letter for that simple deletion. You will do as you wish.

> Your friend,
> Jacques Rivière

[P.S.] You could put something like: "What you called 'reply,' Rivière refused to see as anything else than a personal aggression." The second sentence of mine that you quote would be enough, I think, to release you. I also add the phrase that you gave me to serve as a "hat" in case you should wish to show it to him.)

July 13—Gide agreed to delete the passage suggested by Rivière.[35] If he and Rivière were concerned that Cocteau's reaction might prolong the dispute, they perhaps worried unnecessarily. Cocteau always maintained that he deliberately avoided reading Gide's second open letter.

August 4—In his Carte Blanche column Cocteau wrote: "Chez nous, rien ne compte sans contour. J'emprunte le terme à Gide." This comment was no doubt designed to show the public that he and Gide were still on good terms, and to show Gide that Cocteau had learned the lesson of giving due credit to his sources.

September 6—Before Gide's second open letter appeared, and possibly before Cocteau even knew it had been written, he was already anxious to patch up his quarrel with Gide and wrote him a conciliatory letter. Perhaps significantly, the letter was decorated on the right half of the page with a striking caricature of their mutual friend the Countess Anna de Noailles, who had been the original intermediary in the controversy over the borrowed phrase in *Le Coq et l'Arlequin*.

> Aix-en-Provence
> 6 Sept 1919

Mon cher Gide,

Je fais évidemment une chose folle en vous écrivant de la sorte après nos échanges de lettres — mais après un mois de soleil sur une montagne sauvage à traire la chèvre et à manger le chou on perd le sens des perspectives et des convenances. Je suis maintenant à Aix auprès de Darius Milhaud et comme j'ai fait ce dessin en riant et en pensant à vous à "nos rires" à la Comtesse Ananas de Noailles (la fâcherait-il?)[36] je n'hésite pas à vous l'envoyer quitte à l'envoyer "bouteille en mer" — Cachez le dans votre poche — ne le montrez pas à "Blanche d'Auteuil" — ne répondez pas si je vous choque — mais riez une seconde en pensant à moi —

> JC

Permettez à Marc de m'écrire s'il a passé son Bacho.[37]

Aix-en-Provence
Sept. 6, 1919

(My dear Gide,

I am obviously behaving foolishly in writing you this way after our exchange of letters—but after a month of sunshine on a wild mountainside, milking goats and eating cabbages, one loses one's sense of perspective and decorum. Now I am at Aix near Darius Milhaud, and since I made this drawing while laughing and thinking of you, of our "laughs together," of Countess Ananas de Noailles (would it offend her?), I have no hesitation in sending it to you—even if it is like casting a bottle into the sea. Hide it in your pocket—don't show it to [Jacques-Emile] "Blanche of Auteuil"—don't answer if I shock you—but chuckle a moment in thinking of me.

JC

[P.S.] Please let Marc [Allégret] write me whether he passed his Bacho exams.)

October 1—Gide's second open letter to Cocteau appeared in the October 1919 issue of *Ecrits Nouveaux:*

LA NOUVELLE PARADE DE JEAN COCTEAU

Monsieur Jean Cocteau s'est fait une spécialité de la Parade. À la critique que je fis de son livre, sous forme de *lettre ouverte,* dans le Nº de juin de la Nouvelle Revue Française, il riposta par une lettre, que je priai le directeur de cette revue de bien vouloir publier sans commentaires. Il n'y avait point là "générosité" de ma part (et je déplore que M. Rivière, faisant part à M. Cocteau de mes intentions, ait employé ce mot) mais prudence: Je sais de reste, et par expérience qu'à toucher à certaines vogues, et plus elles sont injustifiées, qu'à dénoncer certaines fausses valeurs, et plus elles ont cours — le critique risque de se faire écharper. Il ne m'est jamais apparu que Jean Cocteau dut se considérer comme bridé par le refus d'insertion que lui oppose Jacques Rivière. Celui-ci tenait la dite riposte pour indécente, ne repondant point à ma lettre, et précipitant la discussion sur un terrain peu littéraire où la critique ne pouvait que se fourvoyer — où il ne lui plaisait point de laisser s'aventurer la revue qu'il dirige. Il n'a jamais été dans mon humeur d'exiger rien de personne, non plus à la Nouvelle Revue Française qu'ailleurs: je m'inclinai devant la décision de Rivière. Cependant j'étais officieusement averti que cette "réponse" de Cocteau, si la N.R.F. ne l'acceptait point, paraîtrait ailleurs, et je ne doutai point que le retrait de notre revue ne fit que m'exposer davantage. — Quoi qu'il en soit, et où que dût paraître la protestation de M. Cocteau, (dont entre temps j'avais eu connaissance) j'étais bien fermement résolu à ne point répliquer à mon tour, ne parvenant pas, malgré la persuasion de M. Cocteau, à considérer la

discussion littéraire comme une forme du pugilat. Mais M. Cocteau ne s'en tient pas à la riposte; si injurieuse que fut déjà celle-ci, il l'encadre de commentaires plus injurieux encore; il cite des propos que j'aurais tenus (et j'ai le grand regret de pouvoir me reconnaître beaucoup moins dans les phrases et les idées qu'il me prête, que dans celles que, par ailleurs, il me prend); il fait de certaine entrevue avec moi tel récit, dont le plus poli que j'en pourrai dire, c'est que la version que j'en donnerais, pour être sensiblement différente, n'en serait que plus véridique. J'accepte tout ce qu'il dit ou insinue des défauts de mon caractère; il se peut — mais il fait arme contre moi de ma modération même, mais il éclaire tout ceci d'une manière par trop désinvoltement avantageuse, apportant à camoufler les faits autant d'art qu'à se camoufler lui-même. Il m'oblige à le démasquer.

Il n'est pas donné à chacun d'être original. M. Cocteau n'en est pas à sa première imitation. Ce que ma *lettre ouverte* lui reprochait, ce n'était point tant de s'assimiler l'art d'autrui, que de se donner des airs de chef d'école et d'inventeur; ce n'était point tant de suivre, certes, mais de feindre de précéder.

Je ne parlerais point de l'entrevue que nous eûmes, où je lui donnai connaissance de cette lettre, s'il ne me poussait à le faire par l'habile récit qu'il en donne. Pourquoi me force-t-il à rappeler ses protestations, ses imprécations, le jeu de sa canne-épée, ses supplications, ses serments sur la tête de ses parents... M. Cocteau est un prodigieux acteur. J'étais comme au spectacle et de ma vie, je crois, je n'avais été plus surpris. Je songeais au récit qu'on lit dans Saint-Simon, de son entrevue avec le P. Tellier: "Il me dit tant de choses, si énormes, si atroces, si effroyables et avec une passion si extrême que j'en tombai en véritable syncope" — et je me retenais de lui demander, moi aussi: "Quel âge avez-vous?..." Cela dura deux heures environ, à la suite de quoi je pensai qu'il devait avoir faim et je l'emmenai déjeuner.

Je l'avais un peu calmé en le persuadant qu'il aurait tout loisir pour me répondre, et pour défendre ses principes esthétiques, ainsi qu'il m'annonça qu'il voulait faire — principes que, au demeurant, je n'avais jamais critiqués, puisque aussi bien ce sont les miens. Et c'est bien là pourquoi Cocteau, quittant ce terrain, s'en prend à ma personne, à mon caractère, à la maison que j'ai fait construire! à certaine peinture que j'achète sans me soucier si c'est une grappe de raisin qu'elle représente et pourquoi, fidèle à son habitude, il emprunte certaines phrases de ma lettre pour les rétorquer contre moi.

Ce sont les phrases où je tachais, dans les termes les plus courtois, de dénoncer cette double personnalité de M. Cocteau, l'une réelle, la plus charmante de beaucoup, l'autre d'emprunt, qu'il peine à faire passer pour la vraie.

Au surplus il reconnaît implicitement la justesse de ma critique: Reprenant une phrase de son livre: "L'artiste ne doit jamais sauter de marches," je m'écriais: "Mais qu'avez-vous jamais fait d'autre?"

(et j'ajoutais que je ne lui reprochais certes pas de bondir!). Il proteste. Il explique qu'il n'a pas précisément sauté des marches, mais que s'étant d'abord trompé d'escalier, il a bondi "au risque de se casser le cou" de cet escalier sur un autre... Le malheur c'est qu'au lieu de retomber sur ses pieds, c'est sur les miens qu'il retombe. Il explique ensuite que la lumière "n'y éclaire les marches que par intervalles"; alors je fais jouer l'électricité. Mais voici qu'au lieu de s'excuser, il m'insulte. Je voulais me taire; il me contraint de protester. Ce qu'il souhaite, c'est qu'on parle de lui. Est-il content?

Je m'excuse de fatiguer le lecteur.

ANDRÉ GIDE [38]

(THE NEW PARADE OF JEAN COCTEAU

M. Jean Cocteau has made a specialty of the Parade. To the criticism I made of his book, in the form of an *open letter,* in the June issue of the *Nouvelle Revue Française,* he riposted ungraciously with a letter which I asked the director of that review to be good enough to publish without comment. There was no "generosity" on my part (and I deplore that M. Rivière used this word when informing M. Cocteau of my intentions), but prudence: I know, moreover, and from experience, that the critic risks getting torn to pieces if he tampers with certain fashions, especially when they are unjustified, if he denounces certain false values, especially when they are commonly accepted. It never seemed to me that Jean Cocteau should have considered himself muzzled by Jacques Rivière's refusal of insertion. The latter considered that retort to be improper, not answering my letter in any way, and shifting the discussion onto ground having little to do with literature, where criticism could only go astray—where he had no desire to allow the review he directed to wander. It has never been my nature to insist on anything from anyone, any more at the *Nouvelle Revue Française* than elsewhere: I bowed to Rivière's decision. However, I was officiously warned that Cocteau's "reply," if the *NRF* refused to accept it, would be printed somewhere else, and I had no doubt that the cancellation by our review would only have the effect of exposing me even more. Whatever it might be, and wherever M. Cocteau's protest (about which I had learned in the meantime) should appear, I had quite firmly resolved not to reply in my turn since I cannot, despite M. Cocteau's belief, consider literary discussion a form of boxing. But M. Cocteau does not limit himself to a retort; as insulting as this already was, he frames it with still more insulting comments; he quotes remarks I am alleged to have made (and I regret greatly being able to recognize myself much less in the phrases and ideas he ascribes to me than in those he takes from me elsewhere); he makes such a tale out of a certain interview with me that the most polite thing I can say about it is that the version I would

give, although significantly different, would only be the more in accord with the facts. I accept all that he says or insinuates about the flaws in my character; it may be—but he even turns my moderation against me as a weapon, and throws light on all this in a way which is far too casually to his advantage, using as much art in camouflaging the facts as in camouflaging himself. He obliges me to unmask him.

It is not given to everyone to be original. This is not M. Cocteau's first imitation. What my *open letter* reproached him for was not so much for assimilating the art of others as for giving himself the airs of a chef d'école and inventor; it was not so much for following, to be sure, but for pretending to precede.

I would not speak of the interview we had, in which I made him acquainted with that letter, if he did not push me into doing so by the clever tale he tells of it. Why does he force me to recall his protests, his curses, the play of his sword-cane, his entreaties, his oaths on the head of his parents... M. Cocteau is a prodigious actor. It was as though I were at the theater and in all my life I don't believe I have been more surprised. I thought of the account in Saint-Simon of his interview with Father Tellier: "He told me so many things, so exaggerated, so atrocious, so appalling, and with such extreme passion that I fell into a veritable swoon"—and I too checked myself from asking him: "How old are you?..." All this lasted about two hours, after which I thought he must be hungry and I took him off to lunch.

I had calmed him down a bit by persuading him that he would have every opportunity to reply to me and to defend his esthetic principles, as he announced to me he wished to do—principles which, after all, I had never criticized because they are as a matter of fact my own. And that is exactly why Cocteau, leaving this ground, attacks my person, my character, the house I had built! a certain painting I had bought without bothering my head if it represented a bunch of grapes, and why, faithful to his usual practice, he borrows a number of sentences from my letter to hurl them back on me.

These are the sentences in which I tried in the most courteous terms to expose that double personality of M. Cocteau, one real, the most charming by far, the other borrowed, which he tries hard to pass off as the authentic one.

Besides, he recognizes without question the correctness of my criticism: Taking up a sentence from his book: "The artist must never skip stairs," I exclaimed: "But what else have you ever done?" (and I added that I surely did not reproach him for leaping!). He protests. He explains that he hasn't exactly skipped stairs, but that having at first started up the wrong staircase he jumped, "at the risk of breaking his neck," from that staircase to another... The trouble is that instead of landing on his own feet he lands on mine. He explains afterward that the light "only illuminates the stairs here and there"; so I throw on the lights. But then instead of excusing himself he insults me. I

wanted to keep still; he compels me to protest. What he wishes is to be talked about. Is he happy?

I am sorry for wearying the reader.

ANDRÉ GIDE)

October 8 — Cocteau's resentment toward Gide flared up again in a letter to Jacques-Emile Blanche:

Gide lui, comme d'aucuns se protègent derrière la religion, se drape dans la médiocrité qui lui ralliera aussi pas mal de monde. Son chef d'œuvre sans nicotine est une bonne place forte pour écrire des Lettres Ouvertes. C'est près de Bazin et très près de Bazaine et je trouve naturel que le Coq et l'Arlequin lui déplaise car il peut y lire qu'un artiste qui récule ne trahit pas mais *se* trahit. Du reste son recul c'est du recul sur bien faible distance ce qui s'est remarqué par peu de personnes. Brûlez la page sur Gide — Car mon opinion sur Gide aura toujours l'air d'une rancune — alors qu'au contraire je ne me sens plus la moindre animosité contre l'ami charmant *qui me manque.* (Labyrinthes du cœur). . . .[39]

(Gide himself, the way certain people take shelter behind religion, drapes himself in mediocrity which will also rally quite a few people to his support. His masterpiece without nicotine is a good stronghold from which to write Open Letters. It is close to Bazin and very near to Bazaine, and I find it natural that *Le Coq et l'Arlequin* should displease him because in it he can read that an artist who retreats does not betray, but betrays *himself.* Besides, his retreat is one of very short distance, something that few people have noticed. Burn the page about Gide — For my opinion about Gide will always have the appearance of a grudge — whereas on the contrary I no longer bear the slightest ill feeling toward the charming friend *whom I miss.* (Labyrinths of the heart). . . .)

November 20, 1919 — A month after his second open letter was printed, Gide replied at last to Cocteau's letter of September 6, 1919, in a surprisingly conciliatory tone:

20 Nov. 19

Mon cher Jean

Votre amusante lettre de Septembre ne m'avait point laissé insensible — mais les mêmes raisons que vous aviez de me faire grise mine à ce nombreux déjeuner où nous nous étions rencontré [*sic*] — me retenaient jusqu'à présent d'y répondre. Je déplore que certains passages de votre protestation m'aient mis dans l'obligation de protester à mon tour — je ne l'ai fait qu'à cœur défendant. Devions

[-nous] désormais ne nous lancer que des regards hostiles? Pour ma part je ne saurais, et si je pensais que vous deviez la serrer sans trop de rancune, ma main se tendrait aussitôt...

Blanche me parle d'excellents dessins de vous qu'il me tarde bien de voir.

A. Gide [40]

Nov. 20, 1919

(My dear Jean,

Your amusing letter of September did not leave me at all unmoved —but the same reasons that you had for giving me black looks at that crowded luncheon where we saw each other—kept me from replying until now. I deplore that certain passages of your protest obliged me to protest in my turn—I only did so in self-defense. Should we henceforth exchange only hostile looks? As for me, I wouldn't know how, and if I thought you would shake it without too much ill-feeling, my hand would be offered at once...

Blanche tells me about some of your excellent drawings, which I am most anxious to see.

A. Gide)

With the publication of Gide's second open letter and Cocteau's refusal to be drawn into further open combat, it seemed probable that the incident would fade into oblivion, put down as one more of the squabbles that enlivened the pages of the literary reviews of the day. In fact, the incident only drifted into the background, like a thunderhead on the horizon, where it continued to rumble off and on for the next thirty years. In Cocteau's obsessive return to this incident of his relative youth there is something akin to the so-called persecution complex of Jean-Jacques Rousseau, a figure with whom Cocteau identified himself to a considerable extent.

It is peculiar to Cocteau's psychology that his frequent reminiscences of the *Coq et l'Arlequin* episode convey the impression of (a) a small boy trying earnestly, by repeated assertions of his innocence, to vindicate himself before a stern father, (b) an actor playing to the audience for sympathy, and (c) Cocteau in a hair shirt put on periodically with a martyred air. The incident also served Cocteau as a goad with which he prodded Gide for years afterward to remind the older man of his own loss of dignity during the dispute.

Three years after the *Coq et l'Arlequin* episode Cocteau wrote an article in the *Revue de Genève* for March 1922, constituting the first of many returns to that painful experience. Its tone,

quite typical of Cocteau's response to an affront fancied or real, is a composite of turning the other cheek, tongue in cheek, and sticking out his tongue:

Il faut savoir être injuste. Un homme juste n'aime pas. Que l'amour tombe dans ses balances et vous verrez son bel équilibre les quatre fers en l'air.

C'est pourquoi Gide avait raison d'attaquer mon livre dans une lettre ouverte de la *Nouvelle Revue Française,* pourquoi j'ai eu raison de répondre, pourquoi la *Nouvelle Revue Française* a eu raison de refuser d'insérer ma réponse malgré le Code, pourquoi j'ai eu raison de la publier aux *Ecrits Nouveaux,* pourquoi Gide a eu raison de répondre à ma réponse et pourquoi j'ai eu raison de ne jamais lire ce texte pour mettre un point final.

Gide a son étroitesse. J'ai la mienne. Nous ne sommes ni l'un ni l'autre de la race qui cède. *Le Coq et l'Arlequin* dérange un ordre de choses à quoi Gide participe. Il est naturel qu'il se cabre.[41]

(One must know how to be unjust. A just man doesn't love. Let love drop onto his scales and you will see his beautiful equilibrium go sprawling.

That's why Gide was right to attack my book in an open letter of the *Nouvelle Revue Française,* why I was right to reply, why the *Nouvelle Revue Française* was right in refusing to print my reply, despite the Code, why I was right in publishing it in the *Ecrits Nouveaux,* why Gide was right in replying to my reply, and why I was right in never reading that text to close the matter once and for all.

Gide has his narrowness. I have mine. Neither one of us is of the race which surrenders. *Le Coq et l'Arlequin* upsets an order of things in which Gide participates. It is natural that he bridle.)

On May 9, 1922, Cocteau wrote Gide in a postcard from the Grand Hotel at Le Lavandou: "Avez-vous lu le Nº de la Revue de Genève où je place notre débat sur un plan noble et loin des canailles."[42] ("Have you read the issue of the *Revue de Genève* in which I place our debate on a noble plane and far from the rabble.") Gide's reply, dated May 12, 1922, while generally good-natured in tone, also shows the hackles rising at his memory of the *Coq et l'Arlequin* incident:

12 mai 22

Mon cher Jean

Je m'attristais de vous savoir malade. Que de fois, passant près de la rue d'Anjou... Une névrite, c'est horriblement douloureux, n'est-ce pas? – Il ne m'est pas naturel de me défier, je vous assure,

et ma sympathie pour vous, qui me portait à l'abandon, reste très grande.

Mais ces lignes de la Revue de Genève... quelle plaisanterie!... Evidemment vous placez "notre débat" sur un plan beaucoup plus "noble" que celui où je le maintiens — autant que les questions d'esthétique sont plus nobles que celle de simple police. Vous savez parfaitement (lue ou non ma lettre aux Ecrits Nouveaux) que ce que je reproche à nombre de vos idées, ce n'est pas de différer des miennes; c'est, au contraire, de leur ressembler beaucoup trop. Que ce que je vous reproche c'est d'avoir fait votre pain avec mon blé.

Pour Gabory, je ne sais s'il dit du mal de vous; mais croyez bien que ce n'est pas à moi. Votre palinodie à l'égard de Mendès est d'un terrible exemple pour ceux qui vous écoutent.

Votre nouveau livre — que je n'ai fait qu'entrevoir — m'a paru charmant; encore que tout ne m'y plaise pas également. De toute manière je souhaite de l'avoir; il me sera plus précieux, si je le tiens de vous.

Au revoir. Guérissez-vous et abandonnez-vous au soleil, sur cette plage que je vous envie. Bien affectueusement malgré tout

André Gide [43]

May 12 1922

(My dear Jean,

It saddened me to know you were ill. How many times, passing near the rue d'Anjou... Neuritis is terribly painful isn't it? — It is not usual for me to mistrust myself, I assure you, and my sympathy for you, which led to my lack of restraint, remains very great indeed.

But those lines from the *Revue de Genève*... what a joke!... Evidently you place "our debate" on a far more "noble" plane than I do — insofar as esthetic questions are more noble than those of simple policing. You know very well (whether you read my letter in the *Ecrits Nouveaux* or not) that what I reproach in a number of your ideas is not their difference from my own; on the contrary, it is that they resemble mine far too closely. What I blame you for is for having made your bread with my wheat.

As for Gabory, I do not know if he speaks ill of you; but you may be sure it is not to me. Your retraction about Mendès is a terrible example for those who listen to you.

Your new book — which I have only scanned — seemed charming to me, although I don't like everything in it equally well. In any case, I hope to receive a copy; it will be more precious to me coming from you.

Good-bye. Do get well, and abandon yourself to the sun on that beach which I envy you. Most affectionately in spite of everything,

André Gide)

Encouraged by the warmth of Gide's reply but alarmed at his continuing irritation, Cocteau promptly wrote him a long letter designed to restore harmony once and for all:

Lavandou, Var
15 Mai 1922

Ne disputons plus, cher Gide. Aimons nous. C'est sans doute à cause d'une similitude qui s'exprime autrement que notre amitié se taquine.

Je vous jure sur l'honneur n'avoir jamais lu votre réponse craignant d'exciter en moi de mauvais réflexes. Je vous *affirme* aussi pécher par manque de calcul et non par calcul. Peu importe le reste. Un duel absurde épuiserait à la longue les forces du cœur; or c'est à votre à notre cœur que je fais appel. Oui, j'ai passé 80 jours très durs et votre visite m'aurait plu. Mon regard chargeait Marc de vous le dire.

Au soleil de Lavandou nous retrouverions nos rires et la plante Eugène.

Ecrivez moi.

Je vous embrasse.

Jean

P.S. Je connais certaines de vos récentes préférences poétiques et comme je m'en trouve très loin c'est par simple élan, par dégoût de longues discordes, que je souhaite vous offrir mon livre. C'est un objet amical et, si vous n'y voyez pas ce que j'y vois, le vase quelconque du jour de l'an avec un mot du cœur qui l'accompagne. Ce mot je l'écrirai à notre prochaine rencontre. J'écris à la Sirene qu'on fasse le nécessaire.[44]

Lavandou, Var
May 15, 1922

(Let's not argue anymore, dear Gide. Let's love each other. It is no doubt due to a resemblance that expresses itself differently that our friendship is tormented.

I swear to you on my honor that I never read your reply for fear of provoking bad reactions in myself. I also *assure* you my sinning is from unselfish rather than selfish motives. The rest doesn't matter. An absurd duel would in the long run exhaust the heart's powers; and now it is to your, to our, heart that I appeal. Yes, I spent eighty terribly hard days and I would have enjoyed your visit. My look urged Marc to tell you so.

In the Lavandou sunshine we would rediscover our laughter and the Eugène plant.

Do write to me.

Affectionately,

Jean

P.S. I know some of your recent preferences in poetry, and since I find my own far from yours it is on pure impulse, out of disgust for

long quarrels, that I wish to present my book to you. It is a friendly object and, if you do not see in it what I see, a sort of New Year's Day bouquet with a word from the heart that accompanies it. This word I shall write at our next meeting. I am writing to [Editions de] la Sirène to do what's necessary.)

A preliminary draft of the above letter which is preserved in the Cocteau Archives at Milly-la-Forêt provides an insight into Cocteau's initial reflexes before he curbed his temper in the final version sent to Gide:

Lavandou
15 Mai 1922

Mon cher Gide,

Je connais certaines de vos récentes opinions sur les poètes et comme rien n'y ressemble aux miennes, c'est par simple élan du cœur, par haine des longues discordes que je cherchais à me rapprocher de vous et à vous offrir un livre où ce que j'y vois ne peut vous apparaître. Ne m'avez vous pas dit souvent qu'il existait d'autres lieux de rencontre?

Je vous jure sur l'honneur n'avoir jamais entrouvert le No. des E.N. contenant votre lettre. Un de vos amis m'ayant assuré que c'était une chose "incroyable" "laide" j'évitais, avec cette lecture, des réflexes que même vous n'aviez pu réprimer.

Sans une lettre de vous à Epstein (qu'Epstein croyait une farce) votre mot du 12 m'apprendrait vos griefs.

Stupeur. Personne n'ignore que le Potomak affecte certaines de vos façons mais exprime des idées si peu vôtres qu'elles ne vous frappent en aucune sorte. Ensuite, serai-ce [*sic*] le Coq et l'Arlequin qui ôte *quelque chose* le blé de la bouche à l'ami des musiciens impressionnistes, l'auteur de Chevet de Ravel? (Vous y voisinez avec "Adolphe" ce qui prouve que je ne prouve rien.)

Je parlerais pendant des heures... mais quoi? Votre réponse chercherait à m'atteindre, je répondrais encore, ce duel absurde épuiserait les forces du cœur.

C'est à votre cœur que je fais appel. Finissons en. Voulez vous? Oui, j'ai passé 80 jours atroces et votre visite m'aurait fait du bien. Mon regard chargeait un peu Marc de vous le dire. Au soleil de Lavandou nous retrouverions notre rire et la plante Eugène. Je consens même à croire que notre mal est d'ordre "homéopathique" et que des idées analogues nous éloignent et nous rendent injustes — Mais je ne pourrais plus admettre que vous ne sentiez pas avec quelle passion et quel manque de calcul j'agis toujours.

Je vous embrasse
Jean

P.S. Je vais écrire à la Sirène qu'on vous envoie Vocab[ulaire]. Je vous l'envoie comme un "objet." Si j'avais souhaité vous charmer également à toutes les pages — j'aurais écrit un autre livre — pas *mon* livre. Dans les Fleurs du mal Ste. Beuve remarquait, si je ne me trompe, un joli poème à la lune. Cela rend modeste.[45]

Lavandou
May 15, 1922

(My dear Gide,

I know some of your recent opinions about poets, and since none resemble my own it is on a simple impulse of my heart, out of hatred for long quarrels, that I sought to draw nearer to you and to offer you a book in which what I see cannot be apparent to you. Haven't you often told me there were other meeting places?

I swear to you on my honor that I never opened the issue of the *E[crits]N[ouveaux]* containing your letter. One of your friends having assured me that it was something "unbelievable" and "ugly," I avoided, by not reading it, reactions that even you had been unable to repress.

Without a letter from you to Epstein (which Epstein thought a farce), your note of the 12th would inform me of your grievances.

Amazement. Everyone knows that *Le Potomak* affects some of your manner but expresses ideas so unlike yours that they do not hurt you in the slightest. Besides, how would *Le Coq et l'Arlequin* be able to take something (the wheat from the mouth) from the friend of the Impressionist musicians, from Ravel's bedside table author? (You are in the company there of *Adolphe,* which proves that I prove nothing.)

I could go on for hours... but why? Your reply would try to touch me, I would reply in turn, and this absurd duel would exhaust the heart's powers.

It is to your heart that I appeal. Let's have done with it, shall we? Yes, I went through eighty terrible days, and your visit would have done me good. My look somewhat instructed Marc to tell you so. In the Lavandou sunshine we should rediscover our laughter and the Eugène plant. I even consent to believe that our trouble is "homeopathic" in origin and that analogous ideas drive us apart and make us unjust — But I can no longer accept that you do not recognize the passion and the unselfishness that prompt all my actions.

I embrace you,
Jean

P.S. I am going to write [Editions de] la Sirène to send you *Vocabulaire.* I send it to you as an "object." If I had hoped to charm you equally by every page — I would have written a different book — not *my* book. In *Les Fleurs du mal,* Sainte-Beuve noticed, unless I am mistaken, a pretty poem to the moon. That makes one modest.)

Gide replied briefly but warmly to Cocteau's letter: "Mon Cher Jean, Votre lettre est exquise et vous êtes irrésistible. Je vous embrasse sur le plus azuré de mes papiers. A.G." [46] ("My dear Jean, Your letter is exquisite and you are irresistible. I embrace you on the most azure of my papers. A.G.")

As a comic epilogue to his conciliatory letter of May 15, Cocteau on May 18 addressed a postcard to Gide. On the face of the card he drew a dove of peace laying an egg in flight and ended by drawing a heart. The message, which began with a pun, read:

Ouf! Dites le à Marc

Fini le film
drame et le film où
on reçoit des tartes à la
crême sur la figure.

Entracte.

Le Lavandou (Pathécolor)
Musique de Reyer

Ensuite une
bonne rencontre
Gide — Cocteau [47]

(Ouf! Tell Marc. End of the dramatic film and the film where one gets custard pies in the face. Intermission. Le Lavandou (Pathécolor). Music by Reyer. Followed by a good Gide-Cocteau meeting.)

In his book *Portraits-Souvenir*, which was published in 1935, and which was based on a collection of columns Cocteau had written for *Le Figaro* that year, Cocteau alludes again to Gide in the context of *Le Coq et l'Arlequin*: "Gide me reprochait (à propos d'une note du Coq et l'Arlequin sur le premier jazz) de ne jamais me laisser aller, de ne jamais profiter d'une détente." [48] ("Gide reproached me (with respect to a note in *Le Coq et l'Arlequin* on the first jazz) for never letting myself go, for never unwinding.")

Cocteau's conversation and interviews, as well as his written works, show the scar of his 1919 encounter with Gide. Twenty years later, in a conversation with Claude Mauriac on May 26,

1939, Cocteau spoke at length of Gide and lamented the lack of dignity of Gide's polemic at the end of World War I.[49]

In 1947 Cocteau again brought up in *La Difficulté d'être*, the phrase he had originally borrowed from Gide: "La langue française est difficile. Elle répugne à certaines douceurs. C'est ce que Gide exprime à merveille en disant qu'elle est un piano sans pédales." [50] ("The French language is difficult. It turns up its nose at certain kinds of mellowness. This is what Gide expresses marvelously by saying it is a piano without pedals.")

In the winter of 1952, at the Cap Ferrat home of his friend Mme Francine Weisweiller, Jean Cocteau worked on his *Journal d'un inconnu,* a collection of essays published two years after Gide's death. In a long discussion of Gide, Cocteau once more, with a certain poetic license as to the facts, reverted to *Le Coq et l'Arlequin* controversy of thirty-three years before:

Je venais, en 1916,[51] de publier *Le Coq et l'Arlequin*. Gide en prit ombrage. Il craignait que les jeunes se détournassent de son programme et de perdre des électeurs. Il m'appela comme un élève en faute chez le maître d'école, et me lut une lettre ouverte qu'il me destinait. On m'adresse pas mal de lettres ouvertes. Dans celle de Gide, je figurais en écureuil, et Gide en ours au pied de l'arbre. Je sautais des marches et de branche en branche. Bref, je recevais une semonce et je devais la recevoir en public. Je lui déclarai qu'à cette lettre ouverte je comptais répondre. Il renifla, opina du bonnet, me dit que rien n'était plus riche, ni plus instructif que ces échanges.

On se doute que Jacques Rivière refusa de publier ma réponse dans la N.R.F. où Gide avait publié sa lettre. Elle était assez rude, je l'avoue. J'y constatais que la maison de Gide, Villa Montmorency, ne regardait pas en face, que ses fenêtres donnaient toutes de l'autre côté . . . [Gide] n'avait aucun profit à tirer de ma réponse, sauf d'y répondre, à quoi il ne manqua point. Il chérissait notes et notules, réponses aux réponses. Il répondit à la mienne dans les *Ecrits Nouveaux* qui l'avaient publiée.

Avouerai-je ne l'avoir pas lue? Je tenais à me mettre en garde contre un réflexe, contre une cascade effrayante de lettres ouvertes.[52]

(I had just, in 1916, published *Le Coq et l'Arlequin*. Gide took umbrage at it. He feared that young people would turn away from his program and that he would lose voters. He called me like a naughty schoolboy before the headmaster, and read me an open letter that he intended to send me. People direct quite a few open letters to me. In Gide's I was pictured as a squirrel and Gide as a bear at the foot of the tree. I was skipping steps and leaping from branch to branch. In short, I got a reprimand and I had to get it in public. I declared to him

that I intended to reply to that open letter. He sniffed, nodded his head in agreement, told me that nothing was richer or more instructive than these exchanges.

One suspects that Jacques Rivière refused to print my response in the *NRF*, where Gide had published his letter. It was quite rough, I admit. In it I mentioned that Gide's house, Villa Montmorency, didn't face the street, that the windows all looked out on the other side . . . [Gide] had no advantage to gain from my reply, except to reply to it, which he did not fail to do. He dearly loved notes and notations, replies to replies. He answered mine in the *Ecrits Nouveaux*, which had published it.

Shall I confess to not having read it? I had to put myself on guard against a reflex, against a frightful cascade of open letters.)

In his conversations with Colin-Simard, which were published in 1952, Cocteau again recalled the traumatic encounter with Gide so long before:

J'ai parlé de nos rapports de haine et de grâce parce que je hais la haine, que je déteste les brouilles, et que je me suis toujours arrangé pour ne pas exciter en moi le réflexe de réponse qui pour Gide était irrésistible. Lorsque Gide m'écrivit une lettre ouverte après *Le Coq et l'Arlequin*, je lui répondis par une autre lettre ouverte que Rivière trouva trop dure, et que j'ai publiée dans les *Ecrits Nouveaux*. Gide, comme de juste, répondit à cette réponse. Et pour ne pas nous répondre sans fin, je m'obligeai à ne pas lire cette dernière lettre dont j'ignore encore le contenu.[53]

(I have talked about our relations of hate and grace because I hate hate, detest quarrels, and have always managed myself so as to avoid exciting in myself the response reflex, which for Gide was so irresistible. When Gide wrote me an open letter after *Le Coq et l'Arlequin*, I answered him by another open letter which Rivière found too harsh and which I published in the *Ecrits Nouveaux*. Gide, as usual, replied to this reply. And in order not to answer one another forever I forced myself not to read that last letter, of whose contents I still know nothing.)

In a letter of January 17, 1953, Cocteau wrote a friend: "Vous voyez pourquoi je ne parle pas anglais. Le français c'est le piano sans pédales. L'anglais n'est que pédales."[54] ("You see why I don't speak English. French is the piano without pedals. English is nothing but pedals.") Here Cocteau, again without due credit, borrowed the very epigram of Gide's that had begun the *Coq et l'Arlequin* dispute.

In a foreword to his *Lettre à Jacques Maritain,* dated August 14, 1958, Cocteau refers obliquely to his exchange with Gide nearly forty years before: "Je l'aimais trop pour répondre à sa réponse et adopter la méthode chère à Gide, méthode qui accumule les paperasses, alors que la mienne consiste à brûler le plus possible." [55] ("I liked him too much to reply to his reply and adopt the method dear to Gide, a method that accumulates waste paper, whereas mine consists in burning as much as possible.")

On September 20, 1958, Jean Cocteau delivered an address in Brussels entitled: "Les Armes secrètes de la France." In attendance were Queen Elizabeth of Belgium, and Pierre de Gaulle, who delivered a eulogy of Cocteau. On this occasion Cocteau made two final references to André Gide and to the *Coq et l'Arlequin* dispute. The first is a repetition of the phrase that may be said to have originally opened the dike of animosity between the two men. But this time credit is given to Gide: "comme notre langue même que Gide estimait être du piano sans pédales." [56] The second reference is to the squirrel-bear characterization made by Gide in his first open letter to Cocteau: "Voilà pourquoi ce message risque souvent de me faire mériter le rôle d'écureuil que Gide me distribue, estimant, bien à tort, être un ours au pied de l'arbre." [57] ("That's why this message often risks making me deserve the role of squirrel which Gide assigned me, thinking himself, quite incorrectly, to be a bear at the foot of the tree.")

On this good-natured note Jean Cocteau at last let go of the *Coq et l'Arlequin* episode. It is perhaps significant, as a sign that he had finally made his peace with Gide, and in a sense with himself, that shortly before Cocteau's death in 1963, in the exhaustive television interview [58] he held with Roger Stéphane, the poet did not evoke the *Coq et l'Arlequin* incident or his controversy with André Gide. Both spirits had by now been exorcised.

The Squirrel and the Bear

The *Coq et l'Arlequin* confrontation between Cocteau and Gide is central to a relationship that seesawed between friendship and enmity for nearly forty years. The ancillary letters exchanged by the two writers also furnish evidence bearing on many topics including the evolution and position of the *NRF* and Cocteau's efforts to penetrate that important review.

In the open letters especially are to be found revealing judgments of each writer by the other. Gide often spoke bluntly to Cocteau, and Cocteau replied in kind. Despite the heat of these particular exchanges there was considerable light on both sides. The truth is often painful, and although both Jean Cocteau and André Gide had a certain taste for pain, they were mortal enough to find too much truth hard to bear. In the reciprocal mirrors of their open letters the two authors caught disturbing glimpses of themselves as artists and as men. Cocteau's comment in another context is appropriate: "Les miroirs feraient bien de réfléchir un peu plus avant de renvoyer les images." [1] ("Mirrors would be wise to reflect a little longer before sending back their images.") When they at last turned away after this skirmish, Cocteau and Gide found that their views of each other had been to some extent permanently distorted. With La Fontaine-like irony, Gide had typecast them as The Squirrel and The Bear, respectively, and the labels promised to endure.

The open letters exchanged at the time of the *Coq et l'Arlequin* incident raise certain questions that are central to the rela-

tionship of the two writers. Why should Gide, then fifty years old, and an established author, choose to initiate such an issue over a little book by a colleague, twenty years his junior, who was struggling to find his place in the world of letters? Gide's reasons for his action were at once professional, personal, and practical in nature, although Gide did not necessarily think of them in that order.

Gide enjoyed helping young writers by his honest and generally shrewd criticism of their work. Criticism itself was a creative function for him, and there is little doubt that his desire to help Cocteau find out who he really was, to help him to master his weaknesses and develop his strengths as a gifted young writer, was genuine and lay at the heart of his first open letter.

In addition to these benevolent professional motives for Gide's launching what must have seemed to *NRF* readers an unprovoked attack on Cocteau, certain personal factors must be considered. It is proper to assume that Gide singled out the little phrase Cocteau had borrowed from him for *Le Coq et l'Arlequin* as a literary pretext for his first letter; however, both were practicing homosexuals at the time, and the friction generated by their common interest in the eighteen-year-old Marc Allégret may well have added a personal motive for the attack on Cocteau.

The open letter was one of the forms in which Gide liked to express his literary criticism. Even his protégé Jacques Rivière received an unexpected open criticism from him in the July 1920 issue of *Le Gaulois,* in which he took Rivière to task for deviating from the early *NRF* policies. That letter nearly cost Gide the friendship of Rivière.[2] François Mauriac also complained to Gide about his habit of administering such public criticism to his friends and colleagues.[3] It was characteristic of Gide's sincerity that certain of his own works, such as *Si le grain ne meurt, Corydon, Et nunc manet in te,* and his *Journal,* with their aspect of confession and self-flagellation, resemble extended open letters by Gide to himself. In them he forges weapons that his detractors later turned against him, just as in his 1919 open letters to Cocteau he forged arms that later critics continue to use against the author of *Le Coq et l'Arlequin.*

The polemical techniques Gide employed in his first open letter reveal a skill in this area superior to that of the relatively inexperienced Cocteau. Gide cleverly couples praise with

criticism in his remarks, and assures Cocteau (and *NRF* readers) that his criticism is presented as a sincere and friendly gesture. Throughout the letter Gide adopts the posture of an older teacher reprimanding an unruly pupil. The reprimand would have been milder in effect had it not been public.

Gide's first open letter begins with a compliment to Cocteau on his recent poem *Le Cap de Bonne-Espérance*. Gide says he has read it and has had the double pleasure of hearing it read aloud by Cocteau himself. He then touches on Cocteau's latest work *Le Coq et l'Arlequin*, making a veiled allusion to Cocteau's borrowed aphorisms,[4] and passes on to observations on Cocteau's ballet *Parade*, which had been presented in 1917. In the course of his comments on these three works, Gide states some of his own literary and esthetic doctrines in abbreviated form: "Le vrai spectacle est à l'intérieur," and its corollary that the function of a work of art is to reveal "cette secrète réalité." The statement of this concept, which suggests the growing concern of certain artists with the subconscious even before Freud had been translated into French, indicates that Gide and Cocteau shared similar esthetic convictions in this respect.[5] This is no doubt one of the reasons why Gide could write, in his second open letter to Cocteau, that his own and Cocteau's esthetic principles were very close.

In his first open letter Gide also suggests that an author's best explanation of one of his own works should be the work that follows it. Here again Gide and Cocteau are not far apart. In *Opium*, which Cocteau wrote in 1928 and 1929, he asserts that each of his works goes beyond explanation or contradiction and literally guillotines its predecessor.[6] Gide's letter advises young authors not to defend or explain their works (Gide's anti-preface policy) because this risks limiting their significance for the reader. Cocteau at least paid lip service to this advice, for although he spent considerable time in later years explaining his work, he tried to avoid limiting its meaning to his readers by maintaining that he had put more into his writing than he himself recognized. It was therefore legitimate, according to Cocteau, for different readers or viewers to find different meanings in a given work. In his reply to Gide's criticism, moreover, Cocteau charges that Gide protected himself from the necessity of defending his writings by timidly causing the first editions to appear in extremely small printings.[7]

In this letter Gide praises Cocteau for the charm and brilliance of his poetic gifts, and for his talent as a reader of poetry. He singles out Cocteau's maxims, *Le Cap de Bonne-Espérance*, and certain passages on jazz from *Le Coq et l'Arlequin* for favorable treatment. Commenting on the ballet *Parade*, however, he declares that Cocteau failed to fulfill the real responsibility of the artist: to make clear to his audience that the true spectacle was an inner drama.[8] This concept, nevertheless, was basic both to *David*,[9] the work on which Cocteau had previously collaborated with Stravinsky in 1914 at Leysin, Switzerland, and to the later *Parade*, which made use of an important part of the structural and thematic material of *David*. The very title of *Parade* calls to mind the parade of clowns, "jongleurs," and minstrels through a medieval town to attract an audience to the mystery plays, but the setting and action of *Parade* was contemporary and involved the box office and barker's spiel outside a circus tent. By this means Cocteau intended to impress on his audience that they must visit the inside of the tent to witness the unfolding of the true drama of *Parade*. In this sense, *Parade* was an invitation to live life fully and not to remain on its outer fringes.

The controversial reception given *Parade* at its première in 1917 may have justified Gide's criticism in 1919, but the highly successful revival of *Parade* in 1920 would seem to vindicate the original artistic intentions of Cocteau and his collaborators: Picasso, Diaghilev, and Satie.

Gide's advice to the young Cocteau included a warning not to sacrifice his charm and brilliance for heavier qualities that Cocteau lacked. Gide's characterization of Cocteau as a squirrel, with its implications of quickness and lightness, and of himself as a more slow-moving, heavy-footed bear, also stung Cocteau because it cast him in a frivolous role relative to Gide. Gide reproaches Cocteau for trying to persuade the public that he is a logician when, in Gide's opinion, he is not. Gide also urges Cocteau not to limit his palette to only a few colors, but to let himself go.

Gide attributes a certain hypocrisy, even duplicity, to Cocteau's nature by reproaching him for presenting a false front in order to conceal his true and, what is in Gide's view, Cocteau's best self.[10] When Gide adds very sincerely, "vous vous trompez sur vous-même," he touches a central nerve in Cocteau's sensibilities, one he knows in advance will cause pain.

"Je me dis bien qu'en vous écrivant ceci je vais soulever chez vous une protestation très vive." ("I tell myself that in writing you this I will provoke a sharp protest on your part.") Here was a thrust that did indeed deeply wound Cocteau, especially since it came from the very artist whose advice and example had been a turning point for Cocteau only a few years before. By 1917 Cocteau had started to simplify his handwriting at Gide's urging, purging it of Anna de Noailles's ornate influence. He had also been so affected by Gide's *Paludes* that his subsequent composition of *Le Potomak* marked a genuine reorientation of his career.

It is part of the inner struggle of any young artist to find out who he really is, and it is true that Cocteau in the summer of 1919 had not yet found himself. He had changed direction after his early creations such as *La Lampe d'Aladin*, *Le Prince frivole*, and *La Danse de Sophocle*. Nevertheless, he had not yet "discovered" his major novels, plays, and films, which, according to his esthetic doctrine, "preexisted" and which he felt it to be the archeological role of the poet to unearth. Yet Cocteau felt strongly that he was already a much different and far more mature writer than he had been before the war. He felt he had, in writing *Le Potomak*, closed the door on one phase of his development as an artist, a phase he himself by 1917 regarded as frivolous, immature, and marked by easy and empty glory.

To have Gide, who had helped him to see the error of his early ways, now publicly accuse him of still being mistaken about his true nature, about his true talent and role as a writer, was humiliating and frustrating to Cocteau. It provoked an even more heated response, in Cocteau's open letter, than Gide had anticipated. Yet Gide's criticism remains a shrewd and penetrating observation by one established writer twenty years senior to another. It raised, early in the poet's career, the question: Who is the real Cocteau? And it stated flatly that Cocteau himself did not yet know the answer. Even today, fifty years later, Gide's indirect question still stands, almost as pertinent at the end of Cocteau's brilliant and varied career as it was at the beginning.

Gide also nettled Cocteau by the charge that Cocteau had always run upstairs two at a time, implying that he tried to take shortcuts to success. It was Cocteau's nature to take such a remark in the worst possible way. Gide's reproof seemed espe-

cially unkind to the young poet since it further reminded Cocteau of the quick fame he had won by the reading of his poetry in 1908 while he was De Max's protégé. This was a precocious fame that Cocteau had repudiated long before 1919, and at the urging of Gide himself. These criticisms added to Cocteau's feeling that Gide's entire open letter was a personal, unfair, and unprovoked attack to which he had every right to reply in kind.

Although Gide coupled compliments with criticism, the compliments were ambiguous and the criticisms cut deep. By questioning Cocteau's view of himself, by pointing to the hypocrisy of Cocteau's masks, Gide cast doubt on Cocteau's integrity as an artist. His vocabulary stresses the word "talent" three times in the opening lines of the letter, but the warmth of the word is cooled by the fact that Gide applied it not to Cocteau's writing but to his reading. Gide's deliberate choice of the word "talent" probably carried a pejorative inflection to Cocteau, who drew sharp distinctions between talent and genius. Words with critical or negative nuances abound in Gide's letter: "appréhension," "déconcerte," "concerté," "prétendu," "reproche," "gêne," "erreur." Other phrases subtly emphasize shallow and frivolous aspects that Gide found in Cocteau's writing: "Les plus plaisantes lignes de vous"; "[le] charmant démon des analogies qui me semble particulièrement votre don poétique"; "raffinement de coquetterie." The total effect, unmistakable even if obliquely expressed, was to suggest that Cocteau's talent lay in the direction of artifice rather than art. Although Gide ends his first open letter with an ambiguous compliment for *Le Coq et l'Arlequin,* the letter, taken as a whole, is a bear hug that almost crushes the squirrel.

The question of Gide's motives remains. Why should this eminent man, secure in his career as an author and as director of the *NRF,* suddenly make an apparently unprovoked attack on a young poet who had often acknowledged his debt to the older man? Gide's open letter was not the gratuitous act of a Lafcadio. There were strong personal reasons that counterbalanced the professional motive for his gesture. The fact that both were present is in keeping with the polarity of Gide's nature.

Only one reason, professional in character, is clearly stated by Gide: he wants to advise Cocteau to recognize his talents for what they are, to face himself squarely and to accept himself as

he truly is. This paternalism on the part of Gide is entirely consonant with his life-long willingness to assist and counsel young writers through his personal contacts, his vast correspondence, and the *NRF*. In addressing his comments to Jean Cocteau, Gide was at the same time, by extension, admonishing part of a postwar generation of young writers, often *mondains*, mavericks, or dilettantes whose modernism the dedicated *NRF* authors deplored and found suspect. Gide's open letter to Cocteau therefore gave him an opportunity to express views from which other young writers might profit.

Gide's letter, however, was something like an iceberg. Beneath the spirit of friendly criticism which showed on the surface there were submerged motives of perhaps greater relevance to an understanding of André Gide. There was, for example, the problem of the Surrealists, their disdain for Cocteau, and their ambivalent feelings for Gide. Frederick Brown suggests in his biography of Jean Cocteau [11] that Gide, who was on friendly terms with André Breton at the time, had decided to help Breton and the Surrealists demolish Cocteau. Breton's aversion to Cocteau was already known in literary circles.

In December 1919 Cocteau's friend and mentor Max Jacob wrote Cocteau that he would send a letter defending *Le Coq et l'Arlequin* to Louis Aragon, André Breton, and Philippe Soupault, the editors of the Surrealist review *Littérature*, which had begun publication on March 1, 1919. "Ma lettre," wrote Jacob to Cocteau, "devrait être remise 20 jours avant la parution du numéro, me dit Aragon. Je crois *Littérature* de nos amis (??) – Je doute de tout." [12] ("My letter," wrote Jacob to Cocteau, "should be submitted 20 days before the issue's publication date, Aragon tells me. I think *Littérature* is one of our friends (??) – I am in doubt about everything.")

On December 12, 1919, Jacob sent the following letter to "la direction de *Littérature*":

Mes chers confrères,

Maurice Raynal dans la première chronique de *Littérature* me présente comme un ennemi de Jean Cocteau et comme un détracteur de son livre *Le Coq et l'Arlequin*. Je considère ce livre comme bon et son auteur comme mon ami, ce qui n'empêche ni mon amitié pour tels autres de mes confrères ni mon estime littéraire pour leurs œuvres...

Max Jacob [13]

(My dear Colleagues,
    Maurice Raynal, in the first news section of *Littérature*, presents me as an enemy of Jean Cocteau and as a detractor of his book *Le Coq et l'Arlequin*. I consider this book to be good and its author to be my friend, which doesn't prevent either my friendship for certain other of my fellow authors, nor my literary esteem for their works...

Max Jacob)

    Jacob's mild letter of protest to the editors of *Littérature* questioned their friendship on this occasion with good reason. On personal grounds Breton's animosity for Cocteau had already been set in motion by Jacob himself when he introduced Breton's young friend Raymond Radiguet to Jean Cocteau in June 1919. Patrick Waldberg, an historian of the Surrealist movement, was later told by Breton that when he saw the look that passed between Radiguet and Cocteau at their meeting, he (Breton) knew he had no further place in Radiguet's future. The subsequent abandonment of Breton by Radiguet, and the latter's alliance with Cocteau, was undoubtedly a factor in Breton's unfailing hostility toward Cocteau thereafter. Try as he might, Cocteau, with his remarkable ability to forgive, if not to forget, was never able to charm away Breton's animosity.
    Jacob's doubts about the friendly attitude of his colleagues at *Littérature* were also grounded in the knowledge that Cocteau was persona non grata with the Surrealists as a group, even though he long sought to identify himself with them. Cocteau had prevailed upon the *Littérature* board to accept *Le Coq et l'Arlequin* for publication in their first issue of March 1, 1919. Although Cocteau's name appeared in the table of contents, his text was omitted at the last minute, ostensibly at the request of Erik Satie.[14] Louis Aragon, in a very brief review of *Le Coq et l'Arlequin* that appeared in that issue, pointedly failed to mention Jean Cocteau's name.[15] Other articles in the same issue discussed *Le Bœuf sur le toit*, and *Parade* without mentioning Cocteau by name. On the other hand, the lead article was a fragment of Gide's *Les Nouvelles Nourritures*.[16]
    Relations between Gide and Cocteau had also been recently ruffled by an incident involving Dr. Edmond Bonniot, the husband of Mallarmé's daughter, and at that time executor of Mallarmé's literary estate. In 1919 Jean Cocteau was writing a series of articles called "Carte Blanche"[17] in the news-

paper *Paris-Midi*. In March of that year he announced in his column that his own publishing house, Editions de la Sirène, would shortly publish the quatrains of Mallarmé with illustrations by Raoul Dufy. Dr. Bonniot, as Mallarmé's executor, had previously objected to this project, and had written André Gide on January 10, saying: "Cocteau fait encore des siennes..." Dr. Bonniot asked Gide for the name of a good lawyer to handle a literary suit against Cocteau and the Editions de la Sirène. It was natural that Bonniot should address himself to Gide for several reasons: Gide enjoyed great prestige in the literary world and knew Cocteau personally, but more important, the *NRF* was the publisher at the time of the poetry of Mallarmé. By mid-January Jean Cocteau was no doubt receiving anxious reports from Paul Lafitte, his associate at Editions de la Sirène, who had surely been under pressure from Dr. Bonniot and perhaps even from the *NRF*. In all probability Cocteau had also learned by then of Dr. Bonniot's letter to Gide. In an apparent effort to forestall further trouble, Cocteau wrote Gide on January 20, 1919:

Les Bonniot sont aux prises avec Laffitte — Gaspard Michel a été très, très aimable et habile dans cette affaire délicate. Il s'agissait pour lui de me disculper et de rendre service au ménage. Donnez-lui une *œuvre*, mon cher Gide. . . .

Jean [18]

(The Bonniots are at odds with Laffitte — Gaspard Michel has been very, very kind and resourceful in this delicate business. It was a matter of his clearing me and doing a service to the couple. Give him a real *work*, my dear Gide. . . .

Jean)

With typical adroitness Cocteau attempted in this way to turn defeat into victory. By making Laffitte and Dr. Bonniot appear to be the axis of the controversy he removes himself and Gide from it. His request for a work is calculated to flatter Gide while enabling Cocteau to repay Gaspard Michel for his help. At the same time the introduction of Michel's name serves subtle notice that the Editions de la Sirène has a strong ally in the *Ecrits Nouveaux*, which Michel directed. The quatrain project at Editions de la Sirène was put off, but this incident was one more in the succession of irritating behind-the-scene encounters between Cocteau and Gide that culmi-

nated in their more serious open clash in the summer of 1919.

Possibly the most urgent motive Gide had for attacking Cocteau in his open letter was personal rather than professional in nature. This involved the friendship shared during World War I by André Gide, Jean Cocteau, and Marc Allégret.[19] Marc Allégret says that he had already met Jean Cocteau casually through other friends before André Gide introduced them in 1917. Many years later, Jean Cocteau described the 1917 introduction in his *Journal d'un inconnu*, which was written in 1952, the year after Gide's death. In that work, following a discussion of his controversy with Gide in the summer of 1919 over Cocteau's book *Le Coq et l'Arlequin*, Cocteau added:

Le temps passa. . . . Gide se tenait à l'écart. . . . Il me téléphona et me pria de prendre en charge (mettons Olivier).[20] Son disciple Olivier *s'ennuyait de sa bibliothèque*. Je l'initierais aux Cubistes, à la jeune musique, au cirque dont nous aimions les gros orchestres, les gymnastes et les clowns. Je m'exécutai, avec réserve. Je connaissais Gide et sa jalousie presque féminine. Or, le jeune Olivier trouva fort drôle d'énerver Gide, de lui rabattre les oreilles avec mon éloge, lui déclarant qu'il ne me quittait guère et savait *le Potomak* par cœur. Je ne devais l'apprendre qu'en 1942, avant mon départ pour l'Egypte. Gide se confessa et m'avoua qu'il avait voulu me tuer (*sic*). C'est de cette histoire que naquirent les crocs-en-jambe de son journal. Du moins, les mit-il sur ce compte.[21]

(Time passed. . . . Gide kept on the sidelines. . . . He telephoned me and begged me to take over (let's call him Olivier). His disciple Olivier *was bored with his library*. I was to initiate him in the Cubists, young music, the circus where we loved the big orchestras, the gymnasts, and the clowns. I complied, but with reserve. I knew Gide and his almost female jealousy. Now, young Olivier found it highly amusing to unnerve Gide, to flatten his ears with my praises, telling him that he hardly left my side and knew *Le Potomak* by heart. I was not to learn this until 1942, before my departure for Egypt. Gide confessed himself and assured me he had wanted to kill me (*sic*). It is this story that gave birth to the dirty tricks in his journal. At least, he attributed them to this.)

Cocteau had also in 1952 described his introduction to Allégret by Gide in similar terms during his interview with Colin-Simard. But as he wrote these accounts in 1952 Cocteau's admittedly poor memory for dates confused the correct sequence of events. In one of the two preliminary drafts of his

open letter written in *June* 1919, in reply to Gide's first open letter in the *NRF*, Cocteau included the following comment, which he deleted from the final draft as it was printed in the *Ecrits Nouveaux:*

Un jour vous m'avez amené votre jeune neveu — il était, disiez vous, plein d'ennui pour les livres de votre bibliothèque, reniflait vers nous, cherchait du neuf. Vous me demandiez conseil. Mes conseils furent bons sans doute puisque j'ai en votre neveu un véritable petit ami et qu'il m'écrivit après le Cap et le Coq des lettres que je publierais s'il me fallait régler ma conduite sur la vôtre.[22]

(One day you brought me your nephew — he was, you said, bored stiff with the books in your library, was sniffing in my direction, was searching for something new. You asked me for advice. My advice was doubtless good since I have a real little friend in your nephew, and since after *Le Cap* and *Le Coq* he wrote me some letters that I would publish if I were to regulate my conduct by your own.)

Although Cocteau's 1952 recollections of this episode place it *after* his dispute with Gide in the summer of 1919 over *Le Coq et l'Arlequin,* it is clear from the testimony of Marc Allégret himself, from the preceding passage written in June of 1919, and from Gide's *Journal,* that Gide had brought Cocteau and the young Allégret together *before* the *Coq et l'Arlequin* episode.[23] The jealousy that Cocteau attributes to Gide, and that Gide himself acknowledged, could therefore have been a powerful factor in shaping Gide's decision to criticize Cocteau in his first open letter.

As we know, the June-July 1919 issue of the *Ecrits Nouveaux* carried an eight-page rejoinder by Jean Cocteau to André Gide's first open letter in the *NRF.* Since the *NRF* had refused to print his reply Cocteau determined to make the most of the opportunity for rebuttal offered to him by his friend Gaspard Michel of the *Ecrits Nouveaux.* Instead of directing a simple open letter to Gide, Cocteau gave full vent to his theatricality and to his spleen. His reply was cleverly divided into three separate parts, one might almost say "Acts," to avoid an over-long letter that might bore the readers. Part one was titled *Réponse à André Gide,* and in it Cocteau presents his version of the chain of events leading up to his own reply. The second part, called *Exploit,* was a pseudo-legal notice Cocteau had served on Gaston Gallimard of the *NRF.* It demanded that

Cocteau, as the injured party, be given the right to reply to Gide in the *NRF* itself. In the final section of Cocteau's reply, *Lettre à André Gide,* Cocteau answers Gide's criticisms in detail and at the same time launches a personal attack on the older author.

The Bibliothèque Littéraire Jacques Doucet in Paris has in its manuscript collection two interesting drafts of Cocteau's open letter: Doucet ref. F.D. 1152–3 and 4. Draft F.D. 1152–4 was evidently written before F.D. 1152–3 since the former is written in highly abbreviated sentences scattered at random around the pages, as though to capture first thoughts as they occurred. These drafts reveal the pitch of Cocteau's rage at the time, and far surpass in vituperation the relatively muted open reply that appeared in print. Present in the drafts but omitted from the final text are such comments as the following:

Draft F.D. 1152–4.

(1) Vous venez de m'écrire une lettre ouverte bien dangereuse pour vous car des lecteurs superficiels pourraient croire que vous vous êtes reconnu dans l'Arlequin que j'oppose au Coq. Sinon votre rôle de "Judex" demeure inexplicable – car qui donc force un ami à dire en public du mal d'un ami même s'il le pense à moins de vouloir se venger. . . .

(2) Ce système [d'imbroglio] je le respecte, il est votre manière et votre charme. . . .

(3) Où est Gide? Est-il à la campagne? à Paris? Une lettre arrive de Cuverville mais X l'a vu qui se glissait du côté d'Auteuil sous une cape couleur de muraille. . . .[24]

(4) Gide cultive l'esthétique de l'insuccès? . . .

(5) Vous, Normand, vous êtes fait bâtir à Auteuil une maison à votre image – Elle ne regarde pas en face. . . .

(6) – vos curiosités timides. . . .

(7) Ce petit livre [*Le Coq et l'Arlequin*] été [*sic*] plein d'amour – de piété – comme me l'écrivait votre jeune neveu [Marc Allégret] un Evangile. . . .

(8) Vous me faites penser à un homme qui jugerait les chaises en partant de l'idée d'armoire ou vice versa et qui dirait: cette chaise n'est pas bonne – elle ne ferme pas à clef, ou cette armoire n'est pas bonne, on y est mal assis. . . .

(9) La noblesse de l'écrivain consiste à ne pas déifier ses fautes. . . .

(10) Mais du reste mon cher Gide n'êtes vous pas sans cesse en désaccord avec vous-même? N'êtes vous pas un jeu entre un Huguenot et un écolier?

Draft F.D. 1152-3

(1) Je me demande si votre silhouette ne cache pas une foule de silhouettes — toute une génération; si la Nouvelle Revue Française ne prononce pas le "Allez Messieurs" d'une lutte qui couve depuis des années, et si votre lettre ne va pas me fournir l'honneur d'être porte parole de tout un clan. . . .

(2) . . . Cette pudeur Normande vous donne la renommé [*sic*] d'hypocrite. . . .

(3) . . . N'êtes-vous pas l'apôtre de la contradiction?

(4) . . . Maintenant, permettez-moi, puisque vous me déconseillez la logique en me reconnaissant du lyrisme d'aimer sans réserves "Paludes" et de vous déconseiller la critique. . . .

(5) Vous maniez en virtuose les pédales que la langue Française ne devrait pas avoir comme vous le dites dans mon livre. . . .

(Draft F.D. 1152-4

(1) You have just written me an open letter very dangerous for you since superficial readers could believe that you recognized yourself in the Arlequin whom I oppose to the Coq. If not, your role of "Judex" remains inexplicable — for who forces a friend to speak ill of a friend in public, even if he thinks it, unless out of a desire for vengeance. . . .

(2) I respect this system [of entanglements], it is your style and your charm. . . .

(3) Where is Gide? Is he in the country? In Paris? A letter arrives from Cuverville but X has seen him slipping through Auteuil beneath a wall-colored cape. . . .

(4) Gide cultivates the esthetic of non-success. . . .

(5) You, a Norman, had built at Auteuil a house in your own image. It does not face the front. . . .

(6) — your timid curiosities. . . .

(7) This little book [*Le Coq et l'Arlequin*] was full of love — of piety — as your young nephew wrote me, a Bible. . . .

(8) You make me think of a man who judges chairs by starting with the notion of a closet or vice versa, and who would say: this chair is no good — it doesn't lock, or this closet is no good, you sit uncomfortably in it. . . .

(9) The nobility of the writer consists in not deifying his mistakes. . . .

(10) But besides, my dear Gide, are you not forever out of harmony with yourself? Aren't you a sport between a Huguenot and a schoolboy?)

(Draft F.D. 1152-3

(1) I wonder if your silhouette doesn't conceal a swarm of silhouettes — an entire generation; if the *Nouvelle Revue Française* isn't pronouncing the "Go to it, Gentlemen" of a fight that has been brew-

ing for years, and if your letter isn't going to provide me the honor
of being spokesman for a whole clan. . . .

(2) . . . This Norman *pudeur* gives you the reputation of a hypocrite. . . .

(3) . . . Aren't you the apostle of contradiction?

(4) . . . Now, permit me, since you advise me against logic while acknowledging my lyricism, to like *Paludes* unreservedly and to advise
you against criticism.

(5) You work like a virtuoso the pedals that the French language
is not supposed to have, as you say in my book. . . .)

The content of these passages that Cocteau deleted from the
final text of his open reply to Gide not only affords a more detailed view of his true feelings in the heat of the moment but
serves to explain why Cocteau felt he had already sufficiently
pruned his reply of personal remarks and why he refused to
soften it any further to satisfy Jacques Rivière. Paragraph (1)
was probably deleted by Cocteau for tactical reasons. He, or
friends to whom he read the proposed letter, may have felt on
second thought that suggesting that Gide's silhouette represented a whole generation gave too much weight to his adversary's views. Assigning himself the role of "porte parole de
tout un clan" might have also struck readers as being too
presumptuous. Nevertheless, these statements reveal Cocteau's
acute sense of a literary generation gap between himself and
Gide, and his own ambition to become the recognized spokesman for the young postwar writers and their public.

Cocteau's final text, as it appeared in the *Ecrits Nouveaux* for
June-July 1919, still retained many intemperate comments of
a personal nature. Lashing out at his opponent, Cocteau went
beyond the scope of a literary rebuttal. He belittled Gide's personal taste by charging that he had built at Auteuil a symbolic
villa without windows in the front.[25] With similar effect he reported a disillusioning conversation with Gide about Georges
Braque:

Vous vous êtes même rendu acquéreur d'une toile de Georges
Braque. Lorsque je vous demandai ce qu'elle représentait, si c'était sa
"grappe de raisin," vous me répondites avec impatience que vous ne
saviez pas, et que, du reste, cela vous était égal. Or, tout est là.

(You even acquired a painting by Georges Braque. When I asked
you what it represented, whether it was his "bunch of grapes," you

answered impatiently that you didn't know, and that anyway it was all the same to you. However, that's the whole point.)

Cocteau suggests that Gide is dull: "Bien des nuances, mon cher Gide, qui vous échappent." Nor is innuendo missing from Cocteau's reply: "Je répugne à y chercher la manœuvre que certains y virent." "Gide parle de duel. Il vient de se battre dans un costume blindé. Pourquoi voulez-vous que je m'en prenne aux amis qui lui jouèrent cette farce. . . ." ("I shrink from finding in the letter the intrigue that some people see in it." "Gide speaks of a duel. He has just been fighting in armor. Why do you wish me to blame the friends who played this prank on him. . . .") The implication is that Gide had been duped by others into starting the duel, perhaps by Breton and the Surrealists. Cocteau also points out Gide's timidity and insincerity: "Gide, s'il se sent ours en ma présence, porte tant de miel à ses pattes que je distingue peu les griffes." ("Gide, if he does feel like a bear in my presence, has so much honey on his paws that I scarcely notice the claws.") He ridicules Gide's style both in dealing with people and even in his grammar. "Vous avez, Gide, tout un système de mystères, de réserves, d'imparfaits du subjonctif, d'alibis et d'imbroglios." ("You have, Gide, a complete system of mysteries, of reserves, of imperfect subjunctives, of alibis, and of entanglements.") Gide's good faith in writing his open letter in the first place is bluntly questioned by Cocteau: "Gide se rendant compte du ridicule d'envoyer, ouverte, à un ami, sans que personne le demande, une lettre pareille. . . ." ("Gide, realizing the absurdity of sending such a letter, open, to a friend, without anyone having asked for it. . . .") And a few lines later Cocteau again casts doubt on the sincerity of Gide's intentions: "Cette lettre, disait-il, prenant la voix de Cassandre: 'Je la dois au public'(!?). Ou bien encore: 'La véritable amitié ne se nourrit pas de réticences'" [26] ("'This letter,' said he, adopting Cassandra's voice: 'I owe to the public' (!?). And again: 'True friendship is ill-nourished on reticence.'")

The third part of Cocteau's open letter, "Lettre à André Gide," bears a subtitle to remind the reader that this reply had been refused by the *NRF:* "Destinée au numéro du 1er juillet de *La Nouvelle Revue Française.*" In this part of his letter Cocteau responds to Gide's letter almost item by item. This

entire section of the scenario, from the point of view of style and structure, is a parody on Gide's letter. In part one of his letter Cocteau cast Rivière and Gide in the role of villains who betrayed him by their initial agreement to publish his reply and their later refusal to do so. In part two Cocteau assigned himself the part of the reasonable and innocent party being denied his rights by the powerful *NRF*. In part three Cocteau adopts the tactics of the light man in a judo match who uses his heavier opponent's own weight to overthrow him. He deftly seizes Gide's own phrases from his first open letter and turns them against his aggressor.

For example, the "ours" and "écureuil" figure is reversed: "C'est mon tour, si j'y pense, de m'avouer ours aux pattes lourdes et de suivre dans l'arbre vos cache-cache d'écureuil." ("It is my turn, if I think about it, to acknowledge myself to be a heavy-footed bear and to follow your squirrel's hide-and-seek in the tree.")

Cocteau's passage beginning

Il arrive que ce mélange déconcerte à force qu'on le sent concerté. Ce n'est point que je ne reconnaisse la grâce de vos ivresses pruden-tes, mais certaines d'entre elles me semblent bien moins en rapport avec celui que vous êtes qu'avec celui que vous voudriez qu'on vous crût.[27]

(It happens that this mixture disconcerts through one's sensing it to be concerted. It is not at all that I do not recognize the charm of your prudent raptures, but some of them seem to me much less in harmony with the person you are than with the person you would have us believe you to be.)

is taken almost word for word from Gide's comment about Cocteau's maxims, but it is here used wittily by Cocteau to make a point about the duality of Gide's nature.

Gide had accused Cocteau of having two sides, of holding up masks to conceal his true self, of not knowing himself.[28] Cocteau now replies in kind:

Du reste, mon cher Gide, l'incertitude n'est-elle pas le charme de vos œuvres et de votre style? On pense à une belle baigneuse qui n'ose se jeter à l'eau et qui se mouille les seins en poussant de petits cris.

Il y a en vous du pasteur et de la bacchante.[29]

(Besides, my dear Gide, isn't uncertainty the charm of your work and style? One is reminded of a beautiful woman bather who dares not throw herself into the water and who sprinkles her bosom while uttering little shrieks.

There is in you something of the pastor and of the bacchante.)

This was striking at Gide on religious grounds, since it implied he was a pagan Protestant. Gide's ambiguity and indecisiveness call forth further comment from Cocteau:

Gide aime-t-il X...? Admire-t-il Y...? On l'interroge. Il renifle, se penche, hausse les épaules. Son genou dit que oui, son coude que non.[30]

(Does Gide like X...? Does he admire Y...? Someone asks him. He sniffs, hunches over, shrugs his shoulders. His knee says yes, his elbow says no.)

The thrust of the foregoing remarks by Cocteau is to create an image of Gide as two-faced and confused, both as a person and as an artist — exactly the same charge Gide had first leveled at Cocteau.

Cocteau uses another of the same polemical devices Gide uses in his open letter: criticism mixed with praise, a device Cocteau refers to as "aigre-douce." Cocteau disavows any intention to be personal and claims only to be genuinely critical in his reply. Although he accuses Gide of hypocrisy and cowardice in hiding behind Rivière's dictum, "Je sais fort bien que Gide se réfugiera derrière la phrase où 'généreusement' sonne si faux . . ."[31] ("I know very well that Gide will take refuge behind the sentence in which "generously" sounds so false . . ."), he also acknowledges Gide's good influence on him in the past:

Pour le reproche de sauter des marches, je montais depuis l'enfance un escalier absurde. Vous êtes de ceux m'ayant fait voir qu'il en existait un autre.[32]

(As for your reproach about my skipping stairs, ever since childhood I have been climbing an absurd staircase. You are one of those who made me see that another existed.)

Perhaps the criticism that exasperated Gide the most was Cocteau's charge of superficiality based on ignorance. This

superficiality was of two kinds according to Cocteau. The first was exemplified by Gide's criticism of *Parade before* he had seen it:

Je ne vais pas ratiociner sur *Parade*, notre grand jouet mécanique. Vous suivez une mode qui était d'en dire du mal sans l'avoir vu.[33]

(I am not going to talk endlessly about *Parade*, our big clockwork toy. You are following a fashion, which was to speak ill of it without having seen it.)

The second, and even more damning, kind resulted from Gide's position as an older member of the literary establishment, who had lost touch with the young artists in the "ordre nouveau" and the "mouvement moderne":

Je ne trouve qu'une incompréhension fort excusable chez un écrivain mal renseigné sur le travail des jeunes compositeurs. . . .[34]
Vous vous êtes récemment approché de nos semailles avec un intérêt louable chez un homme qui récolte.
Vous ne regardiez pas certaines audaces. Vous les regardez. Mais vous regardez *du dehors*.[35]

(I only find a lack of comprehension that is altogether understandable in an author who is poorly informed about the work of young writers. . . .
You recently approached our sowing with an interest that is praiseworthy in a man who is gathering his sheaves.
You had not been watching certain audacities. Now you do. But you watch them *from the outside*.)

Gide had ended his first open letter with a protest of his friendly intentions, and Cocteau followed Gide's example in his reply by alluding to the borrowed phrase in *Le Coq et l'Arlequin*:

Dans le Coq et l'Arlequin, j'avais sans m'en rendre compte, emprunté une phrase à votre conversation et vous la restituai, sur votre prière instante, par l'entremise d'un *papillon*. Ce papillon était une preuve de mon amitié. Ne voyez pas autre chose dans cette réponse qu'un papillon aux ailes un peu plus lourdes.[36]

(In the *Coq et l'Arlequin* I had, without being aware of it, borrowed a phrase from your conversation and I gave it back to you promptly at your insistence by means of an *acknowledgment slip*. That *papillon* was a proof of my friendship. You should not see anything else in this reply than a butterfly with somewhat heavier wings.)

There is no doubt that the young Cocteau lost stature and damaged his own case by the personal tone of his reply, a mistake a more mature polemicist might have been expected to avoid. Nevertheless, Cocteau demonstrated surprising skill in literary give and take for one so inexperienced. He effectively turned many of Gide's charges back on the older writer with a clever twist added to Gide's own words.[37] He used a number of the same polemical weapons that Gide used in his open letter: ironic humor, indirection and implication, two-edged compliments, and disparaging statements aimed at discrediting his opponent, all presented in the guise of friendly criticism. Characteristically, the style of Cocteau's reply with its flair and drama makes Gide's letter seem to verge on the pedantic. It was an inspired piece of Cocteau stagecraft to include in his reply a legal writ that contributed to the impression that Gide and the *NRF*, "un groupe fermé," were being put on trial.

Cocteau's motives were manifold in answering Gide's open letter as he did. Honor required a reply to such an unprovoked attack, and the young and aggressive Cocteau was anxious to defend and extend his reputation by capitalizing on the publicity of an open exchange with perhaps the foremost literary figure of the day. Cocteau's drafts of his reply reveal his dream of speaking out for the younger writers and artists as their *chef de file*. In replying to Gide he saw a chance to realize this dream in part, and at the same time to discredit Gide and the *NRF* as symbols of the literary establishment, which so far had paid scant attention to Jean Cocteau. It will be recalled that it was not until 1923 that Cocteau's repeated efforts to have his work published in the *NRF* were finally successful. Up until the time of the open letter exchange with Gide in 1919, only Ghéon's 1912 review of Cocteau's *La Danse de Sophocle* had appeared in the *NRF*.

From a tactical point of view, Gide had, up to this moment, enjoyed the advantage of surprise in the skirmish since it was he who had fired the first volley. Cocteau, however, had now succeeded in enlisting the support of a second literary review, thus broadening his audience, and had obtained eight pages of space for his rebuttal, whereas Gide's letter had only half as many. Gide soon corrected this imbalance by writing a second open letter, published this time in the *Ecrits Nouveaux* instead of in the *NRF*. Cocteau's friend Gaspard Michel

saw to it, however, that the letter was buried in the last few pages of the review, and although the two drafts of Gide's reply are dated in July, Gide had to wait until October for his rejoinder to appear in print.

In his second letter Gide, thoroughly outraged by the impertinence of Cocteau's reply, becomes as vituperative as Cocteau. Irony gives way to sarcasm: "j'ai le grand regret de pouvoir me reconnaître beaucoup moins dans les phrases et les idées qu'il me prête, que dans celles que, par ailleurs, il me prend." [38] The gruff good humor of the first letter has disappeared, and Gide's tone throughout is one of injured dignity moved to rudeness. Instead of the note of friendly intent on which his first letter ended, Gide's second letter ends with a bored yawn: "Je m'excuse de fatiguer le lecteur."

The central thrust of Gide's second letter enlarges on a criticism Gide had made of Cocteau in his first letter, but he now states it quite bluntly:

Il m'oblige à le démasquer.
Il n'est pas donné à chacun d'être original. M. Cocteau n'en est pas à sa première imitation. Ce que ma *lettre ouverte* lui reprochait, ce n'était point tant de s'assimiler l'art d'autrui, que de se donner des airs de chef d'école et d'inventeur; ce n'était point tant de suivre, certes, mais de feindre de précéder.[39]

(He obliges me to unmask him.
It is not given to everyone to be original. This is not M. Cocteau's first imitation. What my *open letter* reproached him for was not so much for assimilating the art of others as for giving himself the airs of a chef d'école and inventor; it was not so much for following, to be sure, but for pretending to precede.)

The charges of unoriginality and plagiarism were repeated:

fidèle à son habitude, il emprunte certaines phrases de ma lettre pour les retorquer contre moi.
Ce sont les phrases où je tâchais, dans les termes les plus courtois de dénoncer cette double personnalité de M. Cocteau, l'une réelle, la plus charmante de beaucoup, l'autre d'emprunt, qu'il peine à faire passer pour la vraie.[40]

(faithful to his usual practice, he borrows a number of sentences from my letter to hurl them back on me.
These are the sentences in which I tried in the most courteous terms to expose that double personality of M. Cocteau, one real, the most

charming by far, the other borrowed, which he tries hard to pass off as the authentic one.)

These charges of borrowing, and of holding up a mask to conceal his true identity, followed Cocteau the rest of his life. It is these reproaches which critics of Cocteau and admirers of Gide alike have been inclined to remember, rather than the highly significant statement about Cocteau also made by Gide in his second letter:

> Je l'avais un peu calmé en le persuadant qu'il aurait tout loisir pour me répondre, et pour défendre ses principes esthétiques, ainsi qu'il m'annonça qu'il voulait faire – *principes que, au demeurant, je n'avais jamais critiqués, puisque aussi bien ce sont les miens.*[41]

> (I had calmed him down a bit by persuading him that he would have every opportunity to reply to me and to defend his esthetic principles, as he announced to me he wished to do – *principles which, after all, I had never criticized because they are as a matter of fact my own.*)

Curiously enough, Gide decided to omit from the final text of his second letter to Cocteau a long passage that appeared in his draft of the letter. This passage deals with the *papillon* in *Le Coq et l'Arlequin:*

> Je passais outre les nombreux "emprunts" de son livre et j'avais eu la bonne grâce de convenir avec lui d'un petit "papillon" qui tout en signalant telle phrase qu'il m'avait prise, détournait l'attention de telles autres phrases que Mr C. sait fort bien que j'aurais également pu revendiquer. Ce "papillon" faisait office de paratonnerre. Mr C. sait fort bien qu'il n'aurait même pas été question de ce papillon si la phrase en question, à laquelle somme toute je ne tenais guère, puisque je n'ai jamais songé à l'écrire, il l'avait empruntée, comme telle autre qu'il me signala lui-même à un de mes livres, et non à ma conversation, de sorte qu'elle engageait une tierce personne par qui Cocteau la connaissait. Quand il fut question de ce papillon je n'avais pas encore lu tout le livre (le Coq et l'Arlequin); il m'apparut hélas! lorsque je l'eus entre les mains que si chaque emprunt plus ou moins bien dissimulé, de ce livre eut fait éclore un papillon ceux-ci auraient rappelé les Morphos dont Darwin parle dans le récit de son voyage "si nombreux qu'ils suffisent à modifier le paysage." C'est ce que j'écrivis ensuite à Cocteau.[42]

> (I disregarded the numerous "borrowings" in his book, and I had had the good grace to agree with him on a little acknowledgment slip which, while calling attention to the sort of phrase he had taken from

me, diverted attention from other such lines to which M. C. knows very well I could equally have laid claim. This *papillon* served the function of lightning rod. M. C. knows very well that there would not even have been an issue over this butterfly if the sentence in question, in which after all I had little interest since I never thought to use it in writing, had been borrowed, as he told me he had done in another instance, from one of my books and not from my conversation, so that it entangled a third person from whom Cocteau learned of it. When the question of this butterfly arose, I hadn't yet read the whole book (*Le Coq et l'Arlequin*); it appeared to me, alas! when I had it in my hands, that if each more or less well-disguised borrowing in this book hatched a butterfly, they would have brought to mind the Morphos Darwin speaks about in the account of his voyage "so numerous they were enough to transform the landscape." This is what I wrote afterwards to Cocteau.)

Also omitted from Gide's final text was a paragraph originally placed at the very end of his letter:

Que Mr C. consente à rester ce qu'il est, un délicieux improvisateur, et personne ne songera jamais à lui chercher avise. Mais les véritables artistes souffriront (ou plutôt ne souffriront pas) de le voir chercher à entraîner l'art dans des milieux et des aventures un peu trop amusantes et où il n'a que faire de se commettre.[43]

(Let M. C. agree to remain what he is, a charming improvisor, and no one will think to look to him for invention. But true artists will suffer (or rather will not suffer) to see him try to drag art into surroundings and adventures which are a little too amusing and where he has no business exposing himself.)

Cocteau answered Gide's second letter by a deafening silence. He did not respond with a second open letter of his own, and he maintained throughout the rest of his life that he never even read Gide's second letter for fear of prolonging a dispute that was painful to him. This attitude is typical of Cocteau who, though highly sensitive, was temperamentally unable to hold a grudge for long.

When the dust had settled, Gide, the more experienced polemicist of the two, had clearly emerged the victor. He had enjoyed the advantage of having the first and the last word. He had made his points in two different reviews as opposed to one for Cocteau, thus doubling his audience. Most important of all, he had applied some labels to Cocteau that clung to him the rest of his life.

Reduced to their essential meaning, Gide's criticisms of Cocteau evaluate him at that time as charming, brilliant, and gifted, but frivolous and light; a plagiarist, an opportunist, and a delightful improvisor; an artist working with too limited a palette who must learn to let himself go; a young man in the throes of a personal and artistic identity crisis who deceived the public by masking his true self. In Gide's opinion Cocteau's duplicity lay in the fact that he refused to recognize these qualities in himself, and tried on the other hand to pass himself off as a serious logician, an innovator, and a *chef d'école* of the avant-garde. It is a tribute to Gide's critical acumen and prestige that literary historians today are still weighing Cocteau in the scales against Gide's judgments of half a century ago. If some of these judgments seem unduly harsh today, it must be remembered that they were conceived in a moment of anger and jealousy and at a time when Gide was under the heavy strain of launching the postwar *NRF*, beginning his masterpiece *Les Faux-Monnayeurs*, and adjusting to the break with his wife in the fall of 1918. It must also be remembered that Gide's judgments were written before Jean Cocteau had published *Thomas l'Imposteur*, *Le Grand Écart*, *Les Enfants terribles*, or produced any of the long list of his major poems, plays, and films that enriched French literature after 1920.

On the other hand Cocteau's similarly biased reply, amplified by his two drafts, portray Gide as dull and heavy, an insincere old man of doubtful esthetic discernment. Ambiguous and hypocritical, Gide is made out to be confused and unsure of himself. Cocteau pointed out Gide's superficiality as a critic, and suggested he was hopelessly out of touch with the modern movements in the arts.

It was no doubt precisely because he found in Gide many of the same flaws Gide had found in him that Cocteau was moved several years later to make the observation:

Ne disputons plus, cher Gide, aimons nous. C'est sans doute à cause d'une similitude qui s'exprime autrement que notre amitié se taquine.[44]

(Let's not argue anymore, dear Gide. Let's love each other. It is no doubt due to a resemblance that expresses itself differently that our friendship is tormented.)

The capacity of one person to hurt another is often a function of their mutual esteem. The actions of a person we neither

like nor respect have little power to disturb us on a personal level. The very violence of Gide's and Cocteau's reaction to each other in the *Coq et l'Arlequin* exchange may, therefore, be a measure of their mutual affection and respect up until that time. Because of their relative ages and positions in the literary world, Cocteau and Gide could no longer afford to ignore each other. Their public contest assumed aspects of the classic struggle surrounding the origins of kingship which Frazer describes in *The Golden Bough*. The young man, eager for power, challenges the old king, seeking to wrest from him the crown of his authority — in this case his authority with "le public jeune."

In the confrontation between Gide and Cocteau an old order rooted in nineteenth-century symbolism was, for the first time in this way, being openly challenged by a new order: the twentieth-century avant-garde.

Jean Cocteau
and the "NRF"

Like any ambitious young French poet in the years just before World War I, Jean Cocteau was eager to make a name for himself. Establishing a reputation for clever conversation in the salons of Mme Mühlfeld, Countess Anna de Noailles, the Princess Murat, Misia Sert, and other society women of his acquaintance was one path to glory, but being written about or getting his poems published was another matter. To this end it was only natural that Cocteau should cultivate the central figures in the major publishing houses. The important thing was to break into print, either in book form or in articles for the influential literary reviews of the period. Of the many publications for which Cocteau wrote during his career, probably no other single periodical was as important to Cocteau, or its sanctions as greatly coveted by him, as *La Nouvelle Revue Française*.

For the young writers in France just before and after World War I the *NRF* assumed the magnitude of a temple, with André Gide, to use the words of his friend Roger Martin du Gard, as its High Priest.

Although a writer's acceptance by the *NRF* did not hinge on the approval of André Gide alone, any writer seeking to have his work published in the *NRF* had to reckon with Gide as one of the prime movers of the review. As Jean Cocteau knew, an outside, or non-staff writer like himself could not be

either encouraged or discouraged by the *NRF* without Gide's knowledge or consent. This was true because the *NRF* editorial staff in the early years worked as a closeknit committee, each member being kept aware of the others' work. The choice of collaborators or contributors, the general tone and specific content of each issue, were usually matters of joint decision. Although Gide did not reserve for himself a position of arbitrary authority and guide the *NRF* with an iron hand, he nevertheless had a dominant voice in deciding with Jacques Copeau and Jean Schlumberger what went into the magazine. Even when Gide was absent from Paris traveling, and could not be consulted as closely as otherwise, he was still consulted and informed. It was only after the death of Jacques Rivière in 1925 that Gide began to pay somewhat less attention to the affairs of the *NRF*.[1]

As the influence of the magazine grew following its birth in 1908, so did the recognition accorded to writers whose works appeared in its pages.

Obstacle after obstacle, many already familiar to the reader, blocked Cocteau's way to the *NRF*. His youth, his *mondain* reputation, his suspiciously quick rise to literary notice following the public reading of his poetry by De Max's friends in 1908,[2] the immaturity of his first two published volumes of poetry, which serious critics had judged to be frivolous and derivative, all worked against him. Even his Catholic tradition may have been a disadvantage initially in gaining acceptance at the *NRF*, for positions of power on the review were held by men of Protestant background, such as Gide, Copeau, Ghéon, and Schlumberger.[3] At another level, the personal conflicts generated, even unintentionally, by the homosexual artist that Cocteau happened to be, were bound to create misunderstandings and frustrations in his dealings with a Jacques Rivière, a Henri Ghéon, or even an André Gide.

Beyond such personal elements was the fact that Cocteau's esthetic doctrine at the beginning of his career appeared on the surface to reject constraint in favor of spontaneity, disorder, and the facile exploitation of natural talent. This was far removed from the relatively stern credo of the *NRF* as evolved by its founders, who saw as part of their mission the creation of a new classicism and the defense of French literature against the Boulevard writers.[4] Wholesome as this goal seems today, the *NRF* was regarded in 1908 with fear and

suspicion by older conservative writers who viewed it as a Trojan Horse, and its then relatively unknown contributors, Gide, Claudel, and Valéry, as literary anarchists.

The first issue of the *Nouvelle Revue Française* in November 1908 carried on page one the following statement to its readers about its aims and general orientation:

Les écrivains que réunit aujourd'hui la *Nouvelle Revue Française* appartiennent à la génération qui dans la chronologie littéraire suivit immédiatement le symbolisme. . . .

. . . C'est l'espoir des fondateurs de cette revue qu'ils aideront à se dégager plus tôt, . . . l'apport nouveau qui doit distinguer les écrivains d'aujourd'hui de ceux de hier.

Si cette revue . . . , n'est pas précisément une "revue de jeunes," elle n'en est pas moins une jeune revue dès à présent ouverte à la génération qui s'élève.

(The writers the *Nouvelle Revue Française* brings together today belong to the generation which, in literary chronology, immediately followed symbolism. . . .

. . . It is the hope of the founders of this review that they will help emerge sooner . . . the new contribution that must distinguish today's writers from those of yesterday.

If this review . . . is not exactly a "review of young people," it is nonetheless a young review open from this moment to the upcoming generation.)

In addition to the founders and editorial committee listed on the masthead, the long list of contributors included Henri Ghéon and Jean Cocteau's close friend Countess Anna de Noailles.

The initial statement by the *NRF* that its doors were open to the new generation of writers sounded like an invitation especially directed to a young poet like Jean Cocteau. But recognition by the serious-minded literary community of the *NRF* was slow in coming. The article entitled "Considérations" by Jean Schlumberger, which appeared in the February 1909 issue of the *NRF,* helps to explain the editorial resistance that Cocteau encountered:

. . . Ce sont les problèmes du moment qui créent des groupements littéraires. Des individus s'y rapprochent à qui une certaine manière est commune, qui ont même public et mêmes ennemis: Lignes offensives et défensives et, si les humeurs s'accordent, *camaraderies.* Mais

ce n'est qu'avec les problèmes vitaux que commencent les amitiés littéraires: unité d'inspiration, sous les réalisations les plus divergentes, unité non de goûts mais de méthode, non de genres, mais de style. Les camaraderies ne survivent pas au désaccord, s'il porte sur une œuvre du jour ou sur une question d'opportunisme. Au contraire ce n'est qu'à l'égard des œuvres significatives – et le plus souvent de celles du passé – que les amitiés sont intransigeantes. Les préférences restent libres, mais point la qualité de l'admiration, non plus qu'un certain sentiment, si l'on peut ainsi dire, de dépendance filiale.

La forte unité d'un groupe n'est faite que de la restriction des libertés individuelles. Ce que la politesse apporte de liant aux relations sociales, la subordination des caprices personnels l'apporte aux œuvres d'art. Il n'y a que records effrénés et que guerre intestine, là où l'exaltation de l'artiste ne connait d'autre règle que son propre plaisir. On rencontre, il est vrai, des chefs d'œuvre nés du désordre, et il peut arriver au génie de braver toute discipline impunément. Mais ce ne sont là que de magnifiques accidents. . . .Ces légitimes protestations contre des contraintes surannées se mêlèrent aux révoltes des improvisateurs et des esprits brouillons contre toute contrainte. . . .

On ne veut rien attendre que du don et pour un peu, l'on déclarerait l'ébauche supérieure à l'œuvre, parce qu'aucun élément réfléchi n'y semble venir troubler le langage ingénu d'un tempérament. . . .

L'effort ne remplace pas le don, mais il l'exploite. Il n'éteint pas la spontanéité, mais la relègue. . . .[5]

(. . . It is the problems of the moment that create literary groupings. In them there draw together individuals who have in common a certain way of doing things, who have the same public and the same enemies: offensive and defensive lines, and, if moods agree with each other, *camaraderie*. But it is only in facing vital problems that literary friendships begin: unity of inspiration, underlying the most divergent forms of expression, unity not of taste but of method, not of genres but of style. Close friendships do not survive disagreement if it bears on a work of momentary interest or on a question of opportunism. On the contrary it is only with respect to significant works – and most often those of the past – that friendships are intransigent. Preferences remain free, but not the quality of admiration, anymore than a certain feeling, if it can be put this way, of filial dependence.

The strong unity of a group is achieved only by restricting individual liberties. The subordination of personal caprices brings to works of art the same binding quality that good manners bring to social relationships. There is only unbridled output and civil warfare

where the artist's exaltation knows no other rule than his own pleasure. One does encounter, it is true, masterpieces born out of chaos,
and it is possible for genius to defy all discipline with impunity.
But these are only magnificent accidents. . . . These legitimate protests against superannuated constraints blended with the rebellions
of the extemporaneous versifiers and the harum-scarum wits set
against all restraint. . . .

People don't want to count on anything except their natural gift,
and for a trifle they would declare the rough draft better than the
final work because no considered element seems to enter in and disturb the artless language of a temperamental type. . . .

Effort does not replace a gift, but it exploits it. It does not extin-
guish spontaneity, but consigns it to its proper place. . . .)

Schlumberger here describes the strong sense of common
purpose, of communal effort, that underlay the original
NRF. His statements extolling the virtue of hard work and
discipline by the artist as opposed to unbridled dependence
on natural talent, were reflections of a Protestant severity and
love of order that were bound to dismay the Catholic-oriented
Cocteau, whose precocious brilliance seemed to feed on disorder. Cocteau was not a team player by instinct or training;
all his life he protested against the encroachment of "les
pluriels" on "le singulier." He was bound to regard discipli-
narian pronouncements such as Schlumberger's with suspicion
and apprehension.

In prefatory remarks to his 1934 article on Jean Cocteau's
La Machine infernale, Jean Schlumberger comments on the early
attitude of the *NRF* editorial board toward Cocteau:

À l'égard de Cocteau, la N.R.F. s'est longtemps tenue sur la réserve. Elle ne savait comment le faire entrer dans les catégories de
son éthique littéraire. Gide, séduit par tant d'esprit et d'impertinence,
était prêt aux compromis, mais les intransigeants l'emportèrent.

Après la reprise de la revue en 1919, c'est entre Gide et Cocteau
que les rapports tournèrent à l'aigre-doux. Non que le jeu mouvant
de leurs susceptibilités et de leurs raccommodements engageait
personnellement les amis de Gide, mais il créait, pour qui n'aime pas
à danser sur des œufs, une gêne que j'ai souvent déplorée.[6]

(With respect to Cocteau, the *NRF* kept on its guard for a long
time. It did not know how to fit him into the categories of its literary
ethics. Gide, seduced by so much wit and impertinence, was ready
to compromise, but the intransigents prevailed.

After the revival of the review in 1919, the relations between Gide

and Cocteau turned bittersweet. Not that the shifting play of their
touchiness and their reconciliations personally involved Gide's
friends, but it created, for whoever didn't like dancing on eggs,
an embarrassment that I often deplored.)

Jacques Rivière, no doubt one of the "intransigeants"
referred to by Schlumberger,[7] wrote an article in the January
1912 issue of the *NRF* titled "De la sincérité envers soi-même."
It was dedicated to Jacques Copeau and, as Schlumberger's
article had done, it spelled out further the *NRF* literary
doctrine of discipline and control that seemed to run counter
to Cocteau's natural tendencies:

> Il semble que pour être sincère il suffise de se laisser aller, de ne
> pas s'empêcher de sentir, de céder à sa spontanéité. On cesse d'être
> sincère au moment où l'on intervient en soi; si je me travaille, je me
> déforme. La sincérité c'est l'abandon à moi-même, l'obéissance au
> cours naturel de mes émotions, une pente aisée, l'accès complaisant
> à ma facilité intérieure. Elle ne me demande aucun effort; je l'exerce-
> rai comme on se détend.
> Pourtant il est plus juste de dire: la sincérité est un perpétuel effort
> pour créer son âme telle qu'elle est. Rien de plus menteur que la
> spontanéité, rien de plus étranger à moi-même. . . .[8]

> (It seems that to be sincere it might suffice to let one's self go, to
> give free rein to feeling, to give in to one's spontaneity. You cease
> to be sincere the moment you intervene with yourself. If I work on
> myself, I deform myself. Sincerity is self-abandonment—following the
> natural trend of my emotions, an easy slope, ready access to my inner
> aptitude. It demands no effort of me; I will make use of it as in relax-
> ing.
> However, it is more correct to say: sincerity is a constant effort to
> create one's soul as it is. Nothing is more deceptive than sponta-
> neity, nothing is more alien to my self. . . .)

Rivière had been appointed Editor of the *NRF* at the end
of World War I. It was after his first meeting with Cocteau in
May 1919 that the latter at once wrote Gide:

> Jacques Rivière était à ma séance lecture du Cap. Son attitude
> vous aurait fait plaisir puisque vous songiez à nous réunir de longue
> date. Sa figure toute jeune, presque de collégien m'a surpris beau-
> coup.[9]

> (Jacques Rivière was at my reading of the *Cap* [*de Bonne-Espérance*].
> His attitude would have pleased you since you had meant for a long

time to have us meet. His very young face, almost that of a schoolboy, surprised me greatly.)

As far back as 1912, however, long before their meeting, the literary concepts of Rivière and Cocteau seem already to have begun divergent courses. The personality conflict between the two men that initially disturbed their relationship was further aggravated by Rivière's unfortunate war experiences. Surrounded by the enemy in a little wood, he had been captured and made a prisoner of war by the Germans. His sense of guilt at having allowed himself to be captured preyed on Rivière's mind. His health, never robust, failed seriously, and by arrangement with the Red Cross he was sent to Switzerland to recuperate. After the war Jacques and Isabelle Rivière attended a party at the home of their friend the artist André Lhote. Among the other guests were Paul Morand and Jean Cocteau, accompanied as usual by Raymond Radiguet. Mme Rivière recalls that while Cocteau read from *Le Diable au corps* Radiguet sat silent and surly as "un petit taureau." [10] Cocteau read so well that Jacques Rivière asked to see the manuscript for the *NRF*. Later that evening, Cocteau, in his bantering and flippant way, told of his own war experiences with the Fusiliers-Marins and Misia Sert's ambulance corps. His light treatment of the war which had caused Jacques Rivière so much physical and mental anguish was more than the Rivières could stomach and they abruptly left the party.

In Philip Kolb's study of the correspondence between Rivière and Marcel Proust, a study in which Mme Isabelle Rivière collaborated, Kolb comments on the intransigence of Rivière's literary judgments, his reaction to Romanticism, and his desire to see a rebirth of psychology in literature. Kolb's work also points out that from Rivière's viewpoint Proust remained his great discovery in contemporary literature, and that it was Rivière's efforts that finally opened the doors of the *NRF* to the author of *À la recherche du temps perdu*.[11] This claim by Rivière contradicts Cocteau's assertion that it was he, not Rivière, who first persuaded Gide to read Proust: "Peut-être, un de ses [Gide] plus grands griefs à mon égard fut-il de l'avoir obligé à lire Proust." [12] ("Perhaps one of his [Gide's] greatest grievances against me was my having forced him to read Proust.")

Their contact with Proust came to be a source of growing

friction between Cocteau and Rivière.[13] By 1922, when Proust
and Cocteau had temporarily fallen out, Rivière wrote Proust:

Je vous suis profondément reconnaissant de la vivacité avec
laquelle vous prenez mon parti contre Cocteau. Soyez sûr, mon
cher Marcel, que si je me suis montré parfois tiède en réponse à son
amabilité c'est parce que je la savais toujours conditionnée par l'espoir
ou par l'attente de quelque compliment public.
Vous me trouverez peut-être bien exigeant mais il faut pour me
toucher des manifestations d'amitié un peu plus désintéressées.[14]

(I am deeply grateful to you for the energy with which you take
my part against Cocteau. You may be sure, my dear Marcel, that
if I have occasionally shown myself to be lukewarm in my response
to his attentions it is because I always knew them to be conditioned by
the hope or expectation of some public compliment.
Perhaps you will think me very exacting, but demonstrations of
friendship must be a little more unselfish if they are to touch me.)

Rivière's note of thanks to Proust had followed a revealing
letter from Proust to Gaston Gallimard:

Je vous dirai (et vous pouvez lui [Jacques Rivière] dire) qu'à son
sujet j'ai entièrement changé d'avis dans la question Cocteau pour
la raison suivante. J'avais chaleureusement recommandé (sur la
demande de Cocteau qui me faisait un grand éloge de Jacques)
son dernier volume de vers. Jacques m'a mis alors dans l'affreuse
position de faire faire (lui, Jacques) un article très désagréable en
me disant que c'était très aimable, ce qui me donne un air faux. Je
n'étais donc que de mieux en mieux disposé pour Cocteau. Mais
celui-ci m'a écrit une lettre, très gentille pour moi, mais très injurieuse pour Jacques et pour la NRF. Cette palinodie (appuyée
sur ce qu'il est dans le Midi réconcilié avec Gide et se croit sans doute
maître du terrain) m'a déplu, et autant j'aurais désiré que Jacques
fasse dire du bien de lui quand il était affectueux, autant je serais
désolé qu'il ait l'air maintenant, par faiblesse, de céder à ses injures.[15]

(I will tell you (and you can tell him [Jacques Rivière]) that I have
completely changed my mind about him in the Cocteau matter for
the following reason. I had warmly recommended (at the request
of Cocteau, who had sung Jacques's praises to me) his last volume of
verse. Jacques then put me in the terrible position of having had him
(Jacques, that is) write a very unpleasant article while telling me
it was very friendly, which makes me seem hypocritical. I was, therefore, only more and more favorably disposed toward Cocteau. But
the latter wrote me a letter, very kind to me, but highly insulting to

Jacques and the *NRF*. This recantation (based on the fact that he [Cocteau] has made up with Gide in the Midi and no doubt thinks himself master of the situation) displeased me, and much as I would have liked Jacques to have had something good said of him [Cocteau] when he was affectionate, I would be equally upset that he [Jacques] appear now, out of weakness, to give way before his [Cocteau's] insults.)

The relationship between Cocteau and Jacques Rivière, from its inception in 1919 until Rivière's death in 1925, was characterized chiefly by reserve on the part of the *NRF* editor. He clearly played an important part in denying Cocteau access to the *NRF* even though, as Rivière reported to Gide, there were times before World War I when the *NRF*, with less than fifteen hundred subscribers, was extremely short of material and needed "des nouvelles étoiles" as writers.[16] Unfortunately for Jean Cocteau, his star was not yet in the ascendancy at the *NRF*.

Jean Schlumberger, Jacques Rivière, Henri Ghéon, and André Gide were not the only *NRF* members to be approached by Cocteau. He also knocked on Jacques Copeau's door in his efforts to gain admission to the review. Copeau, as one of the founders of the *NRF*, and its literary director from 1909 to 1913, was a central figure in the early development of the review. For years he had studied the Parisian theater, first as critic for *L'Ermitage* and later for *La Grande Revue*. Reacting against the gaudy commercialism of the French theaters of the day, as well as against the confusion generated by the various dramatic schools, Copeau was impelled to renovate the French theater according to his own concepts: a return to simplicity as exemplified by the austerity of a bare stage with a permanent set; subordination of mechanics and "trucs" to the text itself, a focus on first principles to bring out the poetry and reality of the play and the humanity of the actors. For Copeau, the *metteur-en-scène* was a priest-like figure who should control the unity of the production and the morality and conscience of his company. Many of Copeau's precepts were expressed in the manifesto he published in the September 1913 issue of the *NRF*.[17] To bring these precepts to life Copeau the same year founded the Théâtre du Vieux-Colombier, but he remained in close touch with his *NRF* friends, Gide and Ghéon.

Cocteau's letters to Gide and Ghéon about this time reflect his interest in working with Copeau. Jean Cocteau expressed his passion for the theater at a very young age. His earliest childhood letters to his mother and grandparents were often enlivened by imaginative dialogues or by sketches of rooms he happened to be living in, which he drew as stage sets, complete with furniture arrangement. By the time he was twenty-three, Cocteau had seen the first professional production for the stage of one of his works. This was a ballet called *Le Dieu bleu*, presented by the Ballets Russes. Two years later, in 1914, Cocteau, Paul Thévenaz, and Igor Stravinsky were together in Leysin, Switzerland, it will be recalled, hard at work on his second ballet titled *David*. From the Grand Hotel at Leysin Cocteau wrote his mother in March describing *David* as brief but important, in Stravinsky's words "une goutte à empoisonner un éléphant." [18] The sketchy plot, which revolved around a clown and three acrobats, was described by Cocteau to Misia Sert in these terms: "Ce n'est pas une danse, mais une acrobatie de gymnasiarque forain. . . . C'est une courte chose sans attrait théâtral (et) une Parade. . . . C'est du music-hall." [19] ("It isn't a dance, but a feat by an itinerant carnival acrobat. . . . It's a short piece without theatrical appeal (and) a Parade. . . . It's music hall stuff.")

It is clear from his letters to Gide in early 1914 that Cocteau hoped to persuade Jacques Copeau to produce *David* at his Théâtre du Vieux-Colombier. In February, Cocteau wrote Gide enthusiastically: "— J'ai vu Copeau — *Ses yeux sont charmants* — cela suffit pour s'entendre." ("— I saw Copeau— What charming eyes he has— That's enough for an understanding.") And in a marginal postscript Cocteau added: "Copeau très sympathique. Je redoutais. (De mon côté je redoute *aussi!*) Cela m'a fait plaisir." [20] ("Copeau very sympathetic. I was awed. (From my side I am awesome *too!*) It was a pleasure.") The following month Cocteau again wrote Gide about *David* and the possibility of a Copeau production:

Le Grand Hôtel
Leysin, Suisse

Cher Gide,
Je ne vous écrivais pas à cause de l'extrême fatigue et des ré-barbatives plumes d'hôtel — Peu à peu on s'accoutume au piano "pathétique" des poitrinaires, aux sautes étranges du climat, au mal

de gorge et à la réverbération. Travail intense — Igor St.[ravinsky] est une dynamo. Il nous étonne.

— David va devenir, je pense, quelque chose d'extraordinaire (ne ressemble à rien) — et si Copeau le monte je lui jure qu'il aura des "salles": — (Hélas je redoute pour lui le goût secret de "l'officiel" et de la *fontaine Médicis*) — Gide j'ai de vous revoir une tendre impatience — Je termine le Potomac [*sic*] — j'aimerais vous rejoindre! — J'ai de la tristesse et de la douceur auprès de P. Je suppose que ce doit être pour tous pareil, mais notre inquiétude ne commence-t-elle pas où la sécurité des autres s'asseoit.

Je vous embrasse.

Jean.[21]

Grand Hôtel
Leysin, Switzerland

(Dear Gide,

I didn't write you because of exhaustion and the grim hotel pens. Little by little one grows accustomed to the "pathetic" piano of the consumptives, to the strange changes in temperature here, to sore throats and to the reverberations. Strenuous work—Igor St [ravinsky] is a dynamo. He amazes us.

I think *David* is going to become something extraordinary (like nothing else), and if Copeau stages it, I swear to him that he will have full houses: (Alas! I fear he may have a secret taste for the "official" and for the *Medici Fountain*.) Gide, I am eagerly and tenderly looking forward to seeing you again. I am finishing the *Potomac* [*sic*]. I would like to join you! I feel both sadness and comfort near P[aul Thévenaz]. I suppose that it is the same for everybody, but don't we begin to feel anxious where other people settle securely?

I embrace you,

Jean)

The Copeau production that Cocteau hoped for never materialized, however. According to Frederick Brown it was Diaghilev who sabotaged the project. Apparently Cocteau's "excessive fondness" for Nijinsky, and his plan to have *David* produced by Copeau's theater rather than by the Ballets Russes prompted Diaghilev to come to Leysin to persuade Stravinsky to drop *David* and finish the score of *Le Rossignol*.[22] The result was that *David* was never completed or produced.

As for the views of André Gide himself on whether or not Cocteau was worthy of admission to the *NRF*, there is reason to believe that he had mixed feelings on the subject, both on the personal and on the professional level. Jean Schlumberger writes that Gide found Cocteau's wit and impertinence appeal-

ing. But at the same time, according to Jean Paulhan, Gide had the uneasy feeling that Cocteau was too clever for him.[23] This concern of Gide's shows through in his open letters to Cocteau in 1919, and also in the recollection of a longtime friend of both Gide and Cocteau who quotes Gide as saying with a wry smile that he hesitated to get too close to Cocteau because Cocteau was the sort of person "qui tirait les couvertures à son côté du lit." [24]

The same friend reports that it was Gide who insisted originally that Cocteau be put to the test before being accepted by the *NRF*, and that he be required to write only book reviews and minor articles until he had served his apprenticeship. Although a certain reserve, even disapproval, marked his opinions of Cocteau's early poetry, there were numerous occasions after 1920 when Gide, and the *NRF*, applauded Cocteau's work. Even Henri Ghéon's 1912 review of *La Danse de Sophocle*, and Gide's open letter of 1919 in which he evaluated *Le Coq et l'Arlequin* and *Parade*, although negative in some respects, were not altogether uncomplimentary.

These two commentaries by Ghéon and Gide were the first serious critical attention Cocteau received in the *NRF*. The fact that the second followed the first by seven years is not to be construed as indifference to Cocteau by the *NRF;* the magazine did not appear from September 1914 through May 1919 as a consequence of World War I. On the contrary, Gide and Rivière's choice of Cocteau as a focus of controversy in the first postwar issue of their magazine is indicative of Cocteau's growth in literary stature since 1912.

It was not until the 1920's that the *NRF* gave regular attention to Cocteau's work. In the *NRF* for April 1920 Paul Morand gave favorable notice to *Adieu New York — le Bœuf sur le toit*, "spectacle-concert organisé par Jean Cocteau à la Comédie des Champs-Elysées." [25] In the February 1921 issue of the *NRF*, following the successful revival of Cocteau's *Parade* at the Théâtre des Champs-Elysées, Georges Auric wrote an enthusiastic article restating many of the points about the "ordre nouveau" in music that Cocteau had made in 1919 in *Le Coq et l'Arlequin*.[26] In his review of Cocteau's volume of poetry *Vocabulaire* in the *NRF* for June 1922, Roger Allard reverts to the earlier criticisms of Ghéon and Gide by accusing Cocteau of a lack of originality and of holding up masks to confuse and conceal.[27] In the *NRF* for November of the same year,

Jacques Rivière, in an otherwise favorable commentary on Cocteau's *Le Secret professionnel,* expressed reservations about Cocteau's concealing his ideas by costuming them. *Le Secret professionnel,* reflecting Radiguet's influences on Cocteau, urged a return to classicism in literature and might therefore be expected to appeal to the classically oriented *NRF.* Rivière also voiced concern at Cocteau's anxiety to be in the avant-garde, his preference for creating to perfecting, and his delight in launching artistic fashions. He also questioned Cocteau's wisdom in constantly lecturing his public.[28]

Cocteau's pique at the *NRF*'s early coolness to his work was expressed in his private letters to his mother, to Marcel Jouhandeau, and to Jacques-Emile Blanche, with whom he traded caustic remarks on all phases of the *NRF* organization: the review itself, the publishing house, and the bookstore. In a letter of August 18, 1915, Blanche complained to Cocteau about the weak *NRF* program to promote its books:

> Les libraires se demandent pourquoi la NRF ne *propose* pas, comme les autres éditeurs. Gide m'a tellement grondé, avant hier, que je n'ose plus rien dire. Il est très fier que les "Caves" ne se soient vendues qu'à 354 exemplaires. Cette attitude, à la Degas me paraît aussi prétentieuse qu'irritante. Comment un livre peut-il *toucher* son public si personne ne l'annonce? [29]

> (Book dealers wonder why the *NRF* doesn't keep them posted the way other publishers do. Gide scolded me so much, day before yesterday, that I don't dare say anything more. He is very proud that the *Caves* [*du Vatican*] only sold 354 copies. This Degas-like attitude seems to me as pretentious as it is irritating. How can a book *reach* its public if no one advertises it?)

And on August 30, 1915, Cocteau replied by demanding of Blanche: "Sont-ils fou à la NRF?" Cocteau goes on to explain that a salesman at the *NRF* bookshop tried to discourage him from buying Gide's translation of *The Brothers Karamazov.*[30] As late as May 1922, a year before the *NRF* first accepted an article by him, Cocteau wrote from Le Lavandou:

Cher Blanchie
... Pour la NRF ne voyez vous pas leur chute? La revue n'existait que comme groupe amical, "intègre" etc.... — une fois le groupe évente il fallait choisir et, là, leur manque de jugement les coule. Faux dada, descente de Montmartre et de Montparnasse — (les

Mendès et les Mauclair du nouveau). Pauvre Gide croit découvrir un grand poète et adopte un laisser pour compte de mots bandes: Gabory. Crème Simon rance ayant trop vite et mal compris ma leçon "anti-moderniste – grâce – banalité – vers réguliers etc...." et la débitant aux Galeries Lafayette. Sous cette forme "confection" elle frappe Gide qui ne la distingue à aucune page de Vocabulaire – Livre date.[31]

(Dear Blanchie,

    . . . As for the *NRF*, don't you see their downfall? The review existed only as a friendly group, "incorruptible," etc.... – once the group let in the air they had to choose, and there their lack of judgment discredits them. Fake Dada, descent from Montmartre and Montparnasse – (the Mendèses and the Mauclairs of the new). Poor Gide thinks he has discovered a great poet and takes up a rejected merchandise of limited words: Gabory. Simon cream turns rancid having too quickly and poorly understood my "anti-modernist lesson – grace – banality – regular verses, etc...," and charging it to the Galeries Lafayette. Under this form of "ready made goods" it strikes Gide, who doesn't discern it on a single page of *Vocabulaire* – historic book.)

Looking back at those early frustrations, Jean Cocteau, in a preface written a year before his death, reminisced ironically about the *NRF:*

Plus grave était l'attitude des encyclopédistes de la *Nouvelle Revue Française,* lesquels (Gide en tête) considéraient comme inacceptable toute entreprise ne répondant pas à la phrase de Copeau: "Laissez-moi un traiteau nu" et réprouvant l'étalage d'un spirituel que ces adeptes de l'austerité combattirent comme Luther et Rancé les pompes de Rome.[32]

(More serious was the attitude of the encyclopedists of the *Nouvelle Revue Française,* who (with Gide at their head) considered unacceptable any enterprise that did not answer to Copeau's statement, "Give me a bare stage," and reproved the display of wittiness that those adepts in austerity fought against in the way Luther and Rancé attacked the pomps of Rome.)

At last, in 1923, the gates of the *NRF* seemed to open wide to Jean Cocteau. The *NRF* year began with a January issue especially devoted to Marcel Proust, and Cocteau was invited to submit an article titled "La Voix de Marcel Proust." Perhaps as a subtle reproof to Gide and the *NRF,* who had originally

rejected the first part of *À la recherche du temps perdu* because they misjudged the quality of Proust's work, considering him too *mondain* to be a serious writer, Cocteau included in his article the pointed reminder: "être mondain n'est pas être frivole." In citing Proust's example he was also, of course, defending himself from the same charge, which critics perennially leveled at him.[33]

NRF reviews of Cocteau's works followed thick and fast. Radiguet's novel *Le Diable au corps* was reviewed by Cocteau in the April issue.[34] In May Paul Fierens wrote a favorable review of Cocteau's poem "La Rose de François": "Mais Jean Cocteau, diriez-vous, fait de la poésie légère. – Hé! tant mieux!"[35] ("But Jean Cocteau, you would say, writes frivolous poetry. – Ha! So much the better!")

The thrust of Jacques de Lacretelle's July review of Cocteau's first novel *Le Grand Ecart* is contained in his statement: "Soit par invention personnelle, soit par une intelligente adoption, il a touché à tout ce que nous avons vu de neuf et d'original dans tous les domaines de l'art depuis dix ans."[36] ("Whether it be by personal invention, or by intelligent adoption, he has touched on everything we have seen that is new and original in every domain of art in the last ten years.")

In September Cocteau's long and beautiful poem *Plain Chant* was reviewed by Paul Fierens with special recognition of its clarity and depth.[37] The December issue carried an effusive article by Henri Pourrat on Cocteau's war novel *Thomas l'Imposteur*.[38] Almost as though to atone for the years of *NRF* editorial indifference and critical footdragging, Pourrat heaps endless praise on Cocteau's second novel. In this instance the praise can be discounted somewhat since the book publishing branch of the *NRF* itself, working for the first time with Cocteau, was the publisher of *Thomas l'Imposteur*. Nevertheless, the editorial committee practice followed by the *NRF* at the time was such that complimentary reviews like Pourrat's, which finished by asserting that *Thomas l'Imposteur* pointed the way for the development of French letters for the rest of the century, could not have appeared without at least the tacit approval of Gide and/or Rivière.

Ironically enough, by 1923 when the *NRF* welcomed Cocteau so enthusiastically, he had already independently achieved a conspicuous literary position by the excellence and audacity of his work in many genres: poetry, novel, ballet, theater, and

criticism.[39] He had also attracted attention as a newspaper collumnist, artist, and founder of three literary reviews, as well as a publishing house. *NRF* recognition, therefore, came a little after Cocteau's initial need for it had disappeared. Nevertheless, it was comforting to Cocteau that it had finally come. And it was especially satisfying for him to realize that just as official *NRF* indifference to his work prior to 1923 had had André Gide's consent, so the 1923 thaw in the *NRF's* attitude toward Cocteau also had to have Gide's blessing.

Les Deux Maisons
Se Touchent

From the time the two writers first met, until Gide's death in 1951, their presence in one another's lives was almost a constant in one way or another. At the concrete level there was a running exchange of social and professional meetings, books, gifts, and correspondence; and at the artistic level there was the literary presence of each author in the other's writing. Due allowance must, of course, be made for gaps occasioned by Gide's peripatetic way of life, the interruptions of two world wars, and the sporadic quarrels that separated the two men from time to time.

The record of their encounters is long, even though incomplete. By 1912, when their paths presumably first crossed, Gide had left his own salon days far behind,[1] whereas Cocteau was still in the midst of his *mondain* period. Yet they knew many of the same society women whose homes were open to the writers and artists of the day, and it is not unlikely that they met from time to time in the salons of the Princess de Polignac, Princess Murat, Countess de Noailles, Mme Mühlfeld, Misia Sert, and others. Jacques Barzun remembers that as a boy of six he met Gide and Cocteau when they called together at his father's house in Passy.

Gide and Cocteau also met at the bookshop of Adrienne Monnier, who was only twenty-three in 1915 when she opened the Amis des Livres at 7 rue de l'Odéon in Paris. For

writers between the two world wars, the shop became a literary proving ground, in contrast to the fashionable society salons of the period. Adrienne Monnier's early malicious appraisals of Jean Cocteau have long been used against him, despite her acknowledgment many years later that they may have been unjust.

Among the authors who gathered at her bookshop were some she judged worthy enough to read their works to peers and colleagues. She describes how one such reading came to pass in 1919: "Cocteau vint me rejoindre et me dit à peu près: 'Gide voudrait que je lise le *Cap* rue de l'Odéon.'" ("Cocteau came over to me and said something like: 'Gide would like me to read *Le Cap* [*de Bonne-Espérance*] at rue de l'Odéon.'")

Adrienne Monnier's reaction was that *Le Cap de Bonne-Espérance* was a good poem, and that if Gide wanted the poem to be read it should be read. She continues her anecdote:

À Gide, notre Cocteau courut dire: "Adrienne Monnier aimerait beaucoup que je lise le *Cap* rue de l'Odéon en votre présence. Vous viendrez, n'est-ce pas?" Gide tout bonnement acquiesça.

Nous vîmes presque tout de suite, Gide et moi, que nous avons été ficelés. Nous en fûmes moins fâchés qu'amusés. . . .[2]

(To Gide our Cocteau ran to say: "Adrienne Monnier would like very much to have me read *Le Cap* at rue de l'Odéon in your presence. You will come, won't you?" Gide simply agreed.

We saw almost at once, Gide and I, that we had been tricked. We were less angered than amused. . . .)

As a penance, Jean Cocteau was obliged to bring chocolate cakes from Rabattet's for everyone, including Marc Allégret, who came with Gide. André Breton and Philippe Soupault, Cocteau's surrealist antagonists, also attended, bristling with hostility.

According to Adrienne Monnier, who worshiped Gide but complained that Cocteau gave her a migraine, Gide and Cocteau also both attended a recital of avant-garde music by Erik Satie at Paul Rosenberg's art gallery early in March 1919.[3]

In his column "Carte Blanche" written for the newspaper *Paris-Midi*, Cocteau wrote under the dateline of March 31, 1919:

Signalons une des lectures intimes de Socrate, rue de l'Odéon, chez Mlle. Monnier, à la maison des Amis du Livre, où les poètes se rencontrent. Madame Balguerie accompagnée par l'auteur. Dans l'assistance, Paul Claudel, André Gide, Francis Jammes.[4]

(We report on one of the intimate readings of Socrates, rue de l'Odéon, at Mlle Monnier's, at the Amis du Livre, where poets meet. Mme Balguerie accompanied by the author. In the audience, Paul Claudel, André Gide, Francis Jammes.)

The two writers also surely met at the home of their mutual friend Jacques-Emile Blanche either in Auteuil or in Offranville. It was here that Gide's friend Edith Wharton recalls she was first introduced to Cocteau. Although no record has been found of a visit by Cocteau to Gide's home at Cuverville, he evidently was a guest at Gide's Villa Montmorency at Auteuil, for his open letter to Gide in 1919 describes both the interior and the exterior of that unusual residence. Gide visited Cocteau in the latter's Paris apartment at 10 rue d'Anjou. It was there that Gide had urged Cocteau to simplify his writing.

In his *Journal* Gide records a number of personal contacts with Jean Cocteau. In an entry dated August 20, 1914, Gide presents a portrait of Cocteau in wartime:

Jean Cocteau m'avait donné rendez-vous à un "thé anglais" au coin de la rue de Ponthieu et l'avenue d'Antin. Je n'ai pas eu de plaisir à le revoir, malgré son extrême gentillesse; mais il est incapable de gravité et toutes ses pensées, ses mots d'esprit, ses sensations, tout cet extraordinaire brio de son parler habituel me choquait comme un article de luxe étalé en temps de famine et de deuil. Il s'est vêtu, presque en soldat, et le coup de fouet des événements lui donne bien meilleure mine; il ne résigne rien, et simplement tourne au martial sa pétulance. Il trouve pour parler des boucheries de Mulhouse des épithètes amusantes, des mimiques; il imite le son du clairon, le sifflement des shrapnells. Puis, changeant de sujet, car il voit qu'il ne m'amuse pas, il se dit triste; il veut être triste du même genre de tristesse que vous, et soudain épouse votre pensée, vous l'explique puis parle de Blanche, puis singe Mme R., puis parle de cette dame, à la Croix-Rouge, qui criait dans l'escalier: "On m'a promis cinquante blessés pour ce matin; je veux mes cinquante blessés." Cependant il écrase un morceau de cake dans son assiette et le déguste à petites bouchées; sa voix a des éclats, des retours; il rit, il se penche et se plie vers vous et vous touche. L'étrange, c'est que je crois qu'il ferait un bon soldat. Lui l'affirme, et qu'il serait courageux. Il y a chez lui

l'insouciance du gavroche; c'est près de lui que je me sens le plus maladroit, le plus lourd, le plus morose.[5]

(Jean Cocteau had arranged to meet me in an "English tearoom" on the corner of the rue de Ponthieu and the Avenue d'Antin. I had no pleasure in seeing him again, despite his extreme kindness; but he is incapable of seriousness, and all his thoughts, his witticisms, his sensations, all the extraordinary brilliance of his customary conversation, shocked me [as would] a luxury article displayed in a period of famine and mourning. He is dressed almost like a soldier, and the fillip of the present events has made him look healthier. He is relinquishing nothing, but simply giving a martial twist to his usual liveliness. When speaking of the slaughter of Mulhouse, he uses amusing adjectives and mimicry; he imitates the bugle call and the whistling of the shrapnel. Then, changing subjects since he sees that he is not amusing me, he claims to be sad; he wants to be sad with the same kind of sadness [that you have], and suddenly he adopts your mood and explains it to you. Then he talks of Blanche, mimics Mme R., and talks of the lady at the Red Cross who shouted on the stairway: "I was promised fifty wounded men for this morning; I want my fifty wounded men." Meanwhile he is crushing a piece of plum cake in his plate and nibbling it; his voice rises suddenly and has odd twists; he laughs, leans forward, bends toward you and touches you. The odd thing is that I think he would make a good soldier. He asserts that he would and that he would be brave too. He has the carefree attitude of the street urchin; it is in his company that I feel the most awkward, the most heavy, the most gloomy.)

And again, on November 15, 1914:

Hier elle [Mme Misia Edwards] n'avait pu se procurer les photos, mais elle attendait, sitôt après le déjeuner, Cocteau, qui devait les apporter. Cocteau est venu après le déjeuner sans les photos, qu'il m'a promises pour demain soir; en attendant il m'a mené à la maison de santé de la rue de la Chaise où nous pourrions parler à une dame de la Croix-Rouge qui avait soigné ces enfants. La dame de la Croix-Rouge n'était pas arrivée et, attendu au Foyer, j'ai dû quitter Cocteau avant de réussir à rien savoir de plus.[6]

(Yesterday she [Mme Misia Edwards] had not been able to get the photographs, but she was expecting Cocteau right after lunch, who was to bring them. Cocteau came after lunch without the photos [of children injured in the war], which he promised me for tomorrow evening. Meanwhile he took me to the clinic on rue de la Chaise, where we could speak with a Red Cross nurse who had taken care of those children. The lady was not there yet, and, expected at the Foyer, I had to leave Cocteau before learning anything.)

Marc Allégret also recalls that during World War I he often accompanied Gide and Cocteau to the theater, to dinners in Parisian bistros, or to places like the Hôtel Meurice, where they once met Cocteau's friend Roland Garros, the famous French war pilot to whom Cocteau dedicated his poem *Le Cap de Bonne-Espérance*.[7]

Gide's *Journal* describes a luncheon with Jean Cocteau and Paul Valéry on November 3, 1920, at Mme Mühlfeld's:

Invité à déjeuner par Mme Mühlfeld, avec Paul Valéry et Cocteau; je vais les retrouver. Je n'avais pas échangé trois phrases que déjà j'étais exaspéré. Sur quelque sujet que se portât la conversation, l'esprit de Valéry et de Cocteau ne s'efforçait que de dénigrer; ils faisaient assaut d'incompréhension, de déni. Rapportés, leurs propos paraîtraient absurdes. Je ne supporte plus cette sorte de paradoxe de salon, qui ne brille qu'aux dépens d'autrui. Péguy disait: "Je ne juge pas; je condamne." Ils exécutèrent ainsi Régnier, Mme. de Noailles, Ibsen. On parla d'Octave Feuillet à qui l'on s'accorda à trouver beaucoup plus de talent qu'à ce dernier, que Valéry déclarait "assommant." Me voyant réduit au silence, car qu'eût servi de protester, Cocteau déclara que j'étais d'une "humeur exécrable." Je n'aurais pu paraître "en train" qu'à condition de faire chorus avec eux et déjà je me reprochais assez d'être venu pour les entendre.

Au demeurant, chacun d'eux, pris à part, est charmant; et pour Valéry spécialement, si je l'estimais moins, je ne souffrirais point tant de ses dénis. Quoi d'étonnant si, après avoir désenchanté le monde autour de lui, après s'être ingénié à se désintéresser de tant de choses, il s'ennuie![8]

(Invited to lunch by Mme Mühlfeld, with Paul Valéry and Cocteau; I go to join them. I had not exchanged three sentences when I was already exasperated. Whatever subject the conversation drifted to, the minds of Valéry and Cocteau strove to disparage; they vied with each other in lack of comprehension, in denial. Repeated, their remarks would seem absurd. I can no longer put up with that sort of drawing-room paradox which shines only at the expense of others. Péguy used to say: "I am not judging; I am condemning." In this way they executed Régnier, Mme de Noailles, Ibsen. Octave Feuillet was brought up and they agreed in granting him more talent than Ibsen, whom Valéry declared "tiresome." Seeing me reduced to silence—for what would have been the good of protesting?—Cocteau declared that I was in a "dreadful mood." I could not have seemed "in good form" except on condition of joining their chorus, and already I was blaming myself enough for having come to hear them.

Yet each one of them, taken separately, is charming; and for

Valéry in particular, if I esteemed him less, I should not suffer so much from his negative attitude. How could it be surprising if, after having disenchanted the world around him, after having strained his wits to lose interest in so many things, he is bored!)

In late December 1924 Gide had been hospitalized in the Diaconesses' nursing home for appendicitis. Cocteau evidently visited him there at least once, judging from the postscript to his letter to Gide in January 1925 thanking him for Gide's translation of Rabindranath Tagore's play *Amal et la lettre du Roi:*

j[an]v[ier] 1925

Mon cher Gide
    Lettre du pauvre sire en réponse à la lettre du roi. J'ai la mal (mis Amal par) du pays — mais où se trouve le pays. C'est grave.
    Je vous embrasse.

Jean

Je ne suis pas repassé aux Diaconesses; parce que Blanche m'a dit que vous en étiez sorti.[9]

January 1925

(My dear Gide
    Letter from the poor man in reply to the king's letter. I am home-sick ("mis Amal par")—but where is my home? It's serious.
    Affectionately,

Jean

    [P.S.] I did not go back to the Diaconesses' because Blanche told me you had left.)

In May 1925 Cocteau was just emerging from the "tunnel" of one of his periodic cures for the opium habit. He had recently moved from the Thermes Urbains hospital on the rue de Chateaubriand in Paris to the Hôtel des Réservoirs in Versailles, where André Gide came to visit him.

Réservoirs (il pleut sans arrêt)
1er mai

Cher André
    Votre lettre m'a bien ému — D'autant plus qu'après mon tunnel (je vous raconterai tout) il ne me reste que le cœur intact. La tête est vide, vide, vide — Je suis mal attaché à la terre — je vole d'une aile et je boitaille — mais le cœur se nourrit de votre lettre. Ma solitude est incroyable — quand je me trouve trop seul je me couche. Vous imaginez ce que serait votre visite!
    Venez donc dîner un soir de la semaine prochaine — C'est encore

le soir que la fatigue me dérange le moins. Retrouverai-je un jour des forces? Des choses comme votre dernière phrase me donnent du courage. Il m'en faut.

Je vous embrasse

Jean

Téléphonez n'importe quel matin. Comment va votre oreille? Les *NRF* vous ont-ils envoyé votre exemplaire de Poésie — comme il est un des luxe j'en doute car on ne me les a même pas envoyés à dédicacer comme je le demande à Hirsch dans chaque lettre.[10]

[Hôtel des] Réservoirs
(it's raining nonstop)
May 1

(Dear André

Your letter touched me very much— All the more so since after my tunnel (I will tell you all about it) only my heart remains intact. My head is empty, empty, empty—I am poorly anchored to earth—I fly on one wing and I hobble around—but my heart is nourished by your letter. My solitude is incredible—when I feel too lonely I go to bed. You can imagine what your visit would mean to me!

Do come to dinner one evening next week. The evening is still the time I am least troubled by fatigue. Will I ever get my strength back? Things like your final sentence give me courage. I need it.

I embrace you,

Jean

[P.S.] Telephone any morning. How is your ear? Did the *NRF* people send you your copy of *Poésie*? Since it's one of the deluxe copies I doubt it, for they haven't even sent them to me for autographing, as I ask Hirsch to do in every letter.)

Another letter from Cocteau to Gide, on May 13, 1925, indicates in the closing line that Gide was expected at Cocteau's the following Wednesday:

Paris
13 mai 1925

Mon cher André

Je devrais vivre dans les chambres d'hôtel et n'en jamais sortir même par lettre. Paris réserve toujours une mauvaise surprise.

Ce qui m'étonne c'est que vous ne sentiez pas que les choses me blessent sur le plan amical. Du reste je veux avoir une otite: avant qu'on me prouve une vraie trahison de Max — je refuse d'y croire — et même si on me la prouve — je croirai qu'il écrivait dans l'hypnose. Pour vous pareil — Malgré que
À mercredi

Je vous embrasse

Jean

Cocteau added in the right margin of this letter:

Voici une des phrases de Max J[acob]: La réalité finit toujours par triompher — ta vie en est un exemple. Car tu es de nous tous le seul qui soit réellement ce qu'il montre. J'ai repris et relu l'article de C[assou]. C'est une bave de Jésuite enragé.

A second note was added by Cocteau at the top of the page, upside down:

Je cite entre autres, pour que vous ne m'accusiez pas de m'inventer des appuis. Max penche vers la personne avec laquelle il se trouve. Mais je le sais exactement à niveau avec moi. D'abord, il m'est impossible d'oublier qu'il a eu le courage de m'écrire presque chaque jour pendant mon supplice — Thermes Urbains.

A final thought was written by Cocteau on the back of the envelope of the letter:

L'article est si clair sans doute qu'Aron m'a téléphoné "combien c'était ennuyeux" et combien Gallimard en était ennuyé aussi, avant que je fasse le moindre signe.[11]

Paris
May 13, 1925

(My dear André,
   I ought to live in hotel rooms and never go out, even by letter. Paris always keeps an unpleasant surprise in store.
   What amazes me is that you did not feel that things hurt me on the level of friendship. Besides, I want to have an otitis: before a real betrayal by Max [Jacob] is proved to me — I refuse to believe it — and even if it is proved — I will believe he wrote under hypnosis. The same for you — even though —
   Until Wednesday.

I embrace you,
Jean

   [P.S.] Here is one of Max J[acob's] comments: "Reality always wins out in the end — your life is an example. Because of all of us you alone are really what you seem to be. I have picked up and reread C[assou's] article. It is the slobbering of an enraged Jesuit."
   [P.S.S.] I cite this among others so that you may not accuse me of inventing supporters. Max inclines toward the person he happens to be with. But I know him to be exactly on my level. First of all, it is impossible for me to forget that he had the courage to write me almost every day during my torture at the Thermes Urbains.
   [P.P.S.] The article is doubtless so clear that Aron phoned me "how troublesome it was" and how much Gallimard was annoyed with it too, before I had lifted a finger.)

In October of 1928 Cocteau had lunch with Gide at the Roquebrune home of Gide's English translator Dorothy Bussy.[12] Gide had also called on Cocteau at Roquebrune in 1928. On November 1 Cocteau wrote his mother: "T'ai-je dit que pendant mes trois jours à Roquebrune Gide avait surgi soudain dans ma chambre?" [13] ("Did I tell you that during my three days at Roquebrune Gide suddenly appeared in my room?")

In the spring of 1929, while undergoing another disintoxication treatment at the Saint-Cloud nursing home, Cocteau was again visited by Gide:

St. Cloud
Mars 1929

Mon cher André,

Votre visite m'a été bien douce et très enrichissante. Comme je vous dois tant de choses et que jadis, sans votre intervention, ma vie se perdait et suivait l'exemple d'une écriture contrefaite, je voulais vous annoncer le vrai bénéfice de ma cure: Le travail me travaille. J'expulse un livre que je souhaitais écrire depuis 1912 (mais je ne pouvais pas). Ce livre sort sans bousculade − il me commande, me maltraite et je fais en 19 jours un travail de plusieurs mois.

Je ne me raconterais pas si je n'avais pas vu la sollicitude avec laquelle vous souhaitiez cette délivrance.

Raïssa M.[aritain] me dit: Ch[arles] D[u] B[os] garde son culte *absolu* de Gide il ne le blâme *que* pour, etc.... − En réponse je lui citais l'étonnante phrase de Chevillard (on exaltait Wagner à table pendant la guerre chez le fils Van Dyck.) "Quel dommage qu'il ne soit pas né à Chatou!"

Je vous aime et vous embrasse. Tendresses à Marc [Allégret].

Jean [14]

Saint-Cloud
March 1929

(My dear André,

Your visit was most pleasant and very enriching for me. As I am indebted to you for so many things, and since in days gone by except for your intervention, my life was being wasted and was patterned on the example of a counterfeit handwriting, I wanted to let you know the real benefit of my cure: work is working me. I am delivering a book [*Les Enfants terribles*] that I had wished to write since 1912 (but could not). This book issues from me without a scuffle − it dictates to me, abuses me, and I am doing several months' labor in nineteen days.

I would not tell about myself if I hadn't seen the solicitude with which you hoped for this delivery.

Raïssa M[aritain] tells me: "Ch[arles] D[u] B[os] maintains his *absolute* cult of Gide, he *only* blames him for, etc...." In reply I quoted to her Chevillard's surprising remark (during the war people were exalting Wagner at meals at young Van Dyck's): "What a pity he was not born at Chatou!"

I like you and I embrace you. Tender regards to Marc [Allégret].

Jean)

An entry in Gide's *Journal* for January 3, 1930, reads:

À Hyères chez les Noailles, où je retrouve Marc, en compagnie de Cocteau et d'Auric. J'arrivais pour déjeuner seulement; je me laisse volontiers retenir à dîner, puis à coucher.[15]

(At Hyères, at the Noailleses', where I find Marc, together with Cocteau and Auric. I had come merely for lunch; I gladly let myself be detained for dinner, then for the night.)

A postcard dated December 26, 1931, from Gide to Cocteau speaks of a meeting with Cocteau and Jean Desbordes, Cocteau's protégé at the time:

Cuverville
26 Déc. 31

Mon cher Jean

Vous vous êtes montré(s) (et D B d [Desbordes]) si ineffablement exquis l'autre matin que je ne vous ai quittés tous deux qu'avec un vif désir de vous revoir. En attendant ce plaisir, qu'a différé la grippe – tous mes souvenirs bien amicaux et mes vœux.

Votre
André Gide [16]

Cuverville
December 26, 1931

(My dear Jean,

You behaved, Desbordes too, in such an ineffably delicious way the other morning that I only left you both with a keen desire to see you again. While awaiting this pleasure, which has been delayed by the flu—all my warmest personal regards and wishes.

Your
André Gide)

The Gide-Cocteau correspondence testifies to another meeting between the two men after Gide's return to France from his wartime absence in North Africa. Pierre Herbart and Gide visited Cocteau at his country home in Milly-la-Forêt, near

Fontainebleau, in 1947, to discuss a contemplated film version of Gide's *récit Isabelle.*[17] By the winter of 1949 Cocteau had entered a frantic period of professional activity. Nevertheless, on his return from a trip to New York he wrote his aging friend and rival to arrange a meeting:

> 36 rue de Montpensier, 1er
> 15 Janvier 1949
> Je retourne à Paris demain
>
> Mon très cher André,
> Je rentre de New York où l'on vous rencontre partout. Hélas, c'est Richard Wright qui a raison et leur rideau d'or vaut le rideau de fer. Je voudrais vous embrasser et parler longuement avec vous de cette étonnante ville ouverte, trop ouverte et pleine de courants d'air.
>
> Je vous embrasse.
> Jean [18]

> 36 rue de Montpensier
> January 15, 1949
> I return to Paris tomorrow.
>
> (My very dear André,
> I have just come back from New York where one meets you everywhere. Alas! Richard Wright is correct and their golden curtain is a match for the Iron Curtain. I would like to hug you and to talk at length about that suprising open city which is too open and full of drafts.
>
> I embrace you,
> Jean)

Gide eagerly replied shortly afterward:

> Cher Jean
> Je songe à vous tristement en apprenant la mort subite de [Christian] Bérard.
> Voudrais vous revoir et ne parviens pas à prendre rendez-vous (l'âge aidant, ça devient une infirmité). Vous me dites de vous téléphoner et je n'ai votre No. ni de Montpensier ni de Milly — où je me souhaite, oubliant l'heure, en face de vous dans un bon fauteuil, écoutant votre "lettre aux Américains" et m'écriant de temps en temps: Oh! non, Jean, vous ne pouvez tout de même pas...
> Plus fatigué qu'il n'est décent de le dire, mais bien votre
> André Gide [19]

> (Dear Jean
> I am thinking of you with sadness, having just learned of the sudden death of [Christian] Bérard.

Would love to see you again but find it difficult to make an appointment (with old age, this is becoming an infirmity). You tell me to telephone you and I have neither your Montpensier number nor the one at Milly—where I wish I were, oblivious of the hour, across from you in a good old easy chair, listening to your "Lettre aux Américains" and exclaiming now and then: "Oh! no Jean, you really can't..." More tired than I can properly say, but very much your

André Gide)

Cocteau answered with two notes:

Très cher André,
  Voici les numéros
          Rue de M.[ontpensier] — Richelieu 55–72
          Milly — le Samedi soir et le Dimanche
          28 — Milly — Setoise
  Impossible de partir pour l'Egypte — le 6 mars — avant de vous avoir embrassé et peut-être lu la lettre.
  La mort de Bérard me laisse comme après une typhoïde.

Jean [20]

(Very dear André,
  Here are the numbers:
          Rue de M[ontpensier]—Richelieu 55–72
          Milly—Saturday evening and Sunday
          28—Milly—Seine et Oise
  Cannot leave for Egypt—March 6th—without embracing you and perhaps reading the letter.
  Bérard's death leaves me like one after a bout of typhoid.

Jean)

Milly Setoise
Fév 1949
Très très cher André
  Nos heures correspondent si mal que j'en arrive à me demander par quel bout saisir le fil de notre rencontre. J'ai presque terminé ma lettre aux Américains et j'aimerais vous la soumettre. Je vous embrasse.

Jean
  Faites moi téléphoner à quelle heure je puis vous appeler moi. [21]

Milly, Seine et Oise
February 1949
(Very very dear André,
  Our hours are so out of joint that I am beginning to wonder how we could eventually get together. I have almost finished my *Lettre aux Américains* and I would like to submit it to you. I embrace you.

Jean

[P.S.] Have someone telephone me what time is best for me to call you.)

Subsequent to these notes, Gide made several trips from the nearby Prefecture of Melun to La Maison du Bailli, as Cocteau's centuries-old home at Milly-la-Forêt was known in the village.[22] As Gide drove down the quiet cobblestone lane which ended at Cocteau's house, he must have been struck by the contrast with some of Cocteau's earlier, less pastoral settings. The narrow doorway in the stone wall, which opened from the lane into a cloistered garden with millstream and *potager* beyond, was very much like the one at Cuverville which had inspired the name for *La Porte étroite*.[23] The peace and silence of Milly could only have made the feverish atmosphere of the old times at Toulon, Paris, and Villefranche seem like a distant nightmare. One catches a glimpse of that frenzied era in an early letter from Cocteau to his friend Marcel Jouhandeau that had described the bedlam at the Hotel Welcome in Villefranche when the U.S. Navy vessel *Pittsburgh* left port:

J'habite un drôle d'endroit — une boite toute suspendue dans les hautes branches d'un arbre de Noël qui flambe. Au premier étage de l'hôtel-bordel, jour et nuit les marins se battent et dansent la danse du ventre. Je n'entends de Jazz que la grosse caisse; c'est comme si on imprimait un journal dans les caves. Bruit de machine, crises de nerfs des poules, chœurs des marins . . . etc. . . . Le départ du Pittsburg était un rêve, avec Marseillaise au ralenti et 12 projecteurs sur les poules en larmes aux fenêtres de l'hôtel — (sic).[24]

(I'm living in a weird place—a box completely suspended in the upper branches of a blazing Christmas tree. On the first floor of the hotel-bordello, day and night the sailors brawl and do the belly dance. The only jazz I hear is the bass drum; it's as though they were printing a newspaper in the cellars. Engine din, the tarts' hysterics, the sailors' choruses . . . etc. . . . The departure of the *Pittsburgh* was a dream, with the "Marseillaise" played in slow time and 12 searchlights on the strumpets sobbing in the hotel windows—(sic).)

Two stone sphinxes flanking the front door at Milly-la-Forêt stared blindly at Gide as he waited for Cocteau to appear, ironic reminders, at the end of his life, of the homosexuality he had long ago described as the "premier sphinx sur ma route," [25] and of the anomaly the two men had in common. Inside the house, however, mementos of Jean Cocteau's

"hâtive et fiévreuse" career engulf the visitor even today. A folding screen at one end of the salon is decorated with snapshots of Cocteau with a revolver, of Albert Einstein sticking out his tongue, of Cocteau's pastel portrait of Colette, and a montage with Picasso's head attached to the tiny Velázquez figure of a little girl. A table holds a plaster cast of Jean Cocteau's hands. Unobtrusively hung on one wall is a small strip of wallpaper from Cocteau's childhood home at Maisons-Laffitte, a talisman which has had its revered place in each house Cocteau occupied. The salon is dominated by exotic flora: two motionless gilt palm trees which frame Christian Bérard's six-by-six-foot sketch for a set of Cocteau's *La Machine infernale*.

One can imagine the thoughts of Gide and Cocteau as side by side they studied this representation of the confrontation between the young, ambitious Oedipus and the sphinx who barred his route. For the second time in a day Gide was faced with a significant image out of his own past. For Cocteau, traveling back in his mind to his confrontations with Gide at the outset of his career, it would have been natural enough for him to identify his eighty-year-old guest as the first sphinx to bar his way on the road to literary success. Yet out of Cocteau's early contest with Gide, as out of Gide's early struggles with his own nature, both artists could now see that much good had come. It was inevitably, therefore, in a mood of reconciliation and reminiscence that the two aging friends and rivals looked forward to these meetings in Cocteau's extraordinary salon.

The salon, which resembles a three-dimensional Douanier Rousseau, swarms with Cocteau's familiars: Life-size animals or fragments of animals are everywhere. "Ils sont tous venus par hasard, apporté par une vague," Cocteau explains, in words like those Gide used to describe the origins of the assorted objects in his rue Vaneau apartment. Two bronze fawns, a pair of papier-mâché roosters, a stuffed owl, a pewter ibis, a ram's head with amethyst-studded horns, an elephant's foot made into a vase, a pair of ostrich legs turned candlesticks, a charcoal sketch of a giraffe, and a live cat curled up asleep in a chair fill the room with a nostalgic clutter. Fertility symbols abound: a chair fashioned from steer horns, four enormous steer horns over the mantel, a bouquet of stag antlers, and the

spiral ivory tooth of a narwhal, the legendary horn of the unicorn, complete the fauna of the remarkable room.

Seated by the fireplace in a deep black leather rocking chair, which nearly tipped over backwards the first time he lowered himself into it, Gide spoke of Cocteau's forthcoming trip to Egypt, a country Gide had visited three years earlier; of plans for a film version of *Les Caves du Vatican;* and of his and Cocteau's activities spanning half a century. It was undoubtedly at these afternoon "rencontres" that Jean Cocteau and André Gide, both mellowed by the years and rendered magnanimous by success, recaptured the warmth that had marked their friendship more than thirty years before.

Only a short time later Gide suffered a heart attack. Cocteau, anxious to see him before leaving for Egypt on March 6 with a troupe of actors, went to call on Gide at his rue Vaneau apartment. Ned Rorem, who was to become another in the long line of Cocteau protégés, called on Cocteau the same day and later wrote in his preface to the English edition of *La Difficulté d'être:* "Tall, thin Cocteau seemed agitated, explained he'd come home only minutes before I rang, had been to check up on *le père Gide,* from whom he'd gotten a *pneumatique* in a disquieting handwriting." [26] Cocteau himself, in his book *Maalesh,* describing the Egyptian tour of his stage company, underlines the element of catharsis in this meeting and in his previous dialogues with Gide at Milly-la-Forêt:

> Gide auquel, hier, j'ai été rendre visite, parce que l'écriture d'une lettre qu'il venait de m'écrire m'avait inquiété, relève, en effet, d'une crise cardiaque assez grave et me parle de l'Egypte. . . . Nous vidons notre sac, comme à ma campagne le mois dernier, où il venait chaque après-midi pendant son séjour à la préfecture de Melun. C'est le fond du sac. Nous finissons par débrouiller ce qui nous avait brouillés, embrouillés, ce qui me vaut les attaques de son journal. Il m'avoue: "J'ai voulu vous tuer." Voilà l'exemple type des dangereuses visites de ces "jeunes" dont je parle dans *La Difficulté d'être.*[27]

> (Gide, to whom I paid a visit yesterday because I was disturbed by the handwriting of a letter he had just sent me, is indeed recovering from a rather serious heart attack and talks to me about Egypt. . . . We unbosom ourselves of all our wrongs, as we did last month at my country house where he came each afternoon during his stay at the Melun prefecture. We get to the bottom of things. We end up by unraveling what had caused our misunderstandings, our entangle-

ments, what earned me the attacks in his *Journal*. He assures me: "I wanted to kill you." There's the typical example of the dangerous visits by those "young people" of whom I speak in *La Difficulté d'être*.)

The meetings of 1949 appear to be the last intimate contact between Jean Cocteau and André Gide, although they saw each other in public at the Comédie-Française shortly before Gide's death and, according to Truman Capote, had a brief chance encounter in Sicily in the spring of 1950.

The paths of the two writers had crossed professionally on many occasions, at the offices of the *NRF*, and at each other's public appearances.[28] For example, with Gide's assistance, Cocteau attended Gide's lecture on the Bengali poet Sir Rabindranath Tagore at the Théâtre du Vieux-Colombier in 1913. On December 1 of that year Cocteau wrote Gide:

> Y vient "elle"? Je redoute.
> D'abord j'irai Jeudi vous entendre. Comment serai-je sûr d'une place? Où retenir? (Le Colombier me demeure inconnu car je me couche tôt, soignant de toutes les maladies la plus féroce: la bonne santé précaire) n'oublions jamais le bossu de Paludes. Donc Vendredi deux heures et le 4 d'une chaise à une estrade.
> J.C.[29]

> (Will "she" be there? I dread it.
> First of all, I'll go to hear you Thursday. How can I be sure of a seat? What about reservations? (The Colombier is still unfamiliar to me since I go to bed early nursing the most ferocious of all illnesses: precarious good health), let's never forget the hunchback in *Paludes*. Friday at two o'clock then, and on [Thursday] the fourth [change seats] from a chair to a dais.
> J.C.)

There were many other private meetings planned by Gide or Cocteau, some of which for one reason or another failed to materialize. Their correspondence refers to a number of such occasions. On December 6, 1913, Cocteau wrote André Gide:

> J'ai peur à mourir de vous mais encore plus de Ghéon après vos craintes. Venez encore seul.
> Cette nuit un cauchemar. Vous n'aimiez pas le livre. C'est pourquoi cette carte.
> À vendredi
> (Je vous écrirai la veille ou l'avant-veille.)
> J.C.[30]

(I am frightened to death by you, but even more by Ghéon after your fears. Come alone again.

Last night a nightmare. You didn't like the book. Hence this card. Until Friday.

(I'll write you a day or two before.)

J.C.)

Just before Christmas 1913, Cocteau wrote Gide again:

Noël déçoit et bourre les souliers de bronchites. — Malgré tout, climat spécial — on aimerait qu'il arrive quelque chose:
Vous voir serait mon seul plaisir.
On m'avait — sadisme — caché (pré-caché) votre visite au plafond. Mon Amyntas, fruit du vol, (?) j'ai dû le rendre.

J.C.[31]

(Christmas is a disappointment and stuffs one's shoes with bronchitis. In spite of everything, special atmosphere, one only wishes something would happen:
To see you would be my only joy.
I had not been told (in advance)—sadism—of your visit to the top flat. My *Amyntas,* stolen fruit (?) I had to return.

J.C.)

In April 1917, Gide wrote Cocteau:

Consternation!
Je souffre depuis mon lever d'une crise de guigne. Un vol d'épreuves à corriger d'urgence (préface aux Fleurs du Mal) s'est abattu sur moi ce matin. Arrivé rue d'Anjou avec une heure de retard... que je suis triste! Mais vous auriez dû laisser quelque indication à votre femme de chambre. Comment vous retrouver à présent? Et je pars demain par le premier train — Si par miracle... vers la fin du jour... un coup de téléphone chez Blanche — chez qui je déjeune —

André Gide [32]

(Consternation!
Ever since getting out of bed I have suffered a streak of bad luck. A flight of page proofs to be corrected at once (preface to the *Fleurs du mal*) alighted on me this morning. Reached rue d'Anjou an hour late... I am so sad! But you should have left some directions with your chambermaid. How can I join you now? And I leave tomorrow by the first train— If by some miracle... toward the end of the day... a telephone call to Blanche's house—where I'll be having lunch—

André Gide)

Cocteau replied apologetically:

Cher Gide,

Quelle déveine! Je ne pensais plus que vous viendriez et j'avais rendez-vous d'affaires à 11 h[eures]¼ — En rentrant à 11 h[eures]½, midi moins le ¼ on m'annonce votre visite — Encore les Eugènes! —— Ne reviendrez-vous pas voir notre Parade? C'est une bonne tranche d'Eugénisme à travers Picasso.

Comme on est bête chez moi — on aurait dû vous dire d'attendre. Cette embrouille retarde les clins d'œil indispensables. Je me réjouissais profondément de vous voir.

Jean [33]

(Dear Gide,

What rotten luck! I didn't think you were going to come and I had a business date at 11:15— When I return at 11:30–11:45 I am told of your visit— The Eugènes again! —— Won't you come back to see our *Parade?* It's a great slice of Eugénism, Picasso-style.

How stupid these people are at my place—they should have asked you to wait. This mixup delays the winks which are absolutely necessary [to understanding]. I was looking forward with joy to seeing you.

Jean)

On May 24, 1918, Cocteau had written Gide announcing the death of Jean Le Roy, a young poet and friend of Cocteau's. Gide responded at once with sympathy:

Cuverville-en-Caux
2 juin 18

Mon cher Jean

Je suis triste de votre tristesse et reste devant vous sans parvenir à trouver les mots de consolation que je voudrais; mais c'est qu'il est certains deuils dont il ne faut point chercher à consoler.

Je reviens à Paris dans dix jours; j'espère vous revoir et déjà vous embrasse.

André Gide [34]

Cuverville-en-Caux
June 2, 1918

(My dear Jean,

I am sad at your sadness and stand before you without finding the words of comfort I seek; but that is because there are a few sorrows that one must not try to comfort.

I return to Paris in ten days; I hope to see you and already embrace you.

André Gide)

In the summer of 1922, when Cocteau was near le Lavandou and Gide was at Porquerolles, an amusing series of notes was exchanged between them in which Cocteau was evidently anxious to cement the friendly relations reestablished by their correspondence of the month before:

> Le Lavandou, Var
> 23 Juin 1922

Mon cher Gide,

Voilà 15 jours, je passe avec Radiguet à St. Clair (qui prolonge en quelque sorte Lavandou) et je lui dis en montrant une maison: "Cette maison devrait être aux Van Rysselberghe." Là-dessus je vole des roses jaunes qui sentaient la pêche. Aujourd'hui, j'étais sur la route avec les Jean Hugo et je croise une dame qui ressemble à Madame V.R. Est-ce elle? Est-ce leur maison? Ce qui ajoute à cet ensemble est la rencontre d'un cycliste qui portait un chapeau et une cape comme vous et qui, du reste, ne vous ressemblait pas par ailleurs.

Condamnez-moi ou donnez-moi une preuve de ma perspicacité.

> Votre
> Jean Cocteau

P.S. La maison est au bord de la route, près de la falaise. Elle est jaune-orange — avec des ouvertures en arcade — des stores ronds — et il y a un bas-relief de St. Jean en bronze près de la porte d'entrée rouge en haut de quelques marches. La maison comporte une autre petite maison de style plus banlieue — en haut du jardin.[35]

> Le Lavandou, Var
> June 23, 1922

(My dear Gide,

A couple of weeks ago I was with Radiguet at Saint-Clair (which is sort of an extension of Lavandou), and I said, pointing out a house: "This house must belong to the Van Rysselberghes." Whereupon I stole some yellow roses which had the fragrance of peaches. Today I was going down the road with the Jean Hugos and I passed a lady who looked like Mme V.[an] R.[ysselberghe]. Is it she? Is it their house? What adds to this pattern was meeting a man on a bicycle who was wearing a hat and cape as you do but who, aside from that, didn't resemble you otherwise.

Scold me, or give me a proof of my perspicacity.

> Your
> Jean Cocteau

P.S. The house stands at the edge of the road, near the cliff. It is yellowish-orange—with arcade-like openings—round windows above —and there is a bronze bas-relief of Saint John near the red front

door at the top of some steps. the property includes another little house of a more suburban style — at the top of the garden.)

Shortly afterwards Cocteau's letter was followed by a second note:

Le Lavandou, Var

Cher Gide,

Un vieillard paralytique m'a dit hier que la maison était bien celle des V.R. Si cela vous embête de m'écrire et si vous écrivez chez eux, présentez donc mes excuses à Madame V.R. La seule modestie (à cause de ma divination étrange — dans les limites où une architecture vous rappelant un style peut être appelée divination) m'ayant empêché de la reconnaître tout à fait sur la route et de la saluer (Proustisme en action) — Je me complaisais dans une atmosphère de rêve.

Pensez à moi comme je pense à vous. Je suis triste de ne pas voir *Saül* — Valéry m'écrit que c'est très beau.

Votre J.C.[36]

Le Lavandou, Var

(Dear Gide,

An elderly invalid told me yesterday that the house was indeed the V[an] R[ysselberghes']. If it is a nuisance for you to write me, and if you are writing me at their house, do present my apologies to Mme V.R. Modesty alone (because of my strange guesswork — to the extent that an architecture's reminding one of a style may be called guesswork) having kept me from completely recognizing her on the road and from greeting her (Proustism in action) — I enjoyed daydreaming away.

Think of me as I think of you. I am sorry not to see *Saül* — Valéry writes me that it is very beautiful.

Your J.C.)

André Gide's reply was brief, nuanced, and cool:

Mon cher Jean,

Ne vous frappez pas. Madame V.R. elle aussi a bien cru vous reconnaître — à cette discretion qui vous relève de cueillir la rose de mon jardin que vous respiriez. Mais à présent la maison du bord de la route est close — dans le sens le moins double du mot.

De Porquerolles je braque vers le Lavandou une lunette d'approche, hélas insuffisante.

Pèle au soleil et demeure votre

A.G.[37]

(My dear Jean,

Don't exercise yourself. Mme V[an] R[ysselberghe] too thought she recognized you — by means of that discretion which kept you from picking the rose of my garden you were sniffing. But now the house at the edge of the road is closed — in the simplest meaning of the word. [Gide plays on words here: "Maison close" also means house of ill repute.]

From Porquerolles I am training a spyglass on Le Lavandou, alas not strong enough.

Blistering in the sun, and remaining always your

A.G.)

Cocteau's response was decorated at the top of the page by his sketch of a wave-like banner inscribed: "Je vous vois," followed by drawings of two hearts.

Le Lavandou, Var.

Mon cher Gide,

Vous êtes trop aimable de m'avoir deviné à travers les mille fautes extravagantes dues au cousin de votre compagnon de voyage. Je venais d'apprendre que vous habitiez en face par Auric. (Il arrive juste.) Il avait rencontré Valéry la veille. A force de coups de soleil j'ai un sale rhume (Prenez garde). Je ne travaille pas, sauf à un livre intitulé "Le Violon d'Ingres" et pour lequel je suis *presque* sûr de votre appui. Il paraît que la critique a été aussi grotesque pour Saül que pour Mâvra que pour mes pièces. Tant mieux — Restons tous jeunes ensemble et aimons nous bien.

Votre

Jean Cocteau

Un jour, venez à la nage — Radiguet qui est myope voit à l'horizon(?) Il essaye de vous découvrir.

P.S. Honte. J'ai respiré la rose, voyant du monde sur la route. L'avant-veille j'avais cueilli. Mais que faire lorsque les billets de banque fleurissent à l'endroit où on a l'habitude de prendre les formules de dépêches.[38]

(I see you.

Le Lavandou, Var

My dear Gide,

You are too kind to have made me out even through the thousand extravagant faults due to the cousin of your traveling companion. I had just learned from Auric that you were living across the way. (He has just arrived.) He had run into Valéry the day before.

Through too much sunburning I've got a nasty cold (watch out!) I am not working, except on a book called *Le Violon d'Ingres* and

for which I am *almost* sure of your support. It seems that the critics have been as grotesque about *Saül* as about *Mâvra* as about my own plays. So much the better—let's all stay young together and be kind to each other.

Your
Jean Cocteau

Swim over to see us someday—Radiguet, who is myopic, scans the horizon(?) He is trying to find you.

P.S. For shame. I sniffed the rose, seeing some people on the road. Two evenings before, I had picked some. But what can one do when bank notes bloom in the place where one is used to getting telegraph forms?)

In the autumn of 1926, Cocteau expressed his regret at having missed Gide and Marc Allégret before leaving for Villefranche:

Villefranche sur mer
A.M. — Octobre 1926

Cher André

Je ne peux vous dire comme je suis triste d'être parti sans vous voir, sans regarder entre vous et Marc les photos merveilleuses dont on me parle.

On a dû vous raconter de moi tant de choses stupides! — La vérité se limite à ceci: mettre un peu d'ordre dans la chambre noire.

Rien ne change et moins que rien mon cœur pour vous après les épreuves du feu et de la glace. Je vous aime et je vous embrasse bien fort.

Jean [39]

Villefranche sur mer
A.M. — October 1926

(Dear André

I can't tell you how sad I am to have left without seeing you, without sitting down between you and Marc looking at the marvelous photos I hear about.

You must have been told so many stupid things about me! The truth is simply this: Putting some order in the darkroom.

Nothing changes, and least of all my heart for you after the trials by fire and ice. I love you and I embrace you very much.

Jean)

Having returned to Paris in November 1926, Cocteau at once wrote Gide:

10 Rue d'Anjou
N.[ovembre] 1926

Mon cher André,

Je suis revenu hier. Déjà malade avec une crise de rhumatismes.
J'ai téléphoné chez vous et j'ai eu la chance d'entendre la voix de
Marc. Je voulais vous remercier, vous dire mon admiration —
le mot est bête — mon émotion profonde. Apprendre, de votre
plume ces douces merveilles, me bouleversait, *m'enchantait.* J'ai lu
à Villefranche, dans le sleeping, dans mon lit de malade — il n'y
avait plus de mer, plus de sommeil, plus de route, plus de maladie —
je lisais, je vous aimais, je souhaitais que votre chère amitié me
soutienne toujours. Après 4 mois de calme "grâce à Dieu" (c'est le
terme exact) — cette lecture est la seule qui me contente. Je vous
embrasse.

Jean [40]

10 rue d'Anjou
November 1926

(My dear André,

I returned yesterday. Already ill with an attack of rheumatism.
I called your house and had the good luck to hear Marc's voice.
I would like to thank you, to tell you my admiration — the word is
stupid — my deep emotion. To learn these tender marvels from your
pen overwhelmed me, *delighted me.* I read at Villefranche, in the sleeping car, in my sick bed — there was no more sea, no more sleep, no
more road, no more illness — I read, I loved you, I hoped your precious friendship would sustain me always. After four months of calm
"thanks to God" (that's the exact term) — this reading is the only
one that pleases me. I embrace you.

Jean)

A letter from Cocteau to Gide in February 1929, written
from the Saint-Cloud clinic where Cocteau was again undergoing disintoxication from opium, asked Gide to visit him:

Clinique de St. Cloud
(à la station du chemin de fer)
Fév. 1929
2 Ave. Pozzo di Borgo
(S et O)

Mon très cher André,

Je lutte contre une grippe — mais c'est du luxe. Je suis encore sorti
d'un remède qui tourne toujours au despote. Cette fois on essaye de
me rendre les nerfs assez solides pour que j'évite son emploi.

Dans mes pires minutes — votre Voyage au Congo me torturait. La
souffrance nous porte plus loin que le "Dire qu'il existe des choses
pareilles." Avez-vous obtenu des résultats?

Cette lettre afin de vous dire que, si c'était possible j'aimerais vous voir avant votre prochain voyage. Marc [Allégret] est-il en Hollande? Je vous embrasse.

Jean [41]

Clinique de Saint-Cloud
(at the railroad station)
February 1929
2 Avenue Pozzo di Borgo
(S et O)

(My very dear André,
   I am fighting the flu—but it's luxury. I have emerged again from a medicine that always turns into a tyrant. This time they are trying to make my nerves strong enough so that I can do without it.
   During my worst moments—your *Voyage au Congo* tortured me. Suffering carries us further than the "To think that such things really exist." Did you get any results?
   This letter is to tell you that, if possible, I'd like to see you before your next trip. Is Marc [Allégret] in Holland? I embrace you.

Jean)

In May of 1929, when Jean Cocteau was staying at Coco Chanel's villa "La Colline" at Roquebrune with Pierre Herbart and Jean Desbordes, André Gide dropped by unexpectedly to call. Cocteau happened to be in Paris on business that day, but Pierre Herbart received the famous caller in his place.[42] Herbart, by Gide's arrangement, later was to become the husband of Elisabeth Van Rysselberghe, mother of André Gide's only child.

After André Gide's return from his war years in Africa, his old friend Paul Valéry planned a reunion in May 1945 to include Jean Cocteau. "Gide, Cocteau . . . ," wrote Valéry, "après tout, gens de l'ancien régime avec moi."[43] Unfortunately, Valéry's final illness prevented the reunion from taking place. In thinking nostalgically of himself, Gide, and Cocteau as part of the same passing artistic generation, he foreshadowed Cocteau's own comment in 1959 after Gide and Valéry were both gone:

Une génération n'est pas faite de personnes du même âge mais de personnes qui vivent et travaillent ensemble même avec de grands écarts d'âge. C'est ainsi que j'estime avoir été de la génération de Gide, de Claudel, de Colette qui ne furent pas de la mienne. Mais j'ai beaucoup vécu auprès d'eux et pour ainsi dire, sur le même bateau. Or depuis quelques temps beaucoup de passagers tombent à la mer.

De l'équipage il restera vite si peu de monde que le bateau ira se
perdre au large et deviendra épave. J'en ai vu disparaître des capi-
taines! Et souvent il m'a fallu prendre le gouvernail alors que je me
reposais jadis sur la science de navigateurs plus avertis que moi! [44]

(A generation is not made up of people of the same age, but of
people who live and work together even though far apart in age.
In this way I consider myself to have been part of the generation
of Gide, Claudel, and Colette, who were not of mine. But I lived a
great deal in their company and so to speak on the same ship. Now,
for some time many passengers have been falling overboard. There
will very soon be so few of the crew left that the ship will go drifting
out to sea and become a derelict. How many captains I have seen dis-
appear! And often I had to seize the helm, whereas I used to trust in
the wisdom of navigators more experienced than I!)

The long record of direct personal contacts between the two
authors was only one aspect of the physical presence each
maintained in the other's life. The meetings and visits, both
social and professional in nature, were supplemented by letters
and gifts. In addition to the many theater "house seats" they
sent each other for performances of their works, they also
remembered each other with various tokens over the years:
photographs, drawings, flowers, and books, which were either
inscribed or formally dedicated by one to the other.

The Milly archives, for example, contain a curious photograph of a male clown in woman's dress, with the fragment of a
handwritten note of advice on the back from Gide to Cocteau.[45]
Pen and ink sketches often enlivened Cocteau's letters to Gide.
By 1913, Jean Cocteau had already conceived and executed
the first of his well-known Eugène cartoons. Two of these
early drawings were given to Gide as part of notes from the
artist himself:

Oui — mais salade Séléné que mangent les veaux lunaires de Wells,
les rennes aux andouillers de cristal, le sylphe de ce froid plafond,
et: Les Eugènes.
Urien en distingue au passage, Tityre la découvre et la note, Les
Mortimer-Menard la négligent.

J.C. [46]

(Yes — but selenic salad eaten by Wells's lunar calves, reindeer with
crystal antlers, the sylph from this cold ceiling, and: the Eugènes.
Urien discerns some on his way, Tityre discovers and notes it, the
Mortimers and Menards disregard it.

J.C.)

The second note read:

> Gardez ce talisman sous votre cape. Pour l'heure il s'amuse à répandre des crises de Foie.
> *Profitons de cette accalmie!*
> — Je pense à notre chère promenade, aux marais Frontins [*sic*] du Jupiter de Philémon, au cryptogame lunaire, au manoir occulte! [47]

(Keep this talisman under your cape. For the time being he is having fun pouring out liver attacks.
Let's take advantage of this lull!
I think of our lovely walk, of the Frontine [*sic*] marshes of Philemon's Jupiter, of the lunar cryptogam, of the secret manor!)

From Rome, where he had gone to work on *Parade* with Picasso, Léonide Massine, and Diaghilev, Cocteau enclosed a cyclamen blossom in a letter to Gide written on or about Good Friday, April 6, 1917:

> Rome — je travaille
> avec Picasso chez
> Diaghilev. Où Ghéon?
>
> Mon cher Gide,
> Ne mettez pas mon silence sur le compte de l'oubli — Mon amitié ne changera plus sinon pour grandir — mais il faudrait se *voir* — impossible de se comprendre épistolairement après des séparations trop longues — Si on se voit *quelques clins d'œil suffisent.* Je traverse une autre crise de "petite mort." Ces phénomènes de nymphe fatiguent beaucoup et rendent triste — J'ai cuilli [*sic*] ce cyclamen dans le kiosque où le pape "joue au bridge" et l'hôtel Minerve ajoute un chapitre aux Caves —
> Je vous raconterai —
>
> Je vous embrasse
> Cocteau
>
> (écrire Hôtel de Russie ou mieux 10 rue d'Anjou — car je rentre apr[ès]-demain.)
> Blanche est un charmeur de gifles — il me semble qu'il en voltige pas mal autour de ses épaules.[48]

Rome — I am working with Picasso
at Diaghilev's. Where's Ghéon?

(My dear Gide,
Don't attribute my silence to forgetfulness. My friendship won't change any more, except to grow, but we ought to *see* each other. Impossible to understand each other through letters after overlong separations. Seeing each other, a *few winks are enough.* I am going

through another crisis of "little death." These nymph phenomena are tiring and sadden one. I picked this cyclamen in the summer house where the Pope "plays bridge," and the Hotel Minerva adds another chapter to the *Caves [du Vatican]*.

I'll tell you about it—

I embrace you,
Cocteau

[P.S.] Write Hôtel de Russie, or better 10 rue d'Anjou since I go home day after tomorrow.

Blanche is a charmer of slaps—it seems to me quite a few flutter about his shoulders.)

In a similar gesture of affection, which may indicate the corresponding importance of each recipient in Cocteau's mind at the time, Cocteau sent his mother a letter on that same Good Friday in which he reports having walked that morning in the garden of the Vatican City, finding bad taste and disorder everywhere. Although the gardens seemed to Cocteau more like Monte Carlo than the Garden of Eden he had expected, he nevertheless sent his mother a souvenir as he had Gide:

J'ai cueilli ces fleurs et ce trèfle pour toi dans le kiosque où le Pape vient jouer au bridge et prendre le thé (sic). Je ne l'ai su qu'après m'être assis sur sa chaise.[49]

(I picked these flowers and this clover for you in the summer house where the Pope comes to play bridge and take his tea (sic). I only learned this after having sat in his chair.)

In a playful mood, Cocteau sent Gide a double exposure snapshot of Cocteau and his friend Countess Edith de Beaumont, who, with her husband, sponsored *Le Bœuf sur le toit* and other works by Cocteau:

Grasse
19 Janvier 1918

— Voilà où nous en sommes, mon pauvre cher Gide — Pensez à l'Eugène d'Offranville! Le Talisman contre la grippe et les trains manqués.

Je pense à vous avec tendresse et mélancolie — si loin l'un de l'autre toujours et pourtant à chaque rencontre le bon fluide circule et la main réchauffe la main. Votre chamois saute dans ma chambre et apporte l'odeur alpicole. Que faites-vous? Travaillez-vous? Moi, j'achève le prologue ou préambule du "Secteur 131" suite du "Cap" et j'essaye de guérir mes rhumatismes —

Ci jointe une photo miracle — gardez la je ne possède que ce détestable exemplaire — Moi l'ange en peignoir éponge et la Vierge Me [*sic*] de Beaumont — la vierge est inscrite dans sa propre tête de mater dolorosa et l'olivier d'une seconde photo qui se superpose me boucle les cheveux.

Vivez heureux je vous embrasse

Jean Cocteau [50]

Grasse
January 19, 1918

(That's the way things are, my dear old Gide. Think of the Eugène at Offranville! The talisman against flu and the missed trains.

I think of you with tenderness and melancholy — always so far from each other and yet at each meeting the good juice flows again and one hand warms the other. Your chamois leaps into my room and brings the alpine fragrance. What are you doing? Are you working? As for me, I am finishing the prologue or preamble to the "Secteur 131," a follow-up to the *Cap* [*de Bonne-Espérance*], and I am trying to cure my rheumatism.

Enclosed is a miraculous snapshot — keep it, I only have this poor copy. I am the angel in the turkish bathrobe and the Virgin is Mme de Beaumont. The virgin is inscribed in her own head of the mater dolorosa; and the olive tree, from the double exposure of a second photograph, makes my hair curly.

Live happily. I embrace you.

Jean Cocteau)

A full-page pen and ink drawing of Countess Anna de Noailles illustrated a letter to Gide from Cocteau written September 6, 1919.[51]

After presenting an address at the Collège de France,[52] Cocteau wrote Gide:

4 Mai 1923

Mon cher Gide,
  Merci pour les belles images. Revenez vite. J'ai vu Marc hier au Collège de France où je parlais vêtu d'une redingote d'apalga. Vous auriez bien ri. Je vous embrasse.

Jean [53]

May 4, 1923

(My dear Gide,
  Thank you for the beautiful pictures. Come back soon. I saw Marc yesterday at the Collège de France where I lectured dressed in an alpaca frock coat. You would have really laughed. I embrace you.

Jean)

First page of letter from Cocteau to Gide of January 19, 1918, with a ferocious Eugène. Its wrench-like, robot hands, saw teeth, and spiked helmet reflect the anti-Prussian mood of wartime France. Photo J. M. Schlemmer.

Edouard Dermit, Jean Cocteau's adopted son, remembers a photograph of André Gide, a gift from Gide himself, which for many years Cocteau kept in his tiny Paris apartment in rue de Montpensier. Cocteau also refers to this photograph in his letter to Gide of February 26, 1945, which was written in that same apartment: "Chaque jour votre cher visage habite ma petite chambre du Palais Royal." [54] ("Each day your dear face lives in my little room of the Palais Royal.")

The letters exchanged between Jean Cocteau and André Gide testify to numerous gifts of books. From Gide's side there came *Thésée, Robert, Morceaux choisis,* and even the catalogue of the 1925 auction of part of Gide's personal library. In addition, Cocteau's personal library at Milly still contains inscribed copies of Gide's *Feuillets d'automne* and of his translation of *Hamlet.* There is no record on either side that Gide sent Cocteau *Les Faux-Monnayeurs.* When a Gide work was not forthcoming quickly enough as a gift from its author, Cocteau was not above writing coquettishly to Gide and asking for it:

Je trouve une trahison que Jehanne-la-Courte mette à fraîchir ses pieds dans vos Caves — et que chez moi nulle couverture orange. Gide est trop sûr du cœur de Jean Cocteau; il en profite.[55]

(I find it treachery that Jehanne-la-Courte is cooling her feet in your *Caves*—while no orange cover at my house. Gide is too sure of Jean Cocteau's heart; he is taking advantage of it.)

At about the same time he wrote Gide again, in a letter which complains chiefly of his poor health and waits until the last line to come to the point:

Maisons Laffitte — S et O
Ouf! Voilà une histoire, mon cher Gide, qui m'a entamé plus qu'à demi. Je crevais, ce qui s'appelle, mais soutenu par un morne élan. Détente atroce. Le Docteur Heckel m'ordonne le bain de soleil. — Naturellement "on" enveloppe la terre d'ouate *comme une chose précieuse* et nul soleil. — Je le guette sur le toit avec un minimum de culotte.
+ Mal aux dents + sinusite + impossibilité gâteuse de lire.
Si votre graisse contre les hautes catastrophes n'est pas une feinte, envoyez une jarre avec l'exemplaire des Caves. De cœur.

Jean
P.S. Rodier (4 Rue de Franqueville) réclame en sourd un Amyntas

que vous lui aviez promis et refuse jusque-là de me rendre le mien
— par égoïsme je viens à son aide.

J.

Eté voir le Pape-Otage en PARLERONS.[56]

Maisons Laffitte — S et O

(Whew! That was a touchy business, my dear Gide, which really
broke me up. I was actually dying, but carried along by a dull impetus.
Terrible unwinding. Dr. Heckel orders me to sunbathe. Of course
"they" wrapped the earth in cotton *like a precious object* and no sun.
I eagerly lie in wait for it on the roof in the briefest of trunks.

+ Toothache + sinusitis + senile inability to read.

If your grease against great disasters is not a fake, send me a jar
with the copy of *Les Caves* [*du Vatican*]. From my heart.

Jean

P.S. Rodier (4 rue de Franqueville) obstinately demands an *Amyntas*
which you promised him and so far refuses to return mine — out of
selfishness I am coming to his rescue.

J.

[P.P.S.] Saw *Le Pape otage.* Let's TALK ABOUT IT.)

For Cocteau's part, he was careful to send Gide an author's
copy of nearly all his major works as they appeared in print.
The Gide-Cocteau correspondence mentions only a few of
them: *Mon Premier Voyage, Le Livre blanc, Vocabulaire, Poésies,
Opéra, La Danse de Sophocle,* and *L'Oiseleur.* That part of André
Gide's personal library now in the Paris home of his daughter,
Mme Catherine Gide, contains not only a number of these
volumes but many others, most containing a handwritten
inscription by Cocteau and often adorned with an original
drawing by the author in pen and ink, pencil, or colored
crayon. The following list of Cocteau's works, with indications
of the inscriptions, is thought to be the complete list of the Cocteau works presently in Mme Gide's library.

La Danse de Sophocle [copy 1]

"Si, si, là bas où je t'aurais rejoint, tu m'aurais reconnu pour ton frère; même il me semble encore que c'est pour te retrouver que je pars. —"
À André Gide
Jean Cocteau

("Yes, yes, down there where I should have joined you, you would have recognized me for your brother; it even seems to me still that it is in order to find you that I leave —"
To André Gide
Jean Cocteau)

La Danse de Sophocle [copy 2]

Συγχίωμαλ!_____   (I make use of along with!)

Συμπασχω!_____   (I feel sympathy with!)

— Jean Cocteau à André Gide et   (Jean Cocteau to André Gide and to
à la mémoire d'André Walter_____   the memory of André Walter_____
1912.   1912.)

Le Coq et l'Arlequin

À André Gide   (To André Gide
"Le piano et le papillon"   "The piano and the butterfly"
ou   or
[printed title:]   [printed title:]
Le Coq et l'Arlequin   *Le Coq et l'Arlequin*
Son ami, de tout cœur   His friend, with all my heart
Jean Cocteau   Jean Cocteau
mars 1919   March 1919)

Le Potomak

À Gide au dessus de la mêlée   (To Gide above the battle
Jean Cocteau   Jean Cocteau
19 Juin 1919   June 19, 1919
[Eugène drawing]   [Eugène drawing])

La Noce massacrée

À Gide qui aimait le "gendarme"   (To Gide who liked the "gen-
cet autre petit jeu de massacre.   darme" this other little game of mas-
Jean Cocteau   sacre.
Juin 1921   Jean Cocteau
                                    June 1921)

Antigone, Les Mariés de la Tour Eiffel

[drawing of a star] Jean   ([drawing of a star] Jean)

Le Secret professionnel

[See Chapter Eight, p. 245]

Le Grand Ecart

À mon cher ami André Gide sans   (To my dear friend André Gide
aucune ombre.   without any shadow.
Jean Cocteau   Jean Cocteau
Mai 1923   May 1923)

Thomas l'Imposteur [57]

[No inscription]

Jean Cocteau

[No inscription. Catalogue from the exhibition of Cocteau's drawings, stage sets, and other documents presented June 15 to 29, 1925, at Galerie Briant-Robert, 7 rue d'Argenteuil, Paris.]

Jean l'Oiseleur

[See Appendix 13]

Opéra

Mon cher André
  Voici l'âme de ma corde en témoignage d'une amitié toujours plus douce et toujours plus forte. [Drawing of star]

Jean
1927

(My dear André,
  Here is the soul of my tightrope, in testimony of a friendship always sweeter and always stronger. [Drawing of star]

Jean
1927)

Le Livre blanc

À mon très cher André Gide de tout cœur

Jean
[Drawing of star and Orphic profile]

(To my very dear André Gide with all my heart.

Jean
[Drawing of star and Orphic profile])

Les Enfants terribles

À mon cher André Gide avec toute ma tendresse.
[Drawing of star]

Jean

(To my dear André Gide with all my affection.
[Drawing of star]

Jean)

Opium

[Although this volume does not have a handwritten inscription by Cocteau, there is in print, immediately after the dedication to Jean Desbordes, the following citation: "Mon cher bon grand fond Malempia." La Séquestrée de Poitiers (D'après l'étude d'André Gide). ("My dear good big deep Malempia." *La Séquestrée de Poitiers* (From the work by André Gide).)]

Essai de critique indirecte

Cher André — chaque minute on vous aime et respecte davantage, et puis vous aimez bien Jeanjean, ce qui me touche plus que tout. Croyez à ma tendresse profonde.

Jean
[Drawing of star]

(Dear André—each minute you are more loved and respected, and then you love Jeanjean, which touches me most of all. Believe in my deep affection.

Jean
[Drawing of star])

Les Chevaliers de la Table Ronde

Mon cher André, vous le savez que je vous aime et que je vous place dans un ciel à part où les étoiles ne sont pas faites d'écritures. Votre

Jean

[Drawing of star]

(My dear André, you know I love you and that I place you in a heaven apart where the stars are not made of writings. Your

Jean

[Drawing of star])

Mon Premier Voyage

(Tour du monde en 80 jours)

Mon cher André
   Ce livre est à vous. Acceptez-le comme je vous l'offre — de tout cœur.

Jean

[Drawing of star]

(My dear André
   This book is yours. Accept it as I give it—with all my heart.

Jean

[Drawing of star])

[In October 1936 Cocteau had gingerly sounded out Gide regarding the suitability of his formal dedication of this volume:]

Mas de Fourques
Lunel (Hérault)
(Cette semaine, à Paris,
où je rentre, à l'hôtel de Castille
37 rue Cambon.)
Oct 1936

Mas de Fourques
Lunel (Hérault)
((This week, in Paris,
where I will return, at the
Hôtel de Castille,
37 rue Cambon.)
October 1936

Mon très cher André
   Je vous ai dédié mon Tour du Monde. Voulez-vous, en passant à la N.R.F., demander le texte de cette dédicace. J'aimerais, par une ligne de vous, savoir si ce témoignage de ma profonde et vieille amitié vous fait plaisir. Je désirais vous garder la surprise — mais sommes toutes, les surprises sont détestables et j'aimerais que nous fussions d'accord. Je vous embrasse.

Jean

[Drawing of star] [58]

My dearest André
   I have dedicated my *Tour du monde* to you. When you pass by the *NRF*, would you ask for the text of this dedication. I would like to know, by a line from you, if this evidence of my deep and old friendship gives you pleasure. I wanted to keep it a surprise for you—but, after all, surprises are detestable, and I would like to be sure we agree. I embrace you.

Jean

[Drawing of star])

Les Parents terribles

Mon cher André
   Je suis votre ami de toujours et de toutes les circonstances. Je vous envoie cette pièce du fond de mon cœur.

Jean

[Drawing of star]

(My dear André,
   I am your friend always and under all circumstances. I send you this play from the bottom of my heart.

Jean

[Drawing of star])

La Fin du Potomak

Mon cher André   (My dear André,
  Que vous dire? Vous savez que je   What to tell you? You know I love
vous aime malgré tout.   you in spite of everything.
               Jean   Jean
      [Drawing of star]   [Drawing of star])

Allégories

À mon très cher André Gide   (To my very dear André Gide
           Jean   Jean
      [Drawing of star]   [Drawing of star])

La Machine à Ecrire

Mon cher André,   (My dear André,
Si profond,   So deep,
si haut, mon   so high, my
    cœur   heart
    ne vous   never leaves
quitte   you
plus   *any*
jamais.   *more.*
           Jean   Jean
      [Drawing of star]   [Drawing of star])

Orphée

À André Gide son ami de toujours.   (To André Gide his friend always.
           Jean   Jean
    [Drawing of star]   [Drawing of star]
           1942   1942
[Drawing of an Orphic face]   [Drawing of an Orphic face])

La Belle et la Bête

Mon cher André   (My dear André,
  Triste échange mais je le fais de   Sad exchange, but I make it with
tout mon cœur.   all my heart.
           Jean   Jean
    [Drawing of star] [59]   [Drawing of star])

In 1925, before leaving for the Congo with Marc Allégret, André Gide sold a large part of his personal library at the Salle Drouot in Paris. Cocteau's receipt of the catalogue for the Gide library sale drew this reply to Gide:

                    Thermes Urbains, 13 Rue Chateaubriand
                           (30 jours sans *âme qui vive*)
Mon cher André,
  Le "Catalogue" m'a (imitation de votre voix): Prodigieusement diverti.

"À André Gide, cette minute d'ombre sempiternellement..."etc.

On s'amuse à voir tomber autour de vous *contournés comme la rose,* ces invraisemblables tarabiscotages. Vos quelques lignes à Maeterlinck sont une merveille — on brûle d'acheter, de connaître le reste.

Je vous souhaite de vendre très cher et de voyager en pensant quelque fois à votre

J.

P.S. On vient de me faire une "opération" très délicate que je vous raconterai un jour *en détail* — car, aprés vente de q.q. livres qu'on ne m'a pas volés, j'irai vous rejoindre au bord du Potomak. Je vous embrasse ainsi que mon cher Marc.[60]

Thermes Urbains, 13 rue Chateaubriand
(30 days without *a living soul*)
(My dear André,

The "Catalogue" was (imitation of your voice): wonderfully entertaining to me.

"To André Gide, this minute of shadow unceasingly...," etc.

It is amusing to see these unlikely overelaborations falling around you, *as convoluted as roses.* Your few lines to Maeterlinck are a marvel —one burns to buy, to know the rest. I hope you fetch enormous prices and will travel, thinking sometimes of your

J.

P.S. I have just had a very delicate "operation" which I will tell you about *in detail* someday—since, after selling some books that were not stolen from me, I will join you on the banks of the Potomak. I embrace you and my dear Marc.)

Gide bluntly gave as one of the reasons for the sale his wish to get rid of books by writers who were no longer his friends. Among the books auctioned off were many works by Claudel, Jammes, Louÿs, and others, often inscribed by the authors. It is no doubt a revealing sign of Gide's regard for Jean Cocteau's works and for the poet himself, despite their quarrels of the previous six years, that Gide did not dispose of any of the numerous books Cocteau had sent him.

The more than one hundred and twenty-four written communications that passed between Gide and Cocteau are of central importance in the history of their friendship. One hundred and fourteen of that number are now available to scholars: eighty-three from Cocteau to Gide, and thirty-one from Gide to Cocteau.[61] Ten communications are still unaccounted for, although they are referred to in the existing correspondence. The correspondence between the two men opened in 1912 with

Cocteau's eloquent and youthful letter of April 20, and closed after nearly forty years with Cocteau's letter of January 2, 1951. About two thirds of the total were written prior to 1926, when *Les Faux-Monnayeurs* was published.

Gide acknowledged to Robert Mallet [62] that his own letters were usually briefer than those of his correspondents, and that although he wrote to many friends, they all felt cheated. According to Mallet, Gide was uneasy when corresponding with a friend such as Valéry, whom he judged to be more brilliant than himself as a private correspondent. Gide seldom took the initiative in writing letters. For the most part he was quite ready to answer his friends, but beyond that he apparently felt little urge to confide in them. [63]

Georges-Paul Collet, in his study "André Gide, épistolier," makes a similar observation about Gide: "Si audacieux dans ses livres, Gide se montrait généralement beaucoup plus réservé dans sa correspondance." [64] ("So audacious in his books, Gide generally showed himself much more reserved in his correspondence.") And further on he adds: "Dans ce domaine [de correspondance] en particulier, Gide avait souvent conscience d'être inférieur à son partenaire." [65] ("In this field [of correspondence] in particular, Gide often had the feeling of being inferior to his partner.")

For his part, Cocteau preferred to keep his letters as short as possible. He discussed his correspondence with Gide at some length when interviewed by Colin-Simard after Gide's death.

Je n'aime pas écrire de lettres, et je les écris très courtes. J'ai remarqué qu'on ne lisait pas les lettres. La preuve, c'est que quand on en retrouve une et qu'on la relit, on constate qu'on y avait lu jadis ce qu'on y cherchait, et que le reste est nouveau.

Sans doute est-ce le bref de mes lettres qui poussait Gide à m'en écrire de courtes, mais sa charmante écriture bouclée et ses enveloppes de couleur me faisaient plaisir. J'étais certain que les phrases ne seraient pas indifférentes.

Toute ma vie j'ai reçu de Gide des lettres exquises et qui ne correspondaient pas aux lettres publiques, notes et notules dont il était maniaque. Cela illustre à merveille ce que j'en ai dit tout à l'heure.

Il semble même que la tendresse de Gide s'exprimait mieux par les lettres que par la présence. Il est possible que cela relève du protestantisme, et qu'il était plus libre de s'exprimer par des jambages que tête à tête.

Il aimait plaire et qu'on lui plaise.

Cet échange de charmes et d'embuscades fonctionnait mal de loin.

J'ai remarqué en outre, puisque vous m'interrogez sur nos différences, que toute sa vie Gide m'a écrit sur le même papier à lettres de luxe, alors que je n'ai jamais eu de papier à lettres ni de table à écrire, et que je m'exprime où je me trouve, avec ce qui me tombe sous la main.

André Gide, certes, était aussi vrai dans ses lettres que dans son Journal, mais sa vérité n'était pas la mienne, et chacun de nous a ses vérités qui ne sont pas celles des autres.[66]

(I don't like to write letters, and I make them very short. I have observed that people don't read letters. The proof is that when you find one again and reread it, you notice that earlier you had read into it what you were looking for, and that the rest is new.

No doubt it was the brevity of my letters that prompted Gide to write me short ones, but his charming, curly handwriting and his colored envelopes gave me pleasure. I was sure the sentences would not be cold.

All my life I have received exquisite letters from Gide which were not like his public letters, notes, and notations with which he was obsessed. That illustrates wonderfully what I just said a moment ago.

It even seems that Gide's affection was expressed better through his letters than by his presence. It is possible that this derives from protestantism, and that he was freer to express himself in writing than in private conversation.

He liked to please and to be pleased by others.

This exchange of charms and ambushes didn't work well at a distance.

I have noticed besides, since you are asking me about our differences, that all his life Gide wrote me on the same deluxe writing paper, whereas I never had either stationery or writing table and I express myself wherever I am with whatever is at hand.

André Gide, to be sure, was as true in his letters as in his *Journal*, but his truth was not mine, and each of us has his truths which are not those of other people.)

All the foregoing characteristics of the two writers appear in the correspondence between them. Cocteau seemed, intentionally or not, to bring out the heavy, morose side of Gide, as Gide himself admitted.

Cocteau, like Gide, was a prolific letter writer. His correspondence with his mother alone exceeds a thousand letters between the years 1906 and 1936, and there were long

stretches when he wrote Mme Cocteau every day. His letters to André Gide represent only a fraction of his total correspondence, but it is clearly a fraction that displays some of Cocteau's best literary qualities: imagination, verve, lapidary and elliptical style, nuance and wit. It also includes traces of the preciosity of immaturity, the shrill anger, the blur of opium, "le désordre," which were a less attractive side of Cocteau.

Both authors exploited the letter as a literary genre in itself, and the numerous drafts and redrafts of important letters on both sides reveal the care with which both Gide and Cocteau composed them. It is very likely that just as Gide wrote his *Journal* with the public in mind, he also composed his letters to Cocteau and others with an eye to later publication. Gide, by temperament more methodical than Cocteau, often kept typed copies of his handwritten letters to Cocteau, or occasionally copied his reply in longhand on the back of a letter received from Cocteau.

Cocteau, on the other hand, seldom kept copies of his personal letters. He wrote with considerable brio, often filling the page with a vortex of postscripts which swirled up one margin and down the other and ended upside down at the top of the page. His early letters to Gide in 1912 and 1913, which might be termed the end of his Anna de Noailles period, were written in gaudy purple ink with four or five outsized words to a line.[67] The rococo handwriting that he had learned from Countess de Noailles required a special pen with a flexible nib and a long rubber tube. His "j's", with their exotic double loops which resembled butterflies about to flutter off the page, were the despair of André Gide, who finally urged him to simplify his handwriting. After 1913, Cocteau's handwriting became simpler, less legible, and more like a schoolboy's scrawl in black ink. Over the years he corresponded with Gide, Cocteau's penmanship often reflects the state of his health and spirits. When influenced by opium, his handwriting became erratic and disjointed, like the asymetrical webs of spiders under narcotics. The written words were then often fragmented into syllables, and numerous errors and corrections marred the pages.

Cocteau's letters to Gide were usually handwritten on plain paper, but, as he himself says, he was inclined to write on any material that lay at hand. The correspondence took many forms: telegrams, *pneumatiques,* postcards, messages on card-

board, letters in books, and even one on a four-of-hearts playing card:

4, 5, 6, 7 Novembre 1922

Mon cher Gide,
 Vos M[orceaux] Choisis me sont revenus d'Auvergne.
 Voilà quatre jours que je me promène avec vous au soleil.
 Que de plaisir et d'amitié profonde.
J.C.
Pramousquier, Var   1922 [68]

4, 5, 6, 7 November 1922

(My dear Gide,
 Your M[orceaux] *choisis* came back to me from Auvergne.
 For the past four days I have been walking in the sun with you.
 What joy and deep friendship.
J.C.
Pramousquier, Var   1922)

The preponderance in the number of letters flowing from Cocteau to Gide is consistent with the greater number of inscribed copies of his own works that Cocteau sent Gide. Cocteau presented Gide with at least twenty-four such volumes, whereas Gide sent Cocteau at least six of his books. Both these figures and the contents and chronological distribution of the letters suggest that it was Cocteau who took the initiative in sustaining the relationship.

It is clear from Cocteau's letters that he was thoroughly familiar with Gide's writing. Cocteau refers to nineteen works by Gide: [69]

Amyntas
Les Cahiers d'André Walter
Les Caves du Vatican
Faits divers
L'Immoraliste
Isabelle
Lord Jim (translation)
Morceaux choisis
Les Nourritures terrestres
Paludes
La Porte étroite
Retour de l'URSS
Robert; Supplément à l'Ecole des femmes

Saül
La Séquestrée de Poitiers
La Symphonie pastorale
Typhon (translation)
Voyage au Congo
Le Voyage d'Urien

Judging from the number of references to Cocteau's work in Gide's letters to him, Gide was also familiar with Cocteau's writing. His letters to Cocteau contain references to:

Antigone
Le Cap de Bonne Espérance
Le Coq et l'Arlequin
La Danse de Sophocle
Le Gendarme incompris
Lettre aux Américains
Mon Premier Voyage
La Noce massacrée
Opium, journal d'une désintoxication
Parade
Poèmes
Vocabulaire

as well as to articles by Cocteau which appeared in *Le Figaro* and *La Revue de Genève*. Gide's *Journal* contains additional references to other works by Cocteau.

Although both writers used their correspondence as a means of expressing certain of their esthetic and literary doctrines, especially in their open letters to each other, Cocteau's letters to Gide also served him in other ways. They gave him an opportunity to rehearse some of his lines before a private but important audience prior to presenting them to a broad public. In this sense the letters, like Cocteau's brilliant private conversation, may be viewed as a proving ground for his developing vocabulary, aphoristic style, and broad literary concepts. To cite only a few instances of this practice:

Speaking of his *La Danse de Sophocle*, Cocteau wrote Gide in June 1912: "elle représente malgré tout une phase de ma courbe." This is a very early expression of Cocteau's lifelong preoccupation with his "courbe" or his "ligne." Cocteau's letters of 1912 and 1913 contain some of the earliest sketches

of the Eugènes which later appear in their fullest expression in *Le Potomak*. In a veiled allusion to the problem of being homosexual, an allusion not lost on Gide, Cocteau wrote him in March 1914: "notre inquiétude ne commence-t-elle pas où le [*sic*] sécurité des autres s'asseoit." The phrase appears again in Cocteau's *Le Potomak* in this form: "Mais de peu les gens se contentent. Leur sécurité s'installe où commence notre inquiétude." [70] ("But people are satisfied with very little. Their security is established at the point where our anxiety begins.")

The same Cocteau letter to Gide, probably written in March 1914 from Leysin, Switzerland, described a blighted love affair in these terms: "Indifférence d'un œil qui vous *inspecte* et qui vous buvait. Molesse [*sic*] d'une main qui ne cherchait que la vôtre —" [71] A similar description appears in *Le Potomak:* "Un œil qui me buvait et qui m'inspecte. Molle, une main qui ne cherchait que la mienne." [72] ("An eye which used to drink me in but which now inspects me. Limp, a hand which used to search only for mine.")

A wartime letter dated 1916 that Cocteau wrote to Gide from the front lines at Nieuportville conveys the atmosphere that he recreated in 1923 in *Thomas l'Imposteur* and illuminates some of the autobiographical aspects of that novel.

1916

Cher Gide,
Vous vous plairiez beaucoup ici — Tranchées Venise arabe à Luna Park — les tirailleurs dansent du ventre et les Zouaves m'offrent des bagues préhistoriques. Le calme n'est pas en pays neutre — on le trouve "mêlé au jeu" comme chante Whitmann [*sic*] et on dort tranquille sous les obus, les bombes, les torpilles.

Je vous raconterai ma nuit de Noël, à 10 mètres des Boches, avec des Mages et des grosses étoiles.

Cœur fidèle
Jean

P.S. où Ghéon? [73]

1916

(Dear Gide,
You would love being here — Arabian Venice trenches at Luna Park — the sharpshooters belly dance and the Zouaves present me with prehistoric rings. Quietness is not to be found in neutral territory — one finds it "mixed in with the game," as Whitman sings, and one sleeps quietly amid the shells, bombs, and mines.

I will tell you about my Christmas Eve, only ten meters from the Boches, with Magi and big stars.

Faithfully and tenderly,
Jean

P.S. Where's Ghéon?)

That extraordinary Christmas night he promised to tell Gide about was fully described in an exquisite letter Cocteau wrote to his mother.[74]

It took the wartime death of a close friend, Jean Le Roy, to bring Cocteau to a first name basis with Gide. In his letter of May 24, 1918, where Cocteau used the salutation "André" for the first time, and in a later preface to a collection of Le Roy's poems, *Cavalier de Frise*, he describes Le Roy in almost identical words, a musical sequence of vowel sounds which evoke the mournful tolling of a bell:

24 Mai 1918

Mon cher André

Je vous écris parce que je souffre. On a tué mon ami Jean Le Roy que j'adorais et pour qui j'étais tout. Le Roy était devenu en quelque sorte mon élève — je mettais en lui ce que du désordre gâche en moi. Il était jeune, beau, bon, brave, génial, simple, c'est ce que la mort aime.

Vous me plaindrez. Chaque jour m'ampute davantage et je n'arrive pas à comprendre que c'est possible.

Je vous embrasse.

Jean [75]

May 24, 1918

(My dear André,

I write you because I am suffering. They have killed my friend Jean Le Roy whom I adored and to whom I was everything. Le Roy had become my pupil in a way — I put into him what was wasted in me by a disorderly life. He was young, handsome, good, brave, full of genius, unaffected, everything Death likes.

You will pity me. Each day I feel his loss more keenly, and I can't grasp that it is *possible*.

I embrace you.

Jean)

The last line of Cocteau's letter to Gide of October 7, 1921, "je change souvent de costume et ne respecte pas mes défroques," is one of those elliptical ambiguities in which Cocteau suggests so much about himself. The paradoxical and protean

aspects of his temperament, his capacity to enjoy both male and female lovers, his ability to embrace such contrasting works as *Requiem* and *Les Enfants terribles* within his creative span, are all implied here in succinct form. Cocteau's statement is especially appropriate to describe his frequent changes of genre, since he did change genres as easily as he changed costume. The statement also applies to his cyclical exploration of the Greek, Biblical, medieval, and modern settings, within which he examined an astonishing variety of forms. "Je change souvent de costume et ne respecte pas mes défroques" also reflects Cocteau's rejection of his early "guides néfastes" in the "enfance hâtive et fiévreuse" he had come to regret: among others, Edouard de Max, Oscar Wilde, Anna de Noailles, Barrès, and, as will be seen later, to some extent Gide himself.

Following an exchange of bristling letters about Cocteau's *Antigone,* a postscript from Cocteau to Gide dated in the winter of 1922–23 [76] uses the expression: "La patine maquille les croûtes." This phrase is repeated by Cocteau in his *Lettre à Jacques Maritain.*[77] Despite the facetious turn Cocteau gives it in his reply to Gide, it is central to Cocteau's esthetic views and to his own creative method. Cocteau believed that, with time, a patina is deposited over the surface of a work of art which conceals its beauty and gives it a commonplace appearance:

> Car, s'il est vrai que la multitude des regards patine les statues, les lieux-communs, chefs d'œuvres éternels, sont recouverts d'une épaisse patine qui les rend invisibles et cache leur beauté.[78]

> (For, if it's true that an accumulation of looks gives patina to statues, commonplaces, eternal masterpieces, are covered by a thick patina that makes them invisible and conceals their beauty.)

In a literary masterpiece this patina often results from changes in language from one epoch to another. Words lose their original meaning, freshness, and brilliance. Part of the poet's task, according to Cocteau, is to take the commonplace objects and experiences of daily life, polish them, remove the patina, and expose the work of art underneath.

> Mettez un lieu commun en place, nettoyez-le, frottez-le, éclairez-le de telle sorte qu'il frappe avec sa jeunesse et avec la même fraîcheur, le même jet qu'il avait à sa source, vous ferez œuvre de poète. Tout le reste est littérature.[79]

(Put a commonplace in position, clean it, rub it, illuminate it in such a way that it strikes us with its youth and with the same freshness, the same flash it had at its beginning; you will be doing poet's work. All the rest is literature.)

A common example of this polishing/revealing process in Cocteau's work is his use of aphorisms, paradoxes, and oxymorons. The echo of Oscar Wilde's witty inversions: "Work is the curse of the drinking class" and "Nature imitates art," is apparent in such an inversion by Cocteau as: "Le temps est un phénomène de perspectives." Paradoxical aphorisms, which are in the spirit of the Wildean inversions, abound in Cocteau's prose:

La faiblesse d'un artiste est de faire école.

Le plus grand chef-d'œuvre de la littérature n'est jamais qu'un dictionnaire en désordre.

Toute musique à écouter dans les mains est suspecte.

Je ne pense pas, donc je suis.

(The weakness of an artist is to create a school.

The greatest literary masterpiece is never anything but a dictionary in disorder.

All music we listen to head in hands is suspect.

I do not think, therefore I am.)

The oxymorons so popular in Greek literature were also appealing to Cocteau, who wrote: "Aller vite lentement," and "l'invisibilité résulte d'une vitesse immobile." His juxtaposition of opposites in the same sentence, "Je suis un mensonge qui dit la vérité," was meant to jostle the reader's imagination into the perception of new relationships between hackneyed words, ideas, or objects that had become "invisible" because they were taken for granted.

The revelation of a work of art (art being a lie which tells the truth) in everyday objects is a constant of Jean Cocteau's esthetic doctrine and method. His distinction between appearances and reality, which Cocteau postulated as "le visible" and "l'invisible," is a mutation of the Platonic concern with form and essence. Much as William Blake saw heaven in a wildflower and the world in a grain of sand, Cocteau recognized

that ordinary things are seldom what they seem to be; a banal object often conceals a higher (or deeper) reality for Cocteau, and he finds countless ways to impress this on his audience. Two examples of this practice are his use in *Orphée* of those commonplaces of modern life, the radio and the mirror. A motion picture of a man listening to a radio would promise to be the most dull and static scene imaginable. Yet Cocteau filmed Jean Marais crouched tensely over the car radio, straining to decipher its message, and succeeded in investing a commonplace object and act with mystery. The example of the mirror again shows Cocteau's ability to "taquiner l'éternité," to touch an ordinary fixture of everyday life and reveal its possibilities for significance. For Cocteau, the mirror, like a painting, takes on the patina of the accumulated looks it has absorbed. He considered it to be a measurer of time, the doorway through which Death comes and goes, a threshold to another world, to a realm of more enduring reality.

Cocteau's extraordinary visual talent gave him the means to exploit more fully than any of his contemporaries the esthetic possibilities of the commonplace. He saw how to restore fresh meanings to words by positioning them on the printed page, a mutation of Mallarmé's example. If he wrote about a ship, Cocteau's words might be arranged on the page to form the outline of a vessel's hull, or if he wrote of a snake, the words would weave across the page in serpentine fashion.

Discovering the artistic forms inherent in everyday objects became an obsession with Cocteau. He created airy, transparent sculptures out of pipe cleaners; and designed book bindings out of packing cartons.[80] In his 1917 ballet *Parade* he elevated the gestures of everyday life to the artistic level of dance. In *La Belle et la Bête,* one of his most successful films, he restored mythological dimensions to what had come to be treated as a children's bedtime story.

One of the reasons why Surrealism appealed to Cocteau was that it sought to destroy established esthetic visions in order to make way for new ones. That is to say, according to Cocteau's doctrine, to recreate the original luster of old visions. Cocteau looked forward to the day when ordinary men, not only poets with their privileged vision of the world, could look at an engine and see a bouquet of roses, or contemplate a rose and see the miracle of an engine.

In a very real sense, Cocteau removed the patina from the

commonplace when he led the way in twentieth-century French letters to a refurbishing of Greek and medieval myths. It is irrevocably to his credit that even before Gide, Giraudoux, and others who also explored this rich vein in the French theater, Cocteau sensed that modern dramatic treatment could lift the myths out of the hitherto popularly accepted category of amusing but irrelevant folk legends. Cocteau's cycle of theatrical works inspired by the Greek myth included *Antigone* (1922); *Orphée* (1926); *Oedipus Rex* (1927); and *La Machine infernale* (1934). Gide's *Philoctète* (1898), never intended for the stage, was only presented once by friends on a private stage. His *Œdipe* (1931) prompted his famous pun to Cocteau: "Il y a une vraie Œdipémie!" Gide's *Perséphone* was first performed in 1934. Jean Giraudoux perhaps explored the Greek myth in modern theatrical terms most successfully of all three authors, but his works came later than Cocteau's: *Amphitryon 38* (1929); *La Guerre de Troie n'aura pas lieu* (1935); *Electre* (1937). Cocteau's art took a giant step forward when it enabled ordinary theater audiences to perceive that the deep psychological and moral truths hidden beneath the patina of the myths had valid meaning for contemporary man.

Removing the patina from ordinary objects was in effect removing the blinders from the eyes of men everywhere. Such a process offered endless possibilities for change and growth, for expanding consciousness. Cocteau's art aimed at making the average man aware of his own capacities which had lain dormant and neglected, his capacities for uncovering beauty, for becoming in a sense a poet. At the esthetic level Cocteau, through visual techniques, was in this way working toward what other writers of his time, such as Gide and Malraux, were doing on a social and moral level: attempting to awaken the ordinary man to his heroic possibilities. Cocteau himself was perhaps not fully conscious of this phenomenon, but the pattern is there.

It emerges clearly in his taking a series of untried young men and helping them, even forcing them, to discover themselves: Raymond Radiguet, Jean Desbordes, Marcel Khill, and Jean Marais, to mention only a few. The example of Edouard Dermit is also an excellent case in point. Deprived of the chance for a higher education by the need to earn his living in the coal mines of Alsace-Lorraine while still a boy, the young Dermit escaped to Paris at every opportunity, bent on a career

as an artist. Through friends he met Jean Cocteau, who engaged him in 1947 as chauffeur-gardener at the country home on the edge of the Fontainebleau forest which Cocteau had recently acquired with Jean Marais. Dermit quickly rose through the ranks of the household. Cocteau, glad to encourage the young man in his artistic career, and always quick to make a work of art of his own from whatever raw material came to hand, asked his friend Picasso to give painting lessons to Dermit. Cocteau later not only arranged a widely publicized *vernissage* for the young artist but entrusted to Dermit the execution of the Cocteau designs for the beautiful Chapelle du Saint Sépulcre at Fréjus. Cocteau also made an important place for Dermit in several of his films: *L'Aigle à deux têtes, Les Enfants terribles, Orphée* and *Le Testament d'Orphée.*[81] Edouard Dermit owes much of his self-discovery to Cocteau, who was the first to see the possibilities beneath the rough patina of the young coal miner. Yet Cocteau also owed a great deal to Dermit, who gave him much-needed affection and loyalty, and who remained Cocteau's companion through the vicissitudes of his old age. Before his death in 1963, Cocteau recognized this debt as well as the evolution of their deepening relationship by naming Dermit his adopted son and literary heir. As part of this responsibility, Edouard Dermit formally administers the vast collection of manuscripts and correspondence in the Archives Cocteau at Milly-la-Forêt.

The letters Cocteau addressed to André Gide were often prompted by the desire to keep Gide informed of his literary activities, since Gide was a powerful friend to have in court at the *NRF.* As early in their correspondence as his second letter to Gide, Cocteau brings his collection of poems *La Danse de Sophocle* to Gide's attention. In thirty-five of his subsequent letters Cocteau refers to his own works, often to those in the process of being written. For example, "Travail intense . . . David va devenir, je pense, quelque chose d'extraordinaire (ne ressemble à rien)" ("Intense work . . . *David* will become, I think, something extraordinary (doesn't resemble anything)"). Later in the same letter Cocteau adds: "je termine le Potomak."[82] In January 1918 Cocteau wrote: "Travaillez-vous? Moi, j'achève le prologue ou préambule du 'Secteur 131' suite du 'Cap.' "[83] ("Are you working? I am finishing the prologue or preamble to 'Secteur 131,' which follows the *Cap*

[*de Bonne-Espérance*].") October 1921: "J'avais commencé mon article (Comoedia) sur les "Mariés" par une citation de vous." [84] ("I had begun my article (in *Comoedia*) on *Les Mariés* [*de la Tour Eiffel*] by quoting you.") Summer 1922: "je ne travaille pas, sauf à un livre intitulé 'Le Violon d'Ingres' et pour lequel je suis *presque* sûr de votre appui." [85] ("I am not working, except on a book called *Le Violon d'Ingres* and for which I am *almost* sure of your support.")

His summer at Le Lavandou with Radiguet in 1922 was a remarkably productive period for Cocteau; his foregoing statement, "je ne travaille pas," was misleading, and probably initiated another "malentendu" between the two authors. At about the same time Cocteau wrote Gide, he also wrote his mother on July 19, 1922, from Pramousquier, using a gray sketchbook cover for stationery:

du roman auquel je travaille passionément . . . Il me donne du plaisir, alors que la poésie est une souffrance et la critique un jeu. Pour la première fois je m'amuse en écrivant.[86]

(of the novel on which I am working passionately . . . It gives me pleasure, whereas poetry is suffering and criticism a game. For the first time I'm having a good time writing.)

The *roman* to which Cocteau refers is his first novel, tentatively titled *Moitié l'ombre,* and later renamed *Le Grand Ecart.* On October 7, 1922, Cocteau wrote his mother with joy and satisfaction:

Le roman repose dans une peau de chamois ficelée de cuir, comme le fromage dans les feuilles de la vigne. Puisse-t-il en sortir aussi fort, aussi doux, et aussi bon. Je n'y tripote plus. Je le laisse travailler seul.[87]

(The novel rests in a chamois skin tied with thongs, like cheese in vine leaves. May it emerge as strong, as sweet, and as good. I am not fiddling with it any further. I leave it to work by itself.)

Only two weeks later, on October 24, 1922, Jean Cocteau was able to write his mother again:

J'écrivais jour et nuit un livre que j'intitule Nouvelle bien qu'il soit plus long que mon roman. Titre Thomas l'Imposteur... Si j'ai réussi c'est un atout énorme dans mon œuvre. Si j'ai manqué, c'est une

mousse au chocolat. Radiguet, qui est un juge sévére trouve que
c'est réussi. N'en parle à personne... Thomas, tu l'as reconnu, c'est
Raoul de Castelnau.[88]

(I worked day and night on a book which I call Novelette even though
it is longer than my novel. Title *Thomas l'Imposteur*... If I have succeeded, it's an enormous trump card in my work. If I've missed out,
it's a chocolate mousse. Radiguet, who is a harsh judge, finds it a
success. Don't speak of it to anyone... Thomas, as you will have
recognized, is Raoul de Castelnau.)

   Cocteau, in this greenest of all his summers, had so far
produced a large book of drawings and two novels. He was
also at work with Arthur Honegger, one of the Groupe des
Six, on an adaptation of *Antigone*. Such good news was too
heavy a secret for Cocteau to keep, and accordingly he wrote
Gide on October 28, 1922:

                       Pramousquier par le Lavandou (Var)
Cher Gide,
   Où êtes vous? Moi je ne peux pas sortir de ce bleu. Si vous n'aimez
pas le Secret Prof[essionnel] envoyez vite tout de même une carte.
Il me suffit que vous en aimiez un bout.
   Le travail dont je vous parlais est un gros album de dessins.
   J'ai fait aussi un petit roman en me laissant aller à tout ce qui
vous semble ma direction naturelle. En outre je termine une Antigone
(adapt[ation]) avec Honegger. Assez parlé de moi.
   Je voudrais savoir ce que vous écrivez, où vous promenez, si vous
avez notre soleil ou la pluie froide? —
   Cette maladie et ce séjour de 5 mois à la mer m'ont DÉNOUÉ QUELQUE
CHOSE.
                       Je vous aime et vous embrasse
                                     Jean Cocteau
Donnez-moi des nouvelles du soldat-ambulant — [89]

                       Pramousquier par le Lavandou (Var)
(Dear Gide,
   Where are you? As for me, I can't get out of this blue. If you don't
like *Le Secret prof[essionnel]*, send a card soon anyway. I just need you
to like a little bit of it.
   The work I mentioned to you is a big album of drawings.
   I have also done a little novel while letting myself go entirely in what
seems to you my natural direction. In addition I am finishing an
Antigone (adapt[ation]) with Honegger. Talked enough about me.
   I'd like to know what you are writing, where you go walking, whether
you have our sunshine or the cold rain?—

This illness and this five-month vacation by the sea have UNKNOTTED
SOMETHING IN ME.
> I like you and embrace you,
> Jean Cocteau
[P.S.] Do give me some news of the wandering soldier—)

Cocteau might well feel something had become unknotted within himself; four important works in three different genres had been delivered in a matter of months. Yet Cocteau in his letter of October 28 to Gide refers casually to "un petit roman," which here seems to allude to his *second* novel, *Thomas l'Imposteur*, without mentioning his earlier work *Le Grand Ecart*. *Thomas l'Imposteur* was published by Gallimard the following year, and it is not unreasonable to think that Gallimard, believing they were publishing Jean Cocteau's first novel, may have been shocked to see *Le Grand Ecart* appear in the Paris bookshops under the Stock imprint several months before *Thomas l'Imposteur* appeared. Such a development would account for the apologetic tone of the following *pneu* from Cocteau to Gide, in the summer of 1923, after Gide evidently treated Cocteau coldly during a visit to the *NRF* offices:

> Eté 23
>
> Mon cher Gide,
> Ne croyez pas que je parlais du Grant-Ecart [*sic*] lorsque je vous écrivais du Lavandou: Je fais un travail qui vous plaira certainement. J'ai fait le G.E. après votre départ de Porquerolles. Je parlais d'un volume de 150 dessins.
> N'ayez donc aucune gêne à me dire votre opinion. Je vous écris ce pneu en pensant tout à coup que votre silence de l'autre jour à la N.R.F. venait peut-être de cette phrase.
>
> Jean
> Le livre à dessin sera la seule réponse possible à vos cartes postales.
> En vous quittant je faisais allusion à un article sur Tabarin qui vous plaisait le jour de notre dispute et que vous opposiez à certaines de mes théories. Ce skating se retrouve dans le G.E.
> Voilà tout. En tout cas je suis bien touché que vous ayez vu la raison du malgré que non erratum.[90]

> Summer 1923
>
> (My dear Gide,
> Don't think I was speaking about the *Grand Ecart* when I wrote you from Le Lavandou. I am working on something which is sure to please you. (I did the *G.E.* after you left Porquerolles.) I was referring to a volume of 150 drawings.

So don't be embarrassed to tell me your opinion. I write you this *pneu* as it suddenly occurs to me that your silence the other day at the *NRF* was perhaps caused by that sentence.

Jean

[P.S.] The book of drawings will be the only possible reply to your postcards.

As I was leaving you I alluded to an article on Tabarin which pleased you the day of our dispute and which you opposed to certain of my theories. This skating appears again in the *G.E.*

That's all. In any case, I am quite touched that you saw the reason for the "malgré que" *non erratum.*)

A few years after this incident, while Cocteau was undergoing a disintoxication cure at a nursing home in Saint-Cloud, he had again written Gide about the labor pains of a new book:

Je ne me raconterais pas si je n'avais pas vu la sollicitude avec laquelle vous souhaitiez cette délivrance.[91]

(I would not tell about myself if I hadn't seen the solicitude with which you hoped for this delivery.)

This balky infant, which had been gestating in Cocteau's mind for seventeen years, proved to be his third novel, and perhaps his greatest in terms of both its intrinsic quality and its relevance to our times: *Les Enfants terribles.*

In his letters to Gide, Cocteau's comments about his works frequently indicate a variety of motives. Sometimes he sought to please Gide, at others to stimulate his interest, or to seek support of a particular work for publication in the *NRF* or by Gallimard. At other times Cocteau candidly asked a favor:

P.S. Romain Rolland me demande des autographes et des dessins pour une vente "Espagne." Croyez-vous qu'Aragon me verrait sans haine? Pouvez-vous tâter ce terrain? Marcel [Khill] a emporté votre lettre à la campagne, sur son cœur. Donc, plus d'adresse exacte, plus de téléphone. Pouvez-vous me renvoyer tout cela?[92]

(P.S. Romain Rolland asks for autographs and drawings from me for a "Spanish" [benefit] sale. Do you think [Louis] Aragon would see me without hatred? Can you feel out this ground? Marcel [Khill] carried your letter off to the country over his heart. So, no more exact address, no more telephone, for you. Can you send me all that again?)

Cocteau frequently invited praise from Gide:

> Mon cher Gide,
>   Pourquoi ce silence? J'ai été bien triste de ne pas vous voir à *Parade*.
> Je vous embrasse.
>
>   Jean [93]

> (My dear Gide,
>   Why this silence? I was very sad not to see you at *Parade*. I embrace
> you.
>
>   Jean)

And in 1927 he wrote:

> Cher André,
>   Vous devinez combien votre lettre me réchauffe. J'eusse aimé
> un petit P.S. sur cet "Opéra" que je vous envoyais *du fond du cœur*.
>   Votre Jean
>   P.S. Tendresses à Marc.[94]

> (Dear André,
>   You can guess how much your letter comforted me. I might have
> liked a little P.S. about that *Opéra* which I sent you *from the bottom of
> my heart*.
>   Your Jean
>   P.S. Love to Marc.)

Sometimes Cocteau combines all the above motives in a single
letter, as he did in January 1919:

> Mon cher Gide,
>   Je suis très ému par votre lettre — Je voudrais que Marc puisse
> avoir le Cap sans attendre — donnez moi donc son adresse. J'aimerais
> vous imaginer en promenade à Cuverville avec le petit livre dans
> votre poche. Vous dites que la mémoire se trouve déçue — mais
> chaque petit bloc de mots ne forme-t-il pas une chanson à retenir?
> J'ai bien souvent entendu [Léon-Paul] Fargue réciter dans la rue
> (d'un air terrible)
>   "Un ours blanc chamarré de moires chromatiques se sèche au
>   soleil de minuit"
>   ou
>   "lorsque nous atterîmes —
>   Je prenais les bruyères de la prairie" — etc. —
> Vous verrez.
> Les Bonniot sont aux prises avec Lafitte. Gaspard Michel a été très,

très aimable et habile dans cette affaire délicate. Il s'agissait pour lui de me disculper et de rendre service au ménage.

Donnez-lui une *œuvre*, mon cher Gide, — il comptait sur le roman et j'ai recopié "Le Balcon" poème pour mettre avec votre No. 2. Merci encore.

Je vous embrasse.
Jean [95]

(My dear Gide,

I am very touched by your letter. I'd like Marc to have the *Cap* [*de Bonne-Espérance*] without delay — please give me his address. I would love to imagine you walking at Cuverville with the little book in your pocket. You say that memory plays tricks — but doesn't each little block of words compose a song to remember? I have very often heard [Léon-Paul] Fargue recite in the street (with a terrible expression):

"Un ours blanc chamarré de moires chromatiques se sèche au soleil de minuit"

or

"lorsque nous atterîmes —
Je prenais les bruyères de la prairie" — etc. —

You'll find out.

The Bonniots are at odds with Lafitte. Gaspard Michel has been very, very kind and resourceful in this delicate business. It was a matter of his clearing me and doing a service to the couple. Give him a real *work*, my dear Gide. He was counting on the novel and I recopied my poem "Le Balcon" to put in your second issue.

Thanks again.

I embrace you.
Jean)

Again, in May 1922, Cocteau addressed a multipurpose letter to Gide in which he stressed the role of Georges Gabory as one of the "jeunes mythomanes" who disturbed his friendship with Gide, alluded to the *Coq et l'Arlequin* episode in a conciliatory manner, and complained of his health. (Appendix 12.)

The most important comments, from Cocteau's point of view, are often casually but significantly dropped at the end of his letter, like an actor's exit lines:

Mon cher Gide:

Rien de vous. Je me baigne au soleil. J'ai l'air d'un boxeur nègre, mais il reste du pâle à l'intérieur.

"Honnête peuple Suisse! Se porter bien ne lui vaut rien... sans

crimes, sans histoire, sans littérature, sans art... un robuste rosier sans épines ni fleurs..." Pourtant on s'y blesse, mais — soi-même — avec, sans doute, le sécateur.

1 – Service: Le Coup de dés, servi, n'est pas en vente. Pourriez-vous me le faire tenir par la NRF?

2 – J'avais écrit à Rivière au sujet de son article "Rossignol." Il confondait l'*à contre cœur* et la *préméditation*. Sa réponse est bonne: Il le fallait pour le public qui ne visite pas la cuisine et juge le plat.

3 – Dernières épreuves du Potomak.

C'est une architecture construite à tâtons et sans connaissance d'avance le nombre d'étages — mais il me semble que — soi-même — sincère, on ne s'égare pas et des caves aux tabatières il y a tout — même l'ascenseur.

Votre Jean [96]

(My dear Gide,

Nothing from you. I am bathing in the sun. My skin looks like a Negro boxer's, but inside I am still pale.

"The upright Swiss! All their good health brings them nothing... no crimes, no history, no literature, no arts... a robust rose bush with neither thorns nor blossoms..." Yet one gets hurt there. But by oneself, probably using the pruning shears.

1. Service: *Le Coup de dés*, printed up, is not yet on sale. Could you arrange for me to get hold of it from the *NRF*?

2. I had written to Rivière about his "Rossignol" article. He confused *"unwillingly"* and *"premeditation."* His reply was good: it was necessary for the public who judges the dish without visiting the kitchen.

3. Final proofs of *Le Potomak*.

It has an architecture built up by feeling my way and without knowing in advance how many stories there would be — but it seems to me that, being honest, one doesn't get lost in it and that from cellar to skylight it is complete — even including an elevator.

Your Jean)

The typical pattern of Cocteau's letters to Gide is displayed by a letter of November 1925, in which Cocteau mingles complaints of his health, gossip, nuanced teasing, and compliments:

25 Novembre 1925

Paris est impossible.

Pesez chaque minute votre chance et trouvez moi un hôtel où je n'aurai plus de rhumatismes. Votre carte arrive apportée par son timbre comme par un papillon.

Quoi de neuf? On raconte que j'entre à Solesmes et que Copeau id. id. — ? C'est faux.

Par contre Valéry est académicien. "Palmes." Je vous embrasse. Je suis furieux de ne pas être avec vous. On gèle — faute de vrai soleil, je retourne à Villefranche Janvier-Février. J'ai fini une pièce "Orphée" que je monte en Avril chez les Pitoëff. Bien triste si vous n'êtes pas dans la salle pour calmer mes crises de nerfs.

Je vous aime.

> Je vous embrasse
>
> Jean [97]
>
> November 25, 1925

(Paris is impossible.

Weigh your luck every minute and find me a hotel where I won't have any more rheumatism. Your card has just arrived, brought by its stamp as though by a butterfly.

What's new? I am said to be entering Solesmes, Copeau too. — ? Untrue.

On the other hand, Valéry is an Academician. "Palmes." I embrace you. I am furious not to be with you. We are freezing. For lack of true sunshine, I return to Villefranche in January/February. I have finished a play, *Orphée,* which I am staging in April at the Pitoëffs' [theater]. Shall be really wretched if you aren't in the house to calm my attacks of nerves.

I like you.

> I embrace you,
>
> Jean)

In sharp contrast to 1922, the year 1944 had been a barren period for Jean Cocteau. His letter to Gide of February 26, 1945, shows Cocteau just emerging from the creative torpor in which the final year of the war had enveloped him:

> 26 Février 1945
>
> 36 rue de Montpensier
>
> Paris

Mon cher André,

Que sont nos petites piques à côté de cette effrayante pelote de foudres? Je pense à vous de tout mon cœur et ne peux m'empêcher de vous l'écrire. Vous êtes une de ces forces qui reposent parce que les armes des hommes ne peuvent rien contre elles. Chaque jour votre cher visage habite ma petite chambre du Palais Royal. Venez vite voir le spectacle de notre panier aux crabes. Travaillez-vous? En ce qui me concerne je n'ose rien entreprendre de grave avec la moitié de ma personne. Le reste se trouve auprès des camarades

d'Alsace et des prisonniers d'Allemagne. Ecrivez moi quatre lignes.
Je vous embrasse fidèlement.

Jean Cocteau [98]

February 26, 1945
36 rue de Montpensier
Paris

(My dear André,

What are our petty squabbles compared to this terrifying ball of
lightning? I think of you with all my heart, and can't keep from
writing it to you. You are one of those forces which are restful because human weapons are powerless against them. Every day your
dear face lives in my tiny room of the Palais Royal. Come soon to
see the spectacle of our basketful of quarrelsome crabs. Are you
working? As for me I dare not undertake anything serious with half
my self. The rest is with comrades in Alsace and prisoners in Germany. Do write a few lines.

I embrace you faithfully.

Jean Cocteau)

By early 1945, with Paris slowly beginning to return to
normal, Cocteau was about to start the crushing schedule of
producing a major film each year from 1945 to 1950, except
for 1946 when he delivered the play *L'Aigle à deux têtes* and the
ballet *Le Jeune Homme et la mort,* in addition to his other literary
work. His frantic round of activity left less time than ever for
correspondence. Dermit remembers how Jean Cocteau's
heart sank when he confronted the mountain of mail that
arrived each morning from every part of the world. The
limitations of energy and health are noticeable in Cocteau's
postwar letters to Gide, although he still wrote nearly three
letters for each of Gide's to him. The records after February
26, 1945, show that twelve letters passed from Cocteau to Gide,
with five from Gide to Cocteau. Half of these related to projects on which the two authors were exploring the possibility
of creative collaboration. The harmonious mood surrounding
these attempts to work together in the closing years of their
relationship was brought to a crescendo by the friendly spirit
of the last two letters exchanged by the two men, one now at
the edge of death and the other in his sixty-second year. In
Gide's letter, written on the last day of the year 1950, there
is no trace of rancor, no ambiguous compliment, none of the
criticism which had often characterized his letters to Cocteau
during the preceding thirty-eight years. The letter has the

candor and warmth of one old friend speaking simply to another:

Dernier jour de l'an 1950

Mon cher Jean

Avant de quitter Paris — si toutefois j'en suis encore capable, — je voudrais vous envoyer une gerbe de souvenirs, d'affectueux messages et de vœux; tardive réponse à votre lettre du mois dernier; mais plus encore réponse à la lettre que je recevais de vous, il y a bien longtemps, après votre première lecture des *Caves*. Vous l'avez sans doute oubliée; moi, pas, car personne ne me parlait aussi bien que vous ne faisiez de mon livre; et j'y repensais avec émotion durant la représentation des *Français*. J'ai du mal à remonter une à une les marches que je viens de dégringoler quatre à quatre. Entre-temps je vous embrasse affectueusement

André Gide [99]

Last day of the year 1950

(My dear Jean,

Before leaving Paris—if, in any event, I am still able to—I should like to send you a nosegay of souvenirs, of affectionate messages and good wishes; a tardy reply to your letter of last month; but even more so to the letter I received from you, long ago, after your first reading of *Les Caves* [*du Vatican*]. You have no doubt forgotten it, but I haven't, for no one spoke to me of my book as well as you did, and I thought of this again with some feeling during the performance at the [Comédie-] Française. I have difficulty in climbing one by one the steps I used to rush down four at a time. Meanwhile I embrace you warmly.

André Gide)

When he read the closing lines of Gide's letter, Jean Cocteau might have recalled with some bitterness Gide's reproach in his open letter thirty years before: "L'artiste ne doit jamais sauter des marches . . . mais qu'avez-vous fait d'autre?" Nevertheless, Cocteau chose to overlook the past and his reply to Gide's gracious letter was equally friendly, complimentary, and soothing:

2 Janvier 1951
Milly — Setoise

Mon très cher André,

Paulhan m'a donné des nouvelles des *Caves* et je suis heureux d'une fin moins conforme à celles dont le public de la rue de Richelieu a l'habitude. Je disais à Paulhan que notre jeunesse de Saint Germain

des Près a pris de la graine depuis Lafcadio ce qui lui donne (à Lafcadio) l'allure d'un très brave type. (Il l'est, du reste.) J'ajoutais que *votre soulier* à vous a semelle de vent. Je vous souhaite encore quelques minutes d'équilibre dans le tohu-bohu mondial.

Je vous embrasse

Jean

P.S. Votre sens du comique théâtral est formidable.[100]

January 2, 1951

Milly — Setoise

(My very dear André,

Paulhan has given me news of *Les Caves* [*du Vatican*], and I am happy about an ending that conforms less to those the public of rue de Richelieu is used to. I told Paulhan that our young people of Saint-Germain-des-Près have taken Lafcadio as an example, which gives him (Lafcadio) the appearance of a very nice chap. (And of course he is.) I added that *your own shoe* has wind for its sole. I wish you a few more minutes of balance in this topsy-turvy world.

I embrace you.

Jean

P.S. Your feeling for comic theater is tremendous.)

From the tone and content of these final letters, both men clearly saw the end of their long relationship drawing near. Barely a month later André Gide was dead.

Invasions, Immunities, Influences

Throughout their friendship, Gide and Cocteau enjoyed a sustained professional contact centered in their theatrical activities. Each made a point of inviting the other to rehearsals or performances of his stage productions.

In 1917, when Cocteau's ballet *Parade* was presented, Cocteau wrote to Gide: "Ne reviendrez-vous pas voir notre Parade? C'est une bonne tranche d'Eugénisme à travers Picasso."[1] Gide replied at once, indicating a desire to see a rehearsal:

Lundi matin

Cher Jean

Il y a des degrés dans l'horrible — comme dit le Poète.

Je précipite mon retour, parce que je supportais mal déjà d'être à Cuverville pendant qu'on vous joue à Paris. Mais d'être à Paris et de ne pas voir votre ballet — cela est tout à fait intolérable.

Dites comment, où, quand? (répétition de préférence) — ou mon amitié ne croit plus à la vôtre.

André Gide[2]

Villa Montmorency

Monday morning

(Dear Jean

There are degrees of the horrible, as the Poet says.

I hasten my return since I could hardly stand being at Cuverville

while you were being performed in Paris. But to be in Paris and not see your ballet — that is altogether intolerable.

Tell me how, where, when? (preferably a rehearsal) — or my friendship won't believe any longer in yours.

André Gide)

Villa Montmorency

Gide apparently was unable to attend as planned, however, and Cocteau sent him a note of reproach:

Mon cher Gide,
   Pourquoi ce silence? J'ai été bien triste de ne pas vous voir à *Parade.*

Je vous embrasse.
Jean [3]

(My dear Gide,
   Why this silence? I was very sad not to see you at Parade.
I embrace you,
Jean)

Gide later made up for this disappointment by attending the successful 1920 revival of *Parade* financed by Cocteau's friend Coco Chanel.

In the autumn of 1925, Cocteau wrote Gide inviting him to attend *Orphée,* the play that the Pitoëffs were to present in 1926 at the Théâtre des Arts.[4]

In 1930, Cocteau sent tickets to Gide and Marc Allégret for his *La Voix humaine,* which had its première on February 17, 1930, at the Comédie-Française.[5] This important recognition of his achievement, like his earlier invitation to address the Collège de France and his later election to the French Academy, represented a moment of triumph to Jean Cocteau, the "cancre de la classe." It was his nature to wish to share that moment with Gide, the "fort en thème" who was at once his friend, his rival, and one of his acknowledged "maîtres." Accordingly, Cocteau wrote Gide:

Je n'ai pas lu Robert en Revue — j'attendais le livre. J'avais doublement raison.

F[évrier] 1930

Cher André,
   Je trouve "Robert" rue d'Anjou et je suis bien ému comme à chaque signe de votre affection. "L'Ecole" [des femmes] est un

livre extraordinaire, une merveille de ce non-moi survolé par un moi sévère. Dans "La Voix humaine" j'essaye d'obtenir cette sorte de force anonyme et je serais heureux de votre présence. J'ai expédié les cartes ce matin (à Marc [Allégret] et à vous).

Je vous embrasse
Jean [6]

(I haven't read Robert in Revue—I was waiting for the book. I was doubly right.

F[ebruary] 1930

Dear André,

   I found *Robert* at the rue d'Anjou, and I was deeply moved as always at every sign of your affection. *L'Ecole* [*des femmes*] is a remarkable book, a miracle of that "non-moi" overflown by a severe "moi." In *La Voix humaine* I try to achieve this kind of anonymous strength, and I would be happy for your presence. I sent the tickets this morning (to Marc [Allégret] and to you).

I embrace you,
Jean)

   In January 1932, Cocteau's film *Le Sang d'un poète* was presented at the Théâtre du Vieux-Colombier. While he was waiting at a nearby café for the film to begin, the sixty-three-year-old Gide meditated on his condition as an aging homosexual. It was a moment of introspection, perhaps brought on by the prospect of shortly seeing Cocteau, also homosexual but still in his prime at only forty-three. Gide's entry in his *Journal* for that night of January 20 follows:

   La chair moins exigeante, tandis que l'âge vient, laisse, il se peut, l'esprit libre. On juge plus sainement de ces choses; mais aussi plus injustement ceux qui sont dominés par les sens. Cette domination, lorsque soi-même on y échappe, on cesse de la comprendre et, partant, de l'admettre chez autrui. Combien d'intransigeances ne sont dues qu'à une froideur de tempérament!

   Ce que j'écris ici me paraît bien banal; je ne l'écris que pour écrire, dans ce café où je suis entré en attendant dix heures, les portes du Vieux-Colombier (où je suis invité pour le film de Cocteau) n'ouvrant pas plus tôt. Et puis il n'est pas du tout vrai que je me sente aujourd'hui moins d'indulgence, à présent que je suis moi-même moins tourmenté. Je me souviens trop bien de ce que c'était de l'être! Mais du moins puis-je mieux comprendre l'incompréhension de ceux qui ne l'ont jamais été, ou qu'un peu.

   Ce que je sais aussi, maintenant que j'ai reçu tant de confidences, c'est combien il suffit peu d'être hétérosexuel pour être... normal;

et combien souvent, tout compte fait, les simples et naturelles pra-
tiques de l'amour physique cèdent à des complications.[7]

(The flesh, less demanding as age comes on, leaves, it may be,
the mind freer. One judges such things more sanely; but also more
unjustly those who are dominated by the senses. When one has
escaped it, one ceases to understand that domination and, consequently, to admit it in others. How many uncompromising judgments are due simply to a cold temperament!

What I am writing here strikes me as very banal; I am writing it
only to write something, in this café where I have come to await
the opening of the Vieux-Colombier's doors at ten o'clock (I am
invited to see Cocteau's film). And besides, it is not at all true that
I feel less indulgent today, now that I am myself less tormented.
I remember too well what it was like to be so! But at least I can better
understand the lack of understanding of those who have never been
so, or only a little.

Another thing I know, now that I have received so many confidences, is how far it is from being sufficient to be heterosexual in
order to be... normal; and how often, all things considered, the simple
and natural practices of physical love yield to complications.)

Gide's *Journal* for July 12, 1937, indicates that he received
an invitation to a rehearsal of Cocteau's *Les Chevaliers de
la Table Ronde*, which was playing at the Théâtre de l'Œuvre.
The spirit of this entry by Gide illustrates the touchiness that
characterized the Gide-Cocteau relationship on both sides.

Invité à la dernière répétition de la pièce de Cocteau. A l'entrée
l'aspect surélégant du public m'a fait fuir; les sourires surtout, les
courbettes. . . . Le lendemain je lisais dans les journaux que, arrivé
trop tard, j'avais dû m'en retourner, n'ayant trouvé place.[8]

(Invited to the last rehearsal of Cocteau's play. At the entrance
the superelegant appearance of the audience made me flee; the
smiles especially, the bows. . . . The next day I read in the papers
that, having arrived too late, I had had to go away, not having found
a seat.)

Cocteau years later tried to offset the derogatory effect
of Gide's comment and to put the record straight:

Je n'aimais pas ses mensonges enfantins (des mensonges de faits).
Il les donnait pour la réalité, et s'y entêtait. Je vous ai déjà dit que
cela le poussait à accuser les autres de mensonges. Exemple: il

venait gentiment assister à toutes les répétitions d'une de mes pièces.
Il écrivit ensuite dans son Journal qu'il ne l'avait jamais vue, et
qu'on lui avait refusé des places au contrôle. Je connaissais tellement
cette méthode que j'en riais et ne m'en affectais pas. Le dommage,
c'est que les écrits restent et beaucoup de gens peuvent croire que
j'ai malhonnêtement fermé ma porte à un homme qui entrait chez
moi comme chez lui.[9]

(I didn't like his childish lies (lies about facts). He gave them out
for reality, and was obstinate about it. I have already told you that
that prompted him to accuse others of lies. Example: he very kindly
came to see all the rehearsals of one of my plays. Afterwards he wrote
in his *Journal* that he had never seen it, and that he had been refused
seats at the box office. I knew that system of his so thoroughly that
it made me laugh and I was not affected by it. The sad thing is, the
writings remain and many people may believe that I rudely closed
my door to a man who entered my home as he did his own.)

A comparison of the two foregoing comments by Gide and
Cocteau shows how Cocteau's accuracy gives way, as it does
on more than one occasion, before the weight of his desire
to justify himself and to throw doubt on the accuracy of Gide's
Journal entries about him.

In January of 1939, Cocteau invited Gide to the dress rehearsal of his play *Les Parents terribles,* which had just reopened
at the Théâtre Bouffes Parisiens, after having been forced
by the Conseil Municipal of Paris to close at the city-owned
Théâtre des Ambassadeurs on the grounds of presenting
incestuous relationships:

> 19, Place de la Madeleine (8e)
> 13 Janvier 1939
>
> Cher André
> Mon silence venait de ce que j'habite la campagne. Est-il possible
> — mais tout est possible au théâtre — que vous n'ayez pas reçu les
> fauteuils pour ma rep.[étition] générale? Si venir voir ma pièce aux
> "Bouffes" vous fait le moindre plaisir, faites le téléphoner à mon
> secrétaire André Goudin. Vous êtes ma vraie famille — Je vous aime
> et je vous embrasse.
>
> Jean[10]

> 19, Place de la Madeleine (8e)
> January 13, 1939
>
> (Dear André
> My silence was due to my living in the country. Is it possible—but
> anything is possible in the theater—that you didn't receive seats

for my dress rehearsal? If it would give you the slightest pleasure to come and see my play at the Bouffes, just have someone phone my secretary André Goudin. You are my real family—I like you and I embrace you.

Jean)

Claude Mauriac tells of seeing Gide and Cocteau at a July 1945 performance of *Richard III:*

Je l'aperçus à sa place de balcon, qui se penchait aimablement et demeurait tourné de côté dans une position fort incommode, pour faciliter le travail d'un operateur qui photographiait non pas lui, André Gide, mais la loge de l'ambassadrice d'Angleterre, Lady Diana Cooper, où trônait Jean Cocteau.[11]

(I saw him in his balcony seat, leaning amiably forward and remaining turned to one side in a very uncomfortable position to facilitate the work of a cameraman who was photographing not him, André Gide, but the loge of the English Ambassadress, Lady Diana Cooper, where Jean Cocteau occupied a place of honor.)

As Gide advanced in years, and failing health hampered his movements, Cocteau's attitude toward him became increasingly sympathetic, almost filial in its gentleness. When Gide expressed interest in attending the showing of a Cocteau film at the Cinéma du Colisée, Cocteau wrote a personal note to the theater manager arranging the best accommodations for his elderly friend.

Cher Monsieur
    Je pense qu'il est fort inutile que je vous demande la grâce d'éviter à André Gide, malade, de faire la queue. Cela va de soi — mais je vous le demande tout de même sachant que vous serez heureux de me rendre ce service et de l'avoir dans votre salle. Ne le placez pas trop près. Merci et du cœur à vous.

Jean Cocteau [12]

(Dear Sir,
    I expect it is quite unnecessary for me to ask you the kindness of letting André Gide, ill, avoid standing in line. That is a matter of course—but I ask it of you anyway knowing you will be happy to render me this service and to have him in your theater. Don't put him too far up front. My heartfelt thanks to you.

Jean Cocteau)

It was no doubt this sort of thoughtful attention on Cocteau's part that prompted Gide to tell Léon Pierre-Quint in 1950: "Oh! Son extrême gentillesse, ses soins attentifs... Vous ne savez pas comme il s'est montré dévoué encore ces derniers temps." [13] ("Oh! His extreme kindness, his careful attentions... You have no idea how devoted he showed himself in the last few years.")

In July 1946, Cocteau wrote Gide after viewing the film version of Gide's *récit La Symphonie pastorale.* Gide replied warmly, expressing regret at not seeing Cocteau at the film.

31 Juillet 46

Charmant ami
    Que n'étais-je avec vous lors de cette projection! J'aurais eu si grand plaisir à vous revoir... Tout ce que vous me dites du film, je le pense aussi (et combien gentil vous êtes de me l'écrire!) — ...

André Gide [14]

July 31, 1946

(Charming friend,
    Why couldn't I have been with you for that showing! It would have given me so much pleasure to see you again... I agree with everything you tell me of the film (and how kind you are to write me about it!) — ...

André Gide)

When Gide's stage version of *Les Caves du Vatican* was presented at the Comédie-Française in December 1950, twenty years after Cocteau's production there of *La Voix humaine,* Cocteau was eager to attend despite his ill health.

Milly (Setoise)
29 Nov 1950

Mon bien cher André,
    Je viens d'être assez malade et je me vante car cela dure et traîne. J'ai dû renoncer au voyage de New York. Si je vous disais que je me soigne pour assister aux Caves. Dans cette époque ignoble (au sens propre du terme) certaines pointes me tiennent encore à cœur et attirent mes ondes. Vous, par exemple, et votre pièce.
    Une ligne me donnant de vos nouvelles me réconforterait mieux que la médecine.

Je vous embrasse
Jean [15]

Milly (Setoise)
November 29, 1950

(My very dear André,

I have just been rather ill, and I am bragging because it still drags on and on. I had to give up the trip to New York. Would you believe that I am taking care of myself so I can attend the *Caves* [*du Vatican*]. In these vile times (in the real sense of the word) certain peaks still touch my heart and attract my waves. You, for example, and your play.

One line giving me your news would strengthen me more than any medicine.

I embrace you,
Jean)

Gide responded at once with warmth:

2 Décembre 50

Cher Jean

Grand réconfort pour moi de vous savoir dans la salle. Je me suis assuré hier qu'une invitation vous parviendrait.

Votre très fatigué
André Gide [16]

December 2, 1950

(Dear Jean,

Great comfort to me to know you will be in the audience. I made sure yesterday that you would receive an invitation.

Your very tired
André Gide)

It was appropriate and at the same time paradoxical that the *Caves* performance proved to be the setting as Gide and Cocteau caught a last glimpse of each other in Paris. In the most hallowed of French theaters, the Comédie-Française, Gide was applauded for a farce that was quite outside the general spirit of his life work; like *Paludes*, "une œuvre à part." Comedy had never been Gide's *forte*, and the irony of this final light touch of Gide's as he left the scene could only delight Jean Cocteau, who had long been criticized by the Gides of his generation for his own lack of seriousness. It seemed as though at the end Gide himself, remembering his advice to Cocteau thirty years before, had finally been able to "se laisser aller"; that he was determined to show that there was, after all, something of "l'écureuil" beneath the austere exterior of "l'ours."

Cocteau's success in the film genre, begun in 1930 with *Le Sang d'un poète,* and further exploited in ensuing years both independently and in collaboration with others, did not pass unnoticed by André Gide.[17] The common interest of both writers in film as an art form led, toward the end of Gide's life, to an effort at professional collaboration between them. There had been other occasions earlier in their careers when Gide and Cocteau had worked together, and the periodic joining of their skills in a common purpose may properly be considered as another way in which the presence of the one was felt in the life and work of the other. The attempted film collaboration between Gide and Cocteau did not bear fruit, but it is a sign of Gide's respect for Cocteau's mastery of filmmaking that it was Gide who took the initiative by approaching Cocteau.

The occasion came shortly after Gide and Pierre Herbart, during a stay in Geneva in December 1946, had finished drafting a scenario based on Gide's *récit Isabelle.* A terse entry in Gide's *Journal* for December 28, 1946, reports: "À Genève: Préface à *l'Anthologie;* Scenario d'*Isabelle.*" An undated letter, probably written in early 1947 by Cocteau, refers to a meeting with Herbart and Gide, at which *Isabelle* was discussed.

> Maison du Bailli, rue de Lau
> Milly (S-et-O)
> Samedi soir

Mon très cher André,
Encore une fois je viens d'avoir la preuve de la noblesse et de l'élégance avec laquelle les choses se résolvent dès qu'on ne se trouve plus dans le "milieu du cinématographe." Je craignais un peu d'avoir à vous parler avec une pleine franchise et de vous confier ma note sur le travail d'*Isabelle.* J'étais absurde. Tout de suite vous vous êtes placé haut et ne vous êtes intéressé qu'à des points de vue qui vous semblaient neufs au lieu de défendre un travail de quatre mois — ce que j'eusse trouvé légitime. Vous m'avez encore une fois donné le spectacle de votre merveilleuse curiosité Goethéenne — plus forte que vos intérêts personnels.

J'ajoute que j'ai admiré Pierre H[erbart]. La jeunesse s'accroche davantage que nous aux détails et je n'ai pas vu l'ombre d'une ombre sur sa figure. . . .

Jean [18]

Maison du Bailli, rue de Lau
Milly (S-et-O)
Saturday evening

(My very dear André,

Once again I have just had proof of the nobility and elegance with which things resolve themselves as soon as one gets outside the "film-maker's world." I was a bit afraid I would have to speak to you in all candor and to give you my memorandum about the *Isabelle* project. I was stupid. You immediately placed yourself on a high plane and concerned yourself only with points of view that seemed new to you, instead of defending a labor of four months—which I would have found justifiable. You have once again given me the spectacle of your wonderful Goethe-like curiosity—stronger than your personal interests.

I must add that I admired Pierre H[erbart]. Young people are greater sticklers for detail than we are, yet I did not see the shadow of a shadow on his face. . . .

Jean)

The preceding letter is most likely the note referred to by Cocteau in his *Journal d'un inconnu* of 1952, where his reservations about the merits of a film version of *Isabelle* are more clearly stated:

Au terme de sa vie, il [Gide] vint dans ma maison de campagne avec Herbart. Il souhaitait que je fisse la mise en scène d'un film qu'il tirait d'*Isabelle*. À l'œil d'Herbart, je devinai qu'il pataugeait. Le film était médiocre. Je le lui expliquai dans une note écrite, et qu'on attendait plutôt de lui un film des *Faux-Monnayeurs,* ou des *Caves.* Il jubilait de m'entendre lire une note. Il empocha cette note. Il est possible qu'on la retrouve dans quelque tiroir.[19]

(Toward the end of his life, he [Gide] came to my country house with Herbart. He wished me to stage a film he was making from *Isabelle.* From the look in Herbart's eye I guessed he was floundering. The film was mediocre. I explained this to him in a written memorandum, and that what people expected from him instead was a film of *Les Faux-Monnayeurs* or of *Les Caves.* He was delighted to hear me read a report. He pocketed that report. It's possible it will be found in some drawer.)

In an interview with Colin-Simard the year after Gide's death, Cocteau had already confirmed that the *Isabelle* project did not work out:

Peu avant de mourir, il [Gide] me demanda de mettre en scène un film qu'il tirait d'*Isabelle*. Je lui expliquai qu'on attendait plutôt de lui un film tiré des *Faux-Monnayeurs* ou des *Caves*, et il se rendit tout de suite à mes raisons.[20]

(Shortly before he [Gide] died, he asked me to stage a film he was making from *Isabelle*. I explained to him that people expected from him instead a film based on *Les Faux-Monnayeurs* or *Les Caves*, and he immediately accepted my reasons.)

A second attempt by Cocteau and Gide at a limited film collaboration centered around Gide's novel *Les Caves du Vatican*. The first sign of Cocteau's interest in a film made from this work appears in his letter to Gide of July 5, 1949:

> Milly, Setoise
> 5 Juillet 1949

Mon très cher André,
　Je ne vois plus cette maison sans vous, sans votre chère présence dans le fauteuil à bascule. J'eusse bien aimé bavarder de l'Egypte et de cet Istanbul où vous avez jeté la consternation — car ils vous croient — et n'osent plus se regarder les uns les autres. On me raconte que vous allez mieux et que vous travaillez aux *Caves*. Enfin! vous ai-je assez supplié de le faire. J'aimerais q.q. lignes pour recevoir des vraies nouvelles de vous et de Lafcadio-film. Ce qu'on rapporte est toujours inexact et la France m'a l'air d'aimer de plus en plus le petit mythe.
　Une carte de vous serait le "tue-mythes" idéal. J'ai terminé les voyages par la Grèce. Tout vous y tire vers le haut, vous allège, lévite. Athènes embaume. L'Egypte et la Turquie vous tirent vers le bas et sentent la mort. Je vous embrasse.

> Jean [21]

> Milly, Setoise
> July 5, 1949

(My very dear André,
　I cannot visualize this house any longer without you, without your dear presence in the rocking chair. I would so much have liked to chat about Egypt and Istanbul, where you caused such consternation — because they believe you and no longer dare to look at each other. I am told you are feeling better and are at work on *Les Caves* [*du Vatican*]. At last! I begged you often enough to do it. I would love a few lines giving some real news about yourself and of the Lafcadio film. What people report is always inaccurate, and it seems to me France likes little myths more and more.
　A card from you would be the ideal "myth-slayer." I finished my

travels in Greece. Everything there draws one upward, lightens and raises one. Athens is a balm. Egypt and Turkey drag one down and smell of death. I embrace you.

Jean)

Jean Denoël reports that at this time Gide was working on a film scenario of *Les Caves.* He had already planned to use Roger Vadim, later a successful film director and husband of Brigitte Bardot, in the role of Lafcadio when he received a second letter from Cocteau proposing Jean Marais for the part:

Milly
S et Oise
Août 1949

Très cher André,

Dans cette maison tout me parle de Gide et je vous vois dans le fauteuil à bascule auprès du feu. J'aimerais vous raconter mes voyages et que vous me racontiez les vôtres. Comment marchent les *Caves?* C'est le rêve de la vie de Jean Marais de tourner ou de jouer ce rôle. Pensez-y, même si nos cinéastes se tournent vers une autre vedette. Marais y serait prodigieux, je vous l'affirme. Naturellement je vous en parle à son insu, car il ne demande jamais rien et crève de peur d'empiéter sur un camarade. Telle est son âme.

Ecrivez-moi quelques lignes – ou demandez à Pierre de me les écrire. Je m'embête loin de vous.

Jean [22]

Milly
S et Oise
August 1949

(Very dear André,

In this house everything speaks to me of Gide and I see you sitting in the rocking chair by the fire. I'd like to tell you about my travels and to have you tell me about yours. How is *Les Caves* [*du Vatican*] going? It is the dream of Jean Marais's life to play this role on the screen or stage. Think about it, even if the producers are inclined toward another star. Marais would be terrific in the part, I assure you. Of course I am mentioning it to you without his knowledge, for he never asks for anything and is deathly afraid of treading on the toes of a colleague. His soul is like that.

Write me a few lines – or ask Pierre to write them. I am bored away from you.

Jean)

Gide's reply was prompt but evasive, the question of casting having now been overshadowed by a more basic problem: *Les Caves du Vatican* was on the Catholic *Index:*

Juan-les-Pins
27 Août 49

Mon cher Jean,
Pour n'avoir pas aussitôt répondu à votre exquise "lettre de retour," il fallait que je fusse bien bas. Quel plaisir j'aurais pris, je prendrai, à écouter vos récits de voyage! Quant aux *Caves,* j'en suis à ne plus savoir où l'on en est. Il se découvre que mon livre est à l'*Index;* danger public, attentatoire. Je suppose que tout va s'arranger; mais cet état d'expectative où l'on me maintient m'exténue. Quant à la "distribution," je n'ai pas attendu votre nouvelle lettre pour y songer; mais ne peux encore rien dire. Trop fatigué pour vous en écrire plus long: juste la force de vous embrasser tout affectueusement.

André Gide [23]

Juan-les-Pins
August 27, 1949

(My dear Jean,
Not to have answered your exquisite "welcome-home letter" at once, I had to be very low. What pleasure I would have had, I will have, in listening to your travel tales! As for [*Les*] *Caves* [*du Vatican*], I hardly know what's going on any more. It appears that my book is on the *Index;* a public menace, challenge to authority. I suppose it will all work out; but this state of expectancy in which they are keeping me is exhausting. With respect to the "casting," I did not wait to receive your latest letter before thinking about it; but as yet I can say nothing. Too tired to write you any more about it: just strength enough to embrace you with great affection.
André Gide)

Jean Cocteau began the new year by writing Gide hopefully that he had taken the first steps to obtain authorization for *Les Caves* to be presented:

15 Janvier 1950
Milly, Setoise

Mon très cher André,
Je ne vous ai pas souhaité ce nouvel an parce que je déteste les "dates." Mais dans cette maison où je vous ai vu cœur à cœur je ne résiste pas à vous embrasser et à vous dire mes vœux de santé profonde.

Jean

J'ai faït des démarches pour obtenir le droit des *Caves.* Cela ne semble pas insoluble. [24]

January 15, 1950
Milly, Setoise

(My very dear André,

I didn't send you New Year's greetings because I hate "dates."
But in this house where I have seen you heart to heart I cannot resist
embracing you and sending you my wishes for your very good health.

Jean

[P.S.] I have taken steps to obtain the clearance for *Les Caves*
[*du Vatican*]. It doesn't seem hopeless.)

The film project ultimately fell through, but Gide retrieved
the situation by arranging for a farce version of *Les Caves*
to be presented in December 1950 at the Comédie-Française.

A letter from Cocteau to Gide in July 1945 establishes the
early stages of another effort at film collaboration between the
two artists prior to their discussions of *Les Caves du Vatican*
and *Isabelle*. Cocteau was summering at the time on the Arcachon basin with Jean Marais and working on his own film
La Belle et la Bête, in which Marais played the lead. The possibility under consideration was an eventual collaboration with
the producer Jean Delannoy on a film version of Gide's *La
Symphonie pastorale* prepared by Pierre Bost and Jean Aurenche.
Both Gide and Cocteau were inclined to move carefully in
planning such a joint enterprise, in view of the unsettled condi-
tions in Paris that summer, so soon after the German sur-
render.

19 Juillet 1945

Mon très cher André

De ma cabane de pêcheurs, malgré le travail de mon film je pense
au mécanisme du vôtre. Mais il importe d'attendre un signe de la
rue Francois 1er. Une affaire qui vous concerne et qui risque de
réunir nos noms exige la plus extrême prudence. L'étude du livre
me donne la certitude que j'avais raison d'éviter les images qui dis-
persent. Votre œuvre ne doit se compliquer d'aucun pittoresque.
Le film s'y trouve enroulé d'un bout à l'autre. Je rentre dans une
quinzaine. Je vous embrasse.

Jean

Mes amitiés à Criel. S'il veut son manuscrit (dont je lui parlerai),
il se trouve dans ma chambre sous la petite table où j'entasse les
lettres. Mon secrétaire le lui remettra. J'ai dû partir par avion en toute
hâte.[25]

July 19, 1945

(My very dear André,

From my fisherman's cabin, in spite of the work on my film, I think about the mechanics of yours. But it is important to wait for a sign from rue François 1er. An enterprise that concerns you and that risks reuniting our names requires the greatest caution. Study of the book confirms my conviction that I was right to avoid images that scatter. Your work should not be complicated by any picturesqueness. The film is wound up in it from one end to the other. I return in a fortnight. I embrace you.

Jean

[P.S.] My best to Criel. If he wants his manuscript (which I will talk about with him), it is in my room under the little table where I stack my letters. My secretary will give it to him. I had to leave by plane in a hurry.)

Although ultimately Cocteau did not officially collaborate on the film, Gide's absence on a trip to Egypt in 1946 offered the younger man occasion to help with it in a minor but significant way. The film featured Michèle Morgan as the blind heroine. Cocteau had followed the progress of the production with interest, and during the filming of the final scenes could not resist urging a few changes on the producer. In a letter to Gide of July 28, 1946, Cocteau confesses: "Comme vous étiez en Egypte — j'ai intrigué pour qu'on supprime le prêche de la fin et qu'on ferme les yeux de la mort qui *regarde.*[26] ("As you were in Egypt, I intrigued to have the sermon cut at the finish and to close the eyes of the dead woman, who seems to be *looking.*") Nothing could have been more appropriate to Cocteau, and to the film's theme, than this inspired final gesture involving both hands and eyes, two physical features that had always been central symbols in Cocteau's esthetic system. Gide's reply three days later indicates that far from resenting this intrusion by Cocteau he welcomed it:

On a supprimé fort heureusement le prêche de la fin. Je n'ai pu obtenir de Delannois [*sic*] certaines coupures, au début, dans l'éducation de l'aveugle, qui me paraissaient très souhaibles [*sic*]. Tant pis! Tel qu'il est le film me paraît assez réussi; ce n'était pas facile; et les responsables à qui j'avais complètement laissé la place, ont fait merveille.

Chaleureusement votre

André Gide

Ai dédicacé pour vous un *Thésée* que vous recevrez bientôt[27]

(They cut out, most fortunately, the sermon at the end. I was unable to get Delannoy to make certain cuts, at the beginning, about the blind girl's education, that seemed to me highly desirable. Too bad! As it stands, the film seems to me to have come off quite well; it wasn't easy; and the responsible people, to whom I gave a completely free hand, worked miracles.

Warmly, your
André Gide

[P.S.] Have dedicated a *Thésée* for you which you will receive soon.)

In addition to the three films already mentioned, there were a number of other projects on which Gide and Cocteau worked together, directly or indirectly.

Jean Cocteau's entire experience with the *NRF* during Gide's lifetime is, of course, a most important example of how the literary lines of the two men frequently intersected. Their correspondence as early as February or March 1914 contains discussions of specific poems of Cocteau's considered for publication in the *NRF:* "P.S. Pour 'des raisons' j'aimerais beaucoup voir aussi paraître: 'Ne sois pas trop intelligent' et 'Les Antipodes.' Que dois-je faire pour les épreuves? — Attendre?" [28] (P.S. For 'certain reasons' I would also very much like to see published: 'Ne sois pas trop intelligent' and 'Les Antipodes.' What shall I do about the proofs? — Wait?)

A postcard from Gide to Cocteau at the beginning of 1914 indicates his impatience to receive some of the poet's work:

Paris
12 janvier 1914

Le plus clair résultat de ça c'est que je ne verrai vos vers que trop tard! Vous ne connaissez pas encore Fargue. Il va mettre douze ans à me les apporter.

André Gide [29]

Paris
January 12, 1914

(The most obvious result of that is that I won't see your verses until too late! You don't yet know Fargue. He'll take a dozen years to bring them to me.

André Gide)

And again from Cocteau, in 1919: "J'ai recopié 'Le Balcon' poème pour mettre avec votre No. 2." [30]

In July of 1946 Cocteau was approached by Gide, through the intermediary of their mutual friend and colleague Jean Denoël, and asked for a contribution to the *NRF*. Cocteau replied to Gide:

Jean Denoël me dit que vous aimeriez avoir un texte de moi. Je corrige un livre d'essais. Je n'ai pas de doubles. Un chapitre vous conviendrait-il? Ecrivez-le moi en quatre lignes. Mon secrétaire doit venir me voir et se chargera de vous le faire parvenir.

Je vous embrasse
Jean [31]

(Jean Denoël says you would like a piece from me. I am correcting a book of essays. I have no copies. Would one chapter suit you? Drop me a line and let me know. My secretary is coming to see me and will undertake to get it to you.

I embrace you,
Jean)

After World War II Jean Cocteau also wrote for *L'Arche,* a monthly literary review for which André Gide served on the Comité de Direction. In the February 1947 issue Cocteau's article "Mesure" [32] immediately preceded an article by Gide which consisted of an exchange of previously unpublished letters between Gide and Marcel Proust.

Between the two wars Cocteau and Gide found other occasions to work together. In 1939, under the aegis of André Gide, the publishing house of Gallimard brought out *Tableau de la littérature française*. This work had been in preparation for several years, and on January 18, 1935, Gallimard had already paid Cocteau 1500 francs for the article he had contributed.[33] As Gide described it in his preface to the book, *Tableau de la littérature française* was "un livre où nombre des meilleurs d'aujourd'hui parleraient des meilleurs d'hier, chacun selon son goût, sa préférence, et ne parlerait que de celui-là seul qu'il a choisi, pour lequel il s'est senti choisi." [34] ("a book in which a number of the best writers of today would discuss some of the best writers of yesterday, each according to his taste, his preference, and would speak only of the one he had chosen, for whom he felt himself chosen.") Jean Cocteau was invited to prepare an essay on Jean-Jacques Rousseau.[35]

In this essay Cocteau deals unsympathetically with Grimm,

Diderot, and the Encyclopedists, with whom he implicitly identifies André Gide. It is enlightening, when reading the Cocteau article, to recall Cocteau's comments to Claude Mauriac in May of 1939, the same year *Tableau de la littérature française* was published. Cocteau and Jean Marais were living at the Hôtel Vatel in Versailles at the time, while Cocteau put the finishing touches to *La Fin du Potomak* and to his new play *La Machine à Ecrire.* Claude Mauriac, who was then working on his book *Jean Cocteau ou la vérité du mensonge,* came to talk with Cocteau. The conversation turned inevitably to the subject of André Gide. Claude Mauriac's notes of the conversation report how Cocteau linked Gide with the Encyclopedists:

Gide défendait les Encyclopédistes contre Rousseau, s'assimilant de bon droit du reste, à Grimm-Diderot et confondant assez justement Cocteau avec Rousseau; qu'il fit, à ce sujet, dépêché par la N.R.F., un très long voyage pour venir le dissuader de publier sa réhabilitation de Rousseau (qui, selon Cocteau, n'avait pas la manie de la persécution, mais était réellement persécuté). Mais Gide ne voulut pas se laisser convaincre et prétendit, comme s'il avait assisté à la chose, que Jean-Jacques était mort d'une ignoble façon – que Cocteau rapporta crûment, mais que je préfère taire. Tout cela avec d'extraordinaires imitations de la voix fusante de Gide, tout cela entremêlé de louanges sur la grandeur de Gide, son génie et sa haute dignité et, aussitôt après, d'extravagantes anecdotes soigneusement choisies ou inventées pour montrer les plus petits côtés de ce grand personnage. . . .) [36]

(Gide defended the Encyclopedists against Rousseau, likening himself with good reason moreover to Grimm-Diderot, and rather correctly identifying Cocteau with Rousseau. In this connection, sent by the *NRF,* Gide made a very long trip to dissuade Cocteau from publishing his rehabilitation of Rousseau (who, according to Cocteau, did not have a persecution complex, but was really persecuted). But Gide wouldn't let himself be convinced and claimed, as though he had been a witness, that Jean-Jacques had died ignobly – which Cocteau reported crudely but which I prefer not to mention. All this with extraordinary imitations of Gide's easy flowing voice, all this mixed with praises about Gide's greatness, his genius and his towering dignity, and, immediately afterward, extravagant tales carefully chosen or invented to show the meanest aspects of this great figure. . . .)

If Cocteau draws certain parallels between Gide and the Encyclopedists, his article also unmistakably reveals his own

identification with Rousseau.[37] Cocteau sees himself, as Rousseau saw himself, as epitomizing the struggle of a "solitaire" against "le monde," of "le singulier" against "le pluriel," a poet pitted against the intellectuals. Cocteau, like Rousseau, had an anti-intellectual aspect to his writing that shows clearly here. Also to be noticed in this essay is a sense of persecution he shares with Rousseau, which he feels led to Rousseau's best writing. Rousseau-Cocteau personifies the "gibier" hounded by hostile critics and an uncomprehending public, the misunderstood poet fated to be "le poète posthume." Both men, Cocteau implies, exemplify "cet équilibre si difficile à maintenir lorsque la route est en l'air sur un fil inconnu au lieu d'être sur le sol et connu d'avance" [38] ("that balance so difficult to maintain when the road is in the air on an unfamiliar thread instead of being on the earth and known in advance"). Central to Cocteau's view of himself at the time are his comments on Rousseau's humanism: "Le cœur seul peut guider la conscience. Dans un siècle de philosophes, il a été au sens classique du terme, le vrai moraliste." [39] ("The heart alone can guide the conscience. In a century of philosophers he was, in the classic sense of the term, the true moralist.") The thrust of the sentence takes on double meaning if Cocteau's name is substituted for Rousseau's, and Gide and the *NRF* take the place of the "philosophes." By way of summation Cocteau closes his article with a self-portrait, but using Rousseau's name:

Jean-Jacques n'eut rien d'un apôtre. Il est homme avec toutes ses faiblesses. Sincère à sa manière, d'une sincérité qui n'est pas celle des saints. Sa vie fut bien moins scandaleuse que celle d'un Richelieu ou d'un Casanova. Il montra constamment du feu; et il suffit de cette petite chose pour bouleverser une époque. Il ne souhaitait rien que d'aimer et être aimé. À cause de cela, il fut haï, persécuté plus qu'aucun homme. Il semble que ce soit surtout ce que le monde ne pardonne pas.[40]

(Jean-Jacques had nothing of the apostle about him. He is man, with all his weaknesses. Sincere in his way, with a sincerity that is not that of the saints. His life was far less scandalous than that of a Richelieu or a Casanova. He constantly showed fire; and this little circumstance was enough to convulse an era. He wished for nothing except to love and to be loved. For that he was hated, persecuted beyond any man. It seems this is above all what the world does not forgive.)

Cocteau did not need to refer to André Gide by name in the Rousseau article in order for Gide to know on which side of the equations Cocteau placed him. To Cocteau, Gide had long personified the "fort en thème" and the critic as opposed to Cocteau's "cancre de la classe" and quarry. In effect it was Gide who had first assigned himself this role during his 1919 exchange of open letters with Cocteau, when he chided the poet for attempting to pass himself off as a logician. No doubt the *Coq et l'Arlequin* episode and his treatment by Gide and Rivière came to Cocteau's mind when he described Grimm's practice of maligning Rousseau in his *Correspondance littéraire* without giving Rousseau a chance to reply:

Il n'y a pas alors de droit de réponse, et si parfois un des abonnés envoie une lettre rectificative, Grimm, aussi habile que les directeurs de journaux modernes, l'escamote et n'en reparle plus.[41]

(Then there is no right of reply, and if perchance one of the sub-scribers should send a correcting letter, Grimm, as clever as the editors of modern newspapers, causes it to vanish and never speaks of it again.)

And yet, if Cocteau saw himself when he peered into Rousseau's mirror, he also caught glimpses of Gide's character in Rousseau as well as in the Encyclopedists. Several of Cocteau's comments in his article about Rousseau point in Gide's direction: "En lui se rencontre un mélange très neuf d'impudeur naturelle et de réserve protestante." ("In him occurs a very new head-on collision between natural shamelessness and protestant reserve.") In his open letter to Gide in 1919, Cocteau had previously commented on the combination in Gide of "bacchante" and "pasteur." "Cet aveugle . . . n'a guère fait de toute sa vie qu'apprendre à se connaître." "Rousseau prend parti sur tous les problèmes qui intéressent son siècle." "Rousseau a commis la pire des imprudences. Il a rendu publique sa vie entière, et il a engagé son œuvre sur sa vie." "Jean-Jacques est beaucoup moins spontané que sincère." [42] ("That blind man . . . has hardly done anything all his life but learn to know who he is.") ("Rousseau takes a stand on all the problems that concern his century.") ("Rousseau committed the worst of follies. He made his entire life public, and he pledged his work on his life.") ("Jean-Jacques is much less spontaneous than sincere.")

Gide's sincerity was an important part of his mystique, both as writer and as critic. In view of such comments, all appropriate to Gide, it is not surprising to read in Cocteau's "Gide vivant" of 1952:

Une des grandes singularités de Gide, c'est d'avoir mêlé en sa personne J.-J. Rousseau et les Encyclopédistes.

Il avait de Rousseau le botanisme et l'enfantillage. Il avait de Diderot et de Grimm, cette rage de chasser à courre et de poursuivre un homme comme une meute. Il en résulte que Gide offre les contradictions les plus vivantes et les plus intransigeantes. Il est cruel et tendre, il chasse les autres et se chasse lui-même. Il préfère les livres aux fleurs et les fleurs aux livres. Il n'a jamais répugné à un certain exhibitionnisme à la Rousseau, mais si on le contourne, on découvrira le sourire de Voltaire.[43]

(One of the most unusual things about Gide is that he blended in himself J.-J. Rousseau and the Encyclopedists.

He had Rousseau's love of botany and child-play. He had Diderot's and Grimm's passion for the hunt and for harrying a man like a pack of stag hounds. The result of this is that Gide presents the most vivid and the most uncompromising contradictions. He is cruel and tender, he hunts others and he hunts himself. He prefers books to flowers and flowers to books. He never shrank from a certain Rousseau-like exhibitionism, but if his outline be traced, one will discover the smile of Voltaire.)

The following year Cocteau repeated his views, with slight variations, in his collection of essays entitled *Journal d'un inconnu:*

Il [Gide] mêlait en sa personne le Jean-Jacques Rousseau botaniste, et le Grimm de chez Mme d'Epinay. Il me rappelait cette interminable, cette harcelante chasse à courre aux trousses d'un gibier maladroit. Il combinait la peur de l'un et la ruse des autres. Il advenait que meute et gibier se confondissent en lui.

Le postérieur de Jean-Jacques, c'est la lune de Freud qui se lève. Gide ne répugne pas à ces exhibitionnismes. Mais si on le contourne, on découvre le sourire de Voltaire.[44]

(He [Gide] blended in his personality Jean-Jacques Rousseau the botanist, and the Grimm of Mme d'Epinay. He reminded me of that harrying stag hunt on the heels of a clumsy quarry. He combined the fear of one with the cunning of the others. It happened that pack and game were intermingled in him.

The rear end of Jean-Jacques is Freud's moon rising. Gide does

not find this sort of exhibitionism repugnant. But if you trace his outline, you find the smile of Voltaire.)

The two preceding passages, written many years after Cocteau's original Rousseau article, illuminate in part Cocteau's polemical intentions in that article, and point up the consistency of his basic attitude toward André Gide. Even while working with Gide on a common project of this sort, Cocteau could not forget Gide's public attack of 1919. Following Péguy's axiom of knowing just how far to go too far, he used the occasion of *Tableau* to help even an old score.

Jean Cocteau's chronic defensiveness about intellectuals, so apparent in his article for Gide on Rousseau, also clearly shows in his preface to his *La Comtesse de Noailles oui et non,* an anthology of earlier essays by Cocteau and one of the last books he composed before his death. Here Cocteau reproves Gide and the *NRF* for having omitted Anna de Noailles from their *Anthologie de la poésie française,* the compilation of which Gide had directed: "Rien ne prouvera aux intellectuels que la comtesse de Noailles soit un très grand poète," Cocteau protests, and then refers acidly to the "encyclopédistes de la Nouvelle Revue Française, . . . (Gide en tête)." [45]

The abbreviated summary of direct and indirect collaborations between Gide and Cocteau in the preceding pages illustrates the ambivalent nature of their relationship. In light of the fact that they were alternately drawn to and repulsed by each other, on the professional as well as the personal level, it would appear that the occasions of their coming together for purposes of collaboration were more calculated than spontaneous. The occasional need or desire for each other's skills and support was never enough to obscure for long from either of them the basic differences in character, age, and artistic temperament which are the determinants of a relationship between two highly creative individuals.

It is usually hazardous to speak of the influence that two great writers have on one another, especially if they are contemporaries. Such influence is difficult to measure because parallels in artistic expression do not necessarily confirm the "invasion," as Cocteau put it, of one creative force by another. In the case of Gide and Cocteau, however, the situation is somewhat different. Since literary influence tends naturally

to flow downstream with time to irrigate succeeding generations of writers, it is not surprising to find that André Gide's impact on a poet twenty years his junior was considerable, and that Cocteau's influence on Gide was correspondingly limited. Moreover, Cocteau himself frequently acknowledged his debt to Gide, in both general and specific terms. Gide's influence on Cocteau was essentially confined to the literary sphere and may be traced through several phases: his effect on Cocteau through the latter's early reading of Gide's work; his influence on the course of Cocteau's literary career at critical junctures; and the total impact of his presence in Cocteau's creative life for nearly forty years. Gide's influence was not always positive and direct. What he said about Cocteau's work often made Cocteau react in an unexpected or reverse way. On these occasions, Gide and Cocteau seemed to play a game of wall and ball, with Gide serving as the wall.

Gide's influence on Cocteau began even before they had met. In his first letter to Gide, written in 1912, Cocteau reports he had taken almost all of Gide's works to Algiers with him:

J'arrive d'Alger si laide et si captivante où j'avais emporté votre œuvre entière. (J'excepte André Walter, difficile à cause des possesseurs prudents et "Amyntas" que mon libraire me procure au retour comme un baume à la molle plaie orientale.) [46]

(I have just arrived from Algiers, that ugly and captivating city, to which I had taken your complete works. (Except for *André Walter*, difficult to borrow because of its prudent owners, and *Amyntas*, which my book dealer has just procured for me on my return to serve as a balm for the soft Oriental wound.))

The letter indicates that Cocteau, like a generation of French youth, identified fervently with the spirit of adolescent revolt in Gide's *Nourritures terrestres*. The tone of the closing lines suggests that Cocteau, who as we know was ten years old when his father died, was disillusioned with his former heroes, such as De Max, Wilde, and Barrès, and was casting about for a fresh literary father image:

Une enfance hâtive et fiévreuse, la rencontre de guides néfastes, en somme un terrible détour . . . me pousse tout à coup en face de votre visage secret, noble et *pur*. Vous rencontrez un Nathaniel

[*sic*] qui se trouve être "enfant prodigue de naissance," mais votre lampe si elle éclaire les marches d'un perron et la grille d'une route est un tendre signal d'*appel*.

(A hasty and feverish childhood, an encounter with baneful guides, in sum a terrible detour . . . thrusts me suddenly before your inscrutable, noble, and *pure* face. You meet in me a Nathaniel who happens to be "a born prodigal son," but if your lamp lights a flight of steps or a fence along the road it is also a gentle, *beckoning* signal.)

Here Cocteau, implying Gide is the older brother and he the younger, gracefully transposes some of Gide's closing words from *Le Retour de l'enfant prodigue* as the older brother sends the younger off to adventure:

"Je tiens la lampe...
— Ah! donne-moi la main jusqu'à la porte.
— Prends garde aux marches du perron."

("I'll hold the lamp..."
"Ah! give me your hand as far as the door."
"Watch out for the porch steps.")

Cocteau's subsequent letters to Gide, as well as to his mother, to Jacques-Emile Blanche, and to others, testify to the fact that he continued during his formative years as a writer to read Gide's work with interest if not always with complete approval.

Perhaps of more lasting significance than the impact of Gide's writing, however, was Gide's function as a catalyst in the realignment of Cocteau's literary values shortly after their acquaintance began. The mixed criticism and encouragement that Cocteau received from Gide and Ghéon after the publication of *La Danse de Sophocle* had been followed by the friendly but blunt advice that Cocteau should simplify his handwriting. Cocteau acknowledges the value of this advice from Gide time and again in his work:

À cette époque ingrate j'aimerais écrire un livre de gratitudes. Entre autres avances de Gide, celle qu'il m'a faite en réformant mon écriture. Je m'étais par stupidité d'extrême jeunesse, fabriqué une écriture. Cette fausse écriture, révélatrice pour un graphologue, me faussait jusqu'a l'âme. Je bouclais d'une petite boucle la grande boucle de mes j majuscules. Un jour qu'il sortait de chez moi Gide,

à la porte, me dit en surmontant une gêne: "Je vous conseille de sim-
plifier vos j." Je commençais a comprendre quelle gloire piteuse
on fonde sur la jeunesse et sur le brio. L'opération de cette boucle
me sauva. Je m'efforçai de reprendre mon écriture véritable et,
l'écriture aidant, je retrouvai le naturel que j'avais perdu.[47]

(To that ungrateful era I would like to write a book of gratitude.
Among other advances from Gide, the one he made me by reforming
my handwriting. In the stupidity of extreme youth I had manu-
factured a handwriting for myself. This false writing, revealing to
a graphologist, made me false to the very soul. I looped a little loop
to the big loop of my capital J's. One day as he was leaving my house
Gide, in the doorway, said to me, overcoming his constraint: "I
advise you to simplify your J's." I was beginning to understand what
a sorry glory was built on youth and brio. The surgery on that loop
saved me. I forced myself to go back to my real handwriting and,
with the help of the handwriting, I recovered the naturalness I
had lost.)

In a comment that no doubt refers back to the Ghéon and
Gide criticisms, Cocteau again reminds Gide of his valuable
suggestion in an undated letter, probably written in the
summer of 1918: "P.S. Ai vu un Ghéon rasé inouï – très
jeune – oublierai-je qu'avec vous il m'a mis le nez dans mes
sottises?"[48] ("P.S. Have seen Ghéon clean-shaven—extraordinary—very youthful—will I ever forget that with you he
rubbed my nose in my own follies?") And again, in 1931:
"Vous m'avez ouvert les yeux sur mes 'J' – à la porte de la
rue d'Anjou avec Ghéon. Je n'oublie pas les bienfaits."[49]
("You opened my eyes to my "J's"—at the door in rue d'Anjou,
with Ghéon. I don't forget good deeds.")

In his collection of self-evaluating essays, *La Difficulté d'être*,
Cocteau further confirms Gide's favorable influence on him
at a critical stage in his development:

Sans nul doute cette ligne menait en ligne droite à l'Académie.
Un jour je rencontrai Gide. Il me fit honte de mon écriture. Je
l'enjolivais d'arabesques. Il est à l'origine d'un réveil en sursaut
dont je devais payer cher le prologue.[50]

(Without any doubt this line was leading straight to the Academy.
One day I ran into Gide. He made me ashamed of my writing. I was
prettifying it with arabesques. He is responsible for startling me
out of a sleep whose prologue cost me dear.)

Only a year before his death Cocteau pointed out once more:

Lorsque je subissais l'influence de la Comtesse [Anna de Noailles], mon écriture compliqua ses jambages. Gide me dit un jour: "Simplifiez votre écriture." Cette remarque m'a davantage rendu service, que bien des critiques d'ordres littéraires. Ensuite mon écriture devint fort illisible, mais vraie. On imagine mal l'importance d'un tel conseil que j'ai souvent donné à de jeunes poètes.[51]

(When I fell under the influence of the Countess [Anna de Noailles], the pothooks of my handwriting became more complicated. Gide said to me one day: "Simplify your writing." That remark was more valuable to me than many literary criticisms. After that my writing became highly illegible, but genuine. It is hard to conceive of the importance of such a piece of advice, which I have often given to young poets.)

The frequency with which Jean Cocteau repeats his gratitude to Gide on this score is a measure of the importance he attached to this advice. "Simplify your writing!" becomes an esthetic imperative in the evolution of Cocteau's work which perhaps even overshadows the importance of the more widely repeated dictum uttered by Diaghilev to Cocteau: "Astonish me!" From Gide's previous and later criticisms of Cocteau's work, as well as from Cocteau's subsequent statements, it is clear that Gide intended that Cocteau should simplify not only his handwriting but also his writing in the fullest sense.

A major reform of Cocteau's work followed his first meeting with Gide. In describing the significance of this meeting Cocteau places Gide with the two other men whom he regularly acknowledges as his masters, one a musician and the other a painter. "Avec certaines rencontres providentielles: Gide, Erik Satie, Picasso. . . ."[52] It should be noted, too, that Gide's name comes first in the succession of good influences. The period 1912 to 1913 was a turning point in Cocteau's career, as his own testimony makes clear. Up until then, Cocteau describes himself as:

chargé d'électricité, je veux dire de poésie informe, incapable de fabriquer un appareil de transmission, dérouté par les éloges suspects et de mauvais livres, je me retournais sur place comme un malade qui essaye de s'endormir. Je trainai, j'étouffai d'orgueil absurde, je m'écœurai, je souhaitai la mort. . . .

Je partis à ma recherche. (Voir Le Potomak.) Ma première rencontre fut Gide. Lui enviai-je assez une enfance protestante! Je le voyais, une bible à la main, patiner singulièrement sur l'eau russe. En belle anglaise il y écrivait son nom. Notre amitié me donna des forces.[53]

(charged with electricity, I mean by that unformed poetry, incapable of building a transmitter, confused by questionable praises and bad books, I tossed and turned like a sick man trying to get to sleep. I languished, I suffocated from absurd pride, I was sick at heart, I longed for death. . . .

I set out on my quest. (See *Le Potomak*.) My first encounter was with Gide. How much I envied him a Protestant childhood! I saw him, Bible in hand, skating oddly on Russian water. In flowing script he wrote his name there. Our friendship gave me strengths.)

Serious critics such as Ghéon and Gide, as well as his own common sense, had brought Cocteau to realize that he was on the wrong track with his first three volumes of verse — "trois niaiseries," as he later called them.[54] Looking back at that period, Cocteau assures his readers: "Ma première évasion importante . . . date de 1912."[55]

Describing his interior disorder at the time, Cocteau writes:

Depuis 1913, je vivais et je mourais de mystère en désordre. *Le Potomak* le prouve. À cette époque je m'exerçais au rêve. J'avais lu que le sucre faisait rêver; j'en mangeais des boîtes. Je me couchais tout habillé deux fois par jour. Je me bouchais les oreilles avec de la cire afin que mes rêves prissent racine plus loin que dans les bruits extérieurs.[56]

(After 1913 I lived and died from mystery in disorder. *Le Potomak* proves it. At that period I practiced the dream. I had read that sugar made one dream; I ate boxes of it. I went to bed fully dressed twice a day. I plugged my ears with wax so that my dreams might take root further away than in external noises.)

This behavior is reminiscent of the conduct of the young André Gide who describes in *Si le grain ne meurt* how he slept on a hard cot and leaped out of bed several times a night to kneel in prayer. It is perhaps revealing of their natures that on these occasions Gide was seeking spiritual grace, whereas Cocteau was in search of esthetic grace.

It was at this moment of crisis that Cocteau visited his friend Jacques-Emile Blanche at Offranville. Blanche later told

François Mauriac how Cocteau there came upon a copy of André Gide's *Paludes* and was overwhelmed by it.[57] Cocteau confirms this more than once:

> J'ai aussi vécu aux environs d'Offranville où habitait Jacques-Emile Blanche. Gide y venait souvent. . . . Ce fut là pour moi le point de départ du Potomak...[58]

> (I also lived near Offranville, where Jacques-Emile Blanche had a home. Gide came there often. . . . That place was for me the starting point of *Le Potomak*...)

> J'y terminai [Leysin] le *Potomak,* commencé à Offranville, chez J.-E. Blanche, sous l'œil de Gide.[59]

> (There [at Leysin] I finished *Le Potomak,* begun at Offranville, in J.-E. Blanche's house, under Gide's eye.)

Mme Catherine Gide's collection in Paris contains a postcard Cocteau sent to Gide from Offranville in October 1913, while he was working on *Le Potomak.* Though brief and elliptical, it shows that *Paludes* was on Cocteau's mind at that time. The card, ornamented by a fat Eugène cartoon, depicted a scene from Varengeville, where Cocteau said Gide had once discovered "une plante Eugène":

> Visites de 5 heures à la Sirène rue G. [recto] Très pour chasse à la panthère de Paludes. [verso]
> [Eugène drawing]

> (Five o'clock visits to the Sirène, rue de G. Very much like panther hunt of *Paludes.*
> [Eugène drawing])

Le Potomak represents a search for artistic identity, a creative crisis brought to a climax by Gide's influence. Conscious of his debt to Gide, and perhaps hopeful of eventual publication by the *NRF,* Cocteau kept Gide informed on *Le Potomak,* writing twice from Switzerland about his progress with the book. When the work was finished in 1914, Cocteau returned to Offranville determined, as he said, to end his self-torture or to be reborn. *Le Potomak* proved to have been a rite of passage for a poet in search of himself.

Unfortunately, World War I intervened before *Le Potomak* could be published. When it finally appeared in 1919, Gide

and Cocteau were already embroiled in their bitter exchange of open letters over *Le Coq et l'Arlequin.* Cocteau sent Gide a copy of *Le Potomak* tersely inscribed: "À Gide au dessus de la mêlée. Jean Cocteau." [60] Despite this meager *envoi,* Cocteau, in his open reply to Gide, acknowledged Gide's favorable influence on him. As Cocteau explained to Jacques-Emile Blanche in a letter of October 1919:

Oui certes! Persicaire comme son nom l'indique est une sorte de Persiflage et, du reste, avec mon souci de justice, j'ai mis dans ma réponse à Gide: *"Vous êtes de ceux m'ayant fait voir"...* rendant ainsi officielle son influence sur moi au moment que j'écrivais le *Potomak.*[61]

(Yes of course! Persicaire, as his name indicates, is a sort of Persiflage, and moreover, with my concern for justice, I put in my reply to Gide: "You are one of those who made me see"... thus making official his influence on me at the time I was writing *Le Potomak.*)

Cocteau's second draft of his open reply to Gide also included this statement, which was omitted from the version printed in *Ecrits Nouveaux* for June-July 1919: "Maintenant, permettez-moi, puisque vous me déconseillez la logique en me reconnaissant du lyrisme d'aimer sans réserves 'Paludes.' " [62] ("Now, permit me, since you advise me against logic but recognize my lyricism, to like *Paludes* without reservation.")

Even the strange names of Cocteau's characters: Persicaire, Argémone, Balsamine, and Pygamon, as he had explained to Blanche, have something in common with Gide's in *Paludes:* Tityre, Hermogène, Potamogéton.[63] Cocteau elaborates in *Le Potomak* itself:

J'étais dans une pharmacie normande avec un ami commun à Gide et à moi.
— Regardez sur les pots lui dis-je, on croirait des noms de Gide. C'est ainsi que je baptisai les personnages du Potomak.
Cette malice amicale et plusieurs autres ne doivent pas être prises en mauvaise part.[64]

(I was in a pharmacy in Normandy with a mutual friend of Gide's and mine.
"Look! on the jars," I said to him, "you'd think they were names of Gide's." That's how I baptized the characters in *Le Potomak.*
That friendly bit of malice and a few others must not be taken amiss.)

Cocteau's decision to caricature certain aspects of Gide's *Paludes* may have originated in his irritation at Gide's criticism of *La Danse de Sophocle* the year *Le Potomak* was begun. In his interview with André Fraigneau for the French Radio in 1951, Cocteau admitted also: "Il y a une espèce de paraphrase un peu moqueuse peut-être, des Nourritures terrestres." [65] Just as Gide's practice was seldom to put poison in his work without including the antidote, so Cocteau, as this passage illustrates, rarely sprinkles his work with vinegar without a smattering of honey to relieve the sting.

Despite superficial differences, *Paludes* and *Le Potomak* treat essentially the same subject: they satirize stagnation and passivity in the individual, and by extension, in society. Both stories are told as histories of the book the reader has in hand, and both Gide and Cocteau poke fun at their heroes, who, disturbed at their own passive attitudes, are unable to communicate their anxiety to even their closest friends. By means of anecdotes about Tityre (in *Paludes*) and the Eugènes (in *Le Potomak*) the two authors burlesque the dilemma of their protagonists.

Both *Paludes* and *Le Potomak* were completed in Switzerland when their respective authors were about twenty-five. Each book is an *œuvre à part* in the work of the two writers. The impact of Gide's unique work *Paludes* on Cocteau's writing of *Le Potomak* has been analyzed by the late Justin O'Brien, who points out the many lines of convergence between the two volumes. [66] "J'ai eu le Paludisme," Cocteau avers in *Le Potomak*. [67] Frederick Brown suggests that Gide was annoyed to see his own style caricatured by Cocteau in *Le Potomak*, [68] and such a thesis is supported by this passage in the draft of a letter from Cocteau to Gide in 1922:

Stupeur. Personne n'ignore que le Potomak affecte certaines de vos façons mais exprime des idées si peu vôtres qu'elles ne vous frappent en aucune sorte. [69]

(Dumbfounded. No one is unaware that *Le Potomak* affects some of your modes but expresses ideas so little yours that they do not impinge on you in any way.)

Although *Le Potomak* includes some persiflage at Gide's expense, it also contains a great deal of serious Cocteau.

Through his advice and example in 1912 and 1913, Gide

initiated a series of reactions in Cocteau which precipitated into action some of his pent-up creative powers. The result is that *Le Potomak* is rich in early expressions of material and themes that Jean Cocteau was to develop subsequently in one genre after another. All the material is present from which poets traditionally spin their magic webs: unrequited love, death, dreams, time, and art, as well as homosexuality, opium, mirrors, sleepwalking, and the antique notion of the poet as a medium. Perhaps no other single work contains so much of Jean Cocteau as this one which was his first book of prose. Distinguished by a disorder of riches, it may well be considered the headwaters of his later works.

In the "Prospectus" of 1916 which precedes *Le Potomak* but which is a part of it, Cocteau offers a thread to guide us through the esthetic labyrinth of such later works as *Le Sang d'un poète, Les Enfants terribles, Orphée,* and others which often initially perplexed, disturbed, and even outraged his public. That guiding thread is Cocteau's highly personal visual orientation. A commonplace crystal paperweight was the key that unlocked for Cocteau a whole world of beauty and mystery. Even the form and substance of the paperweight are meaningful as portents of Cocteau's esthetic evolution: the resolution of natural objects in the six-sided geometric solid is of Cubist inspiration, and crystal became the talisman of the Surrealists. "Comme ceux qui appliquent leur oreille contre un coquillage pour y entendre la mer, j'approchais mon œil de ce cube et j'y pensais découvrir Dieu." [70] ("Like people who place their ear against a shell to hear the sea in it, I brought my eye to this cube and there thought to discover God.")

This simple act sets in motion for Cocteau the dramatic consequence of the monomyth. According to this classic pattern, the mythical hero crosses the threshold to adventure by leaving the familiar world behind and entering the underground world. Here perilous encounters, supernatural helpers, and, if he is worthy, the boon, await him. [71]

The hero cycle, in which the hero crosses the threshold from one world to the other in search of enlightenment, is a recurring structure in many of Cocteau's works: from the waking world to the world of dream as in *Le Sang d'un poète,* from the living world to the world of the dead as in *Orphée,* from the world of light to the world of darkness as in *Œdipe,* from the world of innocence to the world of experience as in *Le*

Grand Ecart. In *Les Enfants terribles* the tragedy involves the inability of the protagonists to cross the threshold from the world of childhood to the world of maturity.

When Cocteau's eyes scanned the distorted images locked in the crystal cube, he, like a true hero of modern myth, crossed the threshold from the outer world to an inner world. From *Le Potomak* on, Cocteau's work largely records the visions of his inner eye gazing on the distorted images that slept within himself, that sleep within each of us. The autobiographical nature of many of Cocteau's works makes this especially clear. The themes of homosexuality in *Le Livre blanc,* of incest in *Œdipe Roi, La Machine infernale, Les Enfants terribles,* and *Les Parents terribles,* of transvestitism in *Le Fantôme de Marseille,* of impersonation in *Thomas l'Imposteur,* of lesbianism in *Le Grand Ecart,* and of addiction in *Opium,* are all reflections of such intimate visions.

In these visions the poet's eye often assumes a genital quality,[72] and the eye, capable of carnal knowledge, becomes a center of focus in Cocteau's work. Œdipus' blinding may thus be interpreted as an act of self-castration in punishment for his incest. In *Le Sang d'un poète* the poet turns voyeur as he places his eye at one keyhole after another. In *Orphée* Death has eyes painted on the outside of her eyelids; Jocasta in *La Machine infernale* speaks of her inner eye, which, in her nightmare, sees the fetus she carries; Picasso has an eye "qui vous fouille"; an ex-lover has an "œil qui vous inspecte" but which formerly "vous buvait." In *Le Livre blanc* Cocteau describes the erotic behavior seen on the far side of a one-way mirror. Mirrors, which exist only by virtue of eyes, become a familiar and significant part of Cocteau's iconography.

For Cocteau the eye does more than record surfaces; it passes beyond the external reality of the everyday, beyond "le visible," to penetrate the patina in search of a new (or an old) reality, "l'invisible." The motion picture camera ideally suited Cocteau in this respect since it was a powerful extension of his eyes, and enabled him to present his own visions in the graphic terms of a fresh genre.

Long before 1930, when he made his first film, many of Cocteau's productions were oriented along visual lines, as his four ballets, five plays, and four miscellaneous stage pieces prior to 1930 testify. It was apparent from the beginning that Cocteau was a person who thought in images. His visual im-

agination, widely recognized as one of Cocteau's distinctive qualities, stems from this fact. The artist Paul Klee said: "I have a think, and then I draw a line around it." Similarly Cocteau wrote in 1928: "J'écris, j'essaye de limiter exactement le profil d'une idée, d'un acte... Je cerne des fantômes, je trouve les contours du vide. Je dessine." [73] ("I write, I try to outline exactly the profile of an idea, of an act... I surround ghosts, I discover the contours of the void. I draw.") With their profuse illustrations, the letters of Jean Cocteau's childhood had anticipated this aspect of his adult correspondence. Drawings by the thousand flowed from his pen during his lifetime, and many were used to illustrate his own books. His style changed with time and ranged from the early posters commissioned by the Ballets Russes, the Eugènes of *Le Potomak,* and the cartoons he signed "Jim" in *Le Mot,* to the stylized sketches in *Opium,* his continuous-line drawings that were related to automatic writing, and highly skilled pen and ink caricatures of friends. Cocteau's graphic art also reflected the evolution of his spirit. In his late years he painted murals for a number of chapels and public buildings as well as for Santo Sospir, the Cap Ferrat home of his friend Mme Alec Weisweiller.

Drawing was a therapeutic necessity to Cocteau. As he explained to his mother in 1922, "Dessiner m'amuse beaucoup et me distrait d'écrire, ou de ne pas écrire." [74] ("Drawing amuses me a great deal and distracts me from writing, or from not writing.") In 1958, Cocteau acknowledged: "une chaise, de l'encre, du papier me fatiguent, alors que peindre des murs et travailler avec mes mains et mes jambes me défatigue" [75] ("a chair, some ink, paper, tire me, but to paint walls and to work with my hands and legs refreshes me").

Jean Cocteau has explained that drawing was his "violon d'Ingres," yet his drawings, like his plays, ballets, films, and the ensemble of his work, reflect his deep natural response to visual stimuli. "Ecrire pour moi c'est dessiner," he wrote in *Opium.* The visual response lies at the heart of his creative process and of his esthetic doctrine that an opaque patina often conceals the work of art in a commonplace. Despite his avowals that he is a poet who also draws, it may not be unreasonable to suggest that Cocteau was really an artist who was also a poet.

In his capacity as artist, poet, or both in one, Cocteau testified to the personal metamorphosis represented by *Le Potomak*

when he wrote: "Dès *Le Potomak*, je décidai de me construire une morale." [76] The act of writing *Le Potomak* was like molting to Cocteau. As he explained to Stravinsky in his 1914 post-dedication to this book: "Igor, je comptais t'offrir un livre et je t'offre ma vieille peau." [77]

Cocteau's *Lettre à Jacques Maritain* elaborated further to his spiritual counselor:

Depuis le Potomak on a vu mon souci de mettre en ordre un désordre fou, de mater du romantisme, de tuer le virtuose, de faire de ma faiblesse un jet comme ce jet d'eau avec lequel les Américains coupent le granit.[78]

(Since *Le Potomak* people have seen my concern for straightening up a wild disorder, for bringing romanticism to heel, for killing the virtuoso, for making out of my weakness a jet like that jet of water with which the Americans cut granite.)

After *Le Potomak* Cocteau intensified his efforts to purge his writing of the picturesque, the sentimental, the "poétique" which he felt the public mistook for "poésie." In a very real sense *Le Potomak* was, as Cocteau asserted, a preface to the rest of his work, a door the hand of André Gide had helped to open.[79]

Gide's advice to Cocteau occasionally found a place in his private letters to the author of *Le Potomak*, as well as in his open letters of 1919. Such advice usually had an effect on Cocteau, but it was not always the effect Gide anticipated. If Gide had helped make Cocteau aware of his need to change, it was a different matter to influence the direction of that change. A word or a phrase from Gide could drive the sensitive younger man in the opposite direction from the one Gide intended. This reverse tropism, Cocteau's leaning away from Gide, was noticed by Jean Marais, who was Cocteau's closest friend from 1937 to 1951, the year Gide died. According to Marais, Gide never forgave Cocteau "for becoming simply Jean Cocteau," instead of submissively following Gide's counsel about his literary career.[80] Paradoxically, in the act of turning away from Gide, Cocteau was also following the advice Gide dispensed to a generation in *Les Nourritures terrestres:* "Jette mon livre."

One of the suggestions Gide made to Cocteau in 1919 was to let himself go, to add more colors to his palette. Cocteau never forgot the advice, but did not always follow it, choosing

instead, despite outward indications of spontaneity and disorder, to establish certain disciplines for himself. It was almost as though Cocteau had read and preferred the very different advice Gide had given Marc Allégret only the year before:

L'art ne s'obtient que par contrainte, et jamais par laisser-aller. Il faut faire de ta vie entière une œuvre d'art — et d'abord soigner le détail.

Si tu veux vraiment tout ça, alors tu es vraiment mon camarade, mon ami. Pourquoi ne t'ai-je pas parlé ainsi plus tôt? Parce que je n'aime donner un conseil que quand je crois qu'il sera suivi.[81]

(Art is obtainable only through restraint, and never through letting one's self go. You must make your entire life a work of art — and first of all pay attention to detail.

If you truly want all that, then you are truly my comrade, my friend. Why haven't I spoken to you sooner this way? Because I don't like to give advice unless I think it will be followed.)

Gide, a few years later, privately reversed his earlier recommendation to Cocteau and commented savagely in his *Journal:* "Si Cocteau se laissait aller, il écrirait des vaudevilles." [82] In 1922, three years after Gide's original advice to let himself go, Cocteau wrote his critical friend: "J'ai fait aussi un petit roman en me laissant aller à tout ce qui vous semble ma direction naturelle." [83] ("I have also done a little novel while letting myself go entirely in what seems to you my natural direction.") This was also a protean reversal by Cocteau. At about the same time he wrote his mother: "Je lutte de toutes mes forces que je ne me laisse pas aller." [84] ("I struggle with all my strength not to let myself go.") The statement, coming from a homosexual and opium addict who was producing several of his most important works that year, has both moral and esthetic overtones.

As early as 1917, however, midway between his completion of *Le Potomak* and the receipt of Gide's open letter of 1919, Cocteau had written to his mother from Rome: "Sachant que ma vie est une fois pour toutes somnanbule, je ne me ronge plus et je me laisse aller. Que Dieu décide — ." [85] ("Knowing that my life is once and for all somnambulistic, I no longer torment myself and I let myself go. May God decide — .") During most of his creative life the question of letting himself go remained a serious moral and esthetic dilemma for Cocteau,

one closely related to the difficulty of being. Cocteau alternated between two convictions: first, the realization that he could be himself only by giving free play to his imagination in art and to his homosexual and narcotic appetites in personal behavior, and second, the recognition, reinforced by critical judgment like that of Rivière and Schlumberger, that discipline was essential to the creation of art and character. On April 7, 1923, after their quarrel over Cocteau's *Antigone* had subsided, Cocteau wrote Gide a letter which poses in facetious terms what was a disturbing problem for Cocteau:

Lettre irrespectueuse
Mon vieux
Tout dépend d'un rayon de soleil. Je suis entièrement pris par le printemps. "Nous" nous foutons du reste. "Nous" ne sommes pas des penseurs. Tout ce que nous avons dit sur la peinture la dernière fois au Louvre ne tient pas debout. Mais pourquoi essayer de mettre au point ces choses avec des mots? La moindre pochade vaut mieux. Je commence à peindre de pratique.
                    dompter [inserted at top of page 2]
Je vais refaire les culs, les cuisses, les arbres et les fleurs, – ou bien ce ne serait pas la peine d'avoir le nez si long. Tant pis! je ne peux plus écrire que comme ça. Pourquoi toujours se retenir? Il n'y a que le plaisir qui compte. J'ai besoin de me laisser aller et d'être comme je suis
                                                        Amicalement
                                                            Jean
         l'Imagination [placed at bottom of page 2] [86]

(Disrespectful letter
Old chap!
Everything hinges on a sunbeam. I am altogether taken over by springtime. "We" don't give a damn about the rest. "We" are not philosophers. All we said about painting at the Louvre last time is only half-baked. But why try to bring these things into focus with words? The most rapid sketch is worth more. I am beginning to paint from memory.
                    Subdue [inserted at top of page 2]
I am going to remake asses, thighs, trees, and flowers—or else there's no use having such a long nose. It can't be helped! I can't write any longer except like that. Why always hold one's self in check? Only pleasure matters. I need to let myself go and to be as
   I am
                                                 Affectionately,
                                                        Jean
         Imagination [placed at bottom of page 2])

The closing line of this letter: "J'ai besoin de me laisser aller et d'être comme je suis," is balanced out by the two words Cocteau places alone at the top and bottom of the second page: "dompter" and "l'Imagination."

In his *Lettre aux Américains,* which was published in 1949, Cocteau included a statement that echoed the Schlumberger-Rivière literary doctrine of self-restraint, rather than Gide's advice to let one's self go:

Plus‚un homme est doué, plus il se surmonte, plus il lutte contre ce don qui prédispose son encre à couler trop vite, plus il s'efforce de la dompter et de la contenir.[87]

(The more gifted a man is, the more he transcends himself, the more he struggles against this gift which predisposes his ink to flow too freely, the more he tries to dominate and contain it.)

In *Le Cordon ombilical,* published in 1962, Jean Cocteau comments on the problem for him of listening to outside voices like Gide's, as well as to that inner voice which dictates to the poet who is both sleepwalker and medium:

Seulement je songe souvent au reproche que Gide me faisait de ne point me *laisser aller* et sans doute suis-je tenté par une école buissonnière, de m'évader momentanément des méthodes rigoureuses que m'impose une obéissance passive à un maître dont je ne suis que le serviteur.[88]

(Only I often think of Gide's reproach that I never *let myself go,* and no doubt I am tempted to run off and play truant, to break myself loose momentarily from the rigorous methods imposed on me by a passive obedience to a master for whom I am only the servant.)

In the same book Cocteau refers to a specific example of his resistance to Gide's influence:

Cependant, certaine désobéissance m'autorisait à user de sources réalistes comme dans *Le Grand Ecart* où Gide — incapable d'admettre que je ne fusse pas aveuglément de sa religion — voyait dans Madeleine Carlier un travesti pareil à celui d'Albertine de Proust et approuvait sans réserve *Thomas l'Imposteur* parce qu'il estimait mon héros appartenir à son mythe.[89]

(However, a certain disobedience allowed me to use some realist sources, as in *Le Grand Ecart* where Gide—unable to admit that I

was not blindly of his persuasion — saw in Madeleine Carlier a transvestite similar to that of Albertine in Proust and approved *Thomas l'Imposteur* unreservedly because he considered my hero to belong to his myth.)

Part of Cocteau's alternating resistance to Gide's literary influence stems from his disillusionment with writers such as Oscar Wilde who had previously left their mark on Cocteau's work. "L'influence d'un écrivain risque de nous donner des tics," he cautioned.[90] It was only long after he was firmly established in the literary world that Cocteau felt secure enough to affirm: "Je suis à l'âge où je ne crains plus d'être envahi par plus fort que moi." [91] ("I am at the age where I no longer fear being invaded by something stronger than I.")

Taking up the theme of "laisser aller" in a less literary and more literal context, Cocteau ascribes his writing of two books specifically to Gide's influence. The first was his *Portraits-Souvenir,* in which Cocteau revisits many scenes from his childhood.

C'est à Gide que je dois ces Portraits-Souvenir si tant est qu'ils méritent de vivre. Gide me reprochait (à propos d'une note du *Coq et l'Arlequin* sur le premier jazz) de ne jamais me laisser aller, de ne jamais profiter d'une détente.[92]

(It is to Gide that I owe these *Portraits-Souvenir,* if indeed they deserve to live. Gide reproached me (concerning a note in *Le Coq et l'Arlequin* about the first jazz) for never letting myself go, for never taking advantage of an unwinding.)

The second book attributed by Cocteau to Gide's influence was the journal of Cocteau's trip around the world in eighty days, *Mon Premier Voyage.* Cocteau's formal dedication of this work to Gide had read:

Mon cher André,
    Un jour vous m'avez reproché d'être trop tendu, de ne pas me laisser aller et vous citiez comme exemple de mon laisser-aller une note du *Coq et l'Arlequin* où je décrivais le premier jazz band.
    Vous nous avez aussi donné l'exemple du voyage.
    Après ces notes de voyages que je vous offre d'un cœur fidèle, le manque de laisser-aller est un reproche que vous ne pourrez plus me faire.

                                                                    J.C.[93]

(My dear André

One day you reproached me for being too taut, for not letting myself go, and you cited as an example of my loosening up a note from *Le Coq et l'Arlequin* where I described the first jazz band.

You have also given us the example of travel.

After these travel notes which I present to you from a faithful heart, you can no longer reproach me for lack of abandon.

J.C.)

A recurring theme in a number of letters between the two writers revolved around Gide's well-known dislike of prefaces, especially those which attempted to explain an author's work. His efforts over many years to enjoin Cocteau from writing the prefaces to which he was addicted are revealed as early as Gide's first open letter of 1919. Cocteau, if not compliant, was sensitive to Gide's point of view in the matter. In 1924 he wrote Gide:

> Le Calme
> Villefranche-sur-Mer
> Août 1924

Mon cher Gide,

D'abord votre Fait Divers est une merveille. Je savais que ma préface vous mettrait de mauvaise humeur — C'est pourquoi elle commence lâchement par un sourire à votre adresse. Duvernois la voulait pour amplifier le texte des "Œuvres Libres" — Ensuite mes amis ont insisté auprès de moi afin qu'elle figure en tête du livre N.R.F.

Ici j'essaye de vivre, ou plutôt j'essaye d'apprendre à vivre à la mort que je porte en moi — c'est atroce. Votre tendresse me réconforte. Souvent votre réserve me peinait. Mais votre bonté envers Thomas, Roméo, les Mariés me donne courage. Comment va Marc? Dites-lui de m'écrire 2 lignes.

Je vous embrasse du fond du cœur.

> Jean [94]

> Le Calme
> Villefranche-sur-Mer
> August 1924

(My dear Gide,

First of all, your "Faits divers" is a wonder. I knew my preface would put you in a bad humor—that's why it begins in a cowardly way with a smile in your direction. Duvernois wanted it to amplify the text of *Œuvres libres*. Afterwards my friends insisted to me that it should appear at the front of the *NRF* book.

Here I am trying to live, or rather I am trying to teach the death that I carry in me how to live — it's terrible. Your tenderness comforts me. Your reserve often pained me. But your goodness toward *Thomas* [*l'Imposteur*], *Roméo* [*et Juliette*], *Les Mariés* [*de la Tour Eiffel*], give me courage. How is Marc? Tell him to drop me a line. I embrace you from the bottom of my heart.

Jean)

The following year Cocteau's *Oiseleur* included this comment:

Gide m'en veut pour mes préfaces et mes notes. Après la publication des *Mariés* il m'écrivit: *Je peste contre votre préface qui attache si court cette chose ailée qui ne demande qu'à voler.* Au fond je l'approuve et je retire des volumes d'ensemble les prospectus dont j'aime à revêtir mes produits lorsque je les offre un par un.[95]

(Gide hates me for my prefaces and my notes. After the publication of *Les Mariés* [*de la Tour Eiffel*] he wrote me: *I storm against your preface which so tightly chains up that winged thing which asks only to fly.* Basically I approve of his view, and I am withdrawing from my collected works the prospectuses with which I like to dress my products when I present them one by one.)

In 1928 Gide wrote one of his celebrated "lettres non-envoyées" to Cocteau expressing peevish disapproval of the attempts by young authors to defend or explain their works. Part of the letter, which Gide claimed not to have sent Cocteau, was nevertheless published the following year in the *NRF*, thus becoming in effect Gide's third open letter to Cocteau in that review:

LETTRE À J.C.
(non-envoyée)

. . . . 1928

Je tiens pour particulièrement maladroites, je vous l'avoue, ces protestations que font entendre certains auteurs (les plus jeunes sont les plus forcenés), chaque fois qu'ils soupçonnent le public ou les critiques de se méprendre sur les intentions de leur dernière œuvre: "Ce n'est pas cela qu'ils ont voulu dire. On voit ici un sens caché; il n'y en a pas. Par contre, il y en avait un là où on n'a pas su le voir. On a pris ceci pour un jeu: c'était très sérieux au contraire. L'on rit, quand il aurait fallu pleurer; et l'on pleure où l'on devait rire..." Mais, parbleu! cher poète, laissez donc les gens se tromper. Si votre œuvre vaut quelque chose, vos lecteurs de demain se chargeront suffisamment de protester contre des mésinterprétations d'au-

jourd'hui. Comment ne comprenez-vous pas que vous occuperez bientôt l'attention d'autant plus qu'on devra vous redécouvrir. Dans les plus belles œuvres du passé, pensez-vous que ce que nous admirons aujourd'hui soit toujours ce que les contemporains de cette œuvre y voyaient? Laissez donc aux journalistes, que demain l'on ne lira plus, l'urgent besoin d'être intégralement compris aussitôt, et félicitez-vous de donner le change, — *du moment que c'est malgré vous*, que vous n'en pouvez mais, et n'avez rien fait pour cela, que de vous offrir aux incompréhensions, le plus simplement, le plus naturellement et sincèrement qu'il se peut. Dans un monde où chacun se grime, c'est le visage nu qui paraît fardé.[96]

(LETTER TO J.C.
(not sent)

. . . . 1928

I find particularly clumsy, I must confess, those protestations raised by certain authors (the youngest are the most frantic) each time they suspect the public or the critics of mistaking the intentions of their latest work: "That's not what they wished to say. One sees here a hidden meaning; there is none. On the contrary, there was one there which passed unnoticed. This was taken for a game; whereas it was very serious. People laugh when they should have cried; and they cry where they were meant to laugh..." But, for heaven's sake! dear poet, let people make their own mistakes. If your work is worth something, tomorrow's readers will undertake well enough to protest against today's misinterpretations. How can you not understand that the more you have to be rediscovered, the sooner you will receive attention. Do you think that what we admire today in the finest works of the past is always what the contemporaries of those works used to see in them? Then leave to journalists, who will not be read tomorrow, the urgent need to be totally understood at once, and congratulate yourself on putting your contemporaries off the scent—*from the moment that it is in spite of yourself* that you are helpless, and have done nothing to this end, except to leave yourself open to misunderstandings the most simply, the most naturally and sincerely as possible. In a world where everyone makes himself up it is the naked face that seems made up.)

A series of letters exchanged by the two writers in 1931 reflects Gide's continued attempts to deflect Cocteau from the hazards of prefaces. In January of that year he composed a letter to Cocteau on three separate postcards in which his anti-preface dogma was reiterated but lightened by an amusing anecdote:

18 janvier [1931]

Mon cher Jean

J'aime à trouver, au seuil de votre livre [*Opium*], le sourire rétracté de notre séquestrée — *Blanche* de son vrai nom; c'est pour rompre les chiens que je l'appelle (tout au contraire) *Mélanie;* mais vous avez su retrouver par delà l'obscurité de ce nouveau nom sa lumière. Je vous sais gré tout amicalement des quelques passages (d'Opium), où (j'ai joie à voir) mon souvenir affleurer; mais puisque vous dites vous être trouvé bien de ce conseil (que j'avais oublié) au sujet de votre écriture, où vous avez senti que je prenais *votre* parti contre vous, vais-je oser aujourd'hui vous dire combien je déplore de vous voir continuer à faire si grand état de l'écho de [97] votre œuvre, ou de son reflet, dans ce monstre informe et vain qu'est le public: — de vous voir dépenser tant de talent à rectifier, expliquer, etc., ce qui n'aurait besoin d'être rectifié et défendu qu'en cas d'*insuffisance.* Seriez-vous modeste!? pour reconnaître si peu que vos œuvres se moquent d'un défenseur, ce défenseur fût-il vous même. Et même il me paraît que ce souci, cette non-acceptation du *habent sua fata libelli* et de l'enseignement secret du *sort* se rattache fort mal à votre éthique, la contredit. Ceci soit dit pour amener une petite histoire [98] que peut-être vous connaissez déjà, un des J. H. Rosny, je ne sais lequel, (ils sont tant!) mettons: l'ainé, — exaspéré par le nombre des fautes d'impression qui émaillaient son dernier livre (il y a longtemps) écrivit un article vengeur qu'il intitula *Mes Coquilles.* Cela parut en "premier Paris," dans... l'Intran, je crois. Mais le sort s'obstina, et, dans le titre même, fit tomber une lettre. On imagine la tête de Rosny, ouvrant le journal et lisant, en gros caractères, à côté de son nom:

Mes Couilles.

Il faut céder... mutuellement

Bien affectueusement
André Gide [99]

January 18, [1931]

(My dear Jean,

I like finding, at the threshold of your book [*Opium*] the retracted smile of our sequestered friend — *Blanche* to use his real name; so as to call off the hounds, I call him, quite the contrary, *Mélanie.* But you knew how to rediscover his light from beyond the obscurity of this new name. I am thankful to you in a friendly way for the several passages in *Opium* where (I have the joy of seeing) my memory cropping up; but since you say you find yourself to be better off as a result of this advice (which I had forgotten) about your handwriting, wherein you felt I was taking *your* side against you, I will venture today to tell you how much I deplore seeing you continue to have such a high opinion of the echo of your work, or of its reflection, in the public, this shapeless and vain monster: — to see you expend so much talent in rectifying, explaining, etc., that which shouldn't need to be

rectified and defended except in case of *inadequacy*. Are you trying to be modest!? by recognizing so slightly that your works scoff at any defender, even if he were yourself. And it even seems to me that this concern, this nonacceptance of the idea that *books have their own destiny,* and of the secret teaching of *fate,* fits in poorly with your ethic, contradicts it. Let this be said to lead into a little story that perhaps you already know: one of the J. H. Rosnys—I don't know which one (there are so many!), let's say the eldest—exasperated by the number of printing errors that marred his last book (a long time ago), wrote a vengeful article entitled *Mes Coquilles.* This appeared as the lead article of a Paris paper, in the *Intran[sigeant],* I believe. But fate persisted, and knocked out a letter in the title itself. You can imagine Rosny's face as he opened the paper and read, in large type, next to his name:

My Balls.

We have to give in... reciprocally.

Very affectionately,

André Gide)

Cocteau's reply the following month must have amazed Gide by its opening avowal that Cocteau never gave a thought to his public. At the same time Gide probably read with mixed feelings Cocteau's phrase, "J'écris pour être relu — jugé en appel," which parallels that of Gide in his *Journal des Faux-Monnayeurs* "Depuis longtemps, je ne prétends gagner mon procès qu'en appel. Je n'écris que pour être relu." [100] Cocteau's letter may also have annoyed him by the ironic allusion to Gide's "lettre non-envoyée" of 1928. Nevertheless the closing lines pay tribute to the effects of Gide's literary discipline on Cocteau:

Grand Hôtel
Toulon, Var.
[3 Février 1931]

Très cher André,

Je suppose que vous avez raison et je me surveillerai — Je vous affirme que je ne pense jamais au public. Non lorsque je ne suis pas poussé par une force qui me domine et qui me dicte, j'avoue aimer bien ce bavardage avec des amis inconnus, avec l'avenir.

Bref laisser des livres comme je souhaite en découvrir des poètes qui m'émeuvent.

Au reste, je ne fais que suivre votre admirable et très cher exemple (peuplier — j'écris pour être relu — jugé en appel — lettres non envoyées — préfaces entre autres la dernière de l'Immoraliste que je dévorais ce matin et que j'ai acheté en même temps que le 14ᵉ volume de Rocambole). Superbe. Fantômas et tout sortant de là.

Ne croyez pas à une lutte! à une riposte. J'approuve de tout mon

cœur ces mises au point – ce tripotage d'une lorgnette jusqu'à ce
que les contours se précisent – c'est, en marge de votre œuvre, la
suite de cette leçon de dessin dont vous parlez et que la France
donne au monde. J'hésite entre deux merveilles: Le Kodak de la
Séquestrée – la carte Joffre-Foch – et la comtesse de Noailles – et
Valéry –

Avez-vous vu le portrait de la comtesse Ananas sur l'Illustration,
en maréchal, en colombe poignardée, avec une satisfaction de pleine
lune – avec sur la figure un "J'y suis" qui sonne comme l'accord
parfait. Je vous embrasse, cher André – ne me grondez plus, ou
plutôt si, grondez-moi. Je vous écoute et j'en tire mes seules disciplines. – Je préparais l'édition définitive du Mystère Laïc. Après
votre lettre j'ai déchiré 8 feuilles – Délice des coupes sombres!
des crayons bleus!

Votre Jean [101]

Grand Hôtel
Toulon, Var
[February 3, 1931]

(Very dear André,

I suppose you are right and I will watch myself. But I assure you I
never think about the public. No – when I am not pushed by a power
which dominates me and gives me orders, I confess I like very much
this chatting with unknown friends, with the future.

In short, to leave behind me books like those I wish to discover by
the poets who move me.

Besides, I only follow your admirable and very beloved example
(a poplar – I write to be reread – judged on appeal – unsent letters
– prefaces, among others the last one for *L'Immoraliste,* which I
devoured this morning and which I bought at the same time as the
fourteenth volume of [Ponson du Terrail's] *Rocambole*). Superb.
Fantômas and everything coming from there.

Don't expect a fight, a retort. I approve with all my heart of this
focusing – this fussing with the lens until the outlines are sharp – it
is, in the margin of your work, the sequel to that drawing lesson you
speak of and which France gives to the world. I hesitate between two
marvels: the Kodak of *La Séquestrée [de Poitiers]* – the Joffre-Foch
map – and the Comtesse de Noailles – and Valéry –

Have you seen the portrait of the Comtesse Ananas on the cover
of *L'Illustration,* with the air of a marshal, a stabbed dove, with a
satisfied look of the full moon – and on her face an "I am there"
that rings like perfect harmony. I embrace you, dear André – don't
scold me any more, or rather yes, do scold me. I listen to you, and I
draw my only disciplines from that. I was preparing the definitive
edition of *Le Mystère laïc.* After your letter I tore up eight pages –
Delight of thinning out! of blue pencils!

Your Jean)

In his interview with Colin-Simard, published in 1952, Cocteau also refers to Gide's reaction to his preface for *Les Mariés de la Tour Eiffel:*

Il faut compter parmi les crises d'élan de Gide vers moi: *Les Mariés de la Tour Eiffel* dont il me reprochait la préface. Pourquoi, me disait-il, attachez-vous par la patte une chose ailée? [102]

(One must count among the bursts of Gide's enthusiasm toward me: *Les Mariés de la Tour Eiffel,* for whose preface he upbraided me. Why, he said to me, do you fasten a winged thing by the foot?)

Cocteau recognized the merit of Gide's view, but could not bring himself to accept it entirely. In the preface to the second volume of his *Poésie critique* Cocteau wrote in 1960:

Je sais que les préfaces alourdissent les livres et attachent, comme le disait Gide, ce qui ne demande qu'à s'envoler. Seulement, arrive le jour où plus n'est besoin de lire les préfaces, où l'œuvre entraîne la préface avec elle et la lâche en plein vol. Jusque-là, j'estime qu'une œuvre a encore besoin de son guide, malgré une tendance têtue à le perdre. [103]

(I know that prefaces weigh down books and fetter, as Gide said, a thing which only asks to fly away. But the day will come when it's no longer necessary to read prefaces, when the work carries the preface along with it and releases it in full flight. Until then, I believe a work still needs its guide, despite a headstrong tendency to lose him.)

It is apparent that Gide's influence made itself felt on Cocteau's work intermittently, both in general and in specific ways, and in positive and negative terms, throughout their long acquaintance. Even their periodic quarrels had a formative effect on Cocteau:

Mes relations avec André Gide furent d'un bout à l'autre un cache-cache de réconciliations, de disputes, de lettres ouvertes, de griefs, . . . Toutes ces petites guerres, escarmouches, duels, et tribunaux, m'ont mieux formé qu'une promenade pacifique. [104]

(My relations with Gide were from beginning to end a hide-and-seek of reconciliations, of disputes, of open letters, of grievances. . . . All these little wars, skirmishes, duels, and tribunals schooled me better than a peaceful promenade.)

In a remark that indicates the intellectual authority that Gide represented for Cocteau and sums up one phase of their long

relationship, Cocteau exclaimed to Léon Pierre-Quint in 1927: "Gide, quel merveilleux professeur!" And in the same interview Cocteau added: "J'ai pour Gide beaucoup de gratitude. J'avais vingt ans et j'en étais à Madame de Noailles, aux grandes portes; il m'a fait connaître la porte étroite." [105] ("I am very grateful to Gide. I was twenty years old and I had arrived at Madame de Noailles, at the great doors; he taught me to know the narrow gate.")

In view of the foregoing review of some of the facts, it is somewhat misleading to read Cocteau's disavowal of influence by Gide. While acknowledging that he had learned much from Gide, Cocteau made this statement to Colin-Simard the year after Gide's death:

Gide ne pouvait m'apprendre quelque chose que par contraste. Ce qu'il m'a appris est immense. Il m'a appris qu'il ne fallait tirer profit de rien, et qu'au lieu de dire à la jeunesse "Quitte ta maison et ta famille," il fallait lui dire "Reste. Sauve-toi à toutes jambes au fond de toi-même."

Gide ne pouvait avoir sur moi influence d'aucune sorte. C'est pourquoi je ne lui en ai jamais voulu de rien.

L'influence étant l'invasion d'une personnalité par une autre personnalité plus forte que la sienne, ceux qui la subissent la considèrent vite comme une maladie, et cherchent n'importe quel moyen de s'en guérir.

André Gide ne pouvait rien prendre dans mes magasins, et je ne pouvais rien prendre dans sa boutique. C'est la raison profonde de notre perpétuelle discorde et de nos excellents rapports. Nous ne vendions pas les mêmes marchandises. [106]

(Gide could only teach me something by contrast. What he taught me is enormous. He taught me that you must not benefit from anything, and that instead of saying to young people "Leave your home and your family," you should say to them "Stay. Take off at full speed into the depths of yourself."

Gide couldn't have any sort of influence on me. That's why I never bore him ill will for anything.

Influence being the invasion of one personality by another personality stronger than one's own, people who experience it quickly take it to be a sickness and look for any possible means of curing themselves.

André Gide couldn't find anything to interest him in my stores, and I couldn't find anything in his boutique. That is the underlying reason for our constant discord and for our excellent relations. We were not selling the same products.)

From a quantitative point of view alone, the extent of André Gide's presence in Jean Cocteau's work is impressive. More than one hundred passages which refer to Gide, several many pages in length, are dispersed among twenty of Cocteau's major critical essays, journals, and prefaces.

In addition to the numerous allusions to Gide and his work that Cocteau published, there were others that he deleted from a given work before publication. One such deletion, in which Cocteau quotes Gide's reply in *Littérature* to a criticism of *La Symphonie pastorale* by Louis Aragon, remains to be seen on the back of page 45 of the manuscript of *Le Secret professionnel*. This manuscript has been deposited in the Bibliothèque de l'Arsenal, Paris, by its owner, Gérard Magistry:

André Gide aimait à dire que s'il couvre chaque fois sa pensée d'un losange de couleur inattendue, ce n'est pas comme on pourrait croire, afin d'atteindre plusieurs publics, mais pour se faire quelques vrais amis qui sachent reconnaître l'unité sous le maillot d'arlequin. C'est une excellente méthode. Mais pourrons-nous y croire depuis certaine lettre de Gide publiée par la revue néo-dadaïste Littérature: Vous me dites que vous n'aimez pas la seconde partie de la Symp. Past. − notez que Gide écrit Sympho. Pastoral − Sy. Past. par désinvolture "moderne" − serait-ce donc que vous aimez la première. J'espère que non. Ce ne serait pas la peine d'avoir écrit *Les Caves* etc. . . .

(André Gide liked to say that if he always covers his thought with a lozenge of unexpected color, it is not, as one might think, in order to reach several publics, but to win some genuine friends who might know how to recognize the unity beneath the harlequin's maillot. It's an excellent method. But can we believe in it after a certain letter from Gide published by the neo-dadaïst review *Littérature:* You tell me you do not like the second part of the *Symp.[honie] Past.[orale]*−note that Gide writes Sympho. Pastoral−Sy. Past. from "modern" breeziness−would it mean then that you like the first? I hope not. It would not have been worth the trouble to write *Les Caves* etc. . . .)

Cocteau's comments on Gide and his work span the entire period of the authors' acquaintance, and they reflect the ups and downs of a relationship which, on the surface, was as changeable as the Paris weather. Cocteau's detractors do both him and Gide a disservice in dismissing his extended, if fragmented, study of Gide as mere name-dropping or flattery on Cocteau's part.

From a qualitative viewpoint, Cocteau's remarks about Gide range from the worshipful to the vindictive. "On ne peut se permettre de juger André Gide en ligne droite," he began his homage to Gide in the *NRF* for November 1951. In keeping with his nature he has more positive, as well as more uncomplimentary, things to say about Gide than Gide has about him. Gide's comments about Cocteau are almost unrelievedly critical. The judgments of both in respect to the other were often colored by personal motives and by the disputes that flared up periodically between them.

Gide brings Cocteau into his work on a number of occasions. It is now well known that the character of Count Robert de Passavant in *Les Faux-Monnayeurs* was inspired in large part by Jean Cocteau.[107]

George Painter also suggests that the character of Icarus in Gide's *Thésée* was inspired in part by the person of Jean Cocteau, although this is a more speculative connection.[108]

Those references by Gide which best illuminate his view of his relationship to Cocteau are the fourteen passages of the *Journal,* the first dated August 20, 1914, and the last April 11, 1948, in which Cocteau is discussed. Cocteau's name appears only incidentally in the extensions of Gide's *Journal:* the *Voyage au Congo,*[109] and *Le Retour du Tchad.*[110] Several of Gide's *Journal* passages concerning Cocteau have been mentioned earlier in this chapter. The balance of Gide's critical comments on Jean Cocteau and his work, comments which found public expression in the *Journal,* are almost uniformly severe. They are considered in the following chapter in conjunction with some of Gide's private judgments on Cocteau, as well as Cocteau's evaluations of Gide and his work.

Jugements sans Appel

The letters exchanged between Cocteau and Gide, their critical works and journals, and their private conversations, all contain judgments about each other. These evaluations are made on both the personal and the professional level, and are often colored by the time and circumstances of their utterance. Personal and professional criticisms are frequently so closely related as to be indistinguishable, and if one of the intermittent quarrels between the two men was under way, it was apt to be reflected in their opinions of the moment. Such opinions, when dictated by personal motives rather than by objective critical appraisal, cannot be considered as final on either side, and at most are only a part of the total evaluation of one writer by the other. Yet these same opinions, once recorded publicly, on occasion provoked further controversy between the two writers. Although Gide and Cocteau restored harmonious personal relations at the end of Gide's life, there is little evidence that their professional appraisal of each other's work underwent significant changes. The original astringent attitudes that grew out of the *Danse de Sophocle,* the *Coq et l'Arlequin,* and the *NRF* episodes had already been through their major modifications by 1923. From then on the two writers' judgments of each other were usually echoes or amplifications of judgments each had previously voiced.

In his first letter to André Gide, in 1912, Jean Cocteau had praised Gide's work in these words:

L'enthousiasme est, il me semble, une des plus hautes formes de l'orgueil. Plus il est fort, plus il prouve le prix instinctif que nous attachons à notre jugement. De là ma gêne.[1]

(Enthusiasm, it seems to me, is one of the highest forms of pride. The stronger it is, the more it proves what instinctive price we set on our judgment. Hence my embarrassment.)

Epigrammatic and elliptical in style from the start, it was also typical of Cocteau that he should assume a deferential tone colored by pride when he addressed a new master. His initial youthful enthusiasm for Gide as a person was soon dashed by Gide's aloofness. On the other hand, Cocteau's anxious solicitations of Gide's judgments of his writings, as for *La Danse de Sophocle*, "Vous détestez donc ce livre jusqu'au silence?"[2] continued for many years.

Shortly after the outbreak of World War I, Cocteau visited his friend Count Louis Gautier-Vignal. The next day he was able to write Gide, with the zeal of a missionary spreading Gide's gospel, that he had introduced Gautier-Vignal to *Les Nourritures terrestres*:

Mon cher Gide,

Hier soir las de ne risquer rien, de mobiliser les Russes et de juger Joffre — j'ai lu les Nourritures à mon hôte qui avait la chance de ne les pas encore connaître. Comme on était loin de la guerre, dans ce climat de la poésie où nul shrapnel ne saurait atteindre!

Je vous admire et je v[ou]s embrasse.

Jean[3]

(My dear Gide,

Last evening, bored at risking nothing, at mobilizing the Russians and at judging Joffre — I read *Les Nourritures* to my host, who was lucky enough not to know them yet. How far away we were from the war, in that atmosphere of poetry which no shrapnel could reach!

I admire you and embrace you.

Jean)

In spite of Cocteau's blandishments, however, Gide had already developed reservations about Cocteau's pattern of expression. Three months after receiving Cocteau's letter, he prefaced an entry in his *Journal* which repeated one of Cocteau's war anecdotes: "Le récit de Jean Cocteau, où, comme dans tous ses récits, l'on entrevoit malaisément le point de départ réel sous l'énorme exagération poétique."[4]

("Jean Cocteau's story, in which, as in everything else he tells, it is hard to distinguish the original germ of reality under the vast poetical exaggeration.") If Gide felt Cocteau was abandoning realism to indulge in excessive poetic license, Cocteau felt Gide was naïve and behind the times. In 1917, Cocteau wrote his mother: "Je me félicite d'avoir été à 'l'école' jeune et de connaître les embûches où tombent naïvement des Claudel ou des Gide, faute d'expérience." [5] ("I congratulate myself on having gone to 'school' young and on being familiar with the ambushes into which the Claudels or Gides naïvely fall for lack of experience.")

Cocteau made a similar point later in a letter to Jacques-Emile Blanche: "J'ai lu cet étrange No. de la N.R.F. qu'ils auraient dû imprimer en Braille puisque tout le monde y est aveugle, à commencer par les jeunes filles de Claudel et de Gide." [6] ("I read that strange issue of the *NRF*, which they should have printed in Braille since everybody there is blind, starting with the young girls of Claudel and Gide.")

Gide's misgivings about Cocteau's literary orientation surface again in his second *Journal* entry about Cocteau in April of 1918. After repeating a Cocteau anecdote about his friend Misia Edwards, Gide adds:

Rien ne m'est plus étranger que ce souci de modernisme qu'on sent incliner toutes les pensées et toutes les résolutions de Cocteau. Je ne prétends point qu'il ait tort de croire que l'art ne respire qu'en sa plus nouvelle apparence. Mais, tout de même, cela seul m'importe que n'emportera pas avec elle une génération. Je ne cherche pas à être de mon époque; je cherche à déborder mon époque. [7]

(Nothing is more foreign to me than this concern for modernism which one feels influencing every thought and every decision of Cocteau. I do not claim that he is wrong to believe that art breathes freely only in its newest manifestation. But, all the same, the only thing that matters to me is what a generation will not carry away with it. I do not seek to be of my epoch; I seek to overflow my epoch.)

Already the fissure was widening between the two writers. They were to become increasingly concerned with their competitive roles as *chefs de file* of the young public.

That same summer of 1918 Cocteau read Gide's translation of Joseph Conrad's *Typhoon*. His reactions were reported in his letter of August 24 to Gide:

Hôtel Brice, Le Piquey,
par Arès, Gironde
24 Août 1918

Mon très cher Gide,

Je viens de lire votre Typhon sur ma côte indigène où je me regarde noircir avec un intérêt de potier. C'est un beau conte, mais je suppose que votre style lui ajoute un relief spécial — Je regrette que vous ne nous donniez pas une grosse pièce — Lord Jim par exemple. Je me console en pensant que ce travail empiéterait sur votre œuvre dont la suite m'intrigue et me laisse impatient.

Ecrivez-vous? Les autres N[ourritures] Terrestres? — et votre poulain sauvage? Que fait-il de ses fortes attaches et de "ses cheveux mal en ordre?" — J'aimerais le revoir, vous revoir, enrichir de plus en plus notre amitié qui me console aux heures tristes.

Je vous embrasse cher Gide. Savez-vous quelque chose de "Blanche au couvent"

Jean.

craint-il encore les mousquetaires en casque à pointe? [8]

Hôtel Brice, Le Piquey,
par Arès, Gironde
August 24, 1918

(My very dear Gide,

I have just been reading your *Typhoon* on my primitive beach where I watch myself turn black with the fascination of a pot-maker. It is a fine tale, but I suspect your style adds a special relief to it. I find it a pity that you do not give us a big chunk—*Lord Jim,* for example. I find consolation in thinking that this labor would encroach on your own work. I am curious and eager for what is still to come.

Are you writing? The other *N[ourritures] terrestres?* And your wild young colt? What is he doing with his strong feelings and his "tousled hair"? I would love to see him again, to see you again, to enrich more and more our friendship which consoles me in my dark hours.

Very best wishes, dear Gide. Do you hear anything of "Blanche in the monastery"?

Jean

[*P.S.*] Does he still fear the musketeers with spiked helmets?)

Cocteau's reaction to *Typhoon* was repeated almost verbatim to his mother and to Jacques-Emile Blanche,[9] and the fact that he gave the same favorable comment on Gide's style to all three is proof of his candor with Gide in this instance.

In 1918 Gide had initiated the friendship between his two young friends Marc Allégret and Jean Cocteau.[10] It was an introduction Gide soon came to regret bitterly, as Allégret

showed signs of breaking out of Gide's orbit and becoming
a satellite to Cocteau's star. In January of 1919 Gide felt obliged
to write Allégret a long letter that was a rehearsal for his open
letter to Cocteau of June 1919. The letter to Allégret castigated
Cocteau mainly on literary grounds, but it reveals how Gide's
personal jealousy affected his critical judgment of Cocteau:

Cuverville 19.1.19

Cher

. . . .

   Cette feuille était pour Jean C[octeau] dont je viens de doubler
le Cap — mais c'est à toi que j'écris d'abord pour désobstruer mon
stylo des réflexions qui se pressent d'abord et dont je ne puis, déjà,
lui faire part. Son absence de personnalité réelle n'a jamais été plus
manifeste que dans ce livre et l'effort même vers le neuf et l'ultra
l'accentue. De plus cette détermination de n'exposer de son émotion
ou de sa pensée que les jalons extrêmes, supprimant la phrase, c'est
à dire l'acheminement d'un point à un autre et du même coup la
démarche qui demeurerait personnelle, fait de son élocution poétique
quelque chose d'on ne peut plus facile à imiter, que déjà sans le
vouloir et sans le savoir, il imite et qui ne laisse percevoir aucune
nuance par où telle suite de mots (je n'ose pas dire: tel vers) de
Cocteau différerait de telle autre suite d'un de ses disciples (garde-toi
d'en être) ou de tel exécrable prédécesseur futuriste (je songe à
Marinetti). Bref, ça n'est pas difficile à faire, et les qualités que malgré
tout j'y trouve, ces dons d'analogie où s'affirme une sensibilité délicate, n'ont rien à voir, ou que fort peu, avec cette disposition typographique où il se voudrait novateur. . . .[11]

Cuverville
January 19, 1919

(Dear

. . . .

   This page was intended for Jean C[octeau], whose *Cap* [*de Bonne-
Espérance*] I have just circumnavigated—but I am writing you first
to flush my pen free of reflections which congest it but which I
cannot, so soon, pass on to him. His lack of real personality has
never been more evident than in this book, and his straining for the
new and the ultra accentuates its absence. Moreover, that determination to expose only the extreme points of his feelings or his
thoughts, compressing the sentence, that is to say his route from one
point to another and at the same time the gait that would remain exclusively his own—makes his poetic style the easiest thing in the world
to imitate, which he himself already imitates without meaning to or
being aware that he does it, and which doesn't permit one to glimpse

any nuance by which such a sequence of words (I dare not say, such verses) by Cocteau would be distinguishable from another such sequence by one of his disciples (take care not to become one) or by some awful Futurist predecessor (I am thinking of Marinetti). In short, that stuff is not hard to do, and the qualities that I find in his work in spite of everything, those gifts for analogy wherein his delicate sensitivity is revealed, have nothing to do, or only very little, with that novel typographical layout that he would like to feel he invented. . . .)

It is a matter for debate whether a private statement like this one, written under pressure of a kind, can be accepted as a more accurate reading of Gide's judgment of Cocteau than his public evaluations. Nevertheless, it is clear that Gide's public attack on Cocteau a few months later in his *NRF* open letter, the most detailed critical comment Gide ever published about Cocteau's work, was motivated in substantial part by personal animosity.

After the *Coq et l'Arlequin* storm had subsided, Gide attended the 1920 revival of Cocteau's ballet *Parade*. His *Journal* for New Year's Day, 1921, records the following appraisal:

Avant mon départ, été voir *Parade* — dont on ne sait ce qu'il faut admirer le plus: prétention ou pauvreté. Cocteau se promène dans la coulisse, où je vais le voir; vieilli, contracté, douloureux. Il sait bien que les décors, les costumes sont de Picasso, que la musique est de Satie, mais il doute si Picasso et Satie ne sont pas de lui.[12]

(Before my departure, went to see *Parade*—of which I don't know what to admire the more: pretense or poverty. Cocteau is walking up and down in the wings, where I go to see him; aged, contracted, painful. He knows that the sets and costumes are by Picasso, that the music is by Satie, but he wonders if Picasso and Satie are not by him.)

In June of the same year Cocteau had sent Gide an inscribed copy of his *La Noce massacrée*. The book included a critical attack on Maurice Barrès, who had preceded Gide as the chief writer to fasten the attention of French youth prior to World War I. Cocteau therefore no doubt expected an enthusiastic reader in Gide. He received instead an equivocal reply that opened and closed on a playful note, but compared Cocteau himself to Barrès and accused Cocteau of going too far in baiting Barrès.[13]

[Septembre 1921]

Voulez-vous jouer massacre avec môa? Mais je ne comprends pas la phrase: "J'ajoute qu'un innocent peut recevoir une balle qui ricoche, *en place de celui qui la lance.*" Qu'est ce que cela veut dire "Et cetera." —

Beaucoup de vrai, ombré d'inadmissibles injustices. Si vous avez mis tant de temps à sortir du portrait de Dorian Gray, c'est que vous étiez entré par la porte de service. Quand on y pénètre avec *Intentions,* plus n'est besoin de chercher d'en sortir; besoin de balayer la pièce simplement.

Mes parents m'avaient élevé, eux aussi dans l'horreur de ce qu'ils appelaient "le malsain." Quand on n'est pas très solide soi-même on a tout le temps peur des *miasmes.* Votre amour de la santé, des tons crus, etc. rappelle l'amour de l'autre pour sa Lorraine... Ne pas laisser le personnage bouffer la personne; tout est là. C'est ce que vous exprimez sagacement: "La sincérité serrée..." Je vous la sers.

Sincerily [*sic*]

A.G.

Mais un abîme entre "franchise" et "sincérité." Agréablement surpris de trouver mon cours après "Hugo hélas!" Somme toute, visites à Barrès — amorcements extrêmes. Vivrai-je assez pour entendre le Gendarme[14] lire le Cap [de Bonne-Espérance]?...

Ce n'est pas le plus ou moins de santé, mais bien l'affectation d'en avoir plus ou moins qui irrite. Et tout autant celle, débile, de vouloir paraître costaud — que celle, bien portant, de vouloir paraître débile.[15]

[September 1921]

(Do you want to play at massacre with me? But I don't understand the sentence: "I would add that an innocent bystander can be hit by a bullet that ricochets, *instead of the one who fires it.*" What does that mean "Et cetera."

Much truth, shadowed by inadmissible injustices. If it took you so long to get out of the *Portrait of Dorian Gray,* it is because you went in through the service entrance. When one goes into it with *Intentions,* there is no further need to look for the way out; simply a need to sweep out the room.

My parents too had brought me up in horror of what they called "the unhealthy." When one is not very solid oneself, there is always a fear of *miasmas.* Your love of health, of raw tones, etc., recalls the other's love for his Lorraine... Not to let the character puff up the person; that's the problem. That is what you wisely express: "oppressive sincerity..." I offer it to you.

Sincerily [*sic*],

A.G.

[P.S.] But an abyss between "candor" and "sincerity." Agreeably surprised to find the extent of my following after "Hugo hélas!" On

the whole, *Visites à Barrès* represents an excessive priming of the pump. Will I live long enough to hear the Gendarme read *Le Cap* [*de Bonne-Espérance*]?...

It isn't the more or less of health, but indeed the affectation of having more or less of it that is irritating. And just as much, the affectation, being frail, of wishing to appear stalwart—as that, being fit, of wishing to seem frail.)

Gide's message had been written on the back of a card depicting the wounded lioness of Ashur-bani-pal, and Cocteau took note of this in the closing line of his querulous reply to Gide's letter:

7/10/21

Yes

Mais ne trichez pas!

Injustices? Bien sûr. "Hugo hélas!" que je trouve parfait révolte la critique. Elle vous reproche d'être "injuste".

Tout notre malentendu vient de ce que vous ne voulez pas comprendre que c'est justement d'avoir pris l'escalier de *service* pour monter et de vouloir redescendre un jour par l'escalier d'honneur qui me distingue des *maîtres*.

Le personnage qui bouffe la personne! C'est vous, vous Gide, qui parlez? Existe-t-il un déméloir? Du reste pourquoi définissez vous "personnage" une personne qui ne pense pas comme vous.

Je ne suis ni fort ni débile. J'ai une résistance incroyable et des rhumes qui me démolissent.

Votre nom après Hugo H? — Mais, mon cher Gide, je ne suis pas cleptomane quoique vous en disiez au jeune docteur Epstein.

"Abîme" entre *ton cru* et *couleur*.

Ce qui sera drôle — juste et injuste — c'est un autre personnage dont l'accent éclairera un côté du Cap comme le Gendarme éclaire un côté (petit) de l'Ecclésiastique. Je le trouverai bien moi-même, car je change souvent de costume et ne respecte pas mes défroques.

Voâla

Jean Cocteau

J'avais commencé mon article (Comoedia) sur les "Mariés" par une citation de vous — Vous voyez que je ne vous traite pas comme la lionne d'Ashur-bani-pal.[16]

October 7, 1921

(Yes.

But no cheating!

Injustices? Of course. "Hugo hélas!", which I find perfect, revolts the critics. They reproach you for being "unjust."

Our entire misunderstanding stems from your not wanting to understand that precisely what sets me apart from the *masters* is that I, having taken the *back*stairs on the way up, wish someday to go back down by the grand staircase.

The character who puffs up the person! Is it you, Gide, speaking? Is there a way to distinguish? Besides, why do you define as a "character" a person who doesn't think the way you do?

I am neither strong nor weak. I have an incredible resistance and colds which pull me down.

Your name after Hugo h[élas]? — But my dear Gide, I am not a kleptomaniac, whatever you may tell young Dr. Epstein.

An abyss between *raw tone* and *color.*

What will be fun—just and unjust—is another character whose accent will illuminate one aspect of the *Cap* [*de Bonne-Espérance*], as the *Gendarme* [*incompris*] illuminates one small aspect of the *Ecclésiastique.* I will surely find it by myself, since I often switch costumes and have no respect for my cast-off garments.

> Voâla,
> Jean Cocteau

[P.S.] I had begun my article (for *Comoedia*) on *Les Mariés* [*de la Tour Eiffel*] by quoting you. You can see that I don't treat you like the lioness of Ashur-bani-pal.)

When Cocteau sent Gide a copy of his *Le Secret professionnel* in September 1922, he included a letter-length inscription complimenting Gide on his *Morceaux choisis* and commenting that Gide's use of "angélisme" was another point they had in common:

> 3 Septembre 1922
>
> Mon cher Gide,
>
> Vous retrouverez ici les quelques pages qui vous plaisent. Je viens de lire vos "Morceaux Choisis" apportés par Auric au bout de la conférence Weimar — que je trouve admirable et que je ne connaissais pas. Auric découvre que vous avez employé "Angélisme" — (mais dans un tout autre sens). Encore une rencontre. Vous finirez par voir dans ces rencontres un pur tissu de sympathie profonde.
>
> Je vous embrasse
> Jean
>
> Avez-vous lu Fantômas? Atroce farce d'avoir arrêté le fragment Lafcadio avant la mort de Fleurissoire. N'ayant pas les Caves, on lit, on s'installe et on reste le bec dans l'eau. Est-ce exprès? [17]

> September 3, 1922
>
> (My dear Gide
>
> You will find here again the few pages that please you. I have just read your *Morceaux choisis,* brought by Auric following the Weimar conference, which I find admirable and which I did not know. Auric

discovers that you have used "Angélisme" (but in a completely different sense). One more meeting. You will end up by seeing in these meetings a pure fabric of deep sympathy.

I embrace you,

Jean

[P.S.] Have you read *Fantômas?* Revolting joke to have ended the Lafacadio fragment before Fleurissoire's death. Not having *Les Caves [du Vatican]* we read, settle down, and remain frustrated. Is it on purpose?)

Gide had already read parts of *Le Secret professionnel* in the review *Ecrits Nouveaux,* apparently with approval since Cocteau wrote his mother to this effect. Gide's entry in his *Journal* for September [10], 1922, also confirms that his first reading of *Le Secret professionnel* had been agreeable. A second reading of the book, however, gave rise to second thoughts, and Gide noted in his *Journal:*

Je relis en volume *le Secret professionnel* de Cocteau que R. Martin du Gard m'avait fait lire dans les *Ecrits Nouveaux.* Comment avais-je pu trouver cela bon? La vanité blessée ne réussit jamais que des grimaces.[18]

(I am rereading in book form Cocteau's *Le Secret professionnel,* which R. Martin du Gard had made me read in the *Ecrits Nouveaux.* How could I have considered it good? Wounded vanity never produces anything but grimaces.)

Only two days later, on September 12, Gide wrote Roger Martin du Gard: "Relu *Le Secret professionnel* que Cocteau vient de m'envoyer — avec exaspération. Evidemment, c'est souvent très bien, très ingénieusement bien; mais je sens partout la ficelle et l'affectation. Il songe à lui sans cesse et sa muse a nom: vanité."[19] ("Reread *Le Secret professionnel,* which Cocteau just sent me—with exasperation. Obviously, it is often very good, very ingeniously good; but I feel trickery and affectation throughout. He thinks of himself constantly and the name of his muse is: vanity.")

A few months later, on January 16, 1923, Gide confided another wry appraisal to his *Journal* concerning Cocteau and his drama *Antigone:*

Eté hier au Vieux-Colombier où la troupe de Dullin donnait l'*Antigone,* ou "la dame de Sophocle," par Cocteau. Intolérablement souffert de la sauce ultramoderne, à quoi est apprêtée cette pièce admirable, qui reste belle, plutôt malgré Cocteau qu'à cause de lui.

On comprend du reste ce qui l'a tenté ici, et il a cuisiné cela avec une habileté consommée; mais ceux qui l'applaudissent étaient ceux qui d'abord considéraient Sophocle comme un maître raseur et que n'a jamais désaltérés "the true, the blushful Hippocrene."

La pièce de Cocteau n'est pas *blushful* du tout. Elle répond au même sentiment qui faisait dire à Stravinsky qu'il collaborerait volontiers à *Antoine et Cléopâtre,* mais seulement si l'on donnait à Antoine l'uniforme d'un "bersaglier" italien.

La patine est la récompense des chefs-d'œuvre.[20]

(Went yesterday to the Vieux-Colombier, where Dullin's company was giving *Antigone,* or "Sophocles' lady," by Cocteau. Suffered unbearably from the ultra-modern sauce in which was served up that wonderful play, which remains beautiful more in spite of Cocteau than because of him. One can understand moreover what tempted him here, and he has cooked it up with consummate cleverness; but those who applaud him are those who to begin with considered Sophocles as a great bore and who have never drunk of "the true, the blushful Hippocrene."

Cocteau's play is not at all *blushful.* It reflects the same feeling that made Stravinsky say he would gladly collaborate on *Antony and Cleopatra,* but only if Antony were given the uniform of an Italian *"Bersaglière."*

Patina is the reward of masterpieces.)

Word of Gide's unfavorable reaction quickly reached Cocteau, who at once sent off an indignant letter to Gide:

10 Rue d'Anjou

Mon cher Gide,

Il est pour moi de grande importance que je sache si un homme comme vous peut croire *une minute sérieusement* qu'un homme comme moi cherche le rire avec "Antigone." (Je ne parle pas des répliques narquoises du chœur, des Pré-Ubuismes de Créon et du soldat comique fort atténué dans mon texte.) Si oui — ce que je me refuse encore à imaginer — ce serait enfin la clef d'un interminable malentendu. La preuve d'un angle visuel qui fausse *tout.*

Votre fidèle
Jean Cocteau

Enlever une patine et montrer les couleurs fraîches fait croire au public qu'on lui montre le plus absurde chromo. Voilà le vrai sens de ce rire.[21]

10 rue d'Anjou

(My dear Gide,

It is of great importance for me to know if a man like you can *seriously* believe *for one minute* that a man like me is looking for laughter

with *Antigone*. (I am not speaking of the chorus' bantering replies, the pre-Ubuismes of Créon, and the comic soldier who is greatly played down in my text.) If so—which I can't yet make myself believe—it would at last give the key to our endless misunderstandings. The proof of a visual angle which distorts *everything*.

Your faithful
Jean Cocteau

[P.S.] To remove a patina and show fresh colors makes the public believe one is showing it the most absurd chromo. That is the real meaning of this laughter.)

Cocteau's letter is particularly significant because its irate tone is a measure of the importance Cocteau attached to Gide's evaluations of his work at that critical time. It also reveals a long-standing awareness on Cocteau's part of the invisible barrier between the two artists.

From Roquebrune Gide replied in language that enlarged on his previous *Journal* entry:

24 [Janvier] 1923
Roquebrune

Mon cher Jean,

Mais non, mais non, il n'y a pas de malentendu — et il n'y en a à jamais eu. Mettons simplement — puisque cela n'est pas volontaire — qu'il y a dans votre *Antigone* quelques insignes maladresses, qui prêtent au malentendu. Il s'agit de savoir si vous vous placez au point de vue de Sophocle — ou de Cocteau. Je sais que vous aimez Sophocle; mais je crains que vous ne l'aimiez surtout quand il danse.

"Patine." Il n'y a que les bons vins qui vieillissent bien. La patine est la récompense des chefs d'œuvre.

Quand il fut question que Stravinski [*sic*] fît la musique d'Antoine et Cléopâtre, je l'allai trouver en Suisse. Il me dit: "Volontiers, mais à condition qu'Antoine porte le costume d'un capitaine de Bersaglieri." Convaincu, ce disant, qu'il allait "dans le sens de Shakespeare."

Or vous savez si j'admire Stravinsky; croyez donc à ma vive affection

A.G.[22]

[January] 24, 1923
Roquebrune

(My dear Jean,

No indeed, no indeed, there is no misunderstanding—and there never has been one. Let's say simply—since it was not intentional on your part—that there are in your *Antigone* several conspicuously awkward things that can give rise to misunderstanding. It is a matter

of knowing whether you place yourself in Sophocles' vantage point
—or in Cocteau's. I know you like Sophocles, but I fear you like him
above all when he dances.

"Patina." Only honest wines age well. Patina is the reward of masterpieces.

When there was a question of Stravinsky's doing the music for
Antoine et Cléopâtre I went to meet him in Switzerland. He said to
me: "Willingly, but on condition that Antony wear the costume of a
captain of the Bersaglière." Convinced, in saying this, that he was
headed "in Shakespeare's direction." Now, you know if I admire
Stravinsky; so please believe in my warm affection.

A.G.)

Gide's ambiguous opening sentence carries the ironic implication that there was no misunderstanding on his part because
he had judged Cocteau correctly from the start. His closing
sentence of that paragraph is a shaft aimed at the old wound
he and Ghéon had inflicted on Cocteau eleven years earlier
in their criticism of Cocteau's *La Danse de Sophocle*.

Cocteau, evidently mollified by the public reaction to
Antigone, chose to disregard Gide's innuendo. A few days later
he replied in a much calmer tone:

29 Janvier 1923

— Non, mon cher Gide, *ni malices, ni maladresses.* L'approbation de
certains esprits et les salles de chaque soir me le confirment. Ce
qui ne m'empêche pas, à mon tour, de vous aimer.

Jean Cocteau

Malentendu sur toute la ligne — *oui.*[23]

January 29, 1923

(No, my dear Gide, *neither tricks nor blunders.* The approval of certain
minds and the houses at each performance confirm this to me. All
of which does not, in my turn, keep me from loving you.

Jean Cocteau

[P.S.] Misunderstanding all along the line—*yes.*)

In another postscript, probably to the above letter, Cocteau
added as an afterthought:

Hiver 1922–1923

P.S. Le vin et les œuvres — c'est le système "asperge du pauvre"
dont vous parlez si bien.

On peut dire aussi: La patine maquille les croûtes etc. . . .

J'ai voulu faire quelque chose — Je l'ai fait. Je l'ai réussi selon moi et selon d'autres — c'est le principal.

Votre Je ...

Antoine Bersaglière — c'est si j'avais fait entrer Ismène et Antigone en tandem — aucun rapport.[24]

Winter 1922–1923

(P.S. Wine and works—that's the "poor people's asparagus" system about which you speak so well.

One can also say: A patina disguises a daub, etc. . . .

I wanted to do something—I have done it. I carried it off successfully in my opinion and that of others—that's the main thing.

Your Je ...

[P.P.S.] Antoine Bersaglière, that's as if I had brought Ismène and Antigone on stage in tandem—no connection.)

All the same, by the time he gave his address on May 3, 1923, at the Collège de France, with young Marc Allégret in the audience, Cocteau had forgiven Gide enough to comment favorably again on his style:

Alors on devine que le langage dont Molière se moque était sans doute l'aïeul du style d'un Mallarmé, d'un Marcel Proust, d'un André Gide, d'un Giraudoux, d'un Jacques Rivière. Il se moquait du neuf comme nos revuistes de fin d'année.[25]

(So we can surmise that the language Molière made fun of was without doubt the ancestor of the style of a Mallarmé, a Marcel Proust, an André Gide, a Giraudoux, a Jacques Rivière. He made fun of everything new like our year-end reviewers.)

Later that same month, on the train back to Paris from Annecy with his wife, Gide read Cocteau's novel *Le Grand Ecart*. The *NRF* was about to publish the twin to this novel, *Thomas l'Imposteur,* and Gide, according to Cocteau's report to Léon Pierre-Quint some years later, had personally noted corrections in *Thomas*.[26] Despite these developments Gide makes no allusion to *Thomas l'Imposteur* in his *Journal* for 1923. His entry for May 18, 1923, speaks only of *Le Grand Ecart,* which had just been published as Cocteau's first novel by Stock.

Lu en wagon *le Grand Ecart* de Jean Cocteau, avec un grand effort d'approbation et de louange; durant le premier quart d'heure du livre, suis arrivé, par bon vouloir, à me donner le change, amusé

d'autre part par l'extrême ingéniosité des images et la brusquerie clownesque de certaines présentations. Mais bientôt l'irritation domine, devant un si constant et si avaricieux souci de ne rien perdre, un si précautionneux faire valoir. Sans cesse, ici, l'art dégénère en artifice. Si Cocteau se laissait aller, il écrirait des vaudevilles.[27]

(Read in the train Jean Cocteau's *Le Grand Ecart,* with a great effort toward approbation and praise; during the first quarter of the book I managed, through goodwill, to deceive myself, amused as I was by the extreme ingenuity of the images and the burlesque brusqueness of certain presentations. But soon irritation dominates before so constant and so avaricious an anxiety to lose nothing, such a wary turning to account. In this book art is constantly degenerating into artifice. If Cocteau let himself go, he would write light comedies.)

In his preface to the original edition of *Les Mariés de la Tour Eiffel,* published by Gallimard in 1924, Cocteau complimented Gide and referred to *Paludes* in his opening sentence: "Toute œuvre d'ordre poétique renferme ce que Gide appelle si justement, dans sa préface de *Paludes: La part de Dieu.*" ("All works of a poetic nature enclose what Gide calls so aptly, in his preface to *Paludes: God's part.*")

In April 1925 Cocteau had just moved from the nursing home where he had undergone an opium cure. Still ailing, he wrote Gide from Versailles ironically prophesying Gide's future place as a Surrealist musician. It was an opinion ventured to tease Gide, whose taste in music centered in Chopin's piano compositions.

Hôtel des Réservoirs, Versailles

Cher André,
     La lettre, dirait Apollinaire, en forme de trompe d'Eustache me fait mal à l'oreille. Que c'est ennuyeux d'être malade — Le Spectacle du Printemps donne une furieuse envie de force — Hélas je me traîne. Si encore nous marchions bras dessus bras dessous. Comme j'aimerais entendre votre orchestre! Notez-le — vous serez le musicien surréaliste.

Je vous embrasse
Jean

J'ai eu pendant 48 jours une brave infirmière qui couchait dans ma chambre et soigne votre famille. Elle ne vous connait pas mais dit: André — en parlant de vous!!! Phrase de mon infirmière: "*Mlle Emilienne d'Alençon s'exprimait affectueusement sur vous et chez M. Gide aussi on vous estime bien* — (sic) *du reste les maisons se touchent.*"[28]

Hôtel des Réservoirs, Versailles

Dear André,

(The letter, Apollinaire would say, in the shape of a Eustachian tube, hurts my ear. How boring it is to be ill. The spectacle of Springtime gives a furious desire for strength — alas, I am dragging about. If only we were still walking arm in arm. How I would love to listen to your orchestra! Mark my word — you will be the surrealist musician.

I embrace you,

Jean

[P.S.] For forty-eight days I had a good nurse who slept in my room and who takes care of your family. She doesn't know you but says André — when speaking of you!!! A comment by my nurse: *"Mlle Emilienne d'Alençon* spoke warmly of you, and they think well of you at M. Gide's too (sic) — *besides, the two houses touch."*)

Cocteau's comment describing Gide as the Surrealist musician may have contained an element of wistfulness, for Cocteau's own relations with Breton and the Surrealists were notoriously poor in spite of his persistent efforts to identify himself with them.

In 1928 there appeared an anonymous book with the title *Le Livre blanc* which dealt openly and in a biographical way with the topic of homosexuality. Despite the lack of signature it was soon common knowledge that the author was Jean Cocteau. The theme of homosexuality had already been developed by Gide in similarly clandestine editions of *Si le grain ne meurt* and, more notably, in *Corydon.* Gide's efforts to win acceptance of homosexuality as being only "contre coutume" and not "contre nature" were part of what André Malraux calls Gide's constant self-justification, and what Roger Martin du Gard describes as "je ne sais quel appel nostalgique du martyre." They were also part of Gide's long and varied attempt, through his work and the example of his life, to demolish the taboos and inequities of the bourgeois society that had produced him. He might therefore have been expected to welcome Cocteau's *Le Livre blanc* as one more weapon in the fight against hypocrisy as he saw it. This, however, was not the case. Gide's *Journal* for October 11, 1929, reads:

Lu *le Livre Blanc* de Cocteau prêté par Roland Saucier en attendant l'exemplaire promis par Cocteau. Que d'agitation vaine dans les drames qu'il raconte! que d'apprêt dans son style! de souci de la galerie dans ses attitudes!... que d'artifices!... pourtant certaines

obscénités sont racontées d'une manière charmante. Ce qui choque, et beaucoup, ce sont les sophismes pseudo-religieux.[29]

(Read Cocteau's *Le Livre blanc,* lent by Roland Saucier until I receive the copy promised by Cocteau. What empty agitation in the tales he relates! what affectation in his style! what a play to the gallery in the poses he strikes!... what artifice!... yet certain obscenities are related in a charming way. What is shocking, and greatly so, is the pseudo-religious sophistries.)

The last lines of this passage in which Gide combines praise for obscenities and indignation at religious sophistries brings to mind the accuracy of Cocteau's observation in his open reply to Gide in 1919 that Gide's spirit was a combination of "pasteur et bacchante."

In February 1930 Gide sent Cocteau a copy of his latest book *Robert,* which the *NRF* published with *L'Ecole des femmes* in that year. Cocteau's thanks were followed by the sort of compliment he turned so well and which was so often a feature of his letters to Gide: " 'L'Ecole' est un livre extraordinaire, une merveille de ce non-moi survolé par un moi sévère." [30] (*"L'Ecole* is a remarkable book, a miracle of that "non-moi" overflown by a severe "moi.")

A Cocteau letter to Gide that summer also ended with a note of praise inspired by Gide's *La Séquestrée de Poitiers:* "Le cher grand bon fond Malempia quel chef d'œuvre!" [31]

After a hiatus of three years in their correspondence Gide took the initiative in 1935 by writing Cocteau a note of congratulation on his circus article [32] in *Le Figaro* for February 16, 1935. Roger Martin du Gard had sent it to Gide on February 18, saying: "Pour distraire votre grippe, à défaut de pouvoir vous envoyer du soleil, voici quelques feux d'artifice de Cocteau, l'habile homme." [33] ("To distract your cold, being unable to send you some sun, here are a few fireworks from Cocteau, the clever man.")

> Cuverville en Caux
> 28 février 35
>
> Mon cher Jean
> Où cette lettre vous parviendra-t-elle? si tant est qu'elle vous atteigne jamais... Je voudrais pourtant que vous sachiez combien j'ai savouré vos exquises, étourdissantes, pages sur le cirque dans le Figaro (?) qu'un ami, fort admirateur de vous, me communique. C'est un émerveillement. J'ai plaisir, en les lisant, à sentir combien je vous reste attaché.
>
> André Gide [34]

Cuverville-en-Caux
February 28, 1935
(My dear Jean,
Where will this letter reach you, if it ever finally does catch up...
Anyway, I wish you to know how much I relished your delightful,
stunning pages on the circus in *Le Figaro* (?) which a friend, who is a
great admirer of yours, sent me. They're a wonder. I enjoy, as I
read them, feeling how deeply I am still attached to you.

André Gide)

In the spring of that same year Martin du Gard sent the con-
valescing Gide some Cocteau clippings, probably also from his
series in *Le Figaro*. Both Martin du Gard's comments in April
to Gide about the quality of the writing and Gide's grudging
approval in May are perhaps all the more sincere for having
been communicated privately:

Nice
30 Avril 1935
Pour vous distraire votre convalescence, je vous envoie des coupures,
gardées pour vous. Dans ces souvenirs de Cocteau, il y a des pages
prestigieuses. Et un effort de retour sur soi, de purger les excès
de jeunesse, qui m'a fort touché.

R.M.G.[35]

Nice
April 30, 1935
(In order to distract you during your convalescence I am sending
you some clippings I have kept for you. In these souvenirs of Cocteau's there are some marvelous pages. And an effort to reflect
seriously on his conduct, to purge the excesses of youth, that has
touched me deeply.

R.M.G.)

5 Mai 35
Merci pour les découpures. Cocteau, moins éblouissant un peu que le
premier (sur le cirque); prestigieux encore et avec un tas de qualités
presque morales, assez inattendues (je devrais dire: inespérées).

André Gide [36]

May 5, 1935
(Thanks for the clippings. Cocteau, a little less dazzling than the first
(on the circus); still marvelous and with lots of almost ethical qualities,
quite unexpected (I should say: unhoped for).

André Gide)

The circus, like the theater and the skating rink, had made a
deep impression on Cocteau in childhood. The red and gold

colors, the movement, sounds and scents, and above all the people of the circus, stayed with Cocteau forever. They are woven constantly into his work along with his angels, orphic profiles, and animals in a dream-like profusion that gives the ensemble of Cocteau's work the literary ambience of Chagall's murals. Cocteau perennially identified himself with the tightrope walkers of the circus, and the motif of the poet, avant-garde artist, opium smoker, and homosexual struggling to keep his balance on "la corde raide" is one of Cocteau's most esthetically graphic and psychologically revealing images to describe the tension of his existence.

The following year, in 1936, Gide's *Retour de l'URSS* was published. Surrealism already seemed far behind, and Communism had for many years become the focus of attention of intellectuals and artists of the avant-garde. Gide had become deeply involved in exploring the Communist ethic, drawn partly by his concern for social justice, partly by his broadly humanistic curiosity, and partly by that drive for self-justification which found expression in his persistent efforts to disturb established social values. Cocteau, on the other hand, had studiously avoided becoming an artist *à cause* concerned with social or political problems. Beauty, esthetics, and their moral derivatives were always the center of his artistic concentration. The few articles he wrote for Louis Aragon's Communist daily *Ce Soir* in 1937 were to be the highwater mark of his participation in communist-oriented activity. It was accordingly with some relief that he was able to commend Gide, in a letter of 1936, for the disenchantment with Russian Communism that Gide described in his *Retour de l'URSS:*

Mon cher André

Votre "Retour" est brave, noble, charmant comme vous — c'est vous. C'est ce qui rend la vie possible et ce qui ôte les malaises du désordre. Je vous aime et je vous embrasse. Votre

Jean [37]

(My dear André,

Your *Retour* is courageous, noble, charming as you are — it is you. That is what makes life possible and what removes the discomforts of disorder. I like you and I embrace you.

Your
Jean)

A few months later Gide received a copy of Cocteau's *Mon Premier Voyage*,[38] which described the trip he had made around

the world in eighty days with Marcel Khill in 1936. The trip, based on Jules Verne's famous story, had been organized by the newspaper *Paris-Soir,* and it gave Cocteau the chance to make his first major trip outside France. Travel had become another link between Gide and Cocteau who dedicated this book to him. Gide acknowledged the courtesy in his letter of March 30:

Cuverville
30 mars 37

Mon cher Jean

Je ne vous ai pas assez remercié de votre livre. Je viens de le relire tout entier — avec désespoir. Qu'est-ce que nous foutons dans ce climat crépusculaire? Quand des Kuala Lumpur nous attendent... Je rentre à Paris dans quelques jours; si je savais que vous y êtes, je voudrais vous revoir. Je ne sais même plus votre adresse! C'est honteux. La N.R.F. fera suivre, j'espère.

Je vous embrasse
André Gide [39]

Cuverville
March 30, 1937

(My dear Jean,

I have not thanked you enough for your book. I have just reread it through—with despair. Why are we idling around in this gloomy atmosphere when Kuala Lumpurs are waiting for us? I'll be back in Paris in a few days; if I knew you were there, I would like to see you again. I don't even know your address anymore! How shameful. I hope the *NRF* will forward this.

I embrace you,
André Gide)

During the year 1939 with war threatening Europe, Claude Mauriac kept a journal of his many conversations with André Gide. This journal was the basis of Mauriac's *Conversations avec André Gide,* which was published in 1951. The journal records a warm appraisal of Cocteau by Gide on April 28, 1939:

Nous parlons aussi de Cocteau. Son [Gide's] visage s'éclaire d'une véritable affection. "Quel être charmant! Je l'aime bien tout de même, je l'aime malgré tout... Car on ne saurait en vouloir longtemps à un ensorceleur de cette espèce." Il me dit qu'il n'a jamais pu prendre tout à fait au sérieux l'œuvre et l'homme.[40]

(We also speak of Cocteau. His [Gide's] face lights up with real affection. "What a delightful person! I like him very much anyway;

I like him in spite of everything... Because you couldn't hold a grudge for long against a charmer of that sort." He tells me that he has never been able to take the work and the man entirely seriously.)

A month later Claude Mauriac was at Versailles to visit Cocteau and gather material for the book that was published in 1945 as *Jean Cocteau ou la vérité du mensonge*. The evening of May 26 Cocteau regaled Claude Mauriac with a three-hour monologue that touched frequently on Gide. Mauriac was skeptical at the time about the sincerity of Cocteau's professed friendship for Gide:

Il y a dans son verbe, bien cachée sous l'amitié qu'il dit éprouver pour Gide, et dissimulée aussi par une drôlerie à l'air bon enfant, une malveillance certaine et dont les raisons ne me semblent pas désintéressées. J'ai pressenti la jalousie − et mon cœur s'est par moment serré, tant la gêne était forte, et je ne sais quelle inexprimable angoisse.

En attendant, c'est lui, Cocteau, qui accuse Gide de jalousie. Il prétend, comme c'est vraisemblable! que le succès des *Parents terribles* empêche son ami de dormir,[41] et qu'il a aussitôt écrit tout une pièce qu'il essaye vainement de placer de théâtre en théâtre.[42]

(There is in his speech, well hidden beneath the friendship that he claims to feel for Gide, and disguised too by joking in a good-natured manner, a definite unfriendliness, the reasons for which do not seem unselfish to me. I had a presentiment of jealousy−and my heart tightened a moment, the discomfort was so strong−and of some unutterable anguish.

Meanwhile, it is he, Cocteau, who accuses Gide of jealousy. He claims, how plausible it is! that the success of *Les Parents terribles* prevents his friend from sleeping, and that he immediately wrote a play which he is vainly trying to place in theater after theater.)

Cocteau evidently ran through a long repertoire of anecdotes, some amusing, some legendary, but most of them at Gide's expense:

Il [Cocteau] ajoute que c'est lui, Gide, qui avait machiné la candidature de Valéry à l'Académie, avec l'espoir secret d'un échec et que son élection lui fut très désagréable,[43] . . . qu'il mena un double jeu antipathique lors des démêlés que lui, Cocteau, eut avec les Surréalistes.[44]

(He [Cocteau] adds that it's he, Gide, who organized Valéry's candidacy at the Academy with the secret hope of a fiasco, and that

Valéry's election was very disagreeable to him, . . . that he played an unfriendly double game at the time of the disputes that he, Cocteau, had with the Surrealists.)

The following passage was deleted from his *Conversations* by Mauriac prior to publication, but it still exists as part of his original journal of that conversation with Cocteau. It is reported here not because it adds anything new to the knowledge of Gide's character — Gide's own journals are far more explicit in this respect — but because it reveals a distinction between Cocteau's private and public opinions about Gide. "How far to go too far" in public was one thing for Cocteau, but in private was another:

pour montrer les plus petits côtés de ce grand personnage, images attristantes d'un Gide que Ghéon fait renvoyer du pensionnat où il avait réussi pendant la guerre à se faire accepter comme professeur, d'un Gide chassé à coup de pieds d'un cinéma "où il avait fait je ne sais quoi!", d'un Gide surpris avec un petit garçon dans une chambre d'hôtel et s'excusant ainsi: "Je lui faisais seulement raccommoder le bouton." [45]

(to show the meanest aspects of this great person; saddening pictures of a Gide whom Ghéon had expelled from the boardingschool in which he had succeeded in getting himself accepted as a teacher during the war; of a Gide kicked out of a movie theater "where he had done God knows what!"; of a Gide surprised with a little boy in a hotel room and excusing himself by saying: "I was only fixing up his button.")

Later in the conversation Cocteau indulged in his great talent for caricature, "tirer vite, tirer juste," by describing Gide, Claudel, and Valéry with a single phrase for each:

Les maîtres ont du génie, le génie d'enfance, tu comprends: Gide, c'est la vieille Anglaise qui va voir les Pyramides avec un chapeau à voile vert; Claudel, c'est le bébé Cadum, quoi? et Valéry est un gosse dissipé qui lève la main pour sortir. [46]

(The masters have genius, the genius of childhood, you understand: Gide is the old English lady who goes to see the Pyramids with a hat with green netting; Claudel is baby Cadum, what? and Valéry is an inattentive kid who raises his hand to leave the room.)

According to Mauriac, Cocteau felt Gide's work made too many concessions to reality and shied away from venturing

into the unknown. The alleged *acte gratuit* in Gide's *Les Caves du Vatican* made Cocteau laugh because according to Cocteau it was a simple act of hygiene. A really gratuitous act would have been for Lafcadio to hurl a handsome young man from the train instead of an aged nonentity like Fleurissoire.

Gide was also known to express himself in private conversation about Cocteau more freely and in more pejorative terms than he did in public. Roger Stéphane reported that in 1940 when Gide learned Stéphane was friendly with Cocteau, Gide reproached him: "Comment pouvez-vous? Il est vicieux?" [47] And only a few days after Claude Mauriac's session with Cocteau at Versailles, Gide discussed Cocteau with him at some length. The following passage was also deleted by Mauriac from his final journal text for the date of May 31, 1939:

> Cocteau évoqué il est difficile de parler d'autre chose. Gide me félicite de faire un livre sur lui: "C'est un bien curieux personnage, à propos de qui vous aborderez aux plus essentiels sujets... Etonnement de penser qu'il a commencé par admirer Catulle Mendès... C'est inconceivable!... C'est la drogue qui explique le mystère de Cocteau: l'opium supprime la notion du mensonge. Elle efface les limites du vrai et du faux. D'où l'insécurité des rapports que l'on peut avoir avec un Cocteau – d'où sa malhonnêteté profonde, et dont il n'est pas responsable. Ajouter une obsession sexuelle de toutes les minutes – la passion, toujours présente, nécessairement présente..." [48]

> (Once Cocteau is brought up it's hard to speak of anything else. Gide congratulates me on doing a book about him: "He's a very peculiar fellow, in connection with whom you will tackle the most vital subjects... Amazing to think that he began by admiring Catulle Mendès... It's inconceivable!... It is dope that explains Cocteau's mystery: opium suppresses the notion of lying. It obliterates the boundaries of the true and the false. From this comes the insecurity of the relationships one can have with a Cocteau—from this stems his deep dishonesty, for which he is not responsible. Add a sexual obsession on hand every minute—passion always present, of necessity present...")

In evaluating the foregoing statements by Cocteau and Gide to young Claude Mauriac and Roger Stéphane it must be remembered that both Gide and Cocteau knew that Mauriac was gathering information for purposes of publication, that Mauriac was writing a book about each of them.

Cocteau regarded Claude Mauriac's book as a betrayal of friendship. In his *Journal d'un inconnu* (p. 108), Cocteau writes: "On connaît ce livre. L'amitié y éclate sous l'insulte et l'inexactitude. Claude ment et son arme est de m'accuser de mensonge." ("You know this book. Friendship flashes in it beneath insult and inaccuracy. Claude lies, and his weapon is to accuse me of lying.") In fairness to both Jean Cocteau and to Claude Mauriac, who were later reconciled, it should be noted that Mauriac was only twenty-five when he wrote his book on Cocteau. Today, thirty-three years later, he regards that work as a purging of youthful feelings. Mauriac now recognizes Cocteau as a poet of vision who portrayed in *Les Enfants terribles* and *Le Grand Ecart* types of young people who were forerunners of those society is now seeing clearly for the first time. Mauriac believes Cocteau's originality is not yet fully apprehended by critics and public, and that the ensemble of his literary and film work is a unique and major cultural contribution. His most recent work on Cocteau, *Une Amitié contrariée,* presents the fuller appreciation of Cocteau that came with Mauriac's own maturity. In that book, which forms part of Claude Mauriac's meticulous journal over many years, he reports a discussion he had with Gide about Jean Cocteau in 1939. Claude Mauriac speaks first:

C.M.: Plus que son œuvre m'intéresse l'homme. Cet homme qui est le Jean Cocteau que chacun connaît, qui est aussi *un homme* comme les autres, mais plus que les autres capable de prendre conscience de son drame...

(*C.M.:* More than his work it is the man who interests me. This man who is the Jean Cocteau everyone knows, who is also a man like the others, but better able than the others to be aware of his personal tragedy...)

André Gide: Vous ne me ferez pas croire qu'il puisse y avoir drame chez Cocteau. Comment ce personnage qui se donne en spectacle, qui dupe et qui se dupe, pourrait-il vraiment souffrir?

(*André Gide:* You will not convince me that personal tragedy could exist for Cocteau. How could this character who makes a spectacle of himself, who fools others and who fools himself, truly suffer?)

C.M.: Je vous le répète: il souffre parce qu'il est un homme. un homme qui, dans une mesure particulièrement intense, est dévoré

par l'amour. Un homme qui aime, lorsqu'il découvre dans la glace son visage vieilli, souffre. Cocteau est cet homme. Mais il est aussi Jean Cocteau. Vous le jugez sur son apparence.

(*C.M.:* I repeat: he suffers because he is a man, a man who, in a particularly intense way, is devoured by love. A man who loves, when he catches the signs of age in his mirror, suffers. Cocteau is that man. But he is also Jean Cocteau. You are judging him on his appearance.)

André Gide: (entêté, et se refusant à accepter mon argumentation): Je le juge sur son plus constant visage. Il me semble que vous cedez au plaisir de créer le Jean Cocteau de vos désirs. Le vrai Cocteau ne souffre pas.[49]

(*André Gide* (stubbornly, and refusing to accept my argument): I judge him by his most constant expression. It seems to me you are giving in to the pleasure of creating the Jean Cocteau of your own wishes. The real Cocteau does not suffer.)

This dialogue, which took place twenty years after Gide's dispute with Cocteau over *Le Coq et l'Arlequin*, indicates that Gide's early view of Cocteau had generally only hardened with time. His initial concepts of Cocteau as an artist who wore too many masks, who deceived himself, and whose work was not fed by inner springs of discontent, had all received esthetic confirmation in the art of Gide's novel *Les Faux-Monnayeurs*, in which Cocteau's counterpart, the comte de Passavant, played a central role as the spurious artist. Gide's attitudes toward Cocteau had set long before his 1939 conversations with Claude Mauriac. Any subsequent affection and esteem that Gide retained or developed for Cocteau were bound to be above and beyond his basic reservations, however motivated, as to Cocteau's flaws.

Roger Stéphane was later to make one television film about Gide and another on Cocteau. Therefore what was told to Stéphane was said with the awareness it might be for the record. The manner in which Claude Mauriac and Stéphane shuttled back and forth between Gide and Cocteau is reminiscent of the pattern established by Marc Allégret, Pierre Herbart, and Maurice Sachs in their time, a pattern that Cocteau recognized and deplored even though he encouraged it. He later described this problem in his address at Oxford in 1956:

Mes relations avec André Gide furent d'un bout à l'autre un cache-cache de réconciliations, de disputes, de lettres ouvertes, de griefs, dont la source pourrait bien être la bande de jeunes mythomanes qui circulaient entre nous et s'amusaient à brouiller les cartes.[50]

(My relations with André Gide were, from start to finish, a hide-and-seek of reconciliations, quarrels, open letters, and grievances whose source could well have been that band of young mythomaniacs who circulated between us and amused themselves by shuffling our cards).

In June of 1939 André Gide went to visit the Mauriac family at Malagar, their property near Bordeaux. Cocteau followed in spirit and wrote Claude Mauriac a letter complaining of the duplicity of Gide's *Journal:*

Mon cher petit Claude,
   . . . Gide est-il encore auprès de vous? Mon Dieu que son journal attriste (je ne parle pas de ce qui me concerne, mon électricité ne touche jamais sa soie – c'est naturel). Je parle de cette frivolité grave – le diable *par excellence.* . . .[51]

(My dear little Claude,
   . . . Is Gide still with you? My God, how saddening his journal is (I am not referring to the parts about me, my electricity never touches his silk – that's natural). I'm talking about that grave frivolity – the devil *par excellence.* . . .)

The letter illustrates Cocteau's habitual device first used twenty years before in his open letter to Gide, of turning back on Gide the same criticisms Gide makes of him. If Gide accuses him of frivolity, Cocteau returns the compliment. Gide's critical evaluations of Cocteau since 1912 had centered in Cocteau's "légèreté" and "mensonge," the frivolity, artificiality, and unoriginality of his work. They had established Gide as the keynote critic of Cocteau and were widely used by other detractors. As a defense mechanism against such charges, Cocteau quickly developed a response pattern, "son numéro," which is summarized in his "Gide vivant":

L'âme est faible. Il m'a toujours été très dur de m'entendre accuser de mensonge lorsque je disais ma vérité, d'acrobatie lorsque je marchais au bord d'un toit, de prestidigitation lorsque je devenais le véhicule de ce schizophrène que je renferme.
Mais peu à peu, je me suis fait une morale qui consiste à supporter

les injustices, parce que je les estime indispensables à la rigueur d'une œuvre.[52]

(The spirit is weak. It has always been very hard for me to hear myself accused of lying when I was speaking my truth, of acrobatics when I was walking on the edge of a roof, of sleight of hand when I was becoming the vehicle for that schizophrenic who is locked up in me.

But little by little I made a morality for myself which consists in tolerating injustices because I consider them indispensable to the rigor of one's work.)

With the advent of World War II, Gide and Cocteau lost touch with each other. Cocteau first went south to Carcassonne and then returned to Paris for the rest of the war. Gide went to Nice, where he stayed in the apartment of his English translator and friend Dorothy Bussy before proceeding to North Africa.

In June 1942 Gide's article "Trois rencontres avec Verlaine" was published in the review *Fontaine*.[53] Gide's account of his last view of the great poet as a drunken old man harassed by a swarm of cruel children behind the Panthéon does not indicate whether or not Gide came to Verlaine's aid. When Cocteau read the article, he was quick to react in judgment on Gide. In an article of his own he placed himself on the side of Verlaine the *poète maudit*, or *gibier*, a role with which Cocteau liked to identify himself. "Quel spectacle! Et combien je m'étonne que Gide n'en découvre pas la grandeur."[54] ("What a spectacle! And how astonished I am that Gide doesn't see the grandeur of it.")

Cocteau's essay, rich in nuance, strikes at Gide on personal as well as professional grounds: readers are reminded of Gide's repressive Protestantism and of his status as a non-poet verging, in this instance, on the anti-poet. Why didn't Gide rescue Verlaine from his tormentors, as Cocteau declares he would have?

Pourquoi Gide ne s'est-il pas payé ce luxe? Faut-il voir dans sa gêne, dans sa réserve protestante, le réflexe défensif des encyclopédistes en face des turpitudes de Rousseau? Je me le demande. Gide est une énigme. Il se glace assez vite devant le feu.[55]

(Why didn't Gide indulge himself this luxury? Must we see in his discomfort, in his Protestant reserve, the defensive reflex of the Ency-

clopedists in confronting Rousseau's turpitudes? I wonder. Gide is an enigma. He freezes quite quickly before the fire.)

Cocteau's brief tirade brings to mind the central theme of his earlier Rousseau article, which classed Gide with the Encyclopedist persecutors of the author of *Le Contrat social.* Cocteau also heightened the theatricality of the little scene Gide described, by injecting the name of Rousseau, who is buried in the Panthéon. Cocteau finishes his article by likening Verlaine, pitiful as he was when Gide last saw him, to "une étonnante statue que Gide déplorait, place du Panthéon, et que je dresse, vivante, en face des colosses de cendre qui hantent cet illustre mausolée." [56] ("an astonishing statue which Gide deplored, Place du Panthéon, and which I raise up, alive, to confront the colossi of ashes who haunt that illustrious mausoleum.")

When the war had ended and Gide was again back in Paris, Cocteau wrote him his reactions to the film version of Gide's *La Symphonie pastorale:*

J'aurais dû vous téléphoner tout de suite après avoir vu le film — mais je déteste le téléphone et je devais me résoudre à cette cure (sorte de flagellation liquide) — Votre livre est assez robuste pour résister à l'épreuve et même il arrive que Mlle. Morgan en exprime — non pas seulement le personnage mais la noblesse totale. La neige et elle me semblent être les grandes vedettes de l'entreprise. Sauf certaines scènes où les paroles abîment vos silences et "fouillent la plaie" — (ce que vous vous êtes bien gardé de faire) — j'estime que *La Symphonie* vous respecte. J'eusse aimé un film plus radieux et un père moins acteur — une mère moins expressive — Petites chicanes — L'ensemble est beau.[57]

(I should have phoned you just after I saw the film—but I hate the telephone and I had to submit to this cure (a sort of liquid flagellation). Your book is sturdy enough to stand the test, and it even happens that Mlle [Michèle] Morgan expresses the nobleness of the whole work and not just the character she plays. The snow and she seem to be the big stars of the production. Except for certain scenes where the words ruin your silences and "disturb the wound" (something you were very careful not to do), I believe *La Symphonie* respects you. I should have liked a more radiant film and a less theatrical father—a less expressive mother. Niggling criticisms—the ensemble is beautiful.)

Gide had responded: "Tout ce que vous me dites du film, je le pense aussi," [58] and for once the critical opinions of the two artists coincided.

In discussing his own first film, *Le Sang d'un poète*, Cocteau's 1946 preface to the printed version describes certain flaws in his film, flaws of which Gide approved:

> Par exemple, je m'attache aux images. Il en résulte une lenteur presque écœurante. Comme je m'en plaignais à Gide, après une récente reprise, il me répondit que je me trompais, que cette lenteur était un temps à moi, une lenteur inhérente au moi du moment où j'avais tourné le film et qu'on le gâcherait en le changeant de rythme.
>
> Sans doute a-t-il raison. Cette "part de Dieu" dont il parle et dont ce film use et abuse, m'y est sans doute plus sensible. [59]

> (For example, I cling to images. This results in an almost heartrending slowness. As I was complaining about this to Gide, after a recent revival, he replied that I was wrong, that this slowness was a tempo of my own, a slowness inherent in the me of the moment at which I made the film, and that it would be ruined by changing the rhythm.
>
> No doubt he is right. Without doubt I feel in it more that "part of God" about which he speaks and which the film uses and abuses.)

Le Sang d'un poète had been filmed in 1930, but by 1946 the value of flaws that perfect a work of art had become part of Cocteau's esthetic doctrine, a theory of dynamic imperfection. The "part de Dieu," Gide's phrase to describe that part of his creation over which the artist has no control, is also very close to Cocteau's view of the poet as a medium for inner forces whose orders he carries out in his work.

One of Gide's criticisms particularly offended Cocteau by what seemed to him its unfairness: the charge of lightness or lack of gravity. This imputation of lack of serious purpose was anathema to Cocteau. Cocteau felt that he wrote with his blood instead of ink, and his themes of death and disorder invariably had a tragic orientation; for him, writing itself was a life and death struggle. He was convinced that an artist need not be heavy in order to be serious, and he scorned the air of false gravity or "frivolité grave" that he found in Gide's work. In *La Difficulté d'être* of 1947 Cocteau answers Gide's old criticism of lightness, "Je sais que vous aimez Sophocle; mais je crains que vous ne l'aimez surtout quand il danse," ("I know you like Sophocles, but I fear you like

him most of all when he dances"), by citing Joan of Arc and Antigone: "Ces deux anarchistes conviennent à la gravité que j'aime, que Gide me refuse, gravité qui m'est propre et qui ne cadre pas avec celle qu'on a coutume d'appeler par ce nom. C'est celle des poètes." [60] ("These two anarchists fit the gravity that I like, that Gide denies me; gravity suitable to me and that doesn't square with the one usually referred to by that name. It is the gravity of poets.") Here once again, as he so often does when hard-pressed by critics, Cocteau claims poetic immunity.

In 1947, in a letter confirming the abandonment of the project Cocteau and Gide had formed to collaborate on a film version of Gide's *Isabelle*, Cocteau seized the opportunity to bring into the open a matter that had distressed him ever since the publication of Gide's *Journal* in 1930. To Gide he wrote:

Bref votre visite me reste comme un exemple type des motifs qui m'ont toujours empêché de vous en vouloir pour les choses si pénibles que vous dites de moi dans votre journal. J'y distinguais l'injustice des querelles d'amoureux et je n'y veux rien distinguer d'autre.
Je vous aime et je vous embrasse.

Jean

P.S. Je serais très fier et très heureux si vous pouviez, un jour, ajouter quelques notes dans ce sens à votre journal. Car ceux qui vous *croient* et ne font pas que vous lire, me jugent bien mal à travers vos phrases. J'en ai eu souvent des échos et de la peine. Maurice Sachs le jour de "sa mort" m'a expliqué qu'il n'avait fait que suivre votre exemple. Si je vous embête, n'y pensons plus et aimons-nous en cachette. [61]

(In short your visit remains for me as a typical example of the motives that have always kept me from hating you for the very painful things you say about me in your journal. I saw in them the unfairness of lovers' quarrels, and I do not wish to see anything else in them.
I like you and I embrace you.

Jean

P.S. I would be very proud and very happy if you could, someday, add a few notes to this effect to your journal. Because those who *believe* you, and read only you, judge me badly indeed through your comments. I have often heard painful echos as a result. Maurice Sachs, the day of "his death," explained to me that he had only followed your example. If I am a bother to you, let's not think any more about it and let's be friends behind the scenes.)

Cocteau's request seems astonishingly aggressive and naïve at the same time in view of Gide's chronically critical attitude. But Cocteau was now fifty-eight and Gide seventy-eight years old; time was running out. If Gide was ever to balance the harshness of his *Journal* judgments on Cocteau's work by the sort of tribute Cocteau claimed Gide privately paid to his *Thomas l'Imposteur, Roméo et Juliette, Les Mariés de la Tour Eiffel*[62] and *Le Secret professionnel*,[63] it would have to be soon. The gentle tone of Cocteau's request, devoid of all acrimony, and almost like the prodigal son imploring forgiveness, was a sign of the renewed warmth that marked the closing years of their friendship. Gide's reply is not recorded, but Cocteau's plea would seem to have fallen on deaf ears. The *Journal* judgments were never subsequently softened with regard to Cocteau; on the contrary the next year Gide took a final critical slap at Cocteau in his *Journal*. The entry for April 11, 1948, speaks disdainfully of Henri de Montherlant's *Malatesta* and of Cocteau in the same breath:

Décidément je ne peux maintenir mon estime pour un homme aussi précautionneux . . . plus soigneux encore que Cocteau pour l'éclairage de son personnage et soucieux d'autrui (de l'opinion de), avec l'air de planer et de survoler le vulgaire. . . .[64]

(Decidedly I cannot maintain my esteem for so wary a man . . . more painstaking even than Cocteau about the illumination of his personage and anxious about others (about their opinions), who gives the impression of soaring and flying above the common herd. . . .)

From the Cocteau side, some of the most perceptive and revealing judgments on Gide were made by Cocteau after Gide's death in 1951. His long 1952 interview with Colin-Simard, "Gide vivant," and his acceptance addresses at a number of great institutions which had honored him in quick succession in 1955 and 1956, all provided opportunities for posthumous pronouncements about his late friend and rival. The pejorative tone that runs through many of these opinions can doubtless be traced to Cocteau's bitterness that Gide, before his death, had not included anything in his *Journal* to ameliorate his harsh appraisals of Cocteau's works. Forced to explain away this harshness without help from Gide, Cocteau developed two main lines of defense. The first was that Gide's *Journal* entries about him stemmed from jealousy over Marc Allégret.

The second was that a basic misunderstanding existed between him and Gide, the misunderstanding between the *cancre prestigieux de la classe* and the *fort en thème,* between the Rousseau and the Encyclopedist, between the poet and the intellectual. Cocteau's article "On ne peut se permettre," which appeared in the special *NRF* issue for November 1951, *Hommage à André Gide,* gives a clear view of his feelings in this respect:

> Mes rapports avec Gide ont été de malice et de grâce. Il me taqui-nait et m'aimait, comme en témoignent ses lettres intimes en marge d'un journal où il se montre souvent fort injuste à mon adresse.
> Il fallait le comprendre, ne pas se blesser stupidement des boutades d'une susceptibilité à vif qu'il tenait de Jean-Jacques et qui peuvent surprendre chez un héritier des encyclopédistes. . . .
> De ce perpétuel échange entre un vieux maître et un jeune élève, entre le fort en thème et le cancre prestigieux de la classe, émane un parfum qui déroute l'analyse, sauf si le cœur s'en mêle.[65]

> (My relations with Gide were a mixture of malice and of gracious-ness. He teased me and liked me, as testified to by his intimate letters, marginal to a journal in which he often showed himself extremely unjust toward my skill.
> One had to understand him, not be foolishly wounded by the sallies of a raw sensitivity that he owed to Rousseau and that can be sur-prising in an heir of the Encyclopedists. . . .
> From this perpetual exchange between an old master and a young pupil, between the exemplary student and the amazing class dunce, there emanates a perfume that defies analysis, unless the heart enters in.)

Less than a year later, however, Cocteau's public attitude toward Gide had hardened considerably. He selected some of his favorite vocabulary, by now encrusted with a patina of its own, to explain the enigma of André Gide to Colin-Simard:

> Tout le monde possède un invisible et un visible. L'invisible est le schizophrène qui nous habite . . . le rôle de l'écrivain consiste à l'exploiter en le cachant sous le visible.
> Après la mort, cet invisible prend sa revanche et devient le visible véritable.
> André Gide a toujours voulu être visible . . . être une énigme visible.[66]

> (Everyone has an invisible and a visible. The invisible is the schiz-ophrenic who lives inside us . . . the writer's role consists in exploit-ing it while hiding it under the visible.

After death, this invisible takes its revenge and becomes the genuine visible.
André Gide always wanted to be visible . . . to be a visible enigma.)

Cocteau then predicts that since Gide's lifetime custom was to permit himself to be thoroughly explored and sifted over, nothing is left for his "archeologists" to discover about him. Cocteau quickly points out that Gide was a non-poet: "Sans doute, le vrai drame de Gide est de n'être pas poète. Il voulait être l'architecte et le visiteur de son labyrinthe." [67] ("No doubt Gide's real drama is to not be a poet. He wanted to be the architect and the visitor of his labyrinth.") Later in the interview Cocteau makes another thrust at Gide's Achilles heel as a non-poet:

D'après certaines confidences de Ghéon à l'époque de leur brouille, Gide aurait beaucoup souffert de n'être pas poète . . . une forme propre au poète lui avait semblé insoluble . . . il est probable que la grande guerre des lettres, depuis leurs origines, est celle entre les poètes et ceux qui souffrent de ne l'être pas. [68]

(According to certain confidences from Ghéon at the time of their falling out, Gide had suffered acutely from not being a poet . . . a form appropriate to the poet had seemed insoluble to him . . . it is probable that the great war of letters, since their beginnings, is the one between those who are poets and those who suffer because they are not.)

In Cocteau's opinion Gide was physically, not metaphysically, oriented, and preferred sensations to sentiments. With his painful memories of Gide's *Journal* in mind, Cocteau explained to his interviewer:

Son air de sérieux trompait sur son impulsivité qui était extrême. Je sais qu'il regrettait souvent les choses qu'il avait écrites, mais il s'y opiniâtrait, et ne les corrigeait pas afin de les affubler de cet air sérieux dont je parle. [69]

(His serious manner was misleading as to his impulsiveness, which was extreme. I know that he often regretted the things he had written, but he stubbornly persisted, and did not correct them in order to dress them up in that serious manner I am speaking of.)

In an effort to clarify the basic distinction between his own literary doctrine and that of Gide, Cocteau told Colin-Simard:

[Gide's] méfiance en face d'œuvres qui n'étaient pas de son règne relevait de la crainte des enfants dans le noir. Il voulait que les drames restassent sur la terre, relevassent de la police et d'une morale conventionnelle.[70]

([Gide's] wariness in the face of works that were not of his kingdom was akin to the child's fear of the dark. He wanted the dramas to stay on the ground, to be answerable to the police and a conventional ethic.)

And in a further statement whose thrust was to suggest that his own originality perhaps exceeded Gide's, a question which today finds supporters on both sides, Cocteau added: "Son jeu consistait à contrecarrer cette morale, mais jamais il ne s'est fait une morale propre à lui-meme, et uniquement réservée à son usage." [71] ("His game consisted of thwarting that morality, but he never created an ethic to suit himself and reserved exclusively for his own use.")

On the matter of homosexuality Cocteau averred:

J'ai toujours mal compris l'étrange manière qu'employait Gide pour défendre ce qu'il est convenu d'appeler les mauvaises mœurs. Son instinct semblait le pousser vers une extrême jeunesse et vers les amours grecques. Or, ce qui importe dans ce domaine, c'est lorsque la force se conjugue avec la force, et non pas lorsqu'une force veut appuyer une faiblesse.[72]

(I've always had trouble understanding the strange manner Gide used to defend what are generally referred to as bad morals. His instinct seemed to push him toward extremely youthful behavior and toward Greek forms of love. Now, what matters in this area is when strength pairs with strength, and not when strength wants to shore up a weakness.)

He continued the discussion, distinguishing carefully between Gide's attitude and his own, and quoting Henri Ghéon's report that Gide confesses his escapades with Arab boys in order to conceal even more sordid affairs: "Gide ne m'a jamais fait de confidences. Il est vrai que j'ai grande pudeur de ces choses, que Gide sentait ma réserve et ne se laissait jamais aller avec moi." [73] ("Gide never confided in me. It's true that I am very modest about those matters, that Gide sensed my reserve and never let himself go with me.")

This passage reflects Jean Cocteau's aversion to being placed

in the same homosexual category as Gide. The strength of
this feeling on his part is even clearer in a letter he wrote to
one of his biographers, Jean-Jacques Kihm, in 1958:

Le mot *pédérastie* est inadmissible en ce qui me concerne. C'est une
insulte à ma morale éducative et même s'il me plaisait de m'expliquer
dans l'ordre sexuel, la conjugaison des forces viriles que représente
pour moi l'homosexualité resterait à des lieux galaxiques du touche-
pipi de Gide et de la police des mœurs.[74]

(The word *pederasty* is inadmissible as far as I'm concerned. It's
an insult to my instructive morality, and even if I cared to explain
myself on the sexual level, the conjugation of virile forces that
homosexuality represents for me would remain light years away
from Gide's prick feeling and the policing of morals.)

Moving on to the question of legends that surrounded the
two authors, Cocteau told Colin-Simard:

Les légendes qui recouvraient Gide et qui me recouvrent sont
d'origine différente. Je déteste les miennes. Gide ne détestait pas
les siennes.[75]

(The legends that covered Gide and that cover me are of different
origins. I detested mine. Gide didn't hate his.)

Both Gide and Cocteau contributed consciously to their
own legends, as all celebrated artists do to some extent, but
Cocteau's myth-making became an obsession in his late years,
when he attempted to impart a different patina to his reputation. His desire to divorce his works from the legends of frivolity and artifice with which Gide had helped endow them, is
manifest in the way he was already rationalizing about his
legend in 1952:

On pourrait dire que mes légendes n'ont pas le moindre rapport
avec mes œuvres, et je m'en félicite, puisque, si on me brûle en
place publique, on brûle de moi une effigie qui ne me ressemble en
aucune façon.[76]

(One could say that my legends haven't the slightest connection
with my works, and I congratulate myself on this, since if they
burned me in the public square, they would burn an effigy of me
which does not resemble me in any way.)

On the other hand, according to Cocteau, Gide's legends were not effigies but solid flesh from which critical attack drew blood.

The question of Gide's sincerity also came under Cocteau's lash in his conversation with Colin-Simard:

Gide était une fraude vivante, il ne pouvait donc pas constater de fraudes en sa personne, et s'il en constatait chez les autres, il se trompait souvent, prenant pour fraude une expression de leur vérité dont il ne les croyait pas capables. . . . Faux jeton est un pléonasme. Gide était un vrai jeton.[77]

(Gide was a living fraud, so he was unable to notice frauds in his own person, and if he noticed them in others, he was often mistaken, taking for fraud an expression of their truth of which he didn't think them capable. . . . False token is a pleonasm. Gide was a genuine token.)

Cocteau's remarks in his interview were not all uncharitable with respect to André Gide. When Colin-Simard reminded him of Gide's comment, "Comédien? Peut-être, mais, c'est moi-même que je joue — les plus habiles sont les mieux compris" ("Actor? Perhaps, but it is myself I play — the cleverest ones are the best understood"), Cocteau agreed at once that it was an excellent statement. He went on to say that Gide "joue à merveille avec les fameuses cartes qu'il a en mains" ("plays wonderfully with the famous cards he holds"). Cocteau could no doubt have made the same statement about himself with equal validity.

Since Cocteau himself was a writer often identified as having a narcissistic obsession with mirrors, he could understand Gide's self-conscious posturing in his works and the deliberate interplay between Gide's art and life. "Il me semble évident que Gide évoluait dans l'existence sans jamais perdre de vue son rôle de littérateur."[78] ("It seems clear to me that Gide developed in life without ever losing sight of his role as a man of letters.")

In an observation which perhaps gives Gide too much credit for scientific method and not enough for concern with esthetics, Cocteau tries to illustrate a basic difference in the two writers' artistic concerns by commenting:

Lorsque Gide nous raconte comment il enfonce la tête des papillons dans le cyanure et comment il les épingle sur le liège, jamais il ne

cherche à résoudre l'énigme des taches de leurs ailes, ni le pourquoi de leur décor.[79]

(When Gide tells us how he sticks the heads of butterflies in cyanide and how he pins them to the cork, he never tries to solve the puzzle of the splashes of color on their wings, or the reason for their *décor*.)

The idea of establishing one's own identity, of achieving unity and harmony with one's self, of integrating the personality, to use Carl Jung's words, was central to the art of both Cocteau and Gide. As homosexual artists, both men felt a particular need to resolve through art some of the problems that beset them in life. Both writers developed formulas that reflect this urgent concern. "Ma vieille formule," Cocteau tells Colin-Simard, " 'Ce que le public te reproche, cultive-le, c'est toi' me semble plus significative que le 'ose devenir ce que tu es' de Gide." [80] ("My old formula . . . 'What the public reproaches you for, cultivate *that;* that's you' seems to me more meaningful than the "dare to become who you are" of Gide.")

When Colin-Simard asked if Cocteau had ever thought to disturb André Gide, who prided himself on being a disturber, Cocteau's reply explains his method of dealing with Gide throughout their acquaintance:

Je distinguais très vite dans son petit œil d'éléphant ce qui l'intriguait de ma personne, et je tâchais de lui servir ce qu'il en voulait entendre et de lui cacher ce qu'il se refusait d'entendre, ce qui le dérangeait.[81]

(I discerned very quickly in his little elephant's eye what intrigued him about me, and I tried to serve him what he wanted to hear and to conceal from him what he refused to hear, what disturbed him.)

In the course of the interview Cocteau gave his opinion of several of Gide's works in their relation to the author:

Gide était beaucoup plus terrestre qu'humain: les *Nourritures Terrestres* est bien le titre qui le résume.
Ce que je préfère dans l'œuvre de Gide est toujours ce à quoi les Gidiens attachent le moins d'importance. Je trouve *La Porte Etroite* et *Robert* des œuvres plus proches de sa personne que celles où il exploite l'immoraliste.[82]

(Gide was much more earthly than human: *Les Nourritures terrestres* is indeed the title that sums him up.

What I prefer in Gide's work is always what Gidians attach least importance to. I find *La Porte étroite* and *Robert* closer to his character than those works in which he exploits the immoralist.)

In a footnote to this statement Cocteau quoted Jean Genêt's comment about Gide: "son immoralité me semble bien suspecte." Cocteau was to elaborate further on this theme in his discourses before the French Academy in 1955 and at the Brussels Exposition in 1958. "Et là encore il me faut citer Genêt à propos de Gide: 'Je n'aime pas les juges qui se penchent amoureusement vers l'accusé.' " [83] "Etant de la race des accusés il m'est impossible de prétendre à celle des juges; surtout de ces juges auxquels Jean Genêt reproche de se pencher amoureusement vers l'accusé." [84] ("And there again I must quote Genêt on Gide: 'I don't like judges who lean amorously toward the accused.' " "As I belong to the race of the accused, it's impossible for me to lay claim to that of the judges; above all that of the judges Jean Genêt reproaches for leaning amorously toward the accused.")

Straining to finish the long interview with Colin-Simard on a note of harmony concerning Gide, Cocteau's final statement had a stoic ring:

Je suis heureux de terminer ces dialogues avec vous par une approbation totale de l' "Ainsi soit-il" d'André Gide.

Je ne me lève jamais sans me dire: "Tu n'y peux rien: accepte."

(I am happy to close these dialogues with you by a total approval of the "So be it" of André Gide.

I never get up without telling myself: "There's nothing you can do about it: accept.")

And in a phrase reminiscent of Montaigne he added: "Vous voyez qu'en fin de compte, nos chiffres si différents arrivent à produire le même total." [85] ("You see that, everything considered, our numbers which are so different finally add up to the same total.")

Cocteau felt he was probably the most famous but least well-known poet in France. It was part of his Rousseau-like mystique to complain that the public, critics, and even friends misunderstood him. When Margaret Crosland attempted the first comprehensive biography of Cocteau, the latter wrote his English translator: "Le livre de Margaret Crosland apporte sa haute pierre d'erreur à la pyramide au centre de laquelle mes secrets

dorment." [86] ("Margaret Crosland's book brings its capstone of error to the pyramid in whose center my secrets sleep.") It was therefore almost inevitable that Cocteau, deeply wounded by François Mauriac's attack on his play *Bacchus*, should deliver a consolidated reply to all his critics at once. This he did in his *Journal d'un inconnu* of 1952, one chapter of which was titled "D'une justification de l'injustice." The first two sections speak of Cocteau's disappointing relationships with Maurice Sachs and Claude Mauriac, two young friends who Cocteau felt had treated him unjustly. The third section deals with André Gide, who, although older, "obéissait au mécanisme de la jeunesse," and is therefore included by Cocteau "dans ce chapitre, où je cherche à excuser mes agresseurs." Cocteau then repeats what his older readers had already heard from him before: Gide's perfidy in the *Le Coq et l'Arlequin* episode, Gide's jealousy over Marc Allégret, Gide's pique at not having read Proust until Cocteau insisted, Gide's resemblance to both Rousseau and Grimm. But true to his conciliatory temperament, Cocteau ended on a note that summed up quite realistically the relationship he shared with Gide: "J'aimais Gide et il m'agaçait. Je l'agaçais et il m'aimait. Nous sommes quittes." [87] ("I liked Gide and he provoked me. I provoked him and he liked me. We are even.") Cocteau's closing paragraph demonstrates his progress in polemics since the days of his open letter exchange with Gide. By taking a balanced view he automatically raises himself to the same level as his judges.

En outre, j'estime que les effluves qui provoquent les attaques d'un certain ordre, émanent beaucoup plus de l'accusé que du juge. Dans une zone où le litige de responsabilité n'existe pas, juge et accusé sont aussi responsables et irresponsables l'un que l'autre.[88]

(Besides, I consider that the emanations that provoke attacks of a certain kind issue much more from the accused than from the judge. In a zone where there is no such thing as litigation of responsibility, judge and accused are both responsible and irresponsible, the one as much as the other.)

André Gide did not live to see Jean Cocteau elected in 1955 to the same seat in the French Academy once held by an early Cocteau model, Edmond Rostand. Cocteau's acceptance speech was a brilliant amalgam of, among other things, gratitude and guilt. He quickly identified himself in his discourse as the

agent of all the prevous *poètes maudits* who had never been received under the cupola. Conscious that Gide had not been admitted to the Academy, Cocteau deliberately worked Gide into his *Discours* a number of times.[89]

Although Gide had influenced Cocteau's development as a writer, Cocteau did not approve of certain aspects of Gide's style, either in Gide's own writing or in his translations of others. Like Gide, Jean Cocteau was fascinated by language, nuances, and the problems of translation. Gide had translated works by many authors, including Blake, Conrad, and Shakespeare, Rilke, Tagore, and Whitman. Cocteau, without training in foreign languages, had nevertheless adapted dramatic works by Shakespeare, Sophocles, Shaw, and Tennessee Williams. He had entered the literary arena during "la révolution du verbe," and as early as 1912 he had written his mother of the need for reforms in writing in order to restore lost nuances: "quelle balance établir entre ces extrêmes puisque la nuance est morte pour toutes les oreilles et tous les yeux"[90] ("what balance to establish between these extremes since nuance is dead for all ears and all eyes").

In his *Journal d'un inconnu* Cocteau expressed envy for Gide's luck in having skilled translators for his work: "La traduction ne se contente pas d'être un mariage. Elle doit être un mariage d'amour. On m'affirme que Mallarmé, Proust, Gide en ont eu la chance. Cette chance, j'ai failli l'avoir avec Rilke."[91] (Translation is not satisfied with being a marriage. It must be a love match. I am told that Mallarmé, Proust, Gide, have had good luck this way. I almost had this luck with Rilke.")

As late as December 28, 1955, Jean Cocteau wrote hopefully to Justin O'Brien, who had made the four-volume English translation of Gide's *Journal:* "J'eusse été si heureux de vous voir et d'apprendre de votre bouche que j'aurais la chance de voir entre vos mains se dissiper les mythes dont je suis recouvert."[92] ("I should have been so happy to see you and to learn from your lips that I would have, in your hands, the good luck to see dispelled the myths that cover me.")

When Cocteau wrote the scenario for his *L'Aigle à deux têtes,* he included in Act II, Scene v, several lines from a French version of Shakespeare's *Hamlet.* He might have been expected to use the translation by André Gide, which had been published in 1944 in a bilingual edition, and a copy of which had been

given him by Gide. Cocteau did not, however, and an exchange of letters between Cocteau and Jean Dauven indicates why.

Dauven had translated a series of English detective stories into French from the original versions by Peter Cheyney. The hero of the stories was Lemmy Caution, who spoke in colorful language. Cocteau had first read Dauven's translations while recovering from his heart attack in 1954, and in September 1955 he wrote Dauven from Saint-Jean-Cap-Ferrat: "la langue française est à moitié morte et . . . exige afin de revivre un peu des efforts qui me fatiguent" [93] ("the French language is half dead and . . . to revive it a little demands efforts that exhaust me). Cocteau then asked Dauven to translate his acceptance address to the French Academy into *argot*. Dauven, who had already written an essay that attacked Gide's translation of *Hamlet*, suggested to Cocteau that it be included in the preface to the translation of the Academy address. After reading the first draft of the preface, Cocteau wrote Dauven:

J'approuve votre attaque contre Gide. C'est justice. Mais ici elle ne venait et ne doit venir que pour appuyer votre thèse de la langue en relief. Il faut donc refondre le tout et prouver que mon argot n'est que le rejeton de Montaigne et n'a que faire avec le pathos de Gide. C'est là notre but. Sinon nous aurons l'air de nous servir d'un prétexte pour égaler Gide alors que votre texte est plus important que le sien.[94]

(I approve of your attack against Gide. It is justice. But here it only occurred, and should only occur, to support your thesis of the language in relief. So we must recast it all and prove that my argot is nothing but the offspring of Montaigne and has nothing to do with Gide's pathos. That's our goal. Otherwise we'll look as though we're using a pretext to equal Gide, whereas your text is more important than his.)

Shortly afterward Cocteau wrote Dauven: "En ce qui concerne les notices il aurait fallu commencer par les erreurs de Gide et arriver au panégyrique de Peter Cheyney — le mien et le vôtre." [95] ("As far as the notices are concerned, they should have begun with Gide's errors and arrived at the panegyric of Peter Cheyney — mine and yours.")

Dauven, however, relates that Cocteau later decided to put the comments about Gide at the end rather than the beginning of the preface for fear of making Gide too conspicuous in relation to Cocteau. "Je vous conseille de mettre Gide à la

fin pour ne pas déranger notre architecture." [96] ("I advise you to put Gide at the end so as not to upset our architecture.")

In December 1955 Cocteau sent Dauven some additional comments:

> Shakespeare s'adressait au grand public populaire davantage qu'à la cour — Les personnages sont des étudiants, des soldats, des truands et princes truands. La traduction de Gide est un monstrueux contresens, une avalanche paresseuse d'adverbes et platitudes. Incroyable succès de ce monument d'absurdité.[97]

(Shakespeare directed himself to the broad public more than to the court. His characters are students, soldiers, beggars, and vagabond princes. Gide's translation is a monstrous misinterpretation, a lazy avalanche of adverbs and platitudes. Unbelievable success of this monument of absurdity.)

In 1956 Cocteau was granted the degree of *docteur ès lettres honoris causa* by Oxford University. André Gide, also at the instigation of Enid Starkie, had been similarly honored there ten years earlier. In his acceptance address Cocteau spoke of his masters: Stravinsky, Picasso, Radiguet, and Satie, but pointedly omitted Gide's name from among those "grandes rencontres qui m'ouvrirent les yeux." His only mention of Gide came in a brief allusion to the young mischief-makers who in years past had circulated between them to stir up trouble. Cocteau's allusion must have reminded some of his audience, such as Enid Starkie, of Gide's 1918 visit to Cambridge with one of those "jeunes mythomanes," Marc Allégret. That escapade had so appalled Gide's wife that as a gesture of despair and renunciation she burned every letter Gide had ever written her.

Cocteau's pride was undoubtedly, and perhaps justifiably, hurt by Gide's refusal to mitigate the severity of his *Journal* judgments of Cocteau. Such was the weight given to Gide's opinions that Cocteau had reason to fear that the *Journal* evaluations, if left intact, might unfavorably affect future readers and result in an a priori condemnation of his art. In Cocteau's eyes Gide's offenses against him thus came full circle: the open letter attack of 1919 was a sin of commission, and Gide's failure to erase his *Journal* censures before his death was a sin of omission. All his life Cocteau had tried to forget the first, but it was impossible to overlook the second. All he

could do was to explain Gide's criticism as a personal vendetta, or retreat to more technical ground as he did in his interviews with André Fraigneau for the French Radio in 1951:

> En ce qui concerne Gide nous avons toujours eu des rapports merveilleux ensemble. Les rapports publics sont moins bons, mais tous les critiques, et même Gide, ont une grande excuse: je suis, je vous le répète, très difficile à suivre parce que je ne m'appuie sur aucun groupe, sur aucune force extérieure.[98]

> (As far as Gide is concerned we've always had wonderful relations together. The public contacts are less good, but all the critics, and even Gide, have a great excuse: I am, I assure you, very difficult to follow because I don't lean on any one group, on any external force.)

After Gide's death, however, Cocteau's homage to Gide in the *NRF* (see Appendix 23) included the following doctrinal paragraph:

> Nul mieux que Gide ne prouve que toute œuvre grave est un autoportrait et que la ressemblance avec celui qui peint est plus importante que la ressemblance avec le modèle, employé par l'artiste au seul titre de prétexte.

> (No one proves better than Gide that every sober work is a self-portrait and that the resemblance to the painter is more important than the resemblance to the model, employed by the artist merely as a pretext.)

Cocteau's insistence on the autobiographical nature of Gide's fiction is surely not unintentional. In a final riposte at the colleague who had ridiculed him as Passavant in *Les Faux-Monnayeurs*, Cocteau turns the force of that ridicule back on Gide. This time there was no answer.

Rivalry—the Root and the Flower

As Editor of the *NRF* for many years before World War II, Jean Paulhan knew both André Gide and Jean Cocteau at first hand for more than a quarter of a century. A few months before his death in 1968 Paulhan was asked to describe with a single word the relationship between Gide and Cocteau. Without hesitation he replied: "Rivalité!" [1]

Cocteau himself used the same word, in an interview with Léon Pierre-Quint, to characterize his relations with André Gide: "Mais je crois qu'avec des hauts et des bas, il y a une rivalité aigüe entre nous — rivalité masquée — car, dans la vie, nous conservons, en apparence, des rapports supportables." [2] ("But I think that with ups and downs there is a keen rivalry between us—masked rivalry—because in life we preserve, on the surface, tolerable relations.")

The word "rival" is also used by André Gide to refer to the counterpart of Jean Cocteau in *Les Faux-Monnayeurs*. In this novel Gide and Cocteau are transposed as the characters of Edouard and the Count Robert de Passavant respectively. [3] Edouard (Gide) is piqued at the wide attention Passavant's (Cocteau's) books receive: "Mais en lisant les articles sur le livre de *son rival*, il a besoin de se redire que peu lui importe." [4] ("But on reading the articles about *his rival's* book, he has to tell himself again that it matters little to him.") Gide uses "rival" again in the same work when he describes Edouard's

diminishing jealousy toward Passavant after winning the young Olivier away from him: "Ce rival, qu'il détestait hier encore, il venait de le supplanter, et trop complètement pour pouvoir plus longtemps le haïr." [5] ("This rival, whom he had hated as recently as yesterday, he had just supplanted, and too completely to be able to hate him any longer.") In the point and counterpoint of the singular friendship between Gide and Cocteau, rivalry was indeed the constant overtone, but the perennial rivalry itself was rooted in something deeper.

After giving his one-word characterization of the dominant aspect of Gide's and Cocteau's relationship, Jean Paulhan added that jealousy tinged both their human relationships and their writing about each other. He attributed this to the homosexual nature of both men, which, without creating a liaison or even a close rapport between them, inevitably colored their contacts with each other. The two writers found their anomaly a barrier instead of a bond, according to Paulhan, because Gide was a violent pederast and Cocteau a gentle homosexual.

Marc Allégret, who probably knew both Cocteau and Gide better than anyone else after 1917, has a somewhat different perspective on the two authors. Allégret sees them as basically divergent in character, and does not think of them primarily as rivals. In Allégret's view Gide remains essentially "un maître difficile" for Jean Cocteau.[6]

The observations of Jean Paulhan and Marc Allégret bracket the range of responses to this question about the Cocteau-Gide relationship. Marcel Jouhandeau, who also knew Gide and Cocteau very well, confirms that although both were of the same class, being homosexuals, they were of different orders. As he pointed out, even though both are birds, the hawk and the sparrow have little in common.[7]

Claude Mauriac was the first author to write serious studies of both Gide and Cocteau, with a separate volume for each. He found them very different people and takes a view, similar to Paulhan's and Jouhandeau's, that there was a basic lack of rapport between Gide and Cocteau. He also observed that Gide was jealous of Cocteau's brilliance and facility, while Cocteau envied Gide's established position as head of the *NRF* and as prewar *chef de file* of the young writers and reading public alike.[8]

Claude Mauriac's father, François Mauriac, began his literary

career at the same time as Jean Cocteau. He followed closely the activities of Gide and Cocteau for forty years, in varying roles as observer, antagonist, and protagonist. He believes that although both men were homosexuals they were of very different temperament.[9] François Mauriac also felt that Gide did not consider Cocteau a serious competitor as a writer; Mauriac himself, nevertheless, at the end of his life considered Cocteau the better writer of the two. His *Nouveaux Mémoires intérieurs* [10] omits a passage that appeared in the manuscript: "L'œuvre de Gide, l'œuvre de Cocteau, qu'est-ce que cela pèse? Qu'est-ce que la mienne pèsera?" (Gide's work, Cocteau's work, what weight have they? What will mine weigh?") François Mauriac explained that he juxtaposed Gide and Cocteau here because he felt they have not yet found their correct place in literature.

Roger Stéphane made a full-length television film portrait of André Gide and another of Jean Cocteau. When he inquired of Cocteau as to the cause of his friction with André Gide, Cocteau explained that Gide was jealous of his success with films and with the young public. Cocteau's explanation, whether justified or not, was a charge he often leveled against Gide.[11]

The testimony of these colleagues and friends of the two authors points up the fundamental nature of their personality conflict, rooted in Gide's pederasty on one side and Cocteau's sodomy on the other. Cocteau, in a letter to André Gide, said their differences were probably "d'ordre homéopathique." [12] The testimony of outside observers indicates also that their rivalry involved antagonistic and narcissistic behavior designed to hold the attention of young readers, young writers, and young friends. Cocteau often commented in later life about the competition for the young public that prevailed between him and Gide: "Gide se fermait chaque fois qu'il craignait que je lui retirasse des électeurs." [13] "S'il m'a attaqué, c'est qu'il craignait que les jeunes ne préférassent mes marchandises aux siennes." [14] ("Gide closed up every time he feared I might draw some of his constituents away from him." "If he attacked me, it's because he was afraid the young people preferred my merchandise to his.") Jean Cocteau had matched Gide's aphoristic formulas aimed at youth with some of his own and offered the following advice to any young man reading his work:

Je lui demande d'essayer de fuir ce pluriel qui le rebute, dans ce singulier que lui offre sa propre nuit. Je ne lui dis pas, comme Gide: "Pars, quitte ta famille et ta maison." Je lui dis: "Reste et sauve-toi dans tes ténèbres. Inspecte-les. Expulse-les au grand jour." [15]

(I ask him to try to flee this plural which rebuffs him, in that singular which his own night offers him. I don't tell him, as did Gide: "Be off, leave your family and your home." I say to him: "Stay, and lose yourself in your shadows. Examine them. Eject them into broad daylight.")

By 1941 Cocteau had reached the zenith of his popularity with the young public. Jean-Jacques Kihm affirms that "En 1941, Jean Cocteau se sentait véritablement maître de la jeunesse . . . la jeunesse d'après-guerre, en se détournant de lui, l'a tué." [16] ("In 1941, Jean Cocteau felt himself really master of the young . . . postwar youth, by turning away from him, killed him.") After Gide's death Cocteau noted that following World War II Gide too had fallen into disfavor with young readers: "En parlant de Gide, je ne songeais qu'au labyrinthe où il attirait les jeunes, où il aimait se perdre avec eux. Le mécanisme de révolte s'est mis en marche après sa mort." [17] ("In speaking of Gide, I was only thinking of the labyrinth into which he drew young people, in which he liked to lose himself with them. The machinery of rebellion began to work after his death.")

In his interview with Colin-Simard in 1952 Cocteau made a statement about Gide's relation to the young that could apply equally well to Cocteau himself:

J'estime qu'un homme doit protéger et garder son enfance, et si André Gide n'avait pas gardé et protégé la sienne, ce n'est pas sa faute, c'est peut-être qu'il n'en a jamais eu. C'est pourquoi il prolongeait sa jeunesse — ce qui n'est pas pareil — et il a prolongé sa jeunesse à l'extrême jusqu'à la mort. Il avait donc les défauts particuliers à la jeunesse, et n'avait pas ses excuses. Il fréquentait les jeunes pour s'en trouver. Seulement les jeunes excusent leurs propres fautes mais ne les excusent pas chez les gens d'âge parce qu'ils les leur rendent visibles. Gide raconte presque toujours les impairs que lui a causés ce mécanisme, et il s'en étonne. Il ne se rend pas compte qu'en le fréquentant, les jeunes cherchaient en lui les secrets de la réussite et de l'âge, et non pas un écho de leurs malaises et de leurs troubles.
Si même André Gide avait ennuyé les jeunes avec une morale qui

lui soit propre et une sorte de sagesse, il est probable qu'il n'aurait pas subi leurs coups après sa mort.[18]

(I believe a man must protect and guard his childhood, and if André Gide did not guard and protect his, it's not his fault, it's perhaps that he never had any. That's why he prolonged his youth —which is not the same thing—and he prolonged his youth to the extreme, until death. Therefore he had the shortcomings particular to youth and didn't have its excuses. He associated with the young in order to acquire some. Except that the young excuse their own faults but don't excuse them in older people because they make them visible to the young. Gide almost always tells of the blunders this system caused him, and he is surprised by it. He doesn't realize that young people, in associating with him, sought in him the secrets of success and age, and not an echo of their uneasiness and their troubles.

If André Gide had so much as annoyed the young with a morality that was his own, and a kind of wisdom, it's probable that he wouldn't have suffered their blows after his death.)

In addition to making the young public into an arena where he contested with André Gide, Cocteau also took issue with Gide in the field of poetry. If Gide, as he had made plain in his open letters to Cocteau, did not accept Cocteau as a logician, Cocteau refused to consider Gide a poet. On the other hand, Cocteau considered himself a poet in every way, and insisted that all his work be classified accordingly: poetry of the novel, poetry of the theater, poetry of the film, poetry of drawing, etc. For him poetry was written in a special language, not simply in the poet's own tongue, and it did not depend on rhyme for its effect. He distinguished sharply between poetry and the poetic, and berated the public for failing to recognize the difference. He defined the nature and role of the poet endlessly in some of his most arresting aphorisms. For Cocteau the poet was an archeologist and a bringer of light from the dark side of man's nature: "Ce doit être . . . le passage de nos secrets à la lumière, véritable travail d'archéologue, qui nous fait prendre pour des prestidigitateurs." "Tout homme est une nuit, . . . le travail de l'artiste sera de mettre cette nuit en plein jour." [19] "Le poète est le véhicule, le médium naturel de forces inconnues qui le manœuvrent." [20] ("It must be . . . the carrying of our secrets to the light, real archeologist's work, which gets us taken for sleight-of-hand artists." "Every man is a night, . . . the artist's work

will be to bring that night into full daylight." "The poet is
the vehicle, the natural medium of unknown forces which
work him.")

This status as a poet in the broadest sense became increasingly important to Cocteau with time, partly because it enabled
him to draw a distinction between his own talents and those of
his literary rival André Gide. In his dialogue with Léon Pierre-
Quint in 1927, Jean Cocteau pointed out: "Gide, lui, comme
les encyclopédistes, a une sorte de jalousie profonde des
poètes." [21] ("Gide, like the Encyclopedists, has a kind of deep
jealousy of poets.") According to Cocteau, who was to be
accorded the title "Le Prince des Poètes" after a violently
disputed election at the Foire aux Poètes de Forges-les-Eaux
in June 1960, the non-poets always accuse poets of not being
poets, hoping by that tactic to reduce the dangerous company
of the men they fear and envy most.

The jealousy of the non-poets, Gide among them, toward
the true poets such as Cocteau was a theme of Cocteau's
Oxford address in 1956:

une âpre jalousie déchaîne les prosateurs contre les poètes, comme si
les poètes étaient — par une injustice native — les possesseurs d'un
fabuleux privilège dont ceux qui ne le possèdent pas prétendent les
dépouiller ou, du moins, les empêcher de jouir.
Barrès et Gide ont beaucoup souffert de cela.[22]

(a bitter jealousy unleashes the prose writers against the poets, as
if poets were — by an inborn injustice — the possessors of a fabulous
privilege which those who don't possess it claim the right to deprive
them of or, at least, prevent them from enjoying.
Barrès and Gide suffered greatly this way.)

In his "Discours sur la poésie" in 1958 Cocteau showed he
had not forgotten the deprecatory treatment accorded his
poetry by André Gide in *Les Faux-Monnayeurs* of 1926. At the
same time Cocteau reproved Jean-Paul Sartre, who had recently referred to him as "Le Prince des faux-monnayeurs":

il [Sartre] me traite de faux-monnayeur, oubliant que les poètes
frappent des médailles à leur effigie alors qu'un faux-monnayeur
frappe les siennes à l'effigie de la Banque de France.
    . . . Barrès . . . Gide . . . Sartre . . . souffrent, en quelque sorte,
d'une nostalgie de n'être pas de la famille maudite. Cela les pousse

à employer, d'une main, contre les poètes, qu'ils caressent de l'autre, des armes courbes et fort dangereuses.[23]

(he [Sartre] treats me like a counterfeiter, forgetting that poets strike medallions in their own image, whereas a counterfeiter strikes his bearing the effigy of the Bank of France.

. . . Barrès . . . Gide . . . Sartre . . . suffer, in some way, from a nostalgia at not belonging to the accursed family. That drives them to use, with one hand, curved and highly dangerous weapons against the poets whom they caress with the other.)

In those areas where professional and personal interests intertwined, the "rivalité aigüe et masquée" made itself felt almost from the beginning. As an established literary figure even before Cocteau met him, André Gide had a formidable head start on his young admirer. Always sensitive to criticism, Cocteau smarted under Gide's early rebukes and was stimulated to make his star outshine that of Gide. Cocteau's sensitivity and aggressiveness in this direction suggest an overcompensation for the inferiority complex, "la timidité" as Edouard Dermit calls it, from which he suffered and which Cocteau described as: "ce fameux complexe d'infériorité dont, certes, on parle beaucoup trop, mais qui existe et qui, plus que l'orgueil, est la cause de bien des misères." [24] ("this famous inferiority complex which, of course, people talk far too much about, but which exists and which, more than pride, is the cause of many miseries.")

Gide's professional stature and his influence on Cocteau in his formative literary years provided a framework of discipline which Cocteau, part "Nathanaël" part "enfant prodigue," alternately rebelled against and was grateful for. In his first letters to Gide, Cocteau chose to cast himself in these roles. In his middle years he wrote Gide: "Je vous dois tant de choses et . . . jadis, sans votre intervention, ma vie se perdrait," [25] and "vous êtes ma vraie famille." [26] ("I owe you so many things and . . . formerly, without your intervention, my life would have been wasted," and "you are my true family.") Shortly before Gide's death Cocteau refers to him, with evident affection in this instance, as "le père Gide." [27] Throughout the relationship there is a mixture of filial respect and rebellion on Cocteau's part, matched by sympathy and criticism on Gide's side, which are natural to a talented and

ambitious son growing up in the shadow of an illustrious literary father.

A pragmatic aspect to the rivalry also soon developed: both Gide and Cocteau knew the value of selecting the right enemy. Gide had once attributed the lack of attention a literary friend received to his failure to learn the art of making enemies. Jean Cocteau acquired the art early, recognizing that an enemy could teach him things a friend never could: "notre pire ennemi sera seul capable de nous comprendre à fond et *vice versa*" [28] ("our worst enemy will be the only one capable of understanding us completely and *vice versa*").

Paul Morand, diplomat and friend of Jean Cocteau, said in his *Monplaisir ...en littérature:* "Mieux vaut étouffer sous l'oreiller du silence que sous les roses. Cocteau le sent. Impossible de durer sans ennemis; c'est par eux que l'on survit; ils sont une assurance sur l'après-vie." [29] ("Better to smother beneath the pillow of silence than beneath roses. Cocteau feels it. Impossible to last without enemies; it's by means of them that we survive; they are insurance on the afterlife.") Cocteau's ambivalent attitude toward Gide in this respect had been reflected in his projected *dédicace* to *Vocabulaire:* "À mon ennemi Gide — Son ami J.C." [30] Cocteau recognized that Gide's reserve and criticism were often more instructive than the praise of close friends. This fact, as well as Gide's literary eminence, helped confirm Cocteau's intuition that Gide would be invaluable as a controversial friend. Intentionally or not, Cocteau kept the controversy alive and in the open by discussing Gide in his works and with interviewers such as Pierre-Quint, Claude Mauriac, Colin-Simard, and André Fraigneau.

During and immediately following World War I, Jean Cocteau searched restlessly for an area where he could capitalize on his assets of youth and talent, for a way to assert his supremacy over his "maître difficile." Modernism and such avant-garde literary movements as Cubism, Dadaism, Futurism, and Surrealism provided appealing vehicles to the young poet then approaching thirty. Participating in these movements one after the other in a broader display of the "sincérités successives" Pierre Herbart later noted in Gide, Cocteau played a central role in the artistic and literary fusion of Montmartre and Montparnasse. With the accelerated movement between Right Bank and Left Bank Paris, studios and art galleries

began to displace the salons of the Faubourg Saint-Germain as the cultural agoras of the city. In the intensive cross-pollination between artists and Parisian society that followed, with its attendant shifts in social and esthetic standards, the contribution of Cocteau, who had a foot in both worlds, cannot be overlooked.

The young literary anarchists such as Aragon, Breton, and Soupault had not yet formally evolved (by the years 1916 to 1917) to their later position as Surrealists. Nevertheless, André Breton and Philippe Soupault, both barely twenty, were already resentful of Cocteau's aggressive brilliance and rebuffed his efforts to identify with their group. On the other hand, the *NRF*, dominated by André Gide, who was then nearing fifty, also rejected Cocteau's overtures.[31] With characteristic pragmatism Cocteau tried to bring anarchists and establishment together in a move that would secure his position with each. It was Jean Cocteau who first introduced Breton and Soupault to André Gide. Soupault explained later to Léon Pierre-Quint that "à une exposition de cubistes chez Rosenberg, Cocteau se précipite sur Breton et sur moi et nous présente à Gide qui vient d'arriver."[32] ("at a Cubist exhibition at Rosenberg's, Cocteau flung himself on Breton and me and introduced us to Gide, who had just arrived.") But Cocteau's maneuver misfired, for instead of winning allies he seemed to succeed only in uniting his antagonists. When the eclectic Dadaist-Surrealist review *Littérature*[33] appeared in March 1919 under the direction of Breton, Soupault, and Aragon, Gide played a conspicuous part in the first issue, but Jean Cocteau was disregarded. Soupault permits a revealing glance behind the scenes of that initial issue of *Littérature* in his interview with Pierre-Quint in 1927. In response to Soupault's request for a text for the new review, Gide had at first proposed fragments of his *Les Nouvelles Nourritures* but then withdrew his offer. Said Soupault:

Or soudain il refusa de me donner son texte. Voici ce qui s'était passé: à cette époque, Marc [Allégret] voyait souvent Cocteau, ne jurait que par lui. Gide, je crois, aurait voulu nous opposer, nous, le "groupe des trois" [Aragon, Breton, Soupault] à Cocteau pour prouver à Marc qu'il y avait d'autres jeunes dans l'avant-garde que l'auteur du *Cap de Bonne-Espérance.* Il s'exprima un jour très librement à ce sujet, chez les Godebski et devant moi: — Marc est complètement subjugué par cet esprit clownesque!

J'étais si ravi de ce propos, car je détestai alors l'esprit de Cocteau. Et le propos parvient, de Marcel Herrand à qui je le répétai, par plusieurs autres bouches, à Cocteau qui s'en plaignait à Gide:

— Mon cher Soupault, me dit Gide, vous êtes trop léger. Je ne pourrai pas collaborer à Littérature.

(Now suddenly he refused to give me his text. Here's what had happened: at that time Marc [Allégret] saw a lot of Cocteau, swore only by him. Gide, I feel, would have liked to set us up against each other, we the "group of three" [Aragon, Breton, and Soupault], against Cocteau, to prove to Marc that there were other young people in the avant-garde besides the author of *Le Cap de Bonne-Espérance*. He expressed himself one day very freely on this subject, at the Godebskis' and in front of me: "Marc is completely captivated by this clownish wit!"

I was so delighted by this comment because I then hated Cocteau's wit. And the comment got back by several other mouths, from Marcel Herrand, to whom I repeated it, to Cocteau, who complained about it to Gide.

"My dear Soupault," Gide told me, "you are too inconsiderate. I will not be able to contribute to *Littérature*.")

Soupault adds that Gide later relented and sent him the fragments of *Les Nouvelles Nourritures*, which appeared in the March issue of the review, but that "après ce premier incident . . . Gide garda toujours une explicable méfiance pour moi, une méfiance qu'il a toujours eue pour le groupe" [34] ("after that first incident . . . Gide always had an understandable distrust of me, a distrust he has always had for the group").

Soupault's conclusion, however, only partly explains Gide's reserve. Both Gide and Cocteau were too independent in spirit, too set in favor of the nonconformist "singulier" as opposed to the conformist "pluriel" (to use Cocteau's words) to accept the dominion of any school, be it Dada or Surrealist. "Respecter les mouvements. Fuir les écoles," warned Cocteau, and then postulated the corollary to this idea in another epigram: "La faiblesse d'un artiste est de faire école." In March 1920 Cocteau broke with Dada and wrote Francis Picabia, editor of the Dada review *391*, to withdraw three poems he had submitted earlier: "Dada, le Dadaïsme me causent un malaise intolérable . . . Tzara désorganise. . . . Rendez-moi les 3 poèmes pour 391." [35] ("Dada, Dadaism, give me an uneasiness that's unbearable . . . Tzara disorganizes. . . . Give me back the 3 poems for *391*.")

On this occasion Cocteau and Gide found themselves on the same side of the barricades. The April 1, 1920, issue of the *NRF* carried a lead article by Gide in which he demolished Dada: "Le jour où le mot: Dada, fut trouvé, il ne resta plus rien à faire." [36] ("The day the word Dada was invented, there was nothing left to be done.")

Soupault's remarks attest to the pivotal position of Marc Allégret in the personal and professional rivalry between Gide and Cocteau. Allégret was the first of what Cocteau later described as "les jeunes mythomanes" who oscillated back and forth in their allegiance to him and to André Gide:

Afin de se rendre intéressant, de jouer un rôle, le jeune homme oisif qui va de l'un à l'autre véhicule des histoires qu'il forge. Peu à peu le doute s'infiltre. La mèche s'enflamme, s'écourte et l'amitié saute. Des lieues morales séparent alors des hommes qu'un contact de cinq minutes réconcilierait. Victimes de mythomanes, il nous a fallu des années pour nous rejoindre et retrouver notre vieille tendresse. Gide voudrait bien ravaler sa langue. Il est trop tard.[37]

(In order to make himself interesting, to play a role, the idle young man who goes from one to the other is a vehicle for the stories he makes up. Bit by bit doubt creeps in. The fuse ignites, shortens, and the friendship blows up. Then moral leagues separate men whom five minutes' contact would reconcile. Victims of mythomaniacs, we took years to get together and reestablish our old tenderness. Gide would like very much to swallow his tongue. It is too late.)

Later there were other young men, usually writers, who for different reasons succeeded Allégret as focal points for the competitive attentions of Gide and Cocteau: Georges Gabory, Maurice Sachs, Pierre Herbart, Claude Mauriac, and Roger Stéphane among them.

Gabory, author of *Essai sur Marcel Proust,* had read many of Proust's proofs at Gallimard. On May 9, 1922, Cocteau had written Gide: "plusieurs personnes me disent que vous protégez le pauvre Gabory et que c'est pour 'vous être agréable' qu'il bave sur moi . . . G. est un gentil poète que je croyais un gentil garçon. J'ai de lui une lettre où il me demande à 'devenir mon disciple' ce qui prouve sa naïveté. J'ai aidé de mon mieux sa 'mise en marche' " [38] ("several people tell me you are protecting poor Gabory and that it is to 'please you' that he slanders me . . . G. is a nice poet whom I thought to be a nice boy. I have a letter from him asking to 'become my

disciple,' which proves how naïve he is. I helped him to get started as best I could"). These comments illustrate an attitude Cocteau shared with Gide: Both authors shunned disciples, yet were glad to help young writers discover and develop their true talents. Gide replied on May 12, 1922, to Cocteau: "Pour Gabory, je ne sais s'il dit du mal de vous, mais croyez que ce n'est pas à moi." [39] ("As for Gabory, I do not know if he speaks ill of you; but be sure it is not to me.")

Maurice Sachs was introduced to Jean Cocteau about 1922 by Gérard Magistry. Sachs was so impressed by Cocteau that he took Gide's picture off his apartment wall at once and replaced it by Cocteau's. [40] Years later, at the time of Sachs's conversion to Catholicism by Jacques Maritain, Cocteau acted as his godfather. Cocteau and Sachs later had a falling out, however, and according to Cocteau, Sachs removed several boxes of Cocteau's personal documents from Cocteau's home without authority. [41] Many of these are still missing, and it is possible that letters between Cocteau and his friends Proust and Gide are among them.

In his *Conversations avec André Gide*, Claude Mauriac comments on the connections between Sachs, Cocteau, and Gide:

Comme je parlais à Gide de cette lettre [from Sachs], . . . il s'écria: "moi, je ne le méprise pas du tout..." Puis il m'en parla avec une gentillesse, mieux: une charité qui me troubla. Sur le vol que lui reproche Cocteau, il ignorait tout: il savait seulement qu'après mille errements, Sachs, désemparé, avait tenté de se refaire une réputation. Il était venu voir Gide qui, à cause de ce qu'il avait appris sur lui (il ne précisa pas) le reçut avec froideur. Mais la sincérité du repentir de Sachs l'émut; il le vit si malheureux qu'il décida de l'aider dans l'œuvre de régénération qu'il voulait accomplir. C'est alors qu'il le fit entrer à la *NRF*. [42]

(As I was speaking to Gide about that letter [from Sachs], . . . he cried: "Me, I'm not contemptuous of him at all..." Then he spoke to me about him with a kindness, better a charity, which troubled me. About the theft for which Cocteau blames him, he knew nothing: he only knew that Sachs, in distress, after a thousand mistaken ideas, had tried to rebuild his reputation. He had come to see Gide, who, because of what he had learned about him (he did not specify details), received him coldly. But the sincerity of Sachs's repentance moved him; he saw he was so unhappy that he decided to help him in the task of regeneration that he wanted to achieve. It was then that he caused him to join the *NRF*.)

Thus Gide, as he had done before with André Breton, gave the aid and comfort of the *NRF* to the bitter adversary of Cocteau.

Long afterwards Cocteau, referring in a letter to the "choses pénibles" Gide had written about Cocteau in his *Journal*, confided to Gide: "Maurice Sachs le jour de 'sa mort' m'a expliqué qu'il n'avait fait que suivre votre exemple." [43] ("Maurice Sachs, the day of 'his death,' explained to me that he had only followed your example.")

Marc Allégret, nevertheless, remains the prototype of all these "jeunes mythomanes" in the sense that he was the individual symbol of the contest between Gide and Cocteau for the affection and support of the youthful public.

Unlike the others, however, Marc Allégret's friendship with Gide and Cocteau had unique consequences in the art of both writers. It prompted Gide to record some of the deepest feelings to be found in his *Journal*, and it affected Cocteau's drama of 1919, *Les Monstres sacrés*, which was also related to the Gide-Allégret-Cocteau episode in spirit if not in fact. The central theme of the play was that of a young troublemaker who sows doubt and discord between man and wife. In Cocteau's drama the characters and events, completely transposed, lose all autobiographical reference to the 1917–1919 Gide-Allégret-Cocteau rivalry. There is no doubt, however, that the two are closely connected in Cocteau's mind, for in *Maalesh*,[44] after speaking of the Allégret incident he says: "Voilà l'exemple-type de ces dangereuses visites de ces 'jeunes.' . . . On arrive au nœud dramatique des Monstres sacrés." ("Here is the typical example of dangerous visits by those young people. . . . We get at the dramatic knot of *Les Monstres sacrés*.")

From the roots of the homosexual jealousy Allégret stimulated, wittingly or unwittingly, between the two authors, there flowered a major work of art, the only one of his works André Gide described as a novel: *Les Faux-Monnayeurs*. This is not to say that Gide's creation stemmed from this source alone. It is quite apparent, however, that without the major theme of homosexual rivalry over young Olivier between the characters of Edouard and Passavant, a rivalry which is the faithful shadow of Gide's own striving against Cocteau for Allégret's allegiance, the novel would not have served Gide's purpose either on the moral or on the artistic level.[45]

According to his *Journal des Faux-Monnayeurs*, Gide began

to write *Les Faux-Monnayeurs* on June 17, 1919. The timing is significant since it followed by only a few days the publication of his first open letter of criticism to Cocteau in the *NRF*. *Les Faux-Monnayeurs* was also a significant turning point for Gide's works. Until *Les Faux-Monnayeurs*, Gide avers in his *Et nunc manet in te,* everything he had written was inclined toward his wife Madeleine.[46] "Jusqu'aux *Faux-Monnayeurs* (le premier livre que j'aie écrit en tâchant de ne point tenir compte d'elle), j'ai tout écrit pour la convaincre, pour l'entraîner." [47] ("Up until *Les Faux-Monnayeurs* (the first book I wrote trying not to take her into consideration), I wrote everything to win her over, to sweep her along.") According to Germaine Brée, *Les Faux-Monnayeurs* is Gide's most original work, and in the opinion of George Painter it ranks as one of the world's greatest works in this genre. For Gide at the time it was also most significant as a tropism away from Madeleine Gide and toward Marc Allégret. The immediate evidence of this turning away (the novel was not completed until 1925) [48] was Gide's departure to England with the adolescent Allégret in June of 1918.[49] As he was a prime genetic element in Gide's creation of *Les Faux-Monnayeurs,* so Cocteau may have been one of the factors that motivated Gide's escape to Cambridge with Marc. Cocteau therefore unintentionally found himself in the wings when Gide acted out the most dramatic incident of his life: his 1918 rupture with Madeleine and her burning of his letters.

Cocteau's version of his role in the Gide-Allégret episode has been described in earlier chapters of this book. In 1927 Cocteau explained it to Pierre-Quint in these terms:

La jalousie de Gide est presque féminine. C'est d'elle que sont parties nos brouilles.

Il y eut une où Marc joue un rôle. Vous le connaissez? Je l'appelle: un coupe-papier... un coupe-papier pour l'édition de luxe. N'est-ce pas? Gide l'a desséché en l'aidant, il a perdu l'émotion humaine. Il la retrouvera. Le méandre de Gide lui est propre. D'autres s'y perdent.[50]

(Gide's jealousy is almost feminine. It was the starting point of our quarrels.

There was one where Marc played a part. Do you know him? I call him a paper knife... a paper knife for deluxe editions. Isn't that so? Gide dried him up by helping him; he has lost his human feeling. He'll find it again. Gide's winding path suits him. Others lose themselves in it.)

Shortly after Gide's death Cocteau's account of the episode became more explicit:

En bref je peux vous dire que la jalousie amicale d'André Gide était quasi féminine, qu'il m'avait donné en charge un de ses jeunes disciples, lequel trouvant drôle de taquiner Gide, lui avait fait de moi tels éloges que Gide en avait pris de l'humeur jusqu'à vouloir me tuer (sic); il me l'a avoué avant mon départ pour l'Egypte.

Après avoir lavé notre linge, nous eûmes toujours des rapports agréables.[51]

(In short I can tell you that the friendly jealousy of André Gide was quasi-feminine, that he had put in my charge one of his young disciples, who, finding it amusing to tease Gide, had sung my praises so that Gide grew angry to the point of wishing to kill me (sic); he admitted it to me before my departure for Egypt.

After having washed our linen, we always had agreeable relations.)

André Gide, in his own interviews with Pierre-Quint in 1927, the year following publication of *Les Faux-Monnayeurs,* added a revealing footnote to his text of the novel:

—Je voudrais vous dire encore quelques mots de la jalousie. J'ai longuement pensé à ce sujet. A vrai dire, la jalousie n'est un sentiment violemment ressenti que dans un puissant amour hétérosexuel: c'est la haine du mâle pour le mâle. Dans les autres amours, la jalousie devient d'une nature différente, et je la crois beaucoup plus rare. Ma haine pour C[octeau], ma plus grande souffrance, mon besoin de cogner, ma vie complètement déréglée, c'était Pygmalion retrouvant sa statue abîmée, son œuvre saccagée, mon travail, mes soins d'éducateur, mon esprit complètement galvaudés par un autre: le "gentil" C[octeau]. Ce n'était pas de la jalousie, c'était autre chose.[52]

(I would like to say a few more words to you about jealousy. I have thought about this subject at great length. To tell the truth, jealousy is a feeling experienced violently only in a powerful heterosexual love: it is the hatred of male for male. In other loves, jealousy assumes a different nature, and I believe it much more rare. My hatred for C[octeau], my greatest suffering, my need to hit, my completely upset life, this was Pygmalion finding his statue destroyed, his work plundered, my work, my pains as an educator, my spirit completely botched by another: the "nice" C[octeau]. That was not jealousy, it was something else.)

In 1939 André Gide revealed the nature and depth of his feelings in the matter even more completely to Claude Mauriac:

Gide se recueille alors un moment, puis il me fit à mi-voix cet aveu surprenant: "[Par Jean Cocteau] j'ai connu ce qu'était la jalousie. À propos de Z... [Allégret]. Il était un peu mon œuvre. Je l'aimais. Il avait dix-huit ans. Voilà qu'il rencontre X... [Cocteau] et que celui-ci déploie pour le séduire une coquetterie satanique. Vous n'imaginez pas quelle séduction il pouvait avoir dans sa jeunesse. Je sentis bientôt Z... se détacher de moi. Il admirait X... et ce prestige dont il le revêtait me rejetait aussitôt parmi les ancêtres dépassés, les ridicules vieilles barbes. C'est horrible, la jalousie. Je crois que j'aurais été jusqu'à le tuer, vous entendez. Je n'en pouvais plus d'angoisse. Par bonheur, Z... fut assez clairvoyant pour ne pas s'abandonner. Je suis presque sûr qu'il ne s'est rien passé entre eux..." [53]

(Gide collected his thoughts for a moment, then in a lowered voice he made this surprising admission to me: "[Through Jean Cocteau] I have known what jealousy was. With respect to Z... [Allégret]. He was in a way my work. I loved him. He was eighteen. Then it came about that he met X... [Cocteau] and that the latter deployed a satanic coquettishness in order to seduce him. You can't imagine how seductive he could be when he was young. I soon felt Z... detach himself from me. He admired X... and that glamor with which he invested him cast me immediately among the obsolete ancestors, the ridiculous graybeards. Jealousy is horrible. I think I would have gone so far as to kill him, you know. I was exhausted from anguish. Fortunately, Z... was shrewd enough not to let himself go. I am almost certain that nothing happened between them...")

The month after this revelation to Claude Mauriac, Gide went to visit the Mauriac family near Bordeaux. In anticipation of his visit, Claude Mauriac reread *Les Faux-Monnayeurs* with astonishment:

Je reconnais dans le personnage de Robert de Passavant certains traits du caractère de X... Bien plus: les confidences que Gide me fit à son propos me donnent la clef des rapports qui se nouent dans le roman entre Passavant et Edouard. Olivier n'est autre que Z... tout ce que Gide m'a avoué, je la retrouve ici, à peine transposé. Ce sont les termes mêmes, bien souvent, que ceux entendus de sa bouche, le jour où il m'a parlé de la jalousie qu'il avait éprouvée.[54]

(I recognized in the character of Robert de Passavant certain traits of the character of X... What is more: Gide's confidences to me about him give me the key to the relationships that are established between Passavant and Edouard in the novel. Olivier is none other than Z... everything Gide has confessed to me, I find here, scarcely trans-

posed. They are quite often the very words I heard from his mouth the day he spoke to me about the jealousy he had felt.)

Claude Mauriac's discovery of the congruence of Gide's personal account with its fictional counterpart in *Les Faux-Monnayeurs* focuses attention on the literary consequences of Gide's relationship to Allégret and Cocteau. Although the "labyrinthes du cœur," as Cocteau described them, perhaps concern us less today than their literary by-products, the first cannot be disregarded except at the cost of not fully appreciating the second.

Even before Gide began work on *Les Faux-Monnayeurs* and its concurrent journal, certain events and sentiments had been recorded in his autobiographical *Journal* for the year 1917. These entries, pushing boldly up through its pages, were early shoots of *Les Faux-Monnayeurs*. On May 5, 1917, already carried away by his affection for young Marc, Gide describes his happiness: "Merveilleuse plénitude de joie." [55] By November 30, 1917, he was moved to write:

Rien du passé ne satisfait plus mon amour. Tout en moi s'épanouit, s'étonne; mon cœur bat; une surabondance de vie monte à ma gorge comme un sanglot. Je ne sais plus rien; c'est une véhémence sans souvenirs et sans rides...[56]

(Nothing of the past satisfies my love any longer. Everything in me blossoms forth; is amazed; my heart beats wildly; an excess of life rises to my throat like a sob. I no longer know anything; it is a vehemence without memories and without wrinkles...)

Barely a week later, however, Gide's serenity was threatened. He confided as much to his *Journal* in a passage that prefigures his later account in the novel of Edouard's call on Robert de Passavant on behalf of young Olivier:

Avant-hier, et pour la première fois de ma vie, j'ai connu le tourment de la jalousie. En vain cherchais-je à m'en défendre. M[arc] n'est rentré qu'à dix heures du soir. Je le savais chez C[octeau]. Je ne vivais plus. Je me sentais capable des pires folies, et mesurais à mon angoisse le profondeur de mon amour. Elle n'a du reste point duré...

Le lendemain matin, C. que j'allais revoir acheva de me rassurer, me racontant, selon son habitude, les moindres paroles et les moindres gestes de leur soirée.[57]

(The day before yesterday, and for the first time in my life, I knew the torment of jealousy. I tried in vain to defend myself against it. M[arc] did not come in until ten P.M. I knew he was at C[octeau's]. I was all on edge. I felt capable of the maddest things, and from my anguish I measured the depth of my love. Besides, it did not last...

The next morning C[octeau], on whom I called, reassured me completely by telling me, according to his habit, every last word and gesture of their evening.)

An entry for January 24, 1918, suggests, nevertheless, that Gide's crisis of jealousy was not yet over: "Je repars demain pour Paris; plein d'angoisse après la lettre de Jean-Paul [Allégret] d'hier, où il me fait part de ses soupçons sur son frère." [58] ("I leave again tomorrow for Paris; full of anxiety after Jean-Paul's letter of yesterday, in which he tells me his suspicions about his brother.") The *Journal* entries for early 1918 continue to reflect Gide's euphoria and his torment:

March 4   Ah! je brame après cette santé, cet équilibre heureux que je goûte auprès de M[arc] et qui fait que, près de lui, même la chasteté m'est facile, et le repos souriant de la chair. . . . Je marchais à grands pas, tout ailé par l'espoir de ma prochaine délivrance, et imaginant M. à mon côté. [59]

(Oh! I cry for that health, that happy equilibrium, which I enjoy in M[arc's] presence and which makes even chastity easy for me when I am with him, and my flesh smilingly at ease. . . . I walked along briskly, winged with the hope of my forthcoming liberation and imagining M. at my side.)

March 8   Em [Madeleine Gide] ne peut savoir combien mon cœur se déchire à la pensée de la quitter, et pour trouver loin d'elle le bonheur. [60]

(Em [Madeleine Gide] can never know how my heart is torn at the thought of leaving her, and in order to find happiness far from her.)

April 20   Je me demande parfois si je n'ai pas grand tort de vouloir corriger M.[arc]; si je n'ai pas, moi, plus à apprendre de ses défauts qu'il n'aurait profit, lui, à acquérir les qualités que je voudrais lui enseigner. Je tiens de ma mère cette manie de toujours vouloir retoucher à ceux que j'aime. Et pourtant ce qui m'attire en M. c'est aussi bien ce que j'appelle ses défauts — [61]

(I occasionally wonder if I am not quite wrong to try to correct M.[arc]; if I have not more to learn from his shortcomings than he would profit from acquiring the virtues I should like to teach him. I inherit from my mother that mania for always wanting to improve those I love. And yet what attracts me in M. is also what I call his shortcomings.)

April 28   Période de dissolution; hantée par le souvenir et le besoin de M.[62]

(Period of dissolution; haunted by the memory and the need of M.)

May 4   Me passer de M. ne me paraît déjà plus possible.[63]

(Getting along without M. has already ceased to seem possible to me.)

May 19   Revu M. deux jours à Limoges, d'où je reviens tout gonflé de bonheur. Je l'attends.[64]

(Saw M. for two days at Limoges, whence I return bursting with happiness. I am awaiting him.)

On June 18, 1918, André Gide left for England with Marc Allégret. Later that summer Cocteau wrote Gide: "Cher Gide, je sens une première zone de malaise disparue entre nous — ," in an apparent allusion to their peaceable resolution to the Allégret problem.[65]

But the beginning of one idyll with young Marc marked for Gide the end of another with his wife Madeleine. Gide later described that painful moment to Roger Martin du Gard, his closest friend, in words like those of a criminal in the dock reenacting his crime:

La veille de quitter Cuverville, le soir, après le repas, je vois encore comment ma pauvre chérie s'est approchée de moi, qui étais resté assis et comment, se penchant vers moi, plongeant son regard dans le mien, elle m'a dit:
— Tu ne pars pas seul, n'est-ce pas?
J'ai balbutié: "Non..."
— Tu pars avec X?
— Oui...
Je vois ce qu'est alors devenu ce pauvre visage qui était pour moi la beauté, l'amour le plus pur de ma vie. Ah, comme j'ai souffert!

J'ai voulu parler. Mais elle m'a arrêté, d'un mot terrible: "Ne dis rien. Ne me dis jamais rien. Je préfère ton silence à ta dissimulation." [66]

(The day before leaving Cuverville, in the evening, after the meal, I still see my poor darling as she came over to me, who had remained seated, and how, leaning toward me, plunging her look into mine, she said to me:
"You are not going away by yourself, are you?"
I stammered: "No..."
"You're going away with X?"
"Yes..."
I see what happened then to that poor face which for me was beauty, the purest love of my life. Ah, how I suffered! I wanted to speak. But she stopped me with terrible words: "Don't say anything. Don't ever say anything to me. I prefer your silence to your deceit.")

Suffering from humiliation and frustration, Gide paced his room all that night. At dawn, on his way out the door, he thrust a letter on Madeleine explaining that he was rotting away in Cuverville with her. On June 18 his regular *Journal* carried the climactic entry: "Je quitte la France dans un état d'angoisse inexprimable. Il me semble que je dis adieu à tout mon passé." [67] ("I am leaving France in a state of inexpressible anguish. It seems to me that I am saying farewell to my whole past.")

Revealing as they are of Gide's feelings toward Marc Allégret at this time, the *Journal* notations for 1917 and 1918 disclose very little of Gide's attitude toward Cocteau. Gide preferred to display the accumulated animosities of a dozen years of contact with Jean Cocteau from behind a thin veil of fiction in his novel, thus objectifying their rancor and achieving the esthetic distance necessary to his art.

In *Les Faux-Monnayeurs* contempt constantly colors Gide's characterization of Passavant, from the initial choice of the name with its triply pejorative pun, to the final comment Armand makes to Olivier: "Au fond, il est à faire vomir, ton Passavant." [68] Gide's (Edouard's) jealousy of Cocteau's (Passavant's) friendship with Allégret (Olivier) is suggested in a passage that supports the assumption that Gide's trip to England with Marc had been undertaken partly to get the boy away from Cocteau's influence: "Je compte, a-t-il ajouté bientôt, sur le dépaysement de sa vie à Cambridge pour empêcher des comparaisons de sa part, qui seraient à mon

désavantage." [69] (" 'I am counting,' he added shortly, 'on the strangeness of his life at Cambridge, removed from his usual surroundings, to prevent comparisons on his part that would be to my disadvantage.' ") This conversation in the novel represents a double transposition by Gide. Here Douviers speaks to Edouard about Laura, but the idea no doubt came from Gide himself with respect to Allégret and Cocteau.

Many of the charges Gide leveled at Cocteau in his open letters of 1919, and in his *Journal* observations over the years, appear in *Les Faux-Monnayeurs*. Edouard incessantly undercuts Passavant's authenticity as a person and as an artist by pointing out his superficiality and opportunism:

Pour Passavant, l'œuvre d'art n'est pas tant un but qu'un moyen. Les convictions artistiques dont il fait montre ne s'affirment si véhémentes que parce qu'elles ne sont pas profondes; nulle secrète exigence de tempérament ne les commande; elles répondent à la dictée de l'époque; leur mot d'ordre est: opportunité.[70]

(To Passavant the work of art is not so much an end as a means. The artistic convictions that he displays are so vehemently asserted only because they are not profound; no secret demand of temperament commands them; they respond to the dictates of the times; their password is "opportunity.")

In Gide's novel Passavant is the chief personification of the counterfeit theme from which the work draws its name. "À vrai dire, c'est à certains de ses confrères qu'Edouard pensait d'abord, en pensant aux faux-monnayeurs; et singulièrement au vicomte de Passavant." [71] ("To tell the truth, it was certain ones of his colleagues who first occurred to Edouard as he thought about counterfeiters; and especially the vicomte de Passavant.") It is Passavant (Cocteau), with his superficial brilliance of manners and wit, who, by analogy, comes to mind when Bernard describes his counterfeit gold piece to Edouard:

"Ecoutez comme elle sonne bien. Presque le même son que les autres. On jurerait qu'elle est en or.... Elle n'a pas tout à fait le poids, je crois; mais elle a l'éclat et presque le son d'une vraie pièce; son revêtement est en or, ... mais elle est en cristal. À l'usage, elle va devenir transparente. Non, ne la frottez pas; vous me l'abîmeriez. Déjà l'on voit presque au travers.[72]

("Listen to how true it rings. Almost the same sound as the others. You'd swear it was gold. . . . It hasn't quite the weight, I think; but it has the luster and nearly the sound of a genuine coin; its coating is of gold, . . . but inside it's crystal. With use it will become transparent. No, don't rub it; you'll spoil it for me. You can already almost see through it.")

If his evaluation applies to the man, it also applies to his work when Gide's implication is carried a step further. Gide presents Passavant as a mediocre poet; Olivier tells his friend Bernard: "cette pièce de vers que tu trouvais qui ressemblait au *Balcon.* Je savais qu'ils ne valaient rien.[73] ("those bits of verse you felt resembled "Le Balcon." I knew they weren't worth anything.") Passavant is also a writer without a future, who caters to the young public by his modernism:

> La Barre fixe.[74] Ce qui paraîtra bientôt le plus vieux, c'est ce qui d'abord aura paru le plus moderne. Chaque complaisance, chaque affectation est la promesse d'un ride. Mais c'est par là que Passavant plaît aux jeunes. Peu lui chaut l'avenir. C'est à la génération d'aujourd'hui qu'il s'adresse (ce qui vaut certes mieux que de s'adresser à celle d'hier) — mais comme il ne s'adresse qu'à elle, ce qu'il écrit risque de passer avec elle.[75]

> (La Barre fixe. What will soon seem oldest is what first will have seemed the most modern. Every accommodation, every pretense, is the promise of a wrinkle. But that's the way Passavant pleases the young. He doesn't give a rap about the future. It's today's generation he speaks to (which is certainly better than addressing yesterday's)—but since he speaks only to it, what he writes risks passing away with it.)

The thought expressed here, suggesting that Passavant (Cocteau) sought to be of, and even ahead of, his time, is an amplification of Gide's *Journal* entry for April 18, 1918, in which he made the widely quoted comment that he did not seek to be of his epoch but to overflow it. Edouard's (Gide's) critical line of reasoning continues in *Les Faux-Monnayeurs:*

> Il le sait et ne se promet pas la survie; et c'est là ce qui fait qu'il se défend si âprement, non point seulement quand on l'attaque, mais qu'il proteste même à chaque restriction des critiques. S'il sentait son œuvre durable, il la laisserait se défendre elle-même et ne chercherait pas sans cesse à la justifier. Que dis-je? Il se féliciterait des méscompréhensions, des injustices.[76]

(He knows it and doesn't set his hopes on survival; and this is why he defends himself so fiercely, not just when he is attacked, but also why he even protests at each reservation by critics. If he felt his work would endure he would let it defend itself and would not endlessly try to justify it. What am I saying? He would congratulate himself on misinterpretations and injustices.)

Gide's last observation was a shrewd one that became more accurate with the passage of time. As Jean Cocteau advanced in years he developed an attitude that had stoic overtones: "Mais peu à peu je me suis fait une morale qui consiste à supporter les injustices, parce que je les estime indispensables à la rigueur d'une œuvre." [77] ("But little by little I made a morality for myself which consists in tolerating injustices, because I consider them indispensable to the rigor of one's work.") Cocteau's decision to make the most of all that comes in life and the least of all that goes, was codified in such aphorisms as: "qui gagne perd," "la leçon de l'échec," and "tu n'y peux rien, accepte." [78] ("Whoever wins loses," "the lesson of failure," and "you can do nothing; accept.") That decision did not convince Gide, however, who saw it as one more of Cocteau's masks, another expression of his hypocrisy: "Pour n'avoir pas à reconnaître ses défaites, il affectait toujours d'avoir souhaité son sort, et, quoi qu'il advint, il prétendait l'avoir voulu." [79] ("In order to avoid recognizing his shortcomings, he always pretended to have wished for his fate, and whatever happened, he claimed to have willed it.")

A lack of originality on the part of Cocteau and his plagiarism of the ideas of others are insinuated by Gide when he has Passavant, the counterfeit author, pass off as his own theories on marine creatures he had acquired from Olivier's brother Vincent. "Il [Passavant] sait admirablement se servir des idées, des images, des gens, des choses; c'est à dire qu'il met tout à son profit." [80] ("He [Passavant] knows wonderfully well how to use ideas, images, people, things; that is to say, he turns everything to his profit.") Olivier naïvely writes Vincent, but the ironic thrust of Gide's thought was that Passavant (Cocteau) was "l'homme reflet" incarnate.

Gide completes his transposed portrait of Jean Cocteau in *Les Faux-Monnayeurs* by describing Passavant as "un compagnon charmant" who tries to stay eternally young; an opium-smoking, frivolous "raffiné" whose wit is at its best in exchanges

with shop clerks.[81] Finally, in another double transposition, Gide puts into the mouth of Olivier's friend Bernard the words Gide himself repeated many years later to Claude Mauriac and to Jean Cocteau:

> "Qu'est-ce que vous pensez du comte de Passavant? . . ."
> "Moi," dit Bernard sauvagement . . . "je le tuerais."[82]
>
> ("What do you think of Count de Passavant? . . ."
> "Me," said Bernard savagely, . . . "I'd kill him.")

It is clear that *Les Faux-Monnayeurs* owes a considerable debt to Jean Cocteau. His position in the novel stands as a confirmation of his rivalry with André Gide for the esteem of Marc Allégret. The novel itself, perhaps the high point in Gide's artistry, was to an important extent the consequence of that rivalry. Through his portrait of Passavant, Gide held Cocteau up as a butt for what the French character most resents: ridicule. The derogatory parody of Cocteau, consisting as it did of a few salient features taken out of the context of his whole life and personality, nevertheless had the weight of a major judgment that cast a critical shadow across Cocteau's brilliant reputation. *Les Faux-Monnayeurs* also substantiates, unequivocally, the earlier postulate that André Gide's abrasive public evaluations of Cocteau's work were personally motivated to a considerable degree. Nevertheless, one must discount Cocteau's repeated claims that only personal animosity of an "ordre homéopathique" lay behind Gide's criticism, for Cocteau, like any artist worthy of the name, would prefer to be condemned on personal rather than on artistic grounds.

Gide's former son-in-law, Jean Lambert, in his *Gide familier*, also recognized the element of jealousy as central to the Gide-Cocteau relationship: "C'est probablement l'écrivain [Cocteau] à l'égard duquel il [Gide] s'est montré le plus constamment injuste. Je n'en vois qu'une raison: Cocteau seul, sur un plan d'ailleurs non littéraire, lui avait donné l'occasion d'être jaloux."[83] ("He [Cocteau] is probably the writer to whom he [Gide] was most consistently unfair. I see only one reason for it: only Cocteau, on a nonliterary level, moreover, had given him occasion to be jealous.")

In addition to its other functions *Les Faux-Monnayeurs* served as a catharsis for Gide through which he purged himself of

his violent jealousy over Allégret's regard for Cocteau. Having won over Allégret following their stay in England, and at the same time having resolved his emotional tension in a work of art, Gide was free to resume more normal relations with Jean Cocteau. It was many years, however, before the two writers succeeded in reviving the spirit of their early friendship.

The question of his relationship with André Gide, and the rivalry, the disputes, the reconciliations which defined it for nearly forty years, continued to concern Jean Cocteau almost to the end of his own life in 1963. It was in 1951, however, that he most fairly summed up his own attitudes toward Gide and toward many of the issues that had concerned them both. The text of this *hommage,* which appeared in *France-Amérique* (March 4, 1951), is less perfunctory and more revealing than the article he wrote for the special *NRF* issue of November 1951 dedicated to the memory of André Gide (see Appendix 23 for the *NRF* article). In effect, these two articles, even though written after Gide's death, may stand as the second and third open letters from Cocteau to Gide. They are far different in tone and content from the first open letter of 1919.

In the *France-Amérique hommage,* which is both a soliloquy and a eulogy, Jean Cocteau, distinguished member of four national literary academies and "mauvais élève," rises above rivalry to pay honest tribute to his fallen rival André Gide, winner of the Nobel Prize for literature and "maître difficile." Here one Proteus praises another, and Sisyphus sings nostalgically of his stone.

Both artists had been honored by Oxford University. Both had, as men and artists, struggled to achieve an inner equilibrium which did not exclude their anomaly. Each had made art his life, and his life a work of art. Each had left his mark on the generations of French youth between the first and second world wars. Both had rebelled against their bourgeois heritage through the acceptable anarchy of art. Both had permanently disturbed the esthetic and ethical values of their times.[84] Both had devoted their careers to the fight against conformity, and to the pursuit of beauty in all its forms. By their deep concerns for the individual, both had won a deserved place among the great humanists of the twentieth century. Beside these impressive accomplishments the divisions between them dwindle to insignificance. Jean Cocteau recognized this, and

in his *hommage* [85] he attempted to synthesize from the ambivalence of his relationship to André Gide a final and enduring harmony:

GIDE EST MORT. VIVE GIDE

Dans cette traversée que nous faisons tous ensemble, voilà encore un homme qui tombe à la mer. Et lequel? Celui qui soutenait et qui surveillait à notre équipage.

On s'étonne toujours de la mort en ce sens qu'une rencontre a l'air d'être une rencontre entre mille autres et que cette rencontre était la dernière, et que notre poignée de main à la porte était un adieu définitif.

En ce qui concerne Gide, la mort est moins définitive que pour la plupart des hommes. Une œuvre nous mange et cherche à se rendre libre, à vivre seule, à se passer du véhicule qui l'expulse et qui, semble-t-il, la dérange. Cela est d'autant plus vrai pour Gide qu'il conservait les lettres, notait le moindre détail de sa route et se mêlait continuellement de ce travail qui sort de notre nuit, du moi inconnu dont nous ne sommes que les archéologues.

Notre dernière rencontre date de l'année dernière.[86] Il séjournait à Melun, à la préfecture, et venait passer la journée dans ma maison de campagne de Seine et Oise. Il voulait que je fisse un film d'*Isabelle*. Je lui prouvai que le public attendait de lui un message plus direct et lui conseillai d'entreprendre le découpage des *Caves du Vatican*.

C'est à la première représentation des *Caves du Vatican,* à la Comédie-Française, que je devais l'apercevoir pour la dernière fois. Il se dissimulait dans une baignoire de droite.

J'appris par une lettre où il se plaignait d'une grande fatigue [87] qu'il ne m'avait pas quitté de l'œil et que mon amusement visible lui avait été un spectacle.

J'étais, je l'avoue, émerveillé de sa jeunesse et qu'un artiste de cet âge et illustre, au lieu de prendre l'air grave auquel s'astreignent tant d'autres, ne cherchait que son plaisir, à se distraire et à nous distraire. Il en résultait un spectacle analogue à quelque *Tour du monde en 80 jours* ou *Chapeau de paille d'Italie,* mais, comme dirait Mallarmé, d'un Jules Verne ou d'un Labiche "de rêve." Car Gide tenait paradoxalement des Encyclopédistes et de ce Jean-Jacques auquel ils firent une chasse cruelle. C'est dire qu'il se chassait lui-même, sans cesse entre la malice des uns et la naïve franchise de l'autre, et, parfois, fort embrouillé dans cette lutte où il s'enferrait et s'attaquait, se perdait et se défendait, accumulait les imprudences et les ruses.

Nul ne classa plus de notes et de notices, de Postcripti à des lettres, de réponses à des réponses. Il conservait des armes et en usait ensuite, autant contre sa propre personne que contre ses adversaires.

Son œuvre est trop célèbre pour que j'en dresse le catalogue. De

l'*Immoraliste* aux *Faux-Monnayeurs* elle a été une bible pour toute la jeunesse d'une époque confuse et soucieuse de se libérer d'un code moral.

Cet immoraliste était un moraliste. Car une morale n'est pas *la morale* et ne relève que d'une ligne profonde à quoi un individu reste fidèle jusqu'à se contredire et à suivre sa pente, quelle qu'elle soit. Chez Gide, les pentes étaient innombrables. Il déclarait "Les extrêmes me touchent." Il n'aurait pu s'engager dans un parti. Son Parti était le sien propre, où il se mouvait seul et décidait seul de ses directives. Il avait *pris son parti,* en quelque sorte. Et grâce à cela, il représentait un des derniers esprits libres d'une époque où le *pluriel* gagne chaque jour du terrain sur le singulier.

Son école était dangereuse, mais il aurait pu dire avec Goethe dont il possédait l'âme attentive "Si des imbéciles se suicident parce qu'ils ont lu Werther, peu importe!"

Après sa pièce, je lui écrivis que le personnage de *Lafcadio* devenait celui d'un brave garçon un peu timide, à cause des excès auxquels parvinrent ses disciples dont les journaux racontent les crimes gratuits et les commandos anarchistes.

Ce qui ressortait du roman, sous l'angle du théâtre (dont la rampe brûle certaines choses et en souligne d'autres) c'est l'extrême gentillesse, l'extrême bonté de l'auteur. Une grâce enfantine et fraîche, éclatait dans l'ensemble et dans les dialogues.

C'est pourquoi j'estime que ce mort est si peu mort. Et, de même qu'à mes yeux Raymond Radiguet garde ses vingt ans et reste à l'âge où je l'ai perdu, de même Gide se fixe en moi sous le signe de ce spectacle de la Comédie-Française, sorte de *charade* géniale à laquelle il assistait, non en auteur mais en spectateur et pareil à ce merveilleux public du guignol de notre enfance.

La cape et le chapeau de berger qu'il arborait, ont couru le monde visible et le monde invisible. Il déracinait, cueillait, ou tuait ou épurgeait parfois un peu vite, mais qu'importe? Il n'y a que le format qui compte. Le format de Gide est monumental. S'il lui arrive de traverser le purgatoire des grands écrivains, on retournera obligatoirement à l'herbier de cet admirable botaniste de l'âme humaine.

JEAN COCTEAU

(GIDE IS DEAD. LONG LIVE GIDE

In the course of this crossing that we all make together, there is one more man who has fallen into the sea. Which one? The one who sustained and looked after our crew.

We are always astonished by death in the sense that one meeting seems to be like a thousand others and that this meeting was the last, and that our handshake at the door was a final leave-taking.

With respect to Gide, death is less final than for most men. A work

gnaws at us and tries to free itself, to live by itself, to do without the vehicle that expels it and, it seems, disturbs it. That is all the more true in Gide's case since he kept letters, noted down the slightest detail of his journey, and interfered constantly with that work which emerges from our night, from the unknown "I" for whom we are only the archeologists.

Our last meeting took place last year. He was vacationing at Melun, at the prefecture, and came to spend the day at my country house in Seine et Oise. He wanted me to make a film of *Isabelle*. I proved to him that the public looked forward to a more direct message from him and advised him to undertake the scenario for *Les Caves du Vatican*.

It was at the first performance of *Les Caves du Vatican*, at the Comédie-Française, that I was to set eyes on him for the last time. He was hiding in a ground-floor box on the right.

I learned from a letter in which he complained of heavy fatigue that he hadn't taken his eye off me and that my obvious amusement had itself been a show for him.

I was, I admit, amazed at his youthfulness and that an artist of that age and renown, instead of taking on the serious manner so many others feel compelled to adopt only sought his own pleasure, to divert himself and to divert us. The result was a show like some *Tour du monde en 80 jours* or *Chapeau de paille d'Italie*, but, as Mallarmé would say, by a "dream-like" Jules Verne or Labiche. For Gide paradoxically derived from the Encyclopedists and from Jean-Jacques whom they cruelly hounded. That is to say that he hounded himself, without respite, between the malice of the former and the naïve candor of the latter, and, sometimes, deeply embroiled in the struggle, in which he would impale himself on his own vanities and attack himself, he lost his way and defended himself, stored up imprudent acts and wily dodges.

No one filed away more notes and reviews, postscripti to letters, replies to replies. He preserved some weapons and used them later on, as much against his own person as against his adversaries.

His work is too famous for me to have to catalogue it. From *L'Immoraliste* to *Les Faux-Monnayeurs* it has been a bible for the entire youth of a period that was confused and anxious to liberate itself from a moral code.

This immoralist was a moralist. Because a moral is not *morals* and is only ascribable to a deep line to which a person remains true to the point of contradicting himself and of following his own bent, whatever it may be. With Gide the bents were innumerable. He declared: "Extremes touch in me." He could not have committed himself to a party. His Party was peculiarly his own, where he moved by himself and he alone decided on his rules of conduct. He had made up *his own mind,* as it were. And thanks to that he represented one of the

last free spirits in an epoch when the *plural* daily gains ground against the singular.

His school was dangerous, but he could have said with Goethe, whose careful spirit he possessed, "If a few imbeciles kill themselves because they've read *Werther*, never mind!"

After his play I wrote him that the character of Lafacadio was becoming that of a fine, somewhat timid boy, on account of the excesses his disciples managed to commit, disciples whose gratuitous crimes and anarchistic commandos are reported in the newspapers.

What was thrown into relief in the novel by the theatrical perspective (where the footlights burn certain things and underline others) is the extreme kindness, the extreme goodness of the author. A child-like, fresh grace sparkled in the work as a whole and in the dialogues.

That's why I consider that this dead man is so little dead. And, just as in my eyes Raymond Radiguet is still twenty years old and stays the same age at which I lost him, so Gide is fixed in me under the sign of this Comédie-Française play, a sort of brilliant *charade* at which he was present, not as an author but as spectator and like that wonderful puppet show audience of our childhood.

The cape and the shepherd's hat that he sported traveled widely through the visible world and the invisible world. He uprooted, plucked, or killed or purged sometimes a bit quickly, but what of it? Only the format counts. Gide's format is monumental. If he happens to cross the purgatory of great writers, we will be obliged to return to the herbarium of that admirable botanist of the human soul.

JEAN COCTEAU

Appendices

APPENDIX 1

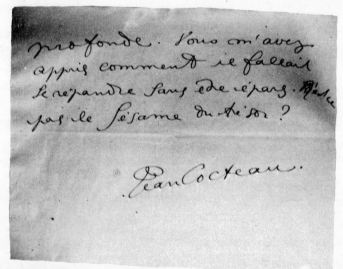

First and last pages of the earliest known letter from Cocteau to Gide. Dated by Gide as April 20, 1912. Doucet Y547.1.

APPENDIX 2

Letter Cocteau to Gide, undated. Postmarked February 5, 1914, Doucet Y547.66.

— J'ai vu Copeau — *ses yeux sont charmants* — Cela suffit pour s'entendre. J'ai "Devenir." L'avez-vous? Si oui vous trouverez même page 96 d'étranges détails sur ma petite jeunesse.

— Le Cinéma des Caves m'enchante. Arnica rythmé par le piano: prodigieux. Protos-Ménalque à suivre partout.

Tendre admiration.
J.

Copeau *très* sympathique. Je redoutais. (De mon côté je redoute *aussi!*) Cela m'a fait plaisir —

Je trouve une trahison que Jehanne-la-Courte mette à fraîchir ses pieds dans vos Caves — et que chez moi nulle couverture orange. Gide est trop sùr du cœur de Jean Cocteau; il en profite.*

(— I saw Copeau — *What charming eyes he has* — That's enough for an understanding.

I have *Devenir*. Do you? If so, you will even find on page 96 some strange details of my dear youth.

I am delighted by the cinema-like *Caves [du Vatican]*. The piano rhythm of Arnica: terrific. Protos-Ménalque to be followed everywhere.

Fondest regards,
J.

[P.S.] Copeau very sympathetic. I was awed. (From my side I am awesome *too!*) It was a pleasure.

I find it treachery that Jehanne-la-Courte is cooling her feet in your *Caves* —while no orange cover at my house. Gide is too sure of Jean Cocteau's heart; he is taking advantage of it.)

*This paragraph, a separate fragment apparently out of place in the Doucet files, should probably be a postscript to letter Cocteau to Gide [May 1914], Doucet Y547.4. (A.K.P.)

APPENDIX 3

Letter Cocteau to Gide [February/March 1914]. Doucet Y547.6.

— il a fallu que le petit "rompe (dit-il) des lances" avec M.C. à mon propos.
M.C. ne saurait m'admettre. "Gide et Ghéon peuvent tout — une phrase
adroite et je n'aurai plus jamais à souffrir d'entendre parler mal de toi."
(Je cite).

Cher Gide — prince d'imbroglio (ou Duc d') *au secours! Je compte sur vous
deux.*

> Tendre gratitude.
>
> Jean

P.S. Pour "des raisons" j'aimerais beaucoup voir aussi paraître: "Ne sois
pas trop intelligent" et "Les Antipodes." Que dois-je faire pour les épreuves?
— Attendre?

(— the little fellow (he said) had to "cross swords" with M.C. about me.
M.C. would never allow me in. "Gide and Ghéon are capable of everything
— one right word and I will never again have to put up with hearing anyone
speak ill of you." (I quote.)

Dear Gide — prince of imbroglio (or Duke of), *help! I am counting on you
two.*

> Deepest gratitude,
>
> Jean

P.S. For "certain reasons" I would also very much like to see published:
"Ne sois pas trop intelligent" and "Les Antipodes." What have I to do about
proofs? Wait?)

APPENDIX 4

Letter Cocteau to Gide [March 1914], Doucet Y547.15.

Mon cher Gide,
    Epoque de l'imbroglio! Quelle douceur! et maintenant quelle amertume
— Mon malaise confus augment [*sic*] de jour en jour — Vous voir m'avait
fait du bien — Je me porte mal. Je souffre. *Je tâtonne dans une morne pénom-
bre.* S'efforcer de rejoindre un amour — y parvenir — et que, juste, alors,
cet amour vous lâche — on en étouffe de déception, de ratage, de fatigue,
de solitude etc, etc... — Indifférence d'un œil qui vous *inspecte* et qui vous
buvait. *Molesse* [*sic*] d'une main qui ne cherchait que la vôtre — c'est atroce —
    Gide, cher Gide, écrivez-moi, vos paroles m'avaient soulagé beaucoup —
                                                                    Jean

(My dear Gide,
    Time of imbroglio! What tenderness! And now what bitterness. My
confused uneasiness increases every day. It did me good to see you.
I don't feel well. I am suffering. *I'm groping my way through a dull twilight.*
To struggle to join one you love, to succeed, only to be dropped by that love,
crushes you with disappointment, failure, exhaustion, loneliness, etc., etc....
The apathy of eyes which now *inspect* you but which once drank you in
thirstily. Slackness of a hand which once eagerly sought yours alone—it's
awful.
    Gide, dear Gide, write to me, your words comforted me greatly—
                                                                    Jean)

APPENDIX 5

Avignon 23 Novembre [1915]

On a découvert récemment par cette fresque du Palais des Papes, l'existence de la Douche Paulhiac au XIVe siècle. Nous avons pensé que ce document d'une grave importance pourrait vous intéresser.

E. Wharton   André Gide

Avignon, November 23 [1915]

(From this fresco in the Palace of the Popes they have recently discovered the existence of the Douche Paulhiac in the fourteenth century. We thought this document, of such grave import, might interest you.

E. Wharton   André Gide)

APPENDIX 6

Letter Cocteau to mother [Christmas 1915]. Archives Cocteau, Milly-la-Forêt.

Ma chère maman,
  Je vais te raconter en détail une Nuit de Noël si grande, si étrange, que j'ai peine à y croire ce matin dans notre camping pluvieux.
  Montre ma lettre à qui m'aime et peut comprendre et voir plus loin que le style nègre-fatigue — je serais bien incapable de recommencer un récit que je n'ose aborder par crainte de littérature ou de confusion. De telles choses, on les parle, on ne les "note" pas. Jamais plus je ne pourrai m'en souvenir sans être "gonflé," empli de ces larmes qui montent "on ne sait pas pourquoi," phrase d'un souverain à son peuple, citation à l'ordre du jour, toile de Cézanne, vers de Rimbaud, et toujours la phrase la plus quelconque, la citation la plus simple, la toile la moins anecdotique, le vers d'apparence le moins significatif.
  À 8 heures casqué, botté, caoutchouté, muni de ma musette et de ma lampe électrique (on s'arrange toujours pour perdre son masque contre le gaz, qui encombre et dégringole comme le manchon d'Anna de Noailles) je grimpe sur mon ambulance et je pars prendre ma garde à N.B.
  Route ténèbre, trous d'obus et ornières molles où on s'enlise si on ne prend pas garde. Relève et permissionnaires, petits groupes tristes qui sortent 3 jours de la taupinière et y retournent ensuite avec résignation, comme à un "atelier," à "la fabrique," au "gagne-pain." À N.B. on cache la bagnole sous un hangar et on entre dans la cave du médecin-chef. Il me reçoit comme on reçoit sur le front, c'est-à-dire royalement. *Rien n'exprime la gentillesse du front,* l'esprit camarade du front. Il arrive d'être bouleversé de cette gentillesse à quoi les villes n'accoutument guère.
  Cave très chaude, trop chaude. "Cabine" du médecin-chef, "cabine" de ses lieutenants, merveilles d'ingéniosité grâce à des pillages, à ce vol officiel, à ce luxe étrange du pays du Front.
  Les 2 lieutenants très chics, *bon chic* sale et franche figure, décorés, drôles, délicieux — 20 zouaves — Ah! les braves types! J'avais apporté 2 bouteilles de Sauterne et du foie gras — ovation — on m'offre une chechia d'honneur, on se souhaite de rejoindre bientôt les familles.
  Salle de festin superbe, aux chandelles. Pinard dans des gourdes zouaves et boches — vaisselle d'aluminium. Au moment de se mettre à table — coup de téléphone. On amène un blessé. Il entre. Le médecin-chef lâche la bousti-faille, se prodigue, le *câline.* C'est un tirailleur — bras cassé. Il tourne de l'œil et s'efforce de sourire. Le médecin-chef qui a voulu que tout le monde y compris les cuisiniers prennent place à table, essaye de lui faire boire quelque chose. Mais il souffre et nous l'emmenons à Zuidcote avec promesse de revenir.
  Course de film américain, passages à niveau qu'on ouvre et ferme soi-même, sentinelles qui surgissent de terre, sanatorium endormi. Je "livre" mon pauvre bougre et nous retournons à N.B. en vitesse.

Les Boches tirent des feux d'artifice pâles qui retombent derrière les dunes et découvrent nos positions. Le vent empêche d'entendre (avions nous cru) le tir des grosses pièces. Enfin notre cave charmante. Je ne me rappelle pas d'avoir été jamais reçu si bien chez personne. On me gâte, me fourre dans mon assiette les plus belles tranches. Un zouave, debout sur sa chaise, imite le gramophone, les oiseaux, la musique arabe, le ténor italien, etc., etc.... les autres se tordent. Les lieutenants font chorus.

La porte s'ouvre. On nous annonce un mort, un caporal parti le matin et qui devait m'offrir des bagues. Pauvre être. Il repose dans la première cave. On le fouille. On ne trouve sur lui que 40 bagues et la photo de Lady Dorothy, jeune anglaise qui se déguise en zouave et visite les lignes grâce au général E. d'O. Il ira rejoindre ses copains dans le petit cimetière, juste contre notre villa, contre ce qui reste de notre villa.

Après l'Ave Maria de Gounod sifflé divinement par un de nos hommes, on se sépare.

Clair de lune tiède, climat spécial de Noël. Les lieutenants ne veulent pas que la fête finisse. On décide de se rendre en première ligne, entendre si les Boches chantent — d'endosser un uniforme de "Zouzou" et on part Iéna — Iéna — Iéna. On passe les 4 sentinelles qui gardent la zone fameuse au bord de l'Yser. Ville détruite — silence fantôme — nous traversons le "Pont Joffre" planches houleuses sur des barques.

Ici commence le front qui se termine à Salonique. *Il commence.* Il ne commence pas vaguement, il y a un premier sac, un premier abri, comme il y aura *un dernier coup de canon* — c'est net comme sur la carte et je t'ai cueilli là une première brindille.

Nous pénétrons alors dans ces catacombes, dans cette "attraction" de Magic City, que l'on visitera au tourniquet après la guerre. Eau à mijambes et sable rose. Pas un coup de canon, pas une torpille. Seulement les "chandelles romaines" qui se balancent et s'éteignent.

Gourbis, cabanes, villes secrètes que révèle une fente lumineuse — un chien qui jappe. Chaque corridor porte un nom. Il y a la rue du capitaine B., le boulevard Babrazzun, l'avenue des Quatre-Cadavres.

Nous arrivons aux 2èmes lignes, à 100 mètres des Boches. Même silence. Il est 4 heures du matin. On barbote en évitant que l'eau clapote et on se courbe lorsque le casque dépasse les sacs. On rencontre des arabes — des rats — des bêtes nouvelles.

1ère ligne.

De 10 en 10 mètres — aux meurtrières — debout — vêtus de peaux de mouton, de ficelle et de journal, les tirailleurs veillent. Ils ne se retournent pas plus à notre passage que dans les cafés maures de Blidah. Ils guettent. Et les Boches guettent. Ils se regardent les yeux dans les yeux. C'est d'une grandeur, d'une puérilité, d'une folie indescriptibles. Nous sommes à 20 mètres des Boches. Boyaux et tunnels — je marche dans une flaque. Un tirailleur se retourne. Il me regarde, il pose un doigt sur ses lèvres; le lieutenant A. me presse l'épaule et me chuchote la bouche contre l'oreille: *"Nous sommes à 8 mètres d'Eux"!* 8 mètres d'Eux! le tirailleur a repris sa pose. Qui a vu ce visage grave, patient, soigneux, terrible, un doigt sur les lèvres a vu *"Servir."*

Les Allemands se taisent, les nôtres se taisent. *C'est la trêve de Noël.* Ce tirailleur, c'est Melchior qui fait signe aux Bergers de se taire dans la crèche.

Ici j'ai cueilli la seconde brindille. Garde-là. C'est une relique.

Je me couche à plat ventre. Je dévore des yeux, des oreilles, ce vide et ce silence. Je ne suis pas suspect de romantisme! Eh bien c'est énorme – énorme de bêtise peut-être, mais énorme. Je ne pouvais m'astreindre à partir.

Enfin il faut battre en retraite. L'aube se lève. Mes compagnons marquent une émotion qui me sera intelligible plus tard et semblent guetter la mienne. Pour éviter l'eau – une rivière jaune – on marche en vue de l'ennemi. Je suis très calme – j'ai confiance dans la "trêve de Noël."

Embouchure du fleuve célèbre – autre pont de planches – clair de lune intense – retour à travers des décombres.

Notre cave est placide. Les Zouaves dorment. On se sèche et les lieutenants me demandent si je désire les suivre à la messe. J'accepte "en rêve." Je marche somnambule. Ils peuvent bien m'emmener au bout du monde.

Petite chapelle froide. 12 poilus. Pas de prêtre. Mes compagnons se décasquent, enlèvent leur Burberrys, se déchargent de leur canne et de leur lampe électrique et... endossent la robe de dentelle.

Tu juges de mon étonnement et de mon respect. Tour à tour l'un faisant communier l'autre ils disent la messe. Jamais *rien* n'aurait pu me faire douter que ces jeunes hommes gais, aventureux, libres de propos et d'allures étaient des prêtres.

La messe dite, ils se métamorphosent, m'emmènent et me tendent leurs étuis à cigarettes – "c'est égal, s'écrie l'un d'eux, en me prenant cordialement sous le bras, voilà une nuit de Noël inoubliable et *bougrement réussie!*"

Il avait raison n'est-ce pas?

Je t'embrasse,
Jean.

P.S. La trêve de Noël était complète. Notre blessé, nos morts étaient dûs à une funeste erreur de patrouille zouave.

Les brindilles étaient à 8 mètres des Boches. La brindille seule, au début de notre front.

[Christmas 1915]

(My dear Mama,

I'm going to tell you all about a Christmas Eve so great, so strange, that I have difficulty in believing it this morning in our rain-soaked camp.

You may show my letter to whoever loves me and can understand and see further than my dead-tired style – I would be quite unable to retell a tale that I hardly dare undertake for fear of embarrassment or "literariness." One speaks of such things but one can't "write" them down. Never again will I be able to remember them without "choking up," brimming with those tears that come flooding "without our knowing why," as they do at a king's words to his people, a citation in the order of the day, a Cézanne canvas, a verse by Rimbaud – and it is always the most ordinary phrase, the simplest citation, the painting with the least narrative aspect, the poem that appears least noteworthy.

At eight P.M., helmeted, booted, and trench-coated, equipped with my musette bag and flashlight (you always manage to lose your gas mask since it's so cumbersome and falls down like Anna de Noailles's muff), I climb into my ambulance and set off to take my tour of duty at N[ieuport] B[ains].

A dark road, shell holes, and mucky ruts you bog down in if you're not careful. Relief troops and soldiers on pass, sad little groups who escape from the molehill and later resignedly come back to it as they would to a "shop," a "factory," or to their "daily job." At N.B. we hide the vehicle under a lean-to and go into the chief medical officer's dugout. He welcomes me the way it's done at the front, that is to say, royally. *Nothing can describe the great kindness of the front,* the comradely spirit of the front. This considerateness, which city life seldom prepares us for, is overwhelming.

Very hot dugout, too hot. "Cabin" of the chief medical officer, "cabin" of his lieutenants, marvels of ingenuity thanks to repeated lootings, a sort of official theft which is a curious luxury of the front area.

The two lieutenants are very chic, *a good chic,* dirty, open faces, decorations, humor, delightful—twenty Zouaves— Ah! what great fellows! I had brought two bottles of Sauterne and some foie gras—cheers—they offer me an honorary tarboosh, we wish each other an early reunion with our families.

Superb banquet hall, with candlelight. Wine from Zouave and Boche canteens—aluminum plates. Just as we sit down at table—the telephone rings. They are bringing us a wounded man. He comes in. The medical officer at once jumps up from his meal, lavishes attention on him, *babies him.* He's a sharpshooter—broken arm. He is fainting and does his best to smile. The doctor, who wanted everyone, including the kitchen help, to take a place at table, tries to get him to drink something. But he is suffering so we take him to Zuidcote, after promising to return.

Wild ride like an American film, railroad grade crossings which we open and close ourselves, sentries who loom up out of the ground, the hospital sound asleep. I "deliver" my poor devil and we rush back to N.B.

The Boches set off some colorless fireworks which fall behind the dunes and reveal our positions. The wind kept us from hearing (so we thought at the time) the fire of the heavy artillery. At last, our charming dugout. I don't recall ever having been so well received by anyone. They spoil me, they load my plate with the tastiest morsels. A Zouave, standing on his chair, imitates a gramophone, birds, Arabian music, an Italian tenor, etc., etc.... the others double up with laughter. The lieutenants chorus requests and applause.

The door opens. They tell us a man is dead, a corporal who went out this morning and who was going to present me with some rings. Poor fellow. He's lying in the outer dugout. They run through his pockets. They only find forty rings on him and a snapshot of Lady Dorothy, the young English-woman who disguises herself as a Zouave and visits the trenches with General E. d'O's permission. The corporal will rejoin his comrades in the little grave-yard close by our villa, near what remains of our villa.

After Gounod's Ave Maria, beautifully whistled by one of our men, we separate.

Warm moonlight, special climate of Christmas. The lieutenants don't want the party to end. We decide to go up to the front line to hear if the Boches are singing—to put on a "Zouzou" uniform and be off to Iéna— Iéna—Iéna. We pass the four sentries guarding the famous zone at the banks of the Yser. Town destroyed—ghostly hush—we cross the "Joffre Bridge," wobbly planks on pontoons.

Here begins the front which ends at Salonika. *It begins.* It doesn't begin

vaguely; there is the first sandbag, the first shelter, just as there is bound to be *a final cannon shot*—it's as clear as on the map. There I picked one of the first twigs for you.

Then we go deeper into those catacombs, that "attraction" of Magic City that we'll pass through a turnstile to visit after the war. Knee-high water and pink sand. Not a sound of cannon, no mines. Only the "Roman candles" which hover in the sky and die away.

Arab huts, shacks, hidden cities revealed by a slit of light—a dog's yelping. Each trench has a name. There is Captain B's Street, Babrazzun Boulevard, the Avenue of the Four Corpses.

We arrive at the second lines, 100 meters from the Boches. Same silence. It is four o'clock in the morning. We paddle along, trying not to splash the water, and bend down when our helmets are above the sandbags. We meet Arabs—rats—new animals.

First line.

Every ten meters—at the loopholes—standing up—wrapped in sheepskins, string, and newspaper, the sharpshooters keep watch. They don't turn around when we pass any more than they do in the Moorish cafés at Blidah. They watch and wait. And the Boches watch and wait. They look each other straight in the eyes. It has a grandeur, a childishness, a madness, which are indescribable. We are twenty meters from the Boches. Approach trenches and tunnels—I step in a puddle. A sharpshooter turns toward me. He stares at me, presses a finger against his lips. Lieutenant A. squeezes my shoulder and whispers with his mouth against my ear: *"We are eight meters from Them!"* Eight meters from Them! the rifleman has resumed his pose. Whoever has seen this grave, patient, careful, terrible face with a finger on his lips knows what it means *"To serve."*

The Germans are silent, our troops are silent. *It is the Christmas truce.* This rifleman is Melchior signaling the shepherds for silence in the manger.

Here I plucked the second twig. Please keep it. It is a relic.

I lie down flat on my stomach. I devour the emptiness and stillness with my eyes and ears. I am hardly one to be accused of romanticism! But just the same it is enormous—enormously stupid perhaps, but enormous. I could not tear myself away.

At last we have to beat a retreat. Dawn breaks. My companions reveal an emotion that I will understand later, and seem to wait watchfully for mine. To avoid the water—a yellow river—we walk in full view of the enemy. I am very calm—I trust in "the Christmas truce."

The famous river mouth—another bridge of planks—intense moonlight—return through ruins.

Our dugout is serene. The Zouaves are asleep. We dry off and the lieutenants ask if I wish to go with them to mass. I accept "as though in a dream." I feel like a sleepwalker. They could very well lead me to the end of the world.

Tiny chapel, cold. Twelve poilus. No priest. My companions remove their helmets, take off their Burberrys, put down their batons and flashlights, and... don the sacramental robes.

You can imagine my astonishment and my respect. They say the mass, each in turn giving Holy Communion to the other. *Nothing* would ever have

made me doubt that these gay and adventurous young fellows, despite their easygoing manners and appearance, were really priests.

The mass over, they changed characters again, took me away and proffered their cigarette cases to me— "Just the same," cries one of them taking me heartily by the arm, "this is an unforgettable and *devilishly successful* Christmas Eve!"

He was right, wasn't he?

Affectionately,
Jean

P.S. The Christmas truce was not broken. Our wounded and dead were due to a fatal error by a Zouave patrol.

The twigs were 8 meters away from the Boches. The single twig was at the beginning of our front.)

APPENDIX 7

Letter Gide to Marc Allégret, April 25, 1918. Collection Marc Allégret, Paris.

Cuverville, 25 avril [19]18

Je t'écrivais hier. Mais voici ta lettre... Et comment ne te récrirai-je pas aussitôt! — Décidément je commence à croire que je pourrai bientôt causer avec toi d'une toute autre façon que je n'ai fait jusqu'alors. Je me persuade que nous avons encore à nous découvrir l'un l'autre — et que de cette découverte dépend notre réelle amitié. Je ne puis éprouver d'amitié vraie pour quelqu'un, sans estime et même sans un grain... d'admiration.

Ne va pas te rassurer trop tôt, car il est vrai que tu m'as fait peur ces derniers temps; et ta lettre, si avidement que je la lise et si rafraîchissante qu'elle soit à mon cœur, ne me tranquillise pas encore complètement. Que je te sais gré de m'écrire ainsi! Et qu'il me tarde de... mais les vraies conversations n'auront lieu qu'en Angleterre, d'ici là je suspends certaines questions au sujet par exemple de ce que tu appelles ton "sens moral" — ... Je renonce, je l'avoue depuis longtemps à comprendre ce que l'on entend par là mais puisque ta lettre m'y pousse je vais te copier aussitôt ces passages de la lettre de D. qui te concernent... "J'avais été frappé depuis longtemps par le manque d'égards de Marc pour les femmes et les jeunes filles du monde d'abord — pour ses aînés ensuite. Souvent il a eu devant moi une conduite de petit butor — Absolument incompréhensible vu son éducation et son raffinement intellectuel. Est-ce une affectation de cynisme?"...

J'ai déjà répondu à D. Je ne veux pas qu'il te juge trop sévèrement. Il saura faire la part de l'éducation — je veux dire: du regimbement contre une éducation souvent absurde — de l'influence et de l'exemple, hélas! Je ne veux pas que son jugement s'élève à l'encontre de l'amitié qui tout naturellement le porte vers toi; mais il dépend de toi de mériter les amitiés que tu souhaites, et ce n'est pas en cachant certains côtés de ta nature, certaines velléités — c'est en ne les *admettant pas*. Je voudrais que tu n'admettes en toi, rien de ce qui *enlaidit*. Et cela enlaidit, mon ami. Comprends-moi, (car souvent, je le sais bien, mon "immoralisme" a pu te donner le change) — C'est sa probité intellectuelle qui pousse en avant mon immoralisme; c'est là le secret de mon livre et ce qui fait son aiguillon. Quant à Lafcadio si tu relis les Caves, tu remarqueras combien soigneusement je mets en avant son *désintéressement*.

C'est contre ce qui enlaidit que je m'insurge; c'est là ce contre quoi je proteste. Et parfois je doute si pour moi toute la morale ne se réduit pas à un intransigeant amour de la beauté. Rien de ce qui est intéressé n'est beau... Et si, dès à présent tu ne te montres pas très strict vis-à-vis de toi-même, très exigeant à te rendre à toi-même des comptes (oh! je parle symboliquement) alors il faut que je te dise adieu.

Je voudrais te donner (mais *tu l'as*) un sens aigu des convenances, un besoin pour toi-même de propreté, de netteté, un souci d'élégance, qui tout de même importe plus que celui des ongles ou des nœuds de cravate.

Vendredi

J'ai dû m'interrompre, bien que le cœur encore plein. J'ose à peine relire ma lettre... Ai-je tort de te parler ainsi, et d'invoquer l'esthétique où d'autres parleraient morale?... Mais non; tu me comprends, n'est-ce pas — et que je te parle ici comme je ne parlerais pas à beaucoup d'autres. Prouve-moi, je t'en prie que je ne me méprends pas en t'estimant.

Ah! que j'ajoute encore ceci: cette exactitude, c'est dans le temps aussi bien que je voudrais te la voir exiger. Que ce soit un duo que nous jouions, ou que tu fasses le soliste à Limoges il s'agit d'aller en mesure, exactement. Il n'y a pas d'harmonie possible sans toi. Le violoniste sent que l'alto, là, près de lui se tient tout près, l'archet au doigt et déjà presque sur la note, dispos à l'attaquer au moment précis qu'il faudra. Parlons sans image, ne charge pas à l'excès ton programme et ne te promets de faire que ce que tu sais que tu pourras exécuter. Mais à cela tiens-toi ferme; cramponne-toi. Ne te laisse pas libre, suivant la disposition de l'instant de faire ou de ne faire point ce que tu te seras proposé. Etre de moins en moins exigeant des autres et de plus en plus exigeant de toi tel doit être ton programme, et c'est le secret de la vraie liberté. Répète-toi ce mot de Baudelaire, lorsqu'on lui demandait comment il faisait pour ne s'ennuyer pas: "C'est que je me pique de faire dans la perfection quoique ce soit que j'entreprenne." Je voudrais que chaque matin, avant de te lever — que dis-je: je voudrais que dès la veille au soir — tu te veuilles et t'exige beau, noble, actif, intelligent. L'art ne s'obtient que par contrainte, et jamais par laisser-aller. Il faut faire de ta vie entière une œuvre d'art — et d'abord soigner le détail.

Si tu veux vraiment tout ça, alors tu es vraiment mon camarade, mon ami. Pourquoi ne t'ai-je pas parlé ainsi plus tôt? Parce que je n'aime donner un conseil que quand je crois qu'il sera suivi.

Ecris-moi. Dis-moi que je ne t'ai ni irrité, ni lassé, j'attends une nouvelle lettre de toi avec une anxieuse impatience.

Ton, qui t'embrasse bien fort,

André Gide

Et n'est-ce pas, tu me rejoindrais même à pied!! Ça va! Ça va!!

Cuverville, April 25, [19]18

(I wrote you yesterday. But now your letter arrives... And how can I keep from writing you again at once! — I definitely begin to feel that I shall soon be able to talk with you in a completely different way than I have up till now. I am convinced that we still have much to discover about each other — and that our real friendship depends on that discovery. I am unable to feel true friendship for someone, unless there be esteem and even a grain of... admiration.

Don't set your mind at rest too soon, because it is true that you have worried me lately; and your letter, as avidly as I read it and as refreshing as it is to my heart, still doesn't completely allay my fears. How grateful I am to you for writing me this way! And how I long to... but our real conversations will only take place in England, and until then I am holding in abeyance certain questions about, for example, what you refer to as your "moral sense"... I have given up, and for a long time past I confess, trying to understand what people mean by that expression, but since your letter urges me to do so I am sending you a copy of the passages from [Marcel] D.[rouin]'s

letter which concern you... "I had been struck for a long time by Marc's lack of respect for women and young society girls first of all — and then for his elders. He has often behaved churlishly in my presence. It's absolutely incomprehensible in view of his education and intellectual refinement. Is it an affectation of cynicism?"...

I have already answered D[rouin]. I don't want him to judge you too harshly. He'll know how to deal with the part involving education — that is to say, the bridling at an education that is often absurd — influence and example, alas! I do not want his judgment to rise up against the friendly feelings that so naturally incline him toward you; but it is up to you to deserve the friendships you hope for, and you will not do this by hiding certain sides of your nature, certain impulses — but by not *allowing them entry*. I would like you not to permit in yourself anything that makes one *ugly*. And that makes one ugly, my friend. Understand me (for often, as I well know, my "immorality" may have thrown you off the track) — it is its intellectual probity that pushes my immorality ahead; that is the secret of my book and what serves as its goad. As for Lafcadio, if you reread *Les Caves* [*du Vatican*], you will notice how carefully I point up his *disinterestedness*.

It is against what makes one ugly that I rebel; that is what I protest about. And sometimes I wonder if for me all morality isn't reducible to an intransigent love of beauty. Nothing selfish is beautiful... And if from now on you do not show yourself to be very strict with yourself, very demanding in bringing yourself to account (oh! I mean symbolically), then I must say goodbye to you.

I would like to convey to you (but *you have it*) a keen sense of the conventions, your need for cleanliness, for clarity, a concern for elegance, which of course means more than worrying about your nails or the knot of your necktie.

Friday

I had to interrupt myself even though my heart was still full. I hardly dare reread my letter... Am I wrong to speak to you this way, and to invoke esthetics where others would speak of morality?... Surely not; you understand me, don't you — and that I speak to you here as I would not to many others. Prove to me, I beg you, that my judgment is not misplaced in thinking highly of you.

Oh! Let me add one more thought: this exactness, I would also like to see you ask it of yourself in respect to time. Whether it be a duet that we were playing, or your performance as soloist at Limoges; it involves keeping time exactly. There is no harmony possible without you. The violinist senses that the alto, there, next to him, is holding himself ready, bow in hand and already almost on the string, prepared to attack it at the precise moment necessary. Let's speak without images. Don't overload your program and don't promise yourself to do anything except what you know you can carry out. But hold fast to that; stick to it like glue. Don't let yourself off, following an impulse of the moment, from doing or not doing whatever you have set yourself. To be less and less demanding of others and more and more demanding of yourself, this should be your policy, and it is the secret of true freedom. Repeat to yourself Baudelaire's reply when he was asked what he did to overcome boredom: "I pride myself on doing to perfection whatever I undertake." I would like it if every morning before getting up — what am I saying:

I would like it if the evening of the day before—you willed and required yourself to be handsome, noble, alert, intelligent. Art is obtainable only through restraint, and never through letting oneself go. You must make your entire life a work of art—and first of all pay attention to detail.

If you truly want all that, then you are truly my comrade, my friend. Why haven't I spoken to you sooner in this way? Because I don't like to give advice unless I think it will be followed.

Write to me. Tell me that I have neither irritated nor wearied you. I await another letter from you with anxious impatience.

Your, who sends warmest greetings,
André Gide

[P.S.] And you would catch up with me, even on foot, wouldn't you!! That's wonderful! Wonderful!!)

APPENDIX 8

Letter Cocteau to Gide [Summer 1918]. Doucet Y547.21.

Bien cher Gide,
J'habite la case de l'Oncle Tom dans un village nègre, au bord du bassin d'Arcachon — je ressemble avec ma barbe qui pousse ma chemise rouge et ma carabine à un héros de livre à 10 centimes "au pays du scalp." — Les Lhote ont une cabane tout près — ils me parlent de J. Rivière, je leur parle de vous et nous vous imaginons heureux ensemble après tant d'aventures — Cher Gide je sens une première zone de malaise disparue entre nous — la bouche ne parle plus loin du cœur et il faudra bientôt que le "cœur parle" — c'est l'essentiel — Merci de votre *crainte* qui n'est pas du *doute*, elle prouve l'amitié véritable. Je sens du reste que je récolte à travers *le silence* les fruits de mon terrible effort — De crise en crise, de fatigue en fatigue, j'arriverai peut-être à cette paix, relative, que goûtent les justes et les travailleurs —

Votre fidèle
Jean

P.S. ai vu Ghéon rasé, inouï — très jeune — oublierai-je qu'avec vous il m'a mis le nez dans mes sottises?

(My very dear Gide,
I'm living in Uncle Tom's cabin in a Negro village on the edge of the Arcachon Basin. With my sprouting beard, my red shirt, and my rifle, I look like a dime novel hero "from the scalp country." The Lhotes have a cabin quite nearby. They talk to me about J. Rivière, I talk to them about you, and we think of your happiness at being together after so many adventures. Dear Gide, I feel a primary zone of uneasiness between us has disappeared. The lips no longer speak when far from the heart, and soon the "heart will have to speak"—that's the main thing. Thanks for your *fear* which is not *doubt*. It is a proof of true friendship. Besides, I feel that through *silence* I am harvesting the fruits of my agonizing effort. From crisis to crisis, one weariness to the next, I may reach that relative peace tasted by the righteous and the toilers.

Your faithful—
Jean

P.S. Seen Ghéon clean-shaven—extraordinary—very youthful—will I ever forget that with you he rubbed my nose in my own follies?)

APPENDIX 9

Letter Gide to Marc Allégret, January 19, 1919. Collection Marc Allégret, Paris.

Cuverville 19.1.19

Cher

Après fouilles dans les dictionnaires et grammaires, je me persuade qu'il fallait: "whether" et non "either" pour le: "si" que nous cherchions à traduire.

Cette feuille était pour Jean C.[octeau] dont je viens de doubler le Cap — mais c'est à toi que j'écris d'abord pour désobstruer mon stylo des réflexions qui se pressent d'abord et dont je ne puis, déjà, lui faire part. Son absence de personnalité réelle n'a jamais été plus manifeste que dans ce livre et l'effort même vers le neuf et l'ultra l'accentue. De plus cette détermination de n'exposer de son émotion ou de sa pensée que les jalons extrêmes, supprimant la phrase, c'est à dire l'acheminement d'un point à un autre et du même coup la démarche qui demeurerait personnelle — fait de son élocution poétique quelque chose d'on ne peut plus facile à imiter, que déjà sans le vouloir et sans le savoir, il imite, et qui ne laisse percevoir aucune nuance par où telle suite de mots (je n'ose pas dire: tel vers) de Cocteau différerait de telle autre suite d'un de ses disciples (garde-toi d'en être) ou de tel exécrable prédécesseur futuriste (je songe à Marinetti). Bref, ça n'est pas difficile à faire, et les qualités que malgré tout j'y trouve, ces dons d'analogie où s'affirme une sensibilité délicate, n'ont rien à voir, ou que fort peu, avec cette disposition typographique où il se voudrait novateur. Le petit livre de Saint Léger Léger était d'une bien plus spéciale saveur; et pour être tout à fait franc, je dois dire que même au *Panorama* de Cendrars, que je viens de lire soigneusement, j'ai pris plus d'amusement et de plaisir poétique.

Cependant je me plonge et m'ébroue dans le Proust, émerveillé souvent et souhaitant d'en lire avec toi maintes pages. Oui, voilà qui est personnel, irrésistiblement naturel, sincère et, partout, inimitable. C'est d'un art prestigieux.

Blanche m'écrit une lettre interminable, éplorée pour me supplier de l'aider à mettre sur pied son *Aymeris*. Il s'agit d'y pratiquer des coupures; il n'a confiance qu'en moi pour le maniement des ciseaux. Il insiste, et de manière si affectueuse et pathétique que je ne me sens guère le cœur de refuser; mais c'est douze jours de travail pour le moins...

Sois toi-même exigeant pour toi. Travaille ferme. Je t'embrasse bien fort et veux que tu me sentes sans cesse ton ami.

André Gide

Cuverville, January 19, 1919

(Dear,

After rummaging through the dictionaries and grammars I am convinced that it should be "whether" and not "either" for the "si" we were trying to translate.

This page was intended for Jean C.[octeau], whose *Cap* [*de Bonne-*

Espérance] I have just circumnavigated—but I am writing you first to flush my pen free of reflections which congest it but which I cannot, so soon, pass on to him. His lack of real personality has never been more evident than in this book, and his straining for the new and the ultra accentuates its absence. Moreover, that determination to expose only the extreme points of his feelings or his thoughts, compressing the sentence, that is to say his route from one point to another—and at the same time the gait that would remain exclusively his own—makes his poetic style the easiest thing in the world to imitate (that he himself already imitates without meaning to or being aware that he does it), and a thing that doesn't permit one to glimpse any nuance by which such a sequence of words (I dare not say, such verses) by Cocteau would be distinguishable from another such sequence by one of his disciples (take care not to become one) or by some execrable Futurist predecessor (I am thinking of Marinetti). In short, that stuff is not hard to do, and the qualities that I find in his work in spite of everything, those gifts for analogy wherein his delicate sensitivity is revealed, have nothing to do, or only very little, with that novel typographical layout that he would like to feel he invented. The little book of Saint Léger Léger had a far more special flavor; and to be entirely candid, I must say that even Cendrars's *Panorama*, which I have just carefully read, amused me more and offered more poetic pleasure.

However, I dive into and wallow in the Proust, often amazed and wishing to read many pages with you. Yes, there is something personal, irresistibly natural, sincere, and, throughout, inimitable. It has a prodigious artistry.

Blanche has written me an interminable letter, tearful, begging me to help him put his *Aymeris* on its feet. It's a matter of making some cuts; he has confidence only in me to use the scissors. He insists, and in such an affectionate and pathetic manner, that I hardly have the heart to refuse; but it means at least a dozen days of work...

Demand much of yourself. Work steadily. I send affectionate wishes and want you to feel always I am your friend.

André Gide)

APPENDIX 10

EXPLOIT *

Signifié le 20-6-9

L'an 1919, le 20 Juin.

À la requête de M. Jean COCTEAU, demeurant à Paris, 10, Rue d'Anjou, et élisant domicile en mon étude.

J'ai Savreux, 10, rue de la Paix, huissier soussigné, dit et rappelé à Gaston GALLIMARD, gérant responsable de la "Nouvelle Revue Française," 35 et 37, rue Madame, Paris, ci-après dénommée la Revue;

Que le n° 69 de la Revue, date du 1er Juin 1919, contient aux pages 125 à 128, sous la rubrique "Lettres Ouvertes" sous le titre "à Jean COCTEAU" et sous la signature "André GIDE," des appréciations sur le requérant et plusieurs de ces œuvres;

Que le requérant s'est rendu à la Revue pour inviter son Directeur à publier une réponse et a remis au dit Directeur la dite réponse;

Que le Directeur, sans contester le consentement de M. A. GIDE à la publication de la réponse, a néanmoins refusé son propre consentement, pour le motif que le requérant n'y aurait pas droit;

Mais que le droit du requérant ne supporte aucun doute, soit aux termes du Code Civil, soit aux termes de la loi sur la presse;

Qu'en premier lieu par la forme donnée à ses critiques, la Revue s'est liée aux écrivains critiques par un quasi-contrat de correspondance;

Qu'en effet l'article relevé par le requérant a paru comme lettre ouverte; que vraisemblablement l'on n'a pas imaginé sans raison de grouper des articles de critique sous ce titre nouveau; que par définition toute lettre appelle implicitement une réponse et toute lettre ouverte appelle une réponse ouverte; qu'autrement le titre de lettres ouvertes, non seulement n'aurait aucun sens mais paraîtrait calculé pour publier, sans appel et par suite sans contrôle, des critiques déguisées à cet effet en apostrophes amicales;

Que faute d'admettre ce quasi-contrat de correspondance entre l'auteur d'une lettre ouverte et son destinataire, l'interprétation contraire mettrait le requérant, ou tout autre écrivain critique par la même voie, dans la nécessité de s'adresser au public par l'organe d'un autre périodique; qu'alors la réponse, affranchie de la réserve qu'impose l'exercice d'un droit conventionnel, prendrait au gré des intéressés les proportions et le ton d'une contre-attaque; qu'ainsi des controverses dégénéreraient en polémiques; et qu'on ne saurait présumer chez les écrivains de la Revue, soit une inconséquence, soit des intentions, aussi mal conciliables avec la bienséance littéraire; Qu'au

---

* This legalistic notice was incorporated by Cocteau in his open letter to André Gide in the *Ecrits Nouveaux* for July-August 1919. He used it as window dressing to amuse readers, but his idea originally was to have the notice served on Gaston Gallimard by an actor from the Comédie-Française. (A.K.P.)

surplus le refus d'insérer la réponse du requérant conférerait à ces écrivains l'immunité reconnue par la loi, en matière de critique, aux seuls titulaires d'une fonction publique ou d'un mandat électif; que cette immunité ne dispense d'ailleurs dans aucun cas d'observer les égards dûs aux personnes sous la sanction des lois; que les écrivains d'une Revue ne tiennent nulle autorité de nul que d'eux-mêmes, et ne peuvent exiger d'aucun tiers la reconnaissance d'un droit quelconque à prononcer des censures unilatérales;

Qu'en deuxième lieu, l'article 13 de la loi du 29 juillet 1881 impose au gérant de la Revue l'obligation d'insérer la réponse du requérant;

Que la simple désignation du requérant dans l'article susvisé lui donne droit à cette insertion, sans qu'aucun autre que lui seul ait à juger de l'utilité, de l'intérêt ou de l'opportunité de la réponse;

Que la réponse déjà remise à la Revue ne contient manifestement rien qui blesse l'intérêt légitime d'aucun tiers;

Que le requérant ne saurait admettre aucune excuse tirée du délai nécessaire pour imprimer sa réponse; que la loi en ordonne la publication, soit dans les trois jours de sa réception, soit dans le plus prochain numéro s'il n'en est pas publié avant l'expiration des trois jours; que la Direction de la Revue a reçu la réponse à la date du 7 juin; et qu'ainsi soit en fait, soit en droit, elle manque de motifs pour se dérober à son obligation;

Pourquoi j'ai fait sommation à Gaston GALLIMARD ès-qualités de:

Publier dans le plus prochain numéro de la "Nouvelle Revue Française," à la même place et en même caractères que l'article susvisé, la réponse dont copie ci-après.

Sous peine de toutes sanctions correctionnelles et actions civiles conformement à la loi...

APPENDIX 11

Letter Gide to Cocteau [1920]. Archives Cocteau, Milly-la-Forêt.

Mardi

Si mal enchaîné, Prométhée, que je ne parviens plus à remettre la main dessus. Et ça m'embête d'aller le relancer au Mercure. Du reste il est si laid... Amyntas ou Saül, se présenterait mieux; si j'avais l'espoir que vous ne les connussiez pas encore...

J'ai repris froid, Dimanche, à ne pas vous trouver sous le plafond.

André Gide

Tuesday

(So poorly chained, Prometheus, that I can no longer put my hand on a copy. And it annoys me to go begging for it at *the Mercure [de France]*. Besides, it's so ugly... *Amyntas* or *Saül* would look better; if I could hope that you didn't already know them...

I took cold again, Sunday, at not finding you beneath the ceiling.

André Gide)

APPENDIX 12

Letter Cocteau to Gide, May 9, 1922. Doucet Y547.86.

9 mai 1922

Mon cher Gide,
    Je ne vous ai pas envoyé "Vocabulaire" par crainte de vous être désagréable car plusieurs personnes me disent que vous protégez le pauvre Gabory et que c'est pour "vous être agréable" qu'il bave sur moi. Naturellement je fais la part de l'étrange déformation que subissent les choses dites, de véhicule en véhicule, mais j'aime mieux savoir de vous et de nul autre si mon livre vous ferait plaisir. G. est un gentil poète que je croyais un gentil garçon. J'ai de lui une lettre où il me demande à "devenir mon disciple" ce qui prouve sa naïveté. J'ai aidé de mon mieux sa "mise en marche." Ai eu de vos nouvelles par Marc. Avez-vous lu le No. de la Revue de Genève où je place notre débat sur un plan noble et loin des canailles. Je vous embrasse.

Jean

    P.S. Votre exemplaire était prêt avec cette dédicace:

à mon ennemi Gide — Son ami J.C.

    Excusez mon écriture. Je me repose au soleil après 80 jours de lit. Jaunisse et névrite. Ma main tremble encore beaucoup.

May 9, 1922

(My dear Gide,
    I did not send you *Vocabulaire* for fear of upsetting you since several people tell me you are protecting poor Gabory and that it is "to please you" that he slanders me. Naturally, I take into account the strange deformation that spoken words undergo from mouth to mouth, but I prefer to learn from you and no one else if my book would give you pleasure. G[abory] is a nice poet whom I thought a nice boy. I have a letter from him asking to "become my disciple," which proves how naïve he is. I helped him to get started as best I could. Had some news of you from Marc. Have you read the issue of the *Revue de Genève* in which I place our debate on a noble plane far removed from the rabble. I embrace you.

Jean

    P.S. Your copy was ready with this dedication:

To my enemy, Gide — His friend J.C.

    Please excuse my handwriting. I am resting in the sun after eighty days in bed. Jaundice and neuritis. My hand still trembles badly.)

APPENDIX 13

Letter, illustrated, Cocteau to Gide [1925], included with proofs or a copy of Le Mystère de Jean l'Oiseleur. *Collection Mme Catherine Gide, Paris.*

Mon cher ami —
Vous retrouverez sous ce carton quelques dessins et des notes où je cherche à tendre des pièges au phototypeur. Peut-être s'y trouve-t-il encore autre chose de moins malicieux: je vous l'offre affectueusement.

JC

P.S. Pourquoi pas ce carton comme couverture? C'est le plus simple.

(My dear friend —
Under this cardboard you will find some drawings and notes in which I try to set traps for the engraver. There may also be something less mischievous: I offer it to you with affection.

JC

P.S. Why not this cardboard for the cover? It's the easiest thing.)

APPENDIX 14

Letter Cocteau to Gide [1925/1926]. Doucet Y547.42.

10 rue d'Anjou

Cher Gide,
  Vous pensez que je suis fier parce que votre paragraphe sur l'homme liqueurs et mon paragraphe sur M. Maskelin se donnent la main! Tout ce que vous dites est vrai, d'un vrai céleste.

Je vous embrasse
Jean

  J'ai été très seul et très triste à cause de deuil qui me touch [*sic*] de près. C'est pourquoi je n'ai pas téléphoné à Marc.

10 rue d'Anjou

(Dear Gide,
  You can imagine how proud I am since your paragraph on the liqueur man and my paragraph on M. Maskelin take each other by the hand! Everything you say is true, of a heavenly truth.

I embrace you,
Jean

  [P.S.] I have been very lonely and very sad because of bereavements closely related to me. That's why I haven't telephoned Marc.)

APPENDIX 15

Letter Cocteau to Gide [early February 1930]. Doucet Y547.68.

Cher André,

Que pensait la R[evue] H[ebdomadaire] en publiant cette merveille — que la générale X lirait comme on écoute Ch[arles] du B[os] chez Maritain? Ce portrait réponse est un prodige de rire contenu.

Je vous embrasse.

Jean

P.S. Tachez de venir une minute à la répétition.

(Dear André,

What was the R[evue] H[ebdomadaire] thinking of when it published that marvel — which General X's wife would read the way they listen to Ch[arles] du B[os] at Maritain's. This portrait-answer is a wonder of restrained laughter.

Fondest regards,

Jean

P.S. Try to come to the rehearsal for a minute.)

APPENDIX 16

Letter Cocteau to Gide, July 14, 1930. Doucet Y547.49.

14 Juillet 1930
Chablis (demain rue Tronchet)

Très cher André,

Lettre bien sinistre de Pierre H[erbart]. Il affirme avoir découvert un Sanatorium dont la cure coûterait cinq mille frs. Grasset prendra son livre (ouvrira même une collection avec) mais je doute fort d'une avance.

Jean Desbordes veut demander une avance à Grasset (promise) et envoyer les 5000 fs. à Pierre. Je trouve que Jean a raison et je ne peux que le louer, mais il est pauvre; son geste serait absurde si Pierre n'allait pas au Sanatorium. Je vous écris en cachette de Jean afin de vous demander conseil et sachant quelle a été votre générosité récente. Ce Sanatorium est-il sérieux? Est-ce possible? Ne fera-t-il pas quelque folie dangereuse sitôt cette somme entre ses mains. Répondez vite.

Je vous aime et vous embrasse.

Jean

P.S. Je me suis permis de faire imprimer un livre blanc à votre nom. Je n'ose refroidir Jean de crainte qu'il ne prenne pas ma prudence pour un manque de générosité — etc...

Le cher grand fond Malempia quel chef d'œuvre!

Chablis (tomorrow No. 1, rue Tronchet)
July 14, 1930

(Very dear André,

A most sinister letter from Pierre H[erbart]. He confirms having found a sanatorium where the cure would cost five thousand francs. Grasset will accept his book (will even begin a new series with it), but I am skeptical about an advance.

Jean Desbordes wants to ask Grasset for an advance (which was promised) and send the five thousand francs to Pierre. I think Jean is right and I can only praise him, but he is poor; his gesture would be absurd if Pierre didn't enter the sanatorium. I am writing you without Jean's knowledge in order to ask your advice and knowing of your recent generosity. Is this sanatorium a reputable place? Is it acceptable? Won't Pierre commit some dangerous folly as soon as the money gets into his hands? Answer quickly.

I like you and embrace you.

Jean

P.S. I took the liberty of having a copy of *Le Livre blanc* stamped with your name.

I do not dare to cool Jean down for fear that he might take my prudence for a lack of generosity — etc....

The dear deep bottom Malempia — what a masterpiece!)

APPENDIX 17

Letter Cocteau to Gide [November/December 1936]. Doucet Y547.69.

Mon cher André,

Votre "Retour" est brave, noble, charmant comme vous — c'est vous. C'est ce qui rend la vie possible et ce qui ôte les malaises du désordre.

Je vous aime et je vous embrasse.

Votre
Jean

P.S. Romain Rolland me demande des autographes et des desseins pour une vente "Espagne." Croyez-vous qu'Aragon me verrait sans haine? Pouvez-vous tâter ce terrain?

Marcel a emporté votre lettre à la campagne, sur son cœur. Donc, plus d'adresse exacte, plus de téléphone. Pouvez-vous me renvoyer tout cela?

(My dear André,

Your *Retour* [*de l'U.R.S.S.*] is courageous, noble, charming as you are — it is you. That is what makes life possible and what removes the discomforts of disorder.

I like you and I embrace you.

Your
Jean

P.S. Romain Rolland asks for autographs and drawings from me for a "Spanish" benefit sale. Do you think Aragon would see me without hatred? Can you feel out this ground?

Marcel [Khill] carried your letter off to the country, over his heart. So, no longer have exact address, no telephone for you. Can you send me all that again?)

APPENDIX 18

Letter Gide to Cocteau, May 17, 1946. Collection J.-J. Kihm and J.-J. Poulet-Allamagny, Paris.

17 Mai [19]46

Mon cher Jean

Vous serez certainement intéressé par ce que le sympathique Camerounien Moudio pourra vous dire. Et je ne doute pas que vous ne puissiez lui être de très bon conseil au sujet du Gala qu'il projette.

Si je n'étais aux trois quarts crevé par un rhume effroyable, vous m'auriez déjà revu — tout attentif et affectueux

André Gide

May 17, 1946

(My dear Jean,

You will certainly be interested by what the congenial Camerounian Moudio will be able to tell you. And I do not doubt that you will be able to give him some very good advice about the Gala he is planning.

If I were not three quarters done in by a frightful cold, you would already have seen me again — all attentive and affectionate.

André Gide)

APPENDIX 19

Letter Gide to Cocteau, July 31, 1946. Archives Cocteau, Milly-la-Forêt.

31 juillet 46

Charmant ami

Que n'étais-je avec vous lors de cette projection! J'aurais eu si grand plaisir à vous revoir... Tout ce que vous me dites du film, je le pense aussi (et combien gentil vous êtes de me l'écrire!) — On a supprimé, fort heureusement, le prêche de la fin. Je n'ai pu obtenir de Delannois [*sic*] certaines coupures, au début, dans l'éducation de l'aveugle, qui me parais-saient très souhaibles [*sic*]. Tant pis! Tel qu'il est le film me paraît assez réussi; ce n'était pas facile; et les responsables à qui j'avais completement laissé la place, ont fait merveille.

Chaleureusement votre
André Gide

Ai dédicacé pour vous un *Thésée* que vous recevrez bientôt.

July 31, 1946

(Charming friend,

Why couldn't I have been with you for that showing! * It would have given me so much pleasure to see you again... I agree with everything you tell me of the film (and how kind you are to write me about it!) — They cut out, most fortunately, the sermon at the end. I was unable to get Delannoy to make certain cuts, at the beginning, about the blind girl's education, that seemed to me highly desirable. Too bad! As it stands, the film seems to me to have come off quite well; it wasn't easy; and the responsible people to whom I left a completely free hand, worked miracles.

Warmly your
André Gide

Have inscribed a *Thésée* for you which you will receive soon.)

* Of *La Symphonie pastorale.* (A.K.P.)

APPENDIX 20

Postcard Cocteau to Gide [late March 1949]. Doucet, Y547.60.

Très cher André,

  Je vous embrasse et parle de vous avec Taha et toute cette Egypte qui vous aime.

Jean

(Dearest André,

  I am embracing you and talking about you with Taha and all Egypt who loves you.

Jean)

Gide's last letter to Cocteau, last day of the year 1950. Archives Cocteau, Milly-la-Forêt.

APPENDIX 22

Letter Cocteau to Gide, January 2, 1951. Doucet Y547.65.

APPENDIX 23

Jean Cocteau's homage to André Gide published in the special commemorative issue of the Nouvelle Revue Française *in November 1951.*

ON NE PEUT SE PERMETTRE...

On ne peut se permettre de juger André Gide en ligne droite. Il fut méandre, et c'était la manière de sa ligne d'être droite. Car l'inflexibilité d'une ligne de cette sorte ne se présente pas géométriquement, mais grâce à l'étrange géométrie et aux perspectives singulières de l'âme humaine.

Arthur Cravan, qui fut à l'origine de Lafcadio, nous rapporte qu'après la visite de Gide sur les quais de la Seine, il le guetta par la fenêtre. Gide, écrit-il, avait le choix entre la merveilleuse vitrine d'une boutique de coquillages et celle d'un bouquiniste. Il hésita et se décida pour le bouquiniste.

Cette note lafcadienne nous présente Gide toujours partagé entre la vie et les textes qui l'exaltent... En voyage, Gide chasse les insectes, les collectionne, herborise, se baigne, entre deux actes de Shakespeare ou deux chapitres de Goethe.

Ces pentes innombrables qu'il résume par cette phrase: *Les extrêmes me touchent,* rendent son œuvre passionnante et nous y attachent.

La voix d'un homme me renseigne beaucoup. Lors de la mort de Proust, c'est sa voix que j'étudiai dans la *Nouvelle Revue Française.* Celle de Gide montait, descendait, glissait, s'amincissait, s'enflait, musicale et tortueuse. Il savait y mettre en relief quelque terme, sur lequel, comme un peintre, il appuyait la touche blanche de l'éclairage, le point que les portraitistes chinois font payer si cher, lorsqu'ils le placent, le dernier jour de pose, dans l'œil du modèle.

Parfois, il semblait que les mots fussent halés par lui des profondeurs d'une citerne.

Mes rapports avec Gide ont été de malice et de grâce. Il me taquinait et m'aimait, comme en témoignent ses lettres intimes en marge d'un journal où il se montre souvent fort injuste à mon adresse.

Il fallait le comprendre, ne pas se blesser stupidement des boutades d'une susceptibilité à vif qu'il tenait de Jean-Jacques et qui peuvent surprendre chez un héritier des encyclopédistes. Ce mélange compose toute la beauté d'un homme qui se tourne autant contre lui que contre les autres. Il juge et se juge d'une plume unique et ne craint jamais de se contredire, n'étant pas l'esclave d'un engagement extérieur à sa personne.

De ce perpétuel échange entre un vieux maître et un jeune élève, entre le fort en thème et le cancre prestigieux de la classe, émane un parfum qui déroute l'analyse, sauf si le cœur s'en mêle.

Nos anicroches sont bien anciennes et Gide m'en parlait comme de vieilles disputes de famille, l'année dernière, pendant ses longues haltes dans ma maison de Seine-et-Oise. Il désirait que je tirasse un film d'*Isabelle.* Je lui conseillai de viser plus haut et de tenter le découpage des *Caves.*

Rien de plus jeune ni de plus désinvolte que ce spectacle des *Caves* à la Comédie-Française. On y retrouvait la joie de notre enfance aux féeries du

Châtelet et à ce *Tour du monde en quatre-vingts jours* où nous eûmes la révèla-
tion du théâtre.

Pas l'ombre de pédantisme. Pas l'ombre de faux sérieux. À peine l'ombre
d'un message, atténuée par le fait que Lafcadio fit école et que ses disciples
ressemblent aux *illuministes* qui voulurent porter les méthodes de Luther à
l'extrême.

Jadis Gide me montra les adorables cimetières de Varengeville et de
Cuverville. Il m'y entretenait, sans crainte, de la mort, et, avant mon départ
pour l'Egypte, il me déclara qu'il "s'amusait" de la grimace que ses crises
donnaient à sa bouche. Il me surprit par une bravade qu'il opposait aux
misères physiques.

Le mélange dont j'ai parlé, il le poussait jusqu'à mélanger prudence,
crainte et parfaite imprudence et méconnaissance du danger que les enfants
possèdent.

Une flamme joyeuse, enfantine, dominait sa cendre et sa braise. On la
voyait dans son regard, ce regard dont la vrille pénétrait toute chose malgré
l'âge et ses lassitudes.

La dernière vision que j'ai de Gide est celle d'un Erasme à calotte noire, en
robe de chambre, au centre de livres et d'objets pensifs, auprès d'un piano où
il se reposait d'exprimer en laissant Chopin s'exprimer à sa place.

Nul mieux que Gide ne prouve que toute œuvre grave est un auto-portrait
et que la ressemblance avec celui qui peint est plus importante que la ressemblance avec le modèle, employé par l'artiste au seul titre de prétexte.

Jean Paulhan m'écrit: "À peine mort, Gide s'est pétrifié, est exactement
devenu de pierre."

J'y reconnais le privilège des souverains que la mort change en gisants, et
qui voyagent sur les eaux profondes.

JEAN COCTEAU.

(ONE CANNOT ALLOW ONE'S SELF...

One cannot allow one's self to judge André Gide in a straight line. He was
a winding path, and the way of his line was straight. For the inflexibility of a
line of this sort does not happen geometrically but thanks to the strange
geometry and to the singular perspectives of the human soul.

Arthur Cravan, who inspired Lafcadio, reports that after Gide's visit on
the quais of the Seine he watched him from the window. Gide, he writes, had
the choice between the marvelous display window of a shell shop and that
of a secondhand bookseller. He hesitated and decided on the bookseller.

That Lafcadian note shows us Gide forever divided between life and the
texts which exalt it... While traveling, Gide pursued insects, collected them,
gathered plants, went swimming, between two acts of Shakespeare or two
chapters of Goethe.

Those countless propensities that he summed up in this sentence, *Extremes
touch in me,* make his work fascinating and attach us to it.

A man's voice teaches me much. When Proust died, it was his voice that I
studied in the *Nouvelle Revue Française.* Gide's rose, fell, glided, thinned out,
swelled, musical and tortuous. He knew how to point up an expression, to
which, like a painter, he applied the highlight, the dot the Chinese portraitists charge so much for when they place it, the last day of the pose, in the
model's eye.

Sometimes it seemed that he hauled the words up from the depths of a cistern.

My relations with Gide were a mixture of malice and of graciousness. He teased me and liked me, as testified to by his intimate letters, marginal to a journal in which he often showed himself extremely unjust toward my skill.

One had to understand him, not be foolishly wounded by the sallies of a raw sensitivity that he owed to Rousseau and that can be surprising in an heir of the Encyclopedists. This blend composes all the beauty of a man who turned as much against himself as against others. He judged and self-judged with a unique pen and never feared to contradict himself, not being in thrall-dom to any commitment outside himself.

From this perpetual exchange between an old master and a young pupil, between the exemplary student and the amazing class dunce, there emanates a perfume that defies analysis, unless the heart enters in.

Our snags go back a long way and Gide spoke with me about them as though they were old family quarrels, last year, during his long stopovers at my home in Seine-et-Oise. He wanted me to make a film from *Isabelle*. I advised him to set his sights higher and to try to do a scenario of *Les Caves* [*du Vatican*].

Nothing more youthful or more unconstrained than the stage version of *Les Caves* at the Comédie-Française. There we found again the childhood joy felt at the fairyland of the Châtelet and at that *Tour du Monde en quatre-vingts jours* where the world of the theater was opened to us.

Not a trace of pedantry. Not the shadow of false sobriety. Scarcely the shadow of a message, attenuated by the fact that Lafcadio had developed a school of followers and that his disciples resemble the illuminists who wished to carry Luther's methods to the extreme.

Long ago Gide showed me the charming cemeteries of Varengeville and Cuverville. He conversed there with me, without fear, about death, and before my departure for Egypt, he told me that he was "amused" at the grimace that his attacks gave to his mouth. He surprised me by his bravado in confronting physical miseries.

The mixture I mentioned, he pushed to the point of mingling prudence and fear with the utter imprudence and oblivion to danger that children possess.

A joyous, childlike flame dominated his ash and his embers. One saw it in his look, that look whose gimlet penetrated everything despite age and its lassitudes.

The last vision I have of Gide is that of an Erasmus in a black smoking cap and a dressing gown, surrounded by books and contemplative objects, near a piano where he rested from expressing himself by letting Chopin express himself instead.

No one proves better than Gide that every sober work is a self-portrait and that the resemblance to the painter is more important than the resemblance to the model, employed by the artist merely as a pretext.

Jean Paulhan wrote me: "Hardly dead, Gide petrified, turned absolutely to stone."

I recognized there the privilege of sovereigns whom death transforms into felled timbers and who voyage over deep waters.

Jean Cocteau)

Chronology of Communications Between Cocteau and Gide, 1912 to 1951

Year	Date	From	To	Reference*
1912	April 20	Cocteau	Gide	Y547.1
1912	June	JC	AG	Y547.2
1912	July 4	JC	AG	Y547.8
[1912]	Saturday	JC	AG	Y547.3
1912	August 6	AG	JC	ML
1913	October 17	JC	AG	ACG
1913	October 22	JC	AG	Y547.5
1913	[November]	JC	AG	Y547.7
1913	December 1	JC	AG	Y547.9
1913	December 6	JC	AG	Y547.10
1913	December 24	JC	AG	Y547.11
1914	January 12	AG	JC	AJC
1914	February 5	JC	AG	Y547.66
1914	[March]	JC	AG	Y547.20
[1914]	[Feb/March]	JC	AG	Y547.6
[1914]	[March]	JC	AG	Y547.15
[1914]	[May]	JC	AG	Y547.4
[1914]	[May]	JC	AG	Y547.66

*All references are to the Bibliothèque Littéraire Jacques Doucet, Paris, unless otherwise noted.

Key

ACG = Archives Catherine Gide, Paris.
AIR = Archives Isabelle Rivière, Dourgne.
AJC = Archives Jean Cocteau, Milly-la-Forêt.
EN = Ecrits Nouveaux.
J.-J. K. = Collection Jean-Jacques Kihm, Paris.
J.-J. P.-A. = Collection Jean-Jacques Poulet-Allamagny, Paris.
ML = Librairie Marc Loliée, Paris, Catalogue 1957.
NRF = La Nouvelle Revue Française.

Year	Date	From	To	Reference*
[1914]	[July]	JC	AG	Y547.13
1914	August 27	JC	AG	Y547.12
[1915]	November 23	AG/EW	JC	AJC
1916	[January]	JC	AG	Y547.14
[1917]	[April 6]	JC	AG	Y547.18
[1917]	[April 17]	AG	JC	AJC
1917	April 16	JC	AG	Y547.16
[1917]	Monday morning [April 23]	AG	JC	AJC
1917	June 3	JC	AG	Y547.17
1918	January 19	JC	AG	Y547.19
1918	May 24	JC	AG	Y547.22
1918	June 2	AG	JC	AJC
[1918]	[Summer]	JC	AG	Y547.21
1918	August 24	JC	AG	Y547.23
1919	January 20	JC	AG	Y547.24
1919	May [3]	JC	AG	Y547.72
1919	May 6	AG	JC	AIR
1919	May 6	JC	AG	Y547.73
1919	[June 15]	JC	AG	D1152-5, A-111-3
[1919]	[June 15]	JC	AG	D1152-6, A-111-3
1919	June 26	AG	JC	AJC
1919	June/July	AG	JC	*NRF*
1919	June/July	JC	AG	*EN*
1919	October	AG	JC	*EN*
1919	July 8	JC	AG	Y547.79
1919	July 11	AG	JC	AJC
1919	September 6	JC	AG	Y547.26
1919	November 20	AG	JC	ACG
[1920]	Tuesday	AG	JC	AJC
[1921]	[September]	AG	JC	ACG
1921	October 7	JC	AG	Y547.27
1922	May 9	JC	AG	Y547.86
1922	May 12	AG	JC	AJC
1922	May 15	JC	AG	Y547.89
1922	[c. May 15]	AG	JC	Y547.89 (Verso)
1922	May 18	JC	AG	Y547.90
1922	June 23	JC	AG	Y547.29
1922	June	JC	AG	Y547.28
1922	June	AG	JC	Y547.28 (Verso)
1922	July/August	JC	AG	Y547.30
1922	September 3	JC	AG	ACG
1922	October 28	JC	AG	Y547.31
1922	Nov. 4, 5, 6, 7	JC	AG	Y547.36
[1923]	[After January 16]	JC	AG	Y547.34
1923	January 24	AG	JC	Y547.34 (Verso)
1923	January 29	JC	AG	Y547.35
1922–1923	Winter	JC	AG	Y547.75

Year	Date	From	To	Reference*
1923	April 7	JC	AG	Y547.37
1923	May 4	JC	AG	Y547.38
1923	Summer	JC	AG	Y547.39
1924	August	JC	AG	Y547.40
1925	January	JC	AG	ACG
[1925]	[January]	JC	AG	ACG
[1925]	[March/April]	JC	AG	Y547.32
[1925]	[April]	JC	AG	Y547.33
[1925]	May 1	JC	AG	Y547.44
1925	May 13	JC	AG	Y547.45
1925	November 25	JC	AG	Y547.41
[1925/ 1926]	–	JC	AG	Y547.42
1926	October AM	JC	AG	Y547.46
1926	N[ovember]	JC	AG	Y547.92
[1927]	–	JC	AG	Y547.43
1928	December	AG	JC	*NRF*
1929	February	JC	AG	Y547.47
1929	March	JC	AG	Y547.48
[1930]	[Early February]	JC	AG	Y547.68
1930	February 11	JC	AG	Y547.67
1930	July 14	JC	AG	Y547.49
1931	January 18	AG	JC	ACG
1931	January 18	AG	JC	AJC
1931	January 18	AG	JC	J.-J. K. and J.-J. P.-A.
1931	February 3	JC	AG	Y547.51
1931	December 26	AG	JC	AJC
1935	February 28	AG	JC	AJC
1936	October	JC	AG	Y547.52
[1936]	[Nov/Dec]	JC	AG	Y547.69
1937	March 30	AG	JC	AJC
1939	January 13	JC	AG	Y547.53
1945	February 26	JC	AG	Y547.54
1945	July 19	JC	AG	ACG
1946	May 17	AG	JC	J.-J. K. and J.-J. P.-A.
1946	July 28	JC	AG	Y547.91
1946	July 31	AG	JC	AJC
[1947]	Saturday night	JC	AG	Y547.55
1949	January 15	JC	AG	Y547.57
1949	February 13	AG	JC	AJC
[1949]	[c. February 15]	JC	AG	Y547.58
1949	February	JC	AG	Y547.59
1949	March 31	JC	AG	Y547.60
1949	July 5	JC	AG	Y547.61
1949	August	JC	AG	Y547.62
1949	August 27	AG	JC	AJC
1950	January 15	JC	AG	Y547.63

Year	Date	From	To	Reference*
1950	November 29	JC	AG	Y547.64
1950	December 2	AG	JC	AJC
1950	Last day of the year	AG	JC	AJC
1951	January 2	JC	AG	Y547.65

Glossary of Persons *

Alençon, Emilienne d'. French poetess and courtesan in pre-World War I Paris.

Ali and Athman. Arab boys described by Gide in *Si le grain ne meurt*. Gide met them in North Africa in 1893 and brought Athman to Paris in 1899.

Allard, Roger (1885–   ). French poet and literary critic.

Allégret, Elie, Pasteur. Father of Marc Allégret and close friend of the Gide family.

Allégret, Marc (1900–   ). Son of Pasteur Elie Allégret, and the adopted son of André Gide. He is now an important film producer in France.

Amrouche, Jean (1906–   ). French poet and editor of Arab origin. From 1943 to 1947 he edited *L'Arche*, which André Gide had founded. In recent years he has been identified with ORTF.

Anglès, Auguste. *Maître de conférences* at the University of Paris and author of a study of the *NRF* since its founding in 1909.

Apelles. Greek artist and court painter to Alexander the Great.

Apollinaire, Guillaume (1880–1918). French poet of Polish and Italian extraction. His poetry and critical works were pivotal to the establishment of Cubism as a literary movement in France.

Aragon, Louis (1897–   ). French poet, long identified as a literary spokesman for the Communist party in France.

Aron, Raymond (1905–   ). French journalist and professor of sociology at the University of Paris. His prolific works have established him as one of the foremost social critics in France.

Aurenche, Jean (1904–   ). French film writer who collaborated with Pierre Bost on the 1946 screen adaptation of André Gide's *La Symphonie pastorale*.

Auric, Georges (1899–   ). French composer, member of the Groupe des Six, and former director of the Opéra de Paris. He composed numerous

---

* The reader will not find in this glossary all names listed in the index. Persons casually mentioned or sufficiently identified in the text, and some too famous to need further comment, have for the most part been omitted. A very few could not be usefully identified.

scores for Cocteau films and won the Cannes Festival Prix de la Musique for his scores for Cocteau's *La Belle et la Bête* and Gide's *La Symphonie pastorale* in 1946.

Barbette (Vander Clyde) (1904–   ). American trapeze artist who delighted French circus audiences of the twenties by his performances disguised as a woman.

Bardot, Brigitte (1934–   ). French film actress celebrated for her creation of sultry roles in post-World War II motion pictures.

Barrès, Maurice (1862–1923). French author who was hailed as the "prince de la jeunesse" about 1890. André Gide, one of his detractors, succeeded Barrès as the intellectual leader of the French youth.

Barzun, Jacques (1907–   ). American professor, educator, and administrator. A wide-ranging and prolific author whose works include important studies of Berlioz, science, and literary movements.

Bataille, Henry (1872–1922). French poet and dramatist whose theatrical work embodied the spirit of the Belle Epoque but lost favor after World War I.

Baudelaire, Charles (1821–1867). French symbolist poet. In *Les Fleurs du mal* he illustrated his esthetic doctrine of correspondences.

Bazaine, Achille François, Marshal (1811–1888). Commanded the French army in Lorraine during the Franco-Prussian War. He is considered to have surrendered ignominiously to the enemy at Metz and was sentenced to death as a traitor.

Bazin, René (1853–1932). French novelist whose work had a strong Catholic orientation.

Beaton, Cecil (1904–   ). Well-known British photographer.

Beaumont, Edith, Countess de. French society woman who, with her husband, Count Etienne de Beaumont, helped finance several works by their friend Jean Cocteau, including *Le Bœuf sur le toit*, for which Darius Milhaud composed the music.

Béhar, Henri C. Co-author with Sprigge and Kihm of a biography of Jean Cocteau.

Bérard, Christian (1902–1949). French artist and stage designer who created the costumes and sets for many ballet and theatrical productions by his close friend Jean Cocteau.

Bernstein, Henri (1876–1953). French dramatist and founder of Le Théâtre Libre who developed the modern theater of psychological analysis.

Blake, William (1757–1827). English poet and artist. André Gide's translation of his *Marriage of Heaven and Hell* (1790) was published in the August 1, 1922, issue of the *Nouvelle Revue Française*.

Blanche, Jacques-Emile (1861–1942). Well-known French society portrait painter and writer. He was a personal friend of both Gide and Cocteau, and his wife was a friend of Cocteau's mother.

Bonniot, Edmond, Dr. Literary executor of Stéphane Mallarmé and husband of Geneviève Mallarmé, the Symbolist poet's daughter.

Bost, Pierre (1901–   ). French man of letters and film writer who collaborated with Jean Aurenche on the film adaptation of André Gide's *La Symphonie pastorale* (1946).

Braque, Georges (1882–1963). French painter who created Analytic and Synthetic Cubism with Picasso from 1908 to 1914 and became a model of the Modern School of Paris.

Brée, Germaine (1907–   ). French literary historian, critic, and educator whose career has centered in the United States. She has written important studies of Proust, Gide, Camus, and Sartre.

Breton, André (1896–1968). French surrealist poet and esthetician whose doctrinal works include *Manifeste du surréalisme* (1924) and *Second Manifeste du surréalisme* (1930).

Brown, Al. American Negro boxer and dope addict whom Cocteau befriended in Paris. With Cocteau's help, Brown made a comeback to become Bantamweight Champion of the World.

Brown, Frederick (1934–   ). American critic, professor of French literature, and author of a biography of Jean Cocteau.

Brynner, Roc. American actor and son of Yul Brynner.

Bussy, Dorothy. British translator of many of André Gide's works. She was the sister of Lytton Strachey.

Campbell, Joseph (1904–   ). American author and professor of mythology and primitive religions. His works include *The Hero with a Thousand Faces* (1949) and *The Masks of God* (1959–1968).

Capote, Truman (1924–   ). American author. His works include *The Grass Harp* (1951) and *In Cold Blood* (1968).

Carlier, Madeleine (Adèle Martin). French actress and youthful sweetheart of Jean Cocteau.

Cassou, Jean (1897–   ). Spanish-born French poet, novelist, and art critic, and director of the Paris Museum of Modern Art from 1946 to 1965.

Castelnau, Raoul de. Frenchman whose experiences in World War I partly inspired the character of Thomas in Jean Cocteau's novel *Thomas l'Imposteur*.

Cendrars, Blaise (1887–1961). Swiss poet and novelist of adventure who, together with Jean Cocteau, founded the publishing firm Editions de la Sirène in 1918.

Chagall, Marc (1887–   ). Russian-born painter who went to Paris in 1910 where he was exposed to Fauvism and Cubism. His work had a marked impact on the Expressionist movement after World War I. André Breton considered Chagall a precursor of Surrealism.

Chanel, Gabrielle (Coco) (1883–1971). Parisian couturière whose designs have influenced women's fashion throughout the world. A friend of Jean Cocteau, she helped finance a number of his theatrical productions.

Chevillard, Camille (1859–1923). French conductor of the Concerts Lamoureux and music director of the Paris Opéra in 1914.

Cheyney, Peter (1891–   ). English author of mystery stories, a number of which were translated into French by Jean Cocteau's friend Jean Dauven.

Chocolat. Negro clown popular during the Belle Epoque. His French circus partner was called Footit.

Chopin, Frédéric (1810–1849). Composer of romantic works for piano. His music was highly regarded by André Gide, whose "Notes sur Chopin" first appeared in *La Revue Musicale* for December 1931.

Claudel, Paul (1868–1955). French author and diplomat whose poetry and theater reflect his strong religious orientation. He was converted to Catholicism following an illumination in Notre Dame on Christmas Day in 1886.

Cocteau, Eugénie. Mother of Jean Cocteau, née Eugénie Lecomte.

Cocteau, Georges. Stockbroker and father of Jean Cocteau.

Cocteau, Marthe. Sister of Jean Cocteau. She became the wife of Count Henri de la Chapelle.

Cocteau, Paul. Brother of Jean Cocteau. He was an aviator in World War I and later married Marcelle Rageot. He died two years before Jean Cocteau after a successful career as a stockbroker.

Colette (Sidonie Gabrielle Claudine Colette) (1873–1954). Perhaps the foremost French woman writer of the twentieth century. She was a close friend of Cocteau and lived near him in the Palais-Royal in post-World War II Paris.

Collet, Georges-Paul. Canadian professor of French literature and editor of the correspondence between André Gide and Jacques-Emile Blanche.

Conrad, Joseph (1857–1924). English novelist and man of the sea, of Polish parentage. André Gide translated his *Typhoon* into French.

Cooper, Lady Diana (1892–   ). Wife of Alfred Duff Cooper, English ambassador to France from 1944 to 1947.

Copeau, Jacques (1879–1949). A founder of the *NRF*, theoretician of the theater, and pioneer among modern *metteurs-en-scène*, Copeau organized the experimental Théâtre du Vieux-Colombier in Paris.

Corre, M. and Mme François. Mme Corre is the niece and literary heir of Henri Ghéon.

Croisset, Francis de (Edgar-Franz Wiener). French dramatist. He and his wife, Marie-Thérèse, became friends of Jean Cocteau. The daughter of Mme Croisset was Marie Laure Bischoffsheim, who later became Vicomtesse de Noailles.

Darbois, Roland. French television producer who collaborated with Roger Stéphane on the production of the Cocteau biography *Portrait Souvenir* for ORTF.

Daudet, Léon (1868–1942). Son of the French writer Alphonse Daudet and brother of Cocteau's friend Lucien Daudet.

Daudet, Lucien (1883–   ). Son of Alphonse Daudet and boyhood companion with whom Jean Cocteau made his first trip to North Africa in 1912.

Dauven, Jean Antoine (1900–   ). French author and translator whom Jean Cocteau asked to translate his Académie Française acceptance speech into argot.

Davray, Jean. French industrialist, man of letters, and director-general of Source Perrier, S.A.

Debussy, Claude (1862–1918). French composer who was a member of Mallarmé's group. The innovative harmonies and literary inspirations of his opera *Pelléas et Mélisande* (1902) most eloquently expressed musical Symbolism.

Delannoy, Jean (1908–   ). French film director and writer who produced the film versions of Jean Cocteau's *L'Eternel Retour* (1943) and André Gide's *La Symphonie pastorale* (1946).

Delay, Jean, Dr. (1907–   ). French psychiatrist and author of the two-volume psycho-biography *La Jeunesse d'André Gide*.

Denoël, Jean (1904–   ). French author and assistant to Gaston Gallimard at Editions Gallimard. He was a friend and colleague of Gide and Cocteau and of many other leading French authors of the twentieth century.

Dermit, Edouard (1924–   ). Literary heir of Jean Cocteau. He now resides in Cocteau's former home near Fontainebleau, where he supervises the Cocteau archives.

Desbordes, Jean. Author of *J'adore* and close friend of Jean Cocteau. He is reported to have died heroically at the hands of the Gestapo in World War II.

Deslys, Mme Gaby. Jazz dance partner of M. Pilcer in a popular music hall act of the eartly twentieth century in Paris.

Diaghilev, Serge (1872–1929). Impresario of the Ballets Russes, who presented a number of Jean Cocteau's early ballets in Paris.

Diderot, Denis (1713–1784). French author and director of the *Encyclopédie*. This project, the most extensive publishing venture undertaken in France up to mid-eighteenth century, is credited with being a prime mover in the intellectual revolution that preceded the French political revolution of 1789.

Dietz, Hermann. Teacher of André Gide at the Ecole Alsacienne, and later of young Jean Cocteau at Val André in Brittany.

Doucet, Jacques (d. 1929). Paris couturier of the early twentieth century. A bibliophile and patron of many writers of the period, he funded the establishment of the Bibliothèque Littéraire Jacques Doucet, which is part of the Bibliothèque Sainte-Geneviève at the University of Paris.

Du Bos, Charles (1882–1939). French writer and convert to Catholicism who campaigned for many years to win André Gide over to the Catholic Church.

Dufy, Raoul (1877–1953). French painter identified with the Fauve movement of 1907 to 1909 in France.

Duhamel, Georges (1884–1966). French writer and member of the Abbaye de Créteil group which subscribed to the *unanimisme* of Jules Romains.

Dullin, Charles (1885–1949). Actor, *metteur-en-scène*, and associate of Jacques Copeau at the Théâtre du Vieux-Colombier. He was a dominating force in the French theater of the 1930's.

Duvernois, Henri (1875–1937). French dramatist and prolific author of short stories.

Edwards, Misia. *See* Misia Sert.

Epinay, Louise de La Live d' (1726–1783). Benefactress of Jean-Jacques Rousseau whom she took under her protection in 1756.

Epstein, Jean, Dr. Physiologist and editor of *Esprits Nouveaux*. Two of his works, *La Lyrosophie* and *La Poésie d'aujourd'hui, un nouvel état d'intelligence*, were published by Cocteau's publishing firm, Editions de la Sirène, in 1922.

Fargue, Léon-Paul (1876–1947). French poet associated with Paul Valéry and Valery Larbaud in the literary review *Commerce* in 1923. His poetry displays both Symbolist and Surrealist influences.

Feuillet, Octave (1821–1890). French idealistic novelist, author of *Roman d'un jeune homme pauvre* (1859).

Feydel, Lucien (1912–   ). French civil servant. Sous-préfet and Secrétaire-Générale de la Seine-Maritime.

Fierens, Paul (1895–1957). Belgian art and literary critic.

Footit. Famous French circus clown of the Belle Epoque whose partner was a Negro performer called Chocolat.

Fraigneau, André. French writer and friend of Jean Cocteau. Together they recorded several important interviews for ORTF.

Frazer, Sir James George (1854–1941). English social anthropologist and author of *The Golden Bough*.

Gabory, Georges. French writer who read some of Proust's manuscripts for the *NRF* and was the author of *Essai sur Marcel Proust*.

Gallimard, Gaston (1881–   ). Administrator of the *NRF* literary review from its founding in 1909, and later of the publishing house of Gallimard, both of which have played a dominant role in the contemporary French literary scene.

Garros, Roland (1888–1918). French aviator in World War I and friend of Jean Cocteau. It is said that when Garros crashed to his death a copy of Cocteau's poem *Le Cap de Bonne-Espérance* was found in his cockpit.

Gaspard Michel, André. Director of the Paris literary review *Ecrits Nouveaux*, in which part of the Gide-Cocteau exchange of open letters appeared in 1919.

Gastambide, Mme René. Current owner of the Gide home at Cuverville in Normandy. The house had been the property of Gide's wife, Madeleine, who bequeathed it to her nephew Dominique Drouin. He sold it to Mme Gastambide.

Gaulle, Pierre de. Brother of General Charles de Gaulle.

Gautier-Vignal, Louis, Count (1888–   ). Scion of a wealthy family from Nice. He became a friend of Jean Cocteau in 1912.

Genêt, Jean (1910–   ). French novelist and dramatist whose early poetry attracted the attention of Jean Cocteau. In 1948, Cocteau came to Genêt's defense in a court action and helped him obtain a pardon from the President of France.

Georgel, Pierre. Conservateur des Musées nationaux. Georgel was one of the literary executors named in Jean Cocteau's testament.

Ghéon, Henri (1875–1944). Physician, drama critic for the *NRF*, and homosexual companion of André Gide.

Gide, Catherine (1923–   ). Daughter of André Gide and Elisabeth Van Rysselberghe.

Gide, Paul. Professor of law and father of André Gide.

Gilson, René. French writer and critic. Author of *Jean Cocteau*, a study of Cocteau's films.

Giraudoux, Jean (1882–1944). French dramatist, novelist, and diplomat. His works reflect his disdain of daily realities and his desire to create a world apart, governed solely by the laws of art and fantasy.

Godebski, Cyprien (Cipa) (1835–1909). Polish-born sculptor and art connoisseur in whose home gathered painters, writers, and musicians. His sister, Misia Sert, was Cocteau's friend.

Grimm, Friedrich Melchior, Baron von (1723–1807). German critic who wrote in the French language and contributed to the *Encyclopédie* project of his friend Denis Diderot.

Hahn, Reynaldo (1874–1947). French musician and boyhood friend of Jean Cocteau.

Herbart, Pierre (1903–   ). French author. His marriage to Elisabeth Van Rysselberghe, at André Gide's instigation, ended in divorce.

Herrand, Marcel. French *metteur-en-scène* who directed several of André Gide's plays in the 1930's.

Hoeck, Mary. One of Cocteau's English translators. He maintained a regular correspondence with her for many years.

Honegger, Arthur (1892–1955). Swiss-French composer and member of the Groupe des Six. He write the score for the opera version of Jean Cocteau's *Antigone* in 1927.

Hugo, Jean (1894–   ). French designer, grandson of Victor Hugo. He and his wife Valentine (née Gross) were for many years friends of Jean Cocteau. Hugo did sets and costumes for several of Cocteau's stage productions.

Jacob, Max (1876–1944). Cubist poet and associate of Picasso, Apollinaire, A. Salmon, and Cocteau. He died during Nazi internment in World War II despite Cocteau's efforts to obtain his release.

Jammes, Francis (1868–1938). French Catholic poet whose intimate verse extolled his Pyrenées background in sensual terms.

Joffre, Joseph, Marshal (1852–1931). French military hero of World War I.

Jouhandeau, Marcel (1888–   ). French author and friend of Jean Cocteau. His wife, Elisabeth Toulemon, who formerly danced under the professional name of Caryathis, inspired many of his novels on conjugal life.

Khill, Marcel. Friend of Jean Cocteau who accompanied the poet on his 1936 reenactment of Jules Verne's *Around the World in Eighty Days*.

Kihm, Jean-Jacques. French teacher, literary commentator, and writer for ORTF, and a biographer and friend of Jean Cocteau.

Klee, Paul (1879–1940). Swiss painter. His work is rare in the annals of twentieth-century art because it owes nothing to the School of Paris and in his own words represents "the pre-history of the visible."

Kolb, Philip (1907–   ). American literary historian and critic of French literature. Author of important studies of Proust and Jacques Rivière.

Labiche (Eugène Marin) (1815–1888). French dramatist and master of light comedy.

Lacretelle, Jacques de (1888–   ). French novelist and friend of André Gide. Gide influenced Lacretelle's literary development in its early stages.

Lafitte, Paul. Associate of Cocteau and Cendrars in their publishing venture, Editions de la Sirène.

Lambert, Jean (1914–   ). French author and faculty member of Smith College. Former husband of Catherine Gide.

Laurens, Paul-Albert. Painter and friend of André Gide. The two young men went to North Africa together in October 1893.

Lebaudy, Max. Wealthy tycoon of the French sugar industry during the Belle Epoque.

Lecomte, André (Uncle André). Uncle of Jean Cocteau.

Lecomte, Eugène. Jean Cocteau's maternal grandfather.

Lecomte, Marianne. Cousin and close childhood friend of Jean Cocteau.

Leopold, Nathan. *See* Loeb, Richard.

Le Roy, Jean (1894–1918). French poet (*Le Cavalier de Frise*, 1924), and friend of Jean Cocteau.

Lhote, André (1885–1962). French painter and friend of both Jean Cocteau and Jacques Rivière.

Loeb, Richard. Together with Nathan Leopold, he was involved in a sensational American kidnapping and murder for "thrills" in 1924. They were defended, and saved from execution, by Clarence Darrow on the grounds of temporary insanity.

Louÿs, Pierre (1870–1925). French poet and novelist who in his youth was a close friend of André Gide. He later associated with Valéry, Hédiard, and Mallarmé in his identification with the Symbolists.

Magistry, Gérard. French man of letters and friend of Jean Cocteau.

Mallarmé, Stéphane (1842–1898). French Symbolist poet and theoretician whose esthetic doctrines appealed strongly to Gide in his formative years.

Mallet, Robert (1915–   ). French educator and author, currently rector of the Academy of the University of Paris. Mallet has edited the correspondence between André Gide and Paul Valéry.

Marais, Jean (1913–   ). Actor and longtime friend of Jean Cocteau. Marais played the leading role in many Cocteau films and plays.

Marinetti, F. T. (1876–1944). Italian writer who initiated the Futurist literary movement.

Maritain, Jacques (1882–1973). French philosopher and writer who has lived and worked in the United States after 1940. A convert to the Catholic Church together with his wife Raïssa, he encouraged the conversion of many French intellectuals to Catholicism in the period following World War I.

Martin, Claude. *Maître de conférences* at the University of Saint-Etienne, France. Author of the critical edition of André Gide's *La Symphonie pastorale* and of *André Gide par lui-même*.

Martin du Gard, Roger (1881–1958). French novelist, Nobel laureate, author of *Les Thibault* (1922–1940). A lifelong friend of André Gide.

Massine, Léonide (1896–   ). Ballet dancer and choreographer of the Ballets Russes.

Mauriac, Claude (1914–   ). French novelist identified with the "Nouveau roman," dramatist, and film critic for *Le Figaro Littéraire*. Son of François Mauriac and friend of both Jean Cocteau and André Gide. Secretary to General Charles de Gaulle from 1946 to 1947.

Mauriac, François (1885–1970). French Catholic novelist and Nobel laureate (1952). His early career included more than one hundred works in poetry, theater, and the novel. In his late years his *Bloc notes* established him as one of France's foremost literary journalists.

Max, Edouard de (1869–1924). The foremost French tragedian of his day. He played the role of Antony in the 1920 production of *Antoine et Cléopâtre*, Gide's translation of the Shakespeare play.

Mendès, Catulle (1841–1909). Author and poet of the Parnassian school who exerted an early influence on Jean Cocteau's work.

Mévil-Blanche, Georges. Nephew of the artist Jacques-Emile Blanche.

Michelet, Jules (1798–1874). Liberal French historian and author.

Milhaud, Darius (1892–   ). French composer and member of the Groupe des Six. Since 1939 a member of the music faculty of Mills College, California.

Modigliani, Amedeo (1884–1920). Italian painter who settled in 1906 in Paris, where he became a friend of Cocteau. He was identified with the School of Paris and became known as a linearist and mannerist. He died of tuberculosis, alcohol, and drugs at the age of thirty-six.

Monnier, Adrienne. Paris book dealer and friend of young writers, whose works she promoted through her shop on the rue de l'Odéon.

Montherlant, Henry de (1896–1972). French novelist, dramatist, and essayist in the French moralist tradition.

Morand, Paul (1888–   ). French author and diplomat whose writing between the two world wars depicts the thirst for new and rapid sensations that characterized the amoral period of the 1920's.

Morgan, Michèle (Simone Roussel) (1920–   ). French film actress. Her performance in the film version of André Gide's *La Symphonie pastorale* won her the award for best actress in the Cannes Film Festival of 1946.

Mortimer-Ménard. Name used by Jean Cocteau to designate a dull, bourgeois prototype in his book *Le Potomak* (1919).

Mühlfeld, Mme. Fashionable Parisian hostess and wife of the literary critic Lucien Mühlfeld. Her salon was frequented by Cocteau, Gide, Valéry, Régnier and other prominent literary figures.

Murat, Marie, Princess. Prominent member of French society with whom Jean Cocteau associated during his summers in Normandy prior to World War I.

Musset, Alfred de (1810–1857). French Romantic poet and dramatist. He had a brief liaison with George Sand.

Nijinsky, Vaslav (1890–1950). Premier danseur of the Ballets Russes, which took Paris by storm in 1909 under the direction of Serge Diaghilev.

Noailles, Anna, Countess de (Princess Brancovan) (1876–1933). Leading French woman poet of the early twentieth century and close friend of Jean Cocteau. Of Rumanian and Greek parentage.

O'Brien, Justin (1906–1968). American scholar, literary historian, and critic of French literature. He translated André Gide's *Journal* into English.

Paulhan, Jean (1884–1968). French writer and advocate of the purification of language. He served as editor in chief of the *NRF* from 1925 until its temporary closing during World War II. From 1953 until his death he shared with Marcel Arland the direction of the new *NRF*.

Péguy, Charles (1873–1914). French poet and essayist who influenced the literature of his time by his works and also through *Les Cahiers de la quinzaine*, a review he founded and edited from 1902 to 1914.

Picabia, Francis (1879–1953). French author, painter, and publisher from 1917 to 1924 of the Dadaist review *391*.

Picasso, Pablo (1881–1973). Spanish painter and sculptor. He designed the sets for Cocteau's Cubist ballet *Parade* in 1917. It was Cocteau's close friendship with Picasso and other artists and writers that enabled him to take

the lead in bridging the cultures of Montmartre and Montparnasse after World War I.

Pierre-Quint, Léon (1845–   ). French literary critic and author of important studies on Marcel Proust.

Pilcer, M. French entertainer and jazz dancer popular in Parisian music halls of the early twentieth century.

Pitoëff, Georges (1884–1939). Russian-born French actor and theatrical director. His wife Ludmilla (1895–1951) was an actress and his collaborator.

Polignac, Princess Edmond de (née Singer). French society woman whose salon was popular with French writers and artists in the Belle Epoque.

Pourrat, Henri (1887–1959). French writer and essayist whose work effectively describes the landscape, customs, and people of his native Auvergne.

Queneau, Raymond (1903–   ). French writer and editor of Editions Gallimard.

Radiguet, Raymond (1903–1923). Precocious author of *Le Diable au corps* and an intimate friend of Jean Cocteau.

Rancé, Armand Jean Le Bouthillier de (1626–1700). French religious reformer.

Ravel, Maurice (1875–1937). French composer. With Debussy he was a leader of the anti-Wagnerian, Impressionist movement in music.

Raynal, Maurice. French art critic of the nineteenth and twentieth centuries.

Régnier, Henri de (1864–1936). French poet and novelist whose work is noted for its delicate, fluid style and who was a leader of the Symbolist movement.

Reverdy, Pierre (1889–1960). French poet who allied himself in 1910 with the Cubist poets and painters who gathered around Picasso at the Bateau-Lavoir in Paris. In 1916 he launched the avant-garde review *Nord-Sud*.

Reyer, Ernest (1823–1909). French operatic composer and critic strongly influenced by Berlioz.

Richelieu, Armand Jean du Plessis, Duke de (Cardinal de Richelieu) (1585–1642). French prelate and statesman. Minister of Louis XIII and in effect ruler of France the last dozen years of his life after the exile of Marie de Médicis.

Rilke, Rainer Maria (1875–1926). German lyric poet whose work blended impressionism and mysticism.

Rivière, Isabelle. French writer on Catholic themes. She was the wife of Jacques Rivière and sister of the novelist Alain-Fournier.

Rivière, Jacques (1886–1925). French writer, critic, and editor of the *NRF* from 1918 until his death in 1925.

Rocher, René. A childhood friend of Jean Cocteau. Rocher later became a well-known actor in France.

Rolland, Romain (1866–1944). French author and Nobel laureate in 1916. His roman-cycle *Jean Christophe* (1904–1912) was a precursor to the extended novels of Jules Romains and Roger Martin du Gard.

Rondeaux, Juliette (1833–1895). Wife of Paul Gide and mother of André Gide.

Rondeaux, Madeleine (Em) (Emmanuèle) (1867–1938). Maiden name of André Gide's cousin who became his wife.

Rorem, Ned (1923–   ). American composer and author who was a friend of Jean Cocteau during the last years of the poet's life.

Rosenberg, Paul. Owner of an art gallery in Paris where poets often read and composers performed their own works between World War I and World War II.

Rosny, J.-H. (*ainé*) (1856–1940). French novelist who collaborated with J.-H. Rosny (*jeune*) from 1886 to 1908 in exploring many types of novel. Both writers were among the first ten members of the Académie Goncourt.

Rostand, Edmond (1868–1918). French dramatist, author of *Cyrano de Bergerac*. He was an early literary model for Jean Cocteau, who later occupied his chair in the Académie française.

Rousseau, Henri (Le Douanier) (1844–1910). French painter whose primitive style united awkward draftsmanship with harmonious colors to convey a strange poetic atmosphere.

Roussel, Raymond (1877–1933). French author who renounced music for a literary career. His major works include *Impressions d'Afrique* (1910) and *Locus solus* (1914).

Sachs, Maurice (1906–1945). French author and onetime friend of Jean Cocteau and André Gide.

Saint-Simon, Louis de Rouvroy, Duke de (1675–1755). French author of *Mémoires* which brilliantly portrayed personalities and events of his era.

Sanouillet, Michel (1924–   ). French author and literary critic. His *Dada à Paris* (1965) is the most comprehensive study to date of the Dadaist literary movement.

Sartre, Jean-Paul (1905–   ). French philosopher and author whose novels and plays were largely responsible for the growth of the Existentialist movement in France after World War II.

Satie, Erik (1866–1925). French composer who collaborated with Cocteau and Picasso by preparing the score for the ballet *Parade* (1917).

Schiffrin, Jacques (d. 1950). French author and publisher who collaborated with André Gide on translations of Pushkin.

Schlumberger, Jean (1877–1968). French author in the classical tradition and a founder of the *NRF*.

Schopenhauer, Arthur (1788–1860). German philosopher and author. His theories influenced André Gide in his twenties.

Sert, Misia (née Godebska). Married at fifteen to Thadée Nathanson. Her second husband was Alfred Edwards, the financier. Her third husband was the Spanish painter José María Sert.

Sokolniska, Mme. A disciple of Sigmund Freud, she disseminated the Austrian psychiatrist's ideas among the Paris literati following World War I.

Soupault, Philippe (1897–   ). French poet and novelist. Co-founder in 1919 with André Breton and Louis Aragon of the Surrealist review *Littérature*.

Sprigge, Elizabeth (1900–   ). English critic and writer. With Henri Béhar and Jean-Jacques Kihm, whom she met at Jean Cocteau's funeral, she subsequently co-authored a biography of Jean Cocteau.

Starkie, Enid (d. 1970). English biographer, professor of Literature at Oxford University, and literary critic who wrote important studies of Baudelaire, Rimbaud, and Gide.

Steegmuller, Francis (1906–   ). American author and critic whose works, besides his fiction, include books about Flaubert, Maupassant, Apollinaire, and Cocteau.

Stéphane, Roger (1919–   ). French television producer whose audio-visual treatment of literary topics has found wide expression on ORTF.

Stravinsky, Igor (1882–1972). Russian composer and conductor. He wrote the score for Jean Cocteau's *Oedipus Rex* (1925) and to him Cocteau dedicated *Le Potomak*.

Tabarin. Seventeenth-century charlatan famous as a farceur.

Tagore, Sir Rabindranath (1861–1941). Bengali poet who was awarded the Nobel Prize for literature in 1913.

Thévenaz, Paul (Paulet). Swiss eurythmics teacher and jack-of-all-arts, including the dance, piano, and drawing. He died in the United States in 1921.

Vadim, Roger (1928–   ). French actor and film director.

Valéry, Paul (1871–1945). French author and esthetician who, as a young poet, felt the influence of Mallarmé. A key to his literary doctrines is the *Introduction à la méthode de Léonard de Vinci* (1894).

Van Rysselberghe, Mme Théo. Wife of the Belgian painter and the maternal grandmother of Catherine Gide.

Vaudoyer, Jean-Louis (1883–1963). French writer, former curator of the Musée des Arts Décoratifs, and former director of the Comédie-Française.

Verlaine, Paul (1844–1896). French Symbolist poet whose early verse is in the Parnassian vein. The originality of his work became more marked after his friendship with Arthur Rimbaud and his conversion to Catholicism.

Verne, Jules (1828–1905). French author best known to English-speaking readers for his *Twenty Thousand Leagues under the Sea* and *Around the World in Eighty Days*.

Vestris, Mme Lucia (1797–1856). English actress and dancer who became manager, with her husband, Charles James Mathews, of the Covent Garden and Lyceum theaters in London.

Waldberg, Patrick. American writer and historian of the Surrealist literary movement in France.

Weisweiller, Francine (Mme Alec Weisweiller, née Worms). She was Jean Cocteau's patron and closest woman friend for the last twenty-three years ot his life. Her brother, Gérard Worms, directed the Editions de Monaco, which published many of Cocteau's works.

Wells, H. G. (1866–1946). British author best known for his fantastic romances, usually based on scientific fact (*The Time Machine*, 1895; *The War Between the Worlds*, 1897).

Wharton, Edith (1862–1937). American expatriate novelist who made her home in France for many years.

Wheeler, Monroe (1900–   ). Art historian and critic identified with the assembling of the permanent collection of the Museum of Modern Art in New York.

Whitman, Walt (1819–1892). American poet (*Leaves of Grass*, 1855) and journalist (director, *The Brooklyn Eagle*). He wished to be known as the poet of the common man.

Wilde, Oscar (1854–1900). English writer whose attitudes and literary style affected Gide and Cocteau at different times in their careers.

Williams, Tennessee (1914–   ). American dramatist whose play *A Street-car Named Desire* was awarded the 1946 Pulitzer Prize for drama.

Wright, Richard (1908–1960). American black novelist whose writing, especially *Native Son* (1940), established him as one of the foremost contemporary authors addressing the problems of black society in the United States.

Notes

CHAPTER 1: Beginnings

1. Gide, *Si le grain ne meurt* (Paris: Gallimard, 1966), p. 9.

2. *Ibid.*, p. 10.

3. The application of Sainte-Beuve's doctrine that the critic must concern himself with the total man in order to understand the artist was at once facilitated and complicated by the advent of Freudian psychology. The temptation to apply Freud's methods to the works of Gide and Cocteau is almost irresistible, although it is a fact that Gide quickly became disillusioned with Freud, and Cocteau's comments about the Austrian psychiatrist are always tinged with hostility.

4. Gide, *Correspondance André Gide–Roger Martin du Gard*, (Paris: Gallimard, 1968), I (1913–1934), 81.

5. Gide, *Journal des Faux-Monnayeurs* (Paris: Gallimard, 1967), p. 85.

6. Jean Delay, *La Jeunesse d'André Gide* (Paris: Gallimard, 1956), I (Vocations III), 135–278.

7. Gide, *Si le grain ne meurt*, p. 82.

8. *Ibid.*, p. 117.

9. *Ibid.*, p. 59.

10. *Ibid.*, p. 98.

11. *Ibid.*, p. 78.

12. *Ibid.*, p. 100.

13. *Ibid.*, p. 189.

14. *Ibid.*, p. 318.

15. *Ibid.*, p. 322. The italics are mine.

16. Jean Schlumberger, *Madeleine et André Gide* (Paris: Gallimard, 1956), p. 220.

17. At the start of his career, apparently in order to add to his image of precocity, Cocteau had created some uncertainty about his true age by claiming to be two years younger than he really was.

18. Jean-Jacques Kihm, Elizabeth Sprigge, and Henri C. Béhar, *Jean Cocteau, l'homme et les miroirs* (Paris: La Table Ronde, 1968), p. 17.

19. Cocteau, *Portraits-Souvenir* (Paris: Grasset, 1953), p. 63.

20. Roger Stéphane, ed., *Jean Cocteau, entretien avec Roger Stéphane*, Collection Portrait Souvenir (Paris: Jules Tallandier, 1964), p. 45.

21. *Ibid.*, p. 44.

22. Cocteau. *Opium, journal d'une désintoxication* (Paris: Stock, Delamain et Boutelleau, 1956), p. 220.

23. Cocteau, *Portraits-Souvenir,* p. 54.

24. The importance to Cocteau of his own childhood experiences gave added meaning to his homage to André Gide in the *NRF* for November 1951 (p. 91). Cocteau there spoke of the farce version of Gide's *Les Caves du Vatican* which had been presented at the Comédie-Française in 1949: "On y retrouvait la joie de notre enfance aux féeries du Châtelet et à ce *Tour du Monde en quatre-vingts jours* où nous eûmes la révélation du théâtre." ("There we found again the childhood joy felt at the fairyland of the Châtelet and at that *Tour du Monde en quatre-vingts jours* where the world of the theater was opened to us.")

25. Cocteau, *La Difficulté d'être* (Paris: Paul Morihien, 1947), p. 56.

26. Cocteau, *Portraits-Souvenir,* p. 44.

27. Cocteau, *La Difficulté d'être,* p. 46.

28. Cocteau, *Portraits-Souvenir,* p. 106.

29. Of Cocteau's remarkable talents, one that revealed itself early in his career was the critical ability to recognize the merit of budding artists in various fields: Picasso in art, *Les Six* among musicians, and even Al Brown, the Negro boxing champion, to name only a few. A skill that flowed naturally from his perception lay in Cocteau's flair for helping such young people to develop and use their creative gifts without making them his disciples. For Cocteau, the perception and the development were creative acts in themselves. Raymond Radiguet, the precocious author of *Le Diable au corps,* stands as the model for this figure in Cocteau's life. Jean Desbordes, author of *J'adore,* was regarded by Cocteau as a reincarnation of Radiguet. Marcel Khill, to whom Cocteau dedicated his *Portraits-Souvenir,* accompanied the poet as Passepartout on his trip around the world in 1936. Jean Marais, who played leading roles in many of Jean Cocteau's films, in 1968 staged the French première of Bernard Shaw's *The Devil's Disciple* at the Théâtre de Paris. The adaptation of the play, made by Cocteau at Marais's request, was one of the poet's last works.

30. Gide, *Si le grain ne meurt,* p. 191.

31. Cocteau, *Portraits-Souvenir,* p. 123.

32. Stéphane, ed., *Jean Cocteau, entretien avec Roger Stéphane,* p. 65.

33. Cocteau's letters to his mother in 1906 speak enthusiastically of the Dietzes and of his friends at the pension. One letter contains a caricature of M. Dietz, and another speaks approvingly of Mme Dietz's liberal religious views. Cocteau wrote his mother reassuringly in September 1906: "Si j'échoue encore cette fois ce ne sera pas faute d'avoir fait l'effort nécessaire. . . ." Archives Cocteau, Milly-la-Forêt. ("If I flunk again this time, it will not be for lack of having made the necessary effort. . . .")

34. Cocteau, *Portraits-Souvenir,* p. 139.

35. Letter Cocteau to mother, undated [summer 1907]. Archives Cocteau, Milly-la-Forêt. The "cher Patron" refers to M. Dietz.

36. Letter Cocteau to mother, undated [summer 1907]. Archives Cocteau, Milly-la-Forêt.

37. Cocteau, *Le Livre blanc* (illus.) (Paris: Editions du Signe, 1930).

38. Letter Cocteau to Gide, undated, Bibliothèque Littéraire Jacques Doucet, Paris, Fonds Gide ref. Y547.18. (All subsequent references to correspondence between Gide and Cocteau in this library will give the word Doucet and the library reference number only.) The "nymph phe-

nomena" probably refers here to Cocteau's disappointing flirtation with Maria Chabelska, a young dancer in the Ballets Russes then in Rome.

39. Gide later explained in his *Journal des Faux-Monnayeurs* (p. 69), "ce n'est pas ce qui me ressemble, mais ce qui diffère de moi qui m'attire" ("it is not what resembles me but what is different from me that attracts me").

CHAPTER 2: *La Danse de Sophocle*

1. Letter Blanche to Cocteau, dated August 22, 1912. Archives Jean Cocteau, Milly-la-Forêt. This letter contains a fatherly lecture to Cocteau on health and hygiene, in which Blanche stresses the relation of physical to mental health, and the importance of bed as a refuge.

2. This portrait now hangs in the Museum of Rouen, along with a study of Cocteau *circa* 1912, a portrait of André Gide *circa* 1912–1913, and a study of Gide and friends at the café Maure at the Paris Exposition Universelle in 1900.

3. Cocteau, *Le Grand Ecart* (Paris: Stock, Delamain et Boutelleau, 1947), pp. 8–9.

4. In later years at Villefranche, Monroe Wheeler of the Museum of Modern Art in New York, and a friend of Cocteau, remembers Cocteau and Georges Auric imitating the voice and manner of André Gide and Oscar Wilde at their meeting in North Africa. (Auric composed the scores for many of Cocteau's stage and screen productions.) Interview with Monroe Wheeler, New York, 1969.

5. Letter Cocteau to Blanche, dated July 1912. Collection Georges Mévil-Blanche, Offranville.

6. Letter Cocteau to Gide, dated April 20, 1912. Doucet Y547.1.

7. Cocteau, *La Comtesse de Noailles oui et non* (Paris: Perrin, 1963), p. 275.

8. Cocteau, "On ne peut se permettre," *Nouvelle Revue Française,* November 1951, p. 91.

9. Letter Cocteau to Blanche, probably July 1912. Collection Georges Mévil-Blanche, Offranville. The book Cocteau refers to here is no doubt his *La Danse de Sophocle.* The "Princesse Marie" mentioned by Cocteau was the Princess Marie Murat. The Croissets were family friends with property near Grasse. Mme Croisset was the mother of Marie-Laure de Noailles, whose husband financed Cocteau's pioneer film *Le Sang d'un poète* in 1930.

10. Letter Cocteau to Gide, dated April 20, 1912. Doucet Y547.1.

11. Telegram Cocteau to Gide, dated July 4, 1912. Doucet Y547.8.

12. Letter Cocteau to Gide, dated "Samedi" [June/early July 1912]. Doucet Y547.3.

13. Extract from letter of Gide to Cocteau, dated August 6, 1912. Catalogue of Librairie Marc Loliée (Paris, 1957), Item #99, p. 11. The original of this letter was bound in a deluxe edition of André Gide's *Amyntas,* the present location of which is unknown.

14. These two copies of *La Danse de Sophocle* are in the library of Mme Catherine Gide, Paris. Both are the 1912 edition published by Mercure de France, Paris. The volume described above is considered to be the first of the two copies sent to Gide, because of the longer *dédicace* and the presence of a June 1912 train schedule filed loosely in the volume, which would suggest the book was received by Gide about that time. The passage Cocteau quotes is from Gide's *Les Nourritures terrestres.*

15. This is similar to Gide's definition of ΣΥΜΠΑΘΕΙΝ as "Souffrir ensemble, vibrer ensemble," in *Les Cahiers et les poésies d'André Walter,* 14th ed. (Paris: Gallimard, 1952), p. 49.

16. Letter Cocteau to Gide. Doucet Y547.2. This letter is dated in Gide's hand as "June 1912," but it was surely written by Cocteau *after* Gide's letter of August 6, 1912. The "jeune barbare" referred to in the postscript is Cocteau himself. "Les Russes" is an allusion to Diaghilev's Ballets Russes, which had recently come to Paris. "Vestris" is a reference to Nijinsky; see also note 20, below.

17. Postcard Cocteau to mother, dated August 13, 1912. Archives Cocteau, Milly-la-Forêt. Edith Wharton first met Cocteau at the Offranville home of Jacques-Emile Blanche. She later traveled in France with Gide, and together they sent a postcard to Cocteau from Avignon in 1915. (Appendix 5.) The "Comtesse" is no doubt Cocteau's friend and model Countess Anna de Noailles.

18. The Ghéon copy of *La Danse de Sophocle* is in the Collection M. and Mme François Corre, Montagne.

19. According to Henri Ghéon's niece, Mme François Corre, Ghéon and Cocteau's friendship deepened in later years. Ghéon was present at Cocteau's "conversion" at the Meudon home of Jacques Maritain in 1925.

20. Letter Cocteau to Ghéon, dated September 5, 1912. Collection M. and Mme François Corre, Montagne. The Fouquières referred to was André Fouquières, an arbiter of society fashion of the day. François Chevassu was the editor of the literary supplement of *Le Figaro.* Lucia Vestris was a dancer and actress whose sensational roles in man's dress attracted wide attention in the early nineteenth century. Bernstein refers to the French dramatist Henri Bernstein.

21. Letter Cocteau to Blanche, dated "Samedi" [1912]. Collection Georges Mévil-Blanche, Offranville. Cocteau's use of "Androgyde" points up his early awareness of Gide's ambivalent sexual character.

22. The collection of M. and Mme François Corre at Montagne includes an undated postcard (probably 1914) from Cocteau to Ghéon:

Je suis ému pour des vers – ému pour le "linoleum." Gide vous dira quel service vous pourrez encore me rendre. L'imbroglio s'embroglie (prononcer ouille).

Votre

J.C.

(I am moved by the verses – moved by the "linoleum." Gide will tell you how you can do me a further favor. The *imbroglio s'embroglie* (pronounced *ouille*).

Your

J.C.)

The same collection contains a note from Cocteau to Ghéon dated January 26, 1914, presumably on the same subject:

Cher Ghéon

J'aimerais vous voir avec Gide pour quelquechose qui vous intéresse – il faudrait aller vite.

J.C.

(Dear Ghéon,
I would like to see you with Gide for something that is of interest to you —we must act quickly.

J.C.)

23. George D. Painter, *Proust, the Later Years* (Boston: Little, Brown, 1965), p. 185.

CHAPTER 3:   *Le Coq et l'Arlequin*

1. Jean Cocteau, "Lettre à Jacques Maritain," *Poésie critique, II* (Paris: Gallimard, 1960), p. 55.

2. "Les Six" was the name given by a journalist to a group of musicians who were colleagues and friends of Jean Cocteau. The original group included Germaine Taillefer, Georges Auric, Louis Durey, Arthur Honegger, Darius Milhaud, and Francis Poulenc. Cocteau was to collaborate with nearly all of these composers in his subsequent ballets and films.

3. Letter Proust to Cocteau, dated February 11, 1919. Printed in *Le Figaro Littéraire*, October 19, 1963, p. 7.

4. Letter Anna de Noailles to Gide, dated "Vendredi 7" [February 1919]. Doucet Y712.21. This letter and Gide's reply have been reproduced in Claude Martin's critical edition of Gide's *La Symphonie pastorale* (Paris: Minard, 1970), pp. 159, 160, 162, 163.

5. Letter Gide to Anna de Noailles, dated February 8, 1919. Archives du Comte Anne-Jules de Noailles, Paris.

6. Inscription in copy of *Le Coq et l'Arlequin* Cocteau sent to Gide in March 1919. Collection Mme Catherine Gide, Paris.

7. *Papillon* in copy of *Le Coq et l'Arlequin* Cocteau sent to Gide in March 1919. Collection Mme Catherine Gide, Paris.

8. Letter Cocteau to Blanche, dated March 1919. Collection Georges Mévil-Blanche, Offranville.

9. Letter Blanche [signed "J"] to Gide, undated. Dated by Gide "fin Mars 1919." Doucet Y547.25. Blanche's article in the *Revue de Paris* for April 1919 mentions *Le Coq et l'Arlequin* very briefly and then only in a footnote.

10. Letter Cocteau to Blanche, undated [March or April 1919]. Collection Georges Mévil-Blanche, Offranville.

11. Letter Cocteau to Gide, dated "Samedi" [May 3, 1919]. Doucet Y547. 72.

12. Letter Rivière to Gide, dated May 5, 1919. Doucet Y547.71.

13. Letter Gide to Cocteau, dated "Mardi matin le 6" [May 1919]. Doucet Y547.74.

14. Letter Cocteau to Gide, dated May 6, 1919. Doucet Y547.73.

15. Letter Gide to Rivière, dated May 6, 1919. Collection Mme Isabelle Rivière, Dourgne.

16. Letter Gide to Rivière, dated "Dimanche" [May 1919]. Collection Mme Isabelle Rivière, Dourgne.

17. Letter Rivière to Gide, dated May 16, 1919. Collection Mme Isabelle Rivière, Dourgne.

18. "Lettre ouverte à Jean Cocteau," *Nouvelle Revue Française*, 63 (June 1919), 125–128. This letter was later published in Gide's *Incidences* (Paris: Gallimard, 1951), pp. 64–66. It also appeared in English translation in his

Pretexts, selected, ed., and introd. by Justin O'Brien (New York: Delta Books, Dell, 1964).

19. *Le Cap de Bonne-Espérance* was a long war poem written by Cocteau during his Cubist period. Published in 1919 by Editions de la Sirène, the poem was dedicated to Cocteau's friend Roland Garros. Cocteau claimed that his poem was found in the cockpit of Garros's plane after it crashed.

20. *Parade* was a satirical ballet with scenario by Cocteau, music by Erik Satie, scenery and costumes by Pablo Picasso, and choreography by Léonide Massine. It was presented by the Diaghilev company in Paris for the first time on May 18, 1917. The New York revival in March 1973 was a triumph.

21. Letter Cocteau to Rivière, undated [June 7, 1919]. Doucet F.D. 1152-7. Faithful to his promise, Cocteau included a favorable comment about Gide's *Notes sur l'Allemagne* in his "Carte Blanche" column for June 9, 1919, which appeared in the newspaper *Paris-Midi*.

22. Letter Rivière to Gide, dated June 11, 1919. Doucet Y547.76.

23. Letter Rivière to Cocteau, dated June 14, 1919. Doucet F.D. 1152-9.

24. Letter Cocteau to Rivière, undated [June 15 or 16, 1919]. Doucet F.D. 1152-8.

25. Letter Cocteau to Gide, undated [June 15, 1919]. Doucet F.D. 1152-6, A-III-3.

26. Letter Isabelle Rivière to Gide, dated June 17, 1919. Doucet Y547.77

27. Inscription in copy of *Le Potomak* Cocteau sent to Gide June 19, 1919. Collection Mme Catherine Gide, Paris.

28. Letter Rivière to Gide, dated June 25, 1919. Doucet Y547.78.

29. "Cher Jean," wrote Gide, "Vous avez écrit à Marc une lettre exquise. Combien je me réjouis de vous revoir Mardi. André Gide." Letter Gide to Cocteau, undated [*c.* June 25, 1919]. Archives Cocteau, Milly-la-Forêt.

30. The *Exploit,* a legalistic notice that Cocteau included at this point in his open letter has been omitted here, but will be found as Appendix 10. Preliminary drafts of Cocteau's letter are in the Doucet Library, Doucet F.D. 1152-3 and 4.

31. Cocteau, "Réponse à André Gide," *Ecrits Nouveaux,* 18–19 (June-July 1919), 153–160.

32. Letter Cocteau to Gide, dated July 8, 1919. Doucet Y547.79.

33. Letter Gide to Cocteau, dated July 11, 1919. Archives Cocteau, Milly-la-Forêt.

34. Letter Rivière to Gide, dated July 12, 1919. Doucet Y547.82.

35. Letter Gide to Rivière, dated July 13, 1919. Collection Mme Isabelle Rivière, Dourgne.

36. Cocteau here plays on words by distorting the Countess de Noailles's first name "Anna" to "Ananas," the French word for "pineapple," a sweet but prickly fruit.

37. Letter Cocteau to Gide, dated September 6, 1919. Doucet Y547.26.

38. Gide, "La Nouvelle Parade de Jean Cocteau," *Ecrits Nouveaux,* 22 (October 1919), 70–72.

39. Letter Cocteau to Blanche, dated October 8, 1919. Collection Georges Mévil-Blanche, Offranville.

40. Letter Gide to Cocteau, dated November 20, 1919. Collection Mme Catherine Gide, Paris.

41. Cocteau, "La Nouvelle Musique en France," *Revue de Genève,* 21 (March 1922), 397–398.

42. Letter Cocteau to Gide, dated May 9, 1922. Doucet Y547.86.

43. Letter Gide to Cocteau, dated May 12, 1922. Archives Cocteau, Milly-la-Forêt.

44. Letter Cocteau to Gide, dated May 15, 1922. Doucet Y547.89. The book Cocteau refers to in the postscript is probably his *Vocabulaire*.

45. Draft of letter Cocteau to Gide, dated May 15, 1922. Archives Cocteau, Milly-la-Forêt. The Epstein Cocteau refers to is probably the same person mentioned in Cocteau's letter to Gide of October 7, 1921, Doucet Y547.24. Cocteau evidently could not decide which phrase to use here so he wrote in "quelque chose" beneath "blé de la bouche."

46. Note Gide to Cocteau, undated [*c.* May 16, 1922]. Doucet Y547.89.

47. Letter Cocteau to Gide, dated May 18, 1922. Doucet Y547.90.

48. Cocteau, *Portraits-Souvenir* (Paris: Grasset, 1953), p. 232.

49. Claude Mauriac, *Conversations avec André Gide* (Paris: Albin Michel, 1951), p. 68.

50. Cocteau, *La Difficulté d'être* (Paris: Paul Morihien, 1947), p. 201.

51. Cocteau's memory here plays him false, as he admits it often does. The original edition of *Le Coq et l'Arlequin* was published in 1918 by Editions de la Sirène, Paris.

52. Cocteau, *Journal d'un inconnu,* Nouvelle Série des Cahiers Verts (Paris: Grasset, 1953), pp. 110–111.

53. Colin-Simard, ed., *Gide vivant — Paroles de Jean Cocteau* (Paris: Amiot Dumont, 1952). This work was published again as part of *Poésie critique, I* (Paris: Gallimard, 1959), pp. 213–214, and also in 1963, shortly after Cocteau's death, as part of his last work, *La Comtesse de Noailles oui et non* (Paris: Perrin), pp. 273–295.

54. Letter Cocteau to Mary Hoeck, dated January 17, 1953. Archives Cocteau, Milly-la-Forêt.

55. Cocteau, *Poésie critique, II*, p. 22.

56. Cocteau, "Les Armes secrètes de la France," *Poésie critique, II*, p. 234.

57. *Ibid.*, p. 244.

58. *Jean Cocteau,* Portrait Souvenir series, directed by Roger Stéphane and Roland Darbois for RTF, 1963.

CHAPTER 4:   The Squirrel and the Bear

1. Cocteau, "Des Beaux Arts considérés comme un assassinat," *Œuvres complètes de Jean Cocteau* (Lausanne: Marguerat, 1946–1951), X, 232.

2. Letter Rivière to Gide, dated August 1, 1920. Doucet Y549.154: "Mais pourquoi, diable! T'es tu cru obligé de désavouer d'une manière aussi dure mon 'manifeste' . . . de 1919? Tu sais que je ne suis pas susceptible; j'ai pourtant eu du chagrin de ce coup de règle que tu m'as appliqué sur les doigts. . . ." ("But why the devil did you feel obliged to disavow my . . . 1919 'manifesto' in such a severe manner? You know I am not thin-skinned; nevertheless, I was vexed by the way you slapped my fingers with a ruler. . . .")

3. Letter François Mauriac to Gide, dated February 5, 1929. Doucet catalogue *François Mauriac,* January 1968, p. 79: "Non, je ne crois pas que vous ayez voulu être perfide — et moi-même je n'ai été sensible à la malice de votre lettre que lorsque je l'ai lue dans la N.R.F. C'est le danger de ces correspondances livrées au public. Vous conviendrez que la même phrase rend un son différent selon qu'elle est dite dans le privé ou qu'elle nous est

adressée à la face du monde!" ("No, I do not believe you meant to be perfidious — and I myself was sensitive to the maliciousness of your letter only when I read it in the *NRF*. That is the danger of these letters that are opened to the public. You will agree that the same sentence has a different sound depending on whether it is said in private or is addressed to us before all the world!")

4. Marcel Proust also praised Cocteau's aphorisms, but without Gide's qualifications. In a note to Cocteau after he had read and reread *Le Coq et l'Arlequin* with a feeling of wonder, Proust wrote his friend: "J'envie vos formules saisissantes. . . ." *Le Figaro Littéraire,* October 19, 1963, p. 7.

5. Members of the *NRF* staff used regularly to analyze their dreams, and, according to Georges Gabory, in 1921 attended weekly meetings at the home of Mme Sokolniska, a student of Freud's newly arrived in Paris. Gabory, *Essai sur Marcel Proust* (Paris: Le Livre, 1926), pp. 28–29.

6. Cocteau, *Opium, journal d'une désintoxication* (Paris: Stock, 1956), p. 47.

7. Many of Gide's books were, in fact, first published serially in the *NRF,* or were first printed in book form in very limited number: *Les Cahiers d'André Walter* about 75 copies; *L'Immoraliste* and *La Porte étroite* 300 copies each; *Si le grain ne meurt* 13 copies, and *Corydon,* published anonymously as *C.R.D.N.,* 22 copies.

8. Contrary to Gide, Marcel Proust was delighted with *Parade.* He wrote Cocteau a congratulatory letter praising the work and the acrobat "dansant 'comme s'il adressait des reproches à Dieu.'" Letter Proust to Cocteau, undated [1917]. Archives Cocteau, Milly-la-Forêt.

9. "Un acrobate ferait la parade du David, grand spectacle supposé donné à l'intérieur; un clown . . . formule moderne du masque antique, chanterait par une porte-voix les prouesses de David et supplierait le public de pénétrer pour voir le spectacle intérieur." Cocteau, *Le Coq et l'Arlequin* (Paris: Editions de la Sirène, 1918), p. 53. ("An acrobat would do the parade for *David,* great show supposedly put on inside; a clown . . . modern formula for the antique mask, would sing through a megaphone about David's exploits and would entreat the public to enter to see the play inside.")

10. Gide had leveled a similar charge years before at Oscar Wilde, an author whose early influence Cocteau spent years trying to shake off: "habile à piper ceux qui font la mondaine gloiré, Wilde avait su créer, par devant son vrai personnage, un amusant fantôme dont il jouait avec espirit" ("clever at decoying those who manufacture worldly glory, Wilde knew how to create, in front of his true personality, an amusing phantom on which he played with wit").

11. Frederick Brown, *An Impersonation of Angels: A Biography of Jean Cocteau* (New York: Viking, 1968), p. 197.

12. *Correspondance Max Jacob, 1921–1924,* ed. François Garnier (Paris: Editions de Paris, 1953), I, 202.

13. *Ibid.,* p. 203.

14. Brown, *An Impersonation of Angels,* p. 189.

15. Louis Aragon, "Le Coq et l'Arlequin," *Littérature,* 1 (March 1919), 19.

16. By November of 1919, however, the young Surrealists were becoming disenchanted with Gide and the *NRF.* An insulting full-page notice in that issue of *Littérature,* signed by Aragon, Breton, and Soupault, included the following remarks:

La Nouvelle Revue Française. Le numéro 72 (nouvelle série) contient:

1º Des considérations d'André Gide qui n'ajoutent rien à notre admiration pour cet auteur . . .

3º Vingt-cinq pages de M. Jacques Rivière (qu'il vaut mieux passer sous silence);

4º Un article de M. André Lhote, qui . . . par l'insuffisance de sa critique n'arrive pas à nous faire oublier la médiocrité de sa peinture; . . .

7º Divers propos insignifiants. . . .

(The *Nouvelle Revue Française*, No. 72 (new series), contains:

1. Some views by André Gide which add nothing to our admiration for that author . . .

3. Twenty-five pages by M. Jacques Rivière (which it is better to pass over in silence);

4. An article by M. André Lhote, who . . . by the inadequacy of his criticism doesn't manage to make us forget the mediocrity of his painting; . . .

7. Various insignificant matters. . . .)

It was probably this issue of the *NRF* to which Cocteau referred in his letter of October 8, 1919, to Jacques-Emile Blanche.

17. The name was originally chosen by Pierre Reverdy as the title for the Surrealist review that was finally published as *Littérature*.

18. Letter Cocteau to Gide, dated January 20, 1919. Doucet Y547.24.

19. Although Allégret is often referred to as Gide's nephew, he was not related to Gide but was a son of Pasteur Elie Allégret, a friend of the Gide family.

20. Cocteau doubtless chose this pseudonym because Olivier was the name by which Gide identified a character inspired largely by Allégret in Gide's novel *Les Faux-Monnayeurs*. In the same novel Cocteau served as the chief point of departure for the character of Robert de Passavant.

21. Cocteau, *Journal d'un inconnu* (Paris: Grasset, 1953), pp. 111, 112.

22. Draft of open letter from Cocteau to Gide, undated [May or June 1919]. Doucet F.D. 1152-4.

23. The Archives Cocteau at Milly-la-Forêt contain a moving letter dated October 15, [1918] from Marc Allégret, then at Grantchester, Cambridge, where he had gone with Gide. In his letter Allégret consoles Jean Cocteau for the wartime death of his aviator friend Roland Garros:

Vous ne sauriez croire quelle admiration j'ai pour lui, et combien je l'aimais depuis ce fameux soir avec Gide, où je l'ai rencontré au Meurice — vous souvenez-vous? C'était pendant un raid — nous étions sur le trotoire [*sic*] devant l'hôtel. Tout d'un coup une auto apparaît, s'arrête. La portière s'ouvre. Vous dites: Garros. Il saute à terre. Cela a été si brusque si puissement [*sic*] grandiose, que j'ai cru voir un nouveau dieu de la mythologie...

(You wouldn't believe what admiration I have for him, and how much I liked him since that famous evening with Gide, when I met him at the Meurice — do you remember? It was during a raid — we were on the sidewalk in front of the hotel. All at once a car appears, stops. The door opens. You say: "Garros." He jumps down. That was so sudden, so vividly grandiose, that I thought I had seen a new god of mythology...)

24. These lines were no doubt inspired by similar comments by J.-E.

Blanche in letters to Jean Cocteau: July 28, [1916]: "Gide erre dans Paris et fait semblant de me croire parti, mais ma maison lui sert d'alibi, à ce prince au manteau couleur de muraille." ("Gide wanders about Paris and pretends to think I'm away, but my house serves as an alibi to this prince with the wall-colored coat.") August 30, 1916: "Gide dans son mantel noir, maître en l'art de l'alibi, rase les murs." ("Gide in his black coat, master at the art of alibis, hugs the walls.") Archives Cocteau, Milly-la-Forêt.

25. Many years later, in an interview recorded for the RTF with Jean Amrouche, Gide admitted that he himself had never liked his Villa Montmorency at Auteuil. *IIe Entretien avec André Gide* (Paris: Discothèque de la ORTF, January-April 1949).

26. Gide had previously written this to Cocteau in his letter dated May 6, 1919. Doucet Y547.74.

27. Cocteau, "Lettre à André Gide," *Ecrits Nouveaux*, 18–19 (June-July 1919), 159

28. In an interview with the author at Dourgne in April 1968 Mme Isabelle Rivière, whose strong Catholic convictions render both Gide and Jean Cocteau anathema to her on religious as well as moral grounds, agreed that both authors held up masks for the public benefit. According to Mme Rivière's view, Cocteau's mask was ugly and his face beautiful; Gide's mask was beautiful but the face ugly.

29. Cocteau, "Lettre à André Gide," p. 159.

30. *Ibid.*, p. 158.

31. *Ibid.*, p. 160.

32. *Ibid.*, p. 159.

33. *Ibid.*

34. *Ibid.*, p. 154. Paraphrasing his comment to Gide in 1919 that as an outsider he did not perceive the true inner spectacle of *Parade,* Cocteau said on September 20, 1958, in an address at Brussels: "Ce qui, Madame, Mesdames, Messieurs, rend la France indéchiffrable à qui l'observe du dehors, c'est que tout ce qui la singularise et pouvait expliquer la place que jalousent ceux qui la condamnent, se dissimule derrière une parade bruyante que les étrangers prennent pour le spectacle intérieur." "Les Armes secrètes de la France," *Poésie critique II* (Paris: Gallimard, 1960), p. 239. ("That which, Madam, ladies and gentlemen, makes France indecipherable to an outside observer is that everything that sets it apart, and could explain the position envied by those who condemn her, camouflages itself behind a noisy parade that strangers take for the interior play.")

35. Cocteau, "Lettre à André Gide," p. 158.

36. *Ibid.*, p. 159.

37. This technique is basic to Cocteau. Justin O'Brien pointed out in respect to Cocteau's work that although Cocteau sometimes borrowed an initial idea from others, he usually modified it by adding something of his own which gave it a new dimension.

38. Gide, "La Nouvelle Parade de Jean Cocteau," *Ecrits Nouveaux* 22 (October 1919), 71.

39. *Ibid.*

40. *Ibid.*, p. 72.

41. *Ibid.* The italics are mine.

42. Gide drew this image from a reading of Darwin's *Voyage* nine years

earlier. See Gide, *Journal, 1889–1939,* Bibliothèque de la Pléiade (Paris: Gallimard, 1951), entry dated June 21, 1910.

43. Gide, "La Nouvelle Parade de Jean Cocteau," preliminary draft for second open letter in *Ecrits Nouveaux,* 22 (October 1919). Reference Doucet Y1528.5.

44. Letter Cocteau to Gide, dated May 15, 1922. Doucet Y547.89.

CHAPTER 5:   Jean Cocteau and the *NRF*

1. Interview with Professor Auguste Anglès, University of Lyon, June 10, 1968.

2. Edouard de Max had played the role of Gygès in the 1901 production of Gide's *Le Roi Candaule,* a work Gide dedicated to him. In his *Portraits-Souvenir,* Cocteau tells that, on his first visit to de Max's apartment, he had found Gide's books piled atop the actor's pale green, rose-ornamented piano. *Portraits-Souvenir* (Paris: Grasset, 1953), p. 158.

3. Although Gide resisted the strenuous efforts of Paul Claudel and other friends to convert him to Catholicism, Ghéon was converted in 1916 and Copeau followed in 1925 and 1926.

4. Statement by Jean Schlumberger in *André Gide,* Portrait Souvenir series, film produced by Roger Stéphane and Roland Darbois for ORTF, December 1965.

5. Jean Schlumberger, "Considérations," *Nouvelle Revue Française,* 1 (February 1909), 5–6.

6. Jean Schlumberger, *Œuvres,* IV (Paris: Gallimard, 1959), 405–407. Many years later, in 1959, Schlumberger sent this comment to Cocteau, who replied: "Je vous remercie d'avoir tiré ces lignes de l'ombre où me voulait mettre la N.R.F. de l'époque. . . ." ("I thank you for having pulled these lines from the shadows in which the *NRF* of that period wished to put me. . . .") Cocteau added defensively that the mannerism and modernism of which he was accused "est le style Giraudoux et de l'Œdipe de Gide, pas le mien." Jean-Jacques Kihm, Elizabeth Sprigge, and Henri C. Béhar, *Jean Cocteau, l'homme et les miroirs* (Paris: La Table Ronde, 1968), p. 416.

7. "Les intransigeants" at that time probably also included Schlumberger himself and Jacques Copeau, as well as Rivière.

8. Jacques Rivière, "De la sincérité envers soi-même," *Nouvelle Revue Française,* 37 (January 1912), 6.

9. Letter Cocteau to Gide, dated "Samedi." Dated by Gide as May 1919. Doucet Y547.72.

10. Interview with Mme Isabelle Rivière, Dourgne, April 1968.

11. *Correspondance Marcel Proust–Jacques Rivière, 1914–1922,* ed. Philip Kolb (Paris: Plon, 1955), p. 268.

12. Cocteau, *La Comtesse de Noailles oui et non* (Paris: Perrin, 1963), p. 276. A fragmentary note from Cocteau to Gide [November 1913] may allude to this effort by Cocteau: "Que de choses à vous dire à propos du 'goût' et du volume de M.P. mais j'étais *ému* de sa présence et sans facilité verbale." Doucet Y547.7. ("So many things to tell you about 'taste' and the volume by M.P., but I was *moved* by his presence and couldn't find the words.")

13. The *NRF* review of Proust's *Du côté de chez Swann* was not written by Rivière but by Schlumberger in the January 1914 issue. Cocteau had reviewed the work two months earlier in the November 23, 1913, issue of

Excelsior, and a review by Jacques-Emile Blanche appeared in *L'Echo de Paris.*

Regardless of whether it was Rivière or Cocteau who initially urged Gide to read Proust's work, the first part of the manuscript for *À la recherche du temps perdu* was submitted by Proust to the publisher Eugène Fasquelle and to the publishing division of the *Nouvelle Revue Française,* for which Gide was a reader. Both Fasquelle and Gide rejected the manuscript, and it was subsequently published by Grasset.

Sometime later, it is said, Gaston Gallimard of the *NRF* bought up the remainder of Proust's book, which, though subsidized by Proust, had not sold well. Gallimard had the volumes brought in a wagon to his premises where the covers were replaced by the *NRF* imprint. Only afterward did he realize to his chagrin that in so doing he had irreparably lost the valuable right to offer the books as the original edition.

14. Kolb, ed., *Correspondance Marcel Proust-Jacques Rivière, 1914–1922,* p. 268.

15. *Ibid.,* p. 268. Cocteau and Gide had in fact renewed their friendship in May 1922. In July and August, Cocteau was at Le Lavandou with Raymond Radiguet, while Gide was nearby at Porquerolles with Roger Martin du Gard.

Jean-Jacques Kihm and Elizabeth Sprigge, in the English language edition of their biography *Jean Cocteau, the Man and the Mirror* (London: Victor Gollancz, 1968), pp. 90–91, reported that Gaston Gallimard asked Cocteau for the manuscript of *Thomas l'Imposteur* at Proust's funeral services. They also reported that André Gide read the proofs and corrected the punctuation of this novel. According to Gaston Gallimard, however, he asked Cocteau for the manuscript after first hearing Cocteau read part of it at Paul Morand's home. Gallimard also advises that Gide did not correct the proofs. Jean Davray, present owner of the manuscript of *Thomas l'Imposteur,* confirms that it bears no notations by Gide.

The revised French edition of the Sprigge-Kihm work, with Béhar, p. 145, has corrected the original version to reflect the foregoing information. It now appears, based on Cocteau's statement to Léon Pierre-Quint, that Gide read the published novel and returned it to Cocteau with marginal notations. The present location of this copy is not known.

16. Letters Jacques Rivière to André Gide. Doucet Y549.104–109.

17. Jacques Copeau, "Un Essai de rénovation dramatique: Le Théâtre du Vieux-Colombier," *Nouvelle Revue Française,* 57 (September 1913), 337–353.

18. Letter Cocteau to mother, dated March 1914. In another letter to his mother a few days later, Cocteau, in his aphoristic, inverted style, describes Stravinsky: "Igor est admirable d'intelligence géniale et de génie intelligent (mariage si rare!)." ("Igor is admirable for genial intelligence and for intelligent genius (such a rare marriage!))." Archives Cocteau, Milly-la-Forêt.

19. Kihm, Sprigge, and Béhar, *Jean Cocteau, l'homme et les miroirs,* p. 75.

20. Letter Cocteau to Gide, dated February 5, 1914. Doucet Y547.66.

21. Letter Cocteau to Gide, undated [March 1914]. Doucet Y547.20. "P" probably refers here to Paul Thévenaz, who later accompanied Jacques Copeau to the United States, where the latter worked from 1917 to 1919.

22. Frederick Brown, *An Impersonation of Angels: A Biography of Jean Cocteau* (New York: Viking, 1968), pp. 93–94.

23. Interview with Jean Paulhan, Boissise-la-Bertrand, March 24, 1968.

24. Interview with Jean Denoël, Paris, May 1968.

25. Paul Morand, "Spectacle-Concert," *Nouvelle Revue Française,* 74 (April 1920), 609–610.

26. Georges Auric, "Théâtre des Champs-Elysées," *Nouvelle Revue Française,* 89 (February 1921), 224–227.

27. Roger Allard, "Vocabulaire," *Nouvelle Revue Française,* 105 (June 1922), 745–747.

28. Jacques Rivière, *"Le Secret professionnel," Nouvelle Revue Française,* 110 (November 1922), 631–633.

29. Letter Blanche to Cocteau, dated August 18, 1915. Archives Cocteau, Milly-la-Forêt.

30. Letter Cocteau to Blanche, dated August 30, 1915. Collection Georges Mévil-Blanche, Offranville.

31. Letter Cocteau to Blanche, dated May 1922. Collection Georges Mévil-Blanche, Offranville.

32. Cocteau, *La Comtesse de Noailles oui et non,* p. 16.

33. Cocteau, "La Voix de Marcel Proust," *Nouvelle Revue Française,* 112 (January 1923), 90–92. The unfortunate title of Cocteau's second book of verse, *Le Prince frivole,* projected an image of its author that critics could hardly resist. Nevertheless, his reputation for frivolity and superficiality were a source of concern to Cocteau even before his literary career was properly under way. In one of the many enlightening and moving letters to his mother, Jean Cocteau wrote from Val d'André in the summer of 1907:

Puisque tu me touches, un mot au sujet de mon avenir... Sache que je suis à ce sujet mille fois moins léger qu'on ne pourrait le croire – Récemment encore j'hésitais sur la voie à suivre mais l'avis péremptoire d'un talent et d'un génie m'a poussé définitivement vers l'idéal que je me forge.

Ne crains rien, il y a sous mon apparente frivolité quelque chose de grand et de profond – que j'ai eu la volonté de masquer parce que comme le dit Bataille: "Dans le monde il faut faire l'idiot pour ne pas avoir l'air d'un imbécile." – J'entends les flatteurs – je ne les écoute pas... et je possède juste assez de raison pour savoir mieux que personne la valeur de ce que je fais.

(Since you press me, a word about my future... Know that I am, on this subject, a thousand times less frivolous than might be supposed– Even recently I hesitated over which path to follow, but the peremptory urging of a talent and a genius has pushed me definitely toward the ideal that I forge for myself.

Don't be afraid, there is beneath my apparent frivolity something big and deep–which I've had the will power to mask because as Bataille says: "In society one has to play the idiot to avoid seeming an imbecile." –I hear the flatterers–I do not listen to them... and I possess just enough rationality to know better than anyone the value of what I'm doing.)

The letter, in the Archives Cocteau, Milly-la-Forêt, is remarkable for showing Cocteau's precocious but balanced awareness of his powers at eighteen, as well as his strong sense of purpose and determination. It also shows that Cocteau had already deliberately adopted the mask of frivolity for which Gide openly criticized him in 1919.

34. Cocteau, "*Le Diable au corps,*" *Nouvelle Revue Française,* 115 (April 1923), 703–705.

35. Paul Fierens, "La Rose de François," *Nouvelle Revue Française,* 116 (May 1923), 836.

36. Jacques de Lacretelle, "*Le Grand Ecart,*" *Nouvelle Revue Française,* 118 (July 1923), 101–103.

37. Paul Fierens, "*Plain Chant,*" *Nouvelle Revue Française,* 120 (September 1923), 350.

38. Henri Pourrat, "*Thomas l'Imposteur,*" *Nouvelle Revue Française,* 123 (December 1923), 756–758.

39. Very early in his career Jean Cocteau became intent on deliberately widening the variety of genres in which he worked. The Archives Cocteau at Milly-la-Forêt contain a letter dated October 6, 1922, to his mother, in which Cocteau, like a literary chef, lists his creations to date using a menu-like format:

Maintenant que j'ai un livre de vers:
Discours du [grand] Sommeil — Cap [de Bonne-Espérance] — Poésies — Vocabulaire

------

Un livre de critique:
[Le] Coq et l'Arlequin — Carte Blanche — Visites à [Maurice] Barrès — [Le] Secret Prof.[essionnel] —

Le Potomak (préface à ces livres)

------

et sans doute bientôt un livre de théâtre avec:
Les Mariés [de la Tour Eiffel] — Antigone — La pièce annamite — Roméo [et Juliette] et Paul et Virginie —

Je veux étudier le roman. —

J'oubliais le livre de dessins. [Added in the right margin of the letter]

Tu vois que tout en me désespérant — rageant — renonçant, le fond de ma nature lutte quand-même — mais il faut que je m'occupe. La méditation me mène toujours au noir.

(Now that I have a book of verse:
Discours du [grand] sommeil — Cap [de Bonne-Espérance] — Poésies — Vocabulaire

------

A book of criticism:
[Le] Coq et l'Arlequin — Carte Blanche — Visites à [Maurice] Barrès — [Le] Secret Prof[essionel]

Le Potomak (preface to these books)

------

and soon no doubt a book of theater with:
Les Mariés [de la Tour Eiffel] — Antigone — the Annamite play *— Roméo [et Juliette]* and *Paul et Virginie —*

I want to study the novel. —

I forgot the book of drawings. [Added in the right margin of the letter]

You see that even though it drives me to despair—raging—giving up, the deepest part of my nature struggles anyway—but I must keep busy. Meditation always leads me to blackness.)

CHAPTER 6: Les Deux Maisons Se Touchent

1. Gide's public image today is apt to be of the man in his late years: bald, austere, and withdrawn, quite removed from the twenty-two-year-old Gide who wrote his friend Paul Valéry in 1891: "Quelques lignes de quelqu'un d'abruti, qui ne lit plus, qui n'écrit plus, qui ne dort plus, ni ne mange ni ne pense—mais court avec ou sans Louÿs dans les cafés ou les salons serrer des mains et faire des sourires." ("A few lines from a brutish person, who no longer reads, no longer writes, no longer sleeps, nor eats nor thinks—but with or without Louÿs makes the rounds of the cafés or salons shaking hands and grinning.") *Correspondance André Gide–Paul Valéry (1890–1942)* (Paris: Gallimard 1955), p. 139.

2. Adrienne Monnier, *Rue de l'Odéon* (Paris: Albin Michel, 1960), p. 107.

3. *Ibid.*, p. 106.

4. Cocteau, "Carte Blanche," *Le Rappel à l'ordre* (1926) (Paris: Stock, Delamain et Boutelleau, 1948), p. 81. Cocteau's comment refers to a musical première on March 21, 1919, of Erik Satie's *Socrate* at which Satie played the piano and Jean Cocteau acted as master of ceremonies.

5. Gide, *Journal, 1889–1939*, Bibliothèque de la Pléiade (Paris: Gallimard, 1951), p. 473. Entry dated August 20, 1914.

6. *Ibid.*, pp. 500–501. Entry dated November 15, 1914.

7. Interview with Marc Allégret, Paris, October 1968.

8. Gide, *Journal*, p. 685. Entry dated November 3, 1920.

9. Letter Cocteau to Gide, dated J[anuary] 1925. Collection Mme Catherine Gide, Paris. I am indebted to Claude Martin and the Information Bulletin of the Association des Amis d'André Gide, No. 9 (October 1970), 5, for this letter and for permission to use it. Tagore's play appeared at the end of 1924, published by the *NRF.*

10. Letter Cocteau to Gide, dated May 1 [1925]. Doucet Y547.44.

11. Letter Cocteau to Gide, dated May 13, 1925. Doucet Y547.45.

12. Letter Cocteau to mother, dated November 1, 1928. Archives Cocteau, Milly-la-Forêt.

13. *Ibid.*

14. Letter Cocteau to Gide, dated March 1929. Doucet Y547.48. Raymond Roussel, whose writing Cocteau had first heard read aloud by André Gide, was also a patient at Saint-Cloud at the time. It was during this cure that Cocteau wrote his *Opium,* the journal of a disintoxication, which he illustrated profusely with strange drawings of people made from opium pipes. A stage version of *Opium,* adapted by Roc Brynner, was successfully presented in London and New York during the 1970 season.

15. Gide, *Journal*, p. 963. Entry dated January 3, 1930.

16. Postcard Gide to Cocteau, dated December 26, 1931, Archives Cocteau, Milly-la-Forêt. A postcard to Desbordes from Gide with the same date is also at Milly.

17. Letter Cocteau to Gide, dated Saturday night [1947]. Doucet Y547.55.

18. Letter Cocteau to Gide, dated January 15, 1949. Doucet Y547.57.

19. Letter Gide to Cocteau, dated February 13, 1949. Archives Cocteau, Milly-la-Forêt.

20. Letter Cocteau to Gide, undated [February 1949]. Doucet Y547.58.

21. Letter Cocteau to Gide, dated February 1949. Doucet Y547.59.

22. Although Cocteau reports daily visits by Gide, according to Jean-Jacques Kihm there were only two such visits. Kihm, *Jean Cocteau, l'homme et les miroirs* (Paris: La Table Ronde, 1968), p. 316.

23. The "porte étroite," "potager," the famous staircase, and the fireplace where Gide's wife burned his letters are all intact in the former home of Madeleine and André Gide at Cuverville. It has recently been handsomely restored by its present owner, Mme Philippe Gastambide. In 1968 the Association des Amis de Cuverville, with Lucien Feydel, Prefect of the Seine-Maritime, as its first president, was organized to preserve the memory of André Gide and to maintain the site of Cuverville. This association was dissolved in 1971.

In anticipation of the Gide Centennial in 1969, the Association des Amis d'André Gide was also created, with M. André Malraux as honorary president and Mme Catherine Gide as president of the Conseil d'Administration. The objectives of this international association are "défendre la mémoire et l'œuvre d'André Gide, d'étudier et réaliser tout ce qui, sous toutes formes et par tous moyens, pourra favoriser la diffusion de l'œuvre d'André Gide et les échanges culturels internationaux . . ." ("to defend the memory and work of André Gide, to study and carry out everything which, in all forms and by all means, can encourage the spread of Gide's work and international cultural exchanges . . .").

24. Letter Cocteau to Marcel Jouhandeau, undated [January 1926]. Fonds Jouhandeau, Bibliothèque Littéraire Jacques Doucet, Paris.

25. *Correspondance André Gide–Roger Martin du Gard* (Paris: Gallimard, 1968), I (1913–1934), 78.

26. Cocteau, *The Difficulty of Being*, trans. Elizabeth Sprigge (New York: Coward-McCann, 1966), p. viii.

27. Cocteau, *Maalesh* (Paris: Gallimard, 1949), p. 26.

28. Letter Cocteau to Gide, dated "Eté [19]23." Doucet Y547.39.

29. Letter Cocteau to Gide, dated December 1, 1913. Doucet Y547.9. The "elle" probably refers to Anna de Noailles, who was also interested in Tagore's work.

30. Letter Cocteau to Gide, dated December 6, 1913. Doucet Y547.10.

31. Letter Cocteau to Gide, dated December 24, 1913. Doucet Y547.11.

32. Letter Gide to Cocteau, undated [early April 1917]. Archives Cocteau, Milly-la-Forêt.

33. Letter Cocteau to Gide, undated; dated by Gide as April 16, 1917. Correct date is probably April 17 or 18. Doucet Y547.16.

34. Letter Gide to Cocteau, dated June 2, 1918. Archives Cocteau, Milly-la-Forêt.

35. Letter Gide to Cocteau, dated June 23, 1922. Doucet Y547.29.

36. Letter Cocteau to Gide, undated; dated by Gide as "June 22." Correct date probably after June 23, 1922. Doucet Y547.28.

37. Letter Gide to Cocteau, undated [end of June 1922]. Doucet Y547.28 (verso).

38. Letter Cocteau to Gide, undated [July 1922]; dated by Gide as July/

August 1922. Doucet Y547.30. The "cousin" referred to is probably Maurice Martin du Gard, then editor of *Les Nouvelles Littéraires,* who was a cousin of Roger Martin du Gard, Gide's companion at Porquerolles at the time.

39. Letter Cocteau to Gide, dated October 1926. Doucet Y547.46.

40. Letter Cocteau to Gide, dated N.[ovember] 1926. Doucet Y547.92. Gide's meditations on the Bible, *Numquid et tu...?,* had recently appeared in the Editions de la Pléiade published by J. Schiffrin. It is perhaps this work of Gide's which evoked such praise from Cocteau. Cocteau's interest in the Roman Catholic church had been rekindled by Jacques Maritain only the year before.

41. Letter Cocteau to Gide, dated February 1929. Doucet Y547.47.

42. Pierre Herbart, *À la recherche d'André Gide* (Paris: Gallimard, 1952), p. 9; and Cocteau, "Gide vivant," *Poésie critique, I* (Paris: Gallimard, 1959), p. 226.

43. *Correspondance André Gide–Paul Valéry (1890–1942),* p. 23.

44. Cocteau, "Préface au passé," *Poésie critique, I,* p. 7.

45. Letter Gide to Cocteau, undated. Archives Cocteau, Milly-la-Forêt.

46. Note Cocteau to Gide, dated October 22, 1913. Doucet Y547.5. Urien is a character in Gide's *Le Voyage d'Urien,* and Tityre is a character in Gide's *Paludes.* Les Mortimer-Ménard are characters in Cocteau's *Le Potomak.*

47. Letter Cocteau to Gide, undated [November 1913]. Doucet Y547.7.

48. Letter Cocteau to Gide, undated [April 6, 1917]. Doucet Y547.18.

49. Letter Cocteau to mother, dated Good Friday [April 6], 1917. Archives Cocteau, Milly-la-Forêt.

50. Letter Cocteau to Gide, dated January 19, 1918. Doucet Y547.19.

51. Letter Cocteau to Gide, dated September 6, 1919. Doucet Y547.26.

52. This address to the students had been arranged by Cocteau's friend Raymond Aron. The speech was later published as "D'un ordre considéré comme une anarchie" in *Le Rappel à l'ordre,* pp. 237–257.

53. Letter Cocteau to Gide, dated May 4, 1923. Doucet Y547.38.

54. Letter Cocteau to Gide, dated February 26, 1945. Doucet Y547.54.

55. This undated note (Doucet Y547.66) was probably written about June 1914, after the publication of the orange-covered first edition of *Les Caves du Vatican.* In a somewhat cruel private joke, forsaking the pseudonym "La Sorcière" by which her friends often referred to her, Cocteau here uses the name Jehanne-la-Courte for his friend Mme Mühlfeld, whose legs were deformed. She had evidently already received a copy of Gide's book.

56. Letter Cocteau to Gide, undated [June 1914]. Doucet Y547.4.

57. Letter Cocteau to Gide, October 1936. Doucet Y547.52.

58. There are three different copies of this work still in Mme Gide's collection: Copy No. A from the original edition published by the NRF in 1923; a copy from the *édition ordinaire,* NRF, 1923; and copy No. 301 from the illustrated edition, NRF, 1927.

59. The "triste échange" probably refers to the gift of *Thésée* Gide promised Cocteau in his letter of July 31, 1946, now in the Archives Cocteau, Milly-la-Forêt.

60. Letter Cocteau to Gide, undated [April 1925]. Doucet Y547.32.

61. Certain letters referred to in the correspondence but now missing, together with others not mentioned but undoubtedly written, consist for the

most part of letters from Gide to Cocteau. The study of this correspondence by Jean-Jacques Kihm, Jean Cocteau, *Lettres à André Gide avec quelques réponses d'André Gide* (Paris: La Table Ronde, 1970), and the article by Arthur K. Peters, "Cocteau et Gide, lettres inédites," in *Jean Cocteau* (Paris: Minard, 1972), contain the complete text in French of all presently known communications between the two men.

62. *Correspondance André Gide–Paul Valéry (1890–1942)*, p. 9.

63. *Ibid.*, p. 240.

64. *Entretiens sur André Gide*, ed. Marcel Arland and Jean Mouton (Paris: Mouton, 1967), p. 73.

65. *Ibid.*, p. 79.

66. Cocteau, "Gide vivant," *Poésie critique, I,* pp. 214–215.

67. See Appendix 1.

68. Letter Cocteau to Gide, dated November 4, 5, 6, 7, 1922. Doucet Y547. 36.

69. In 1950 Raymond Queneau asked a group of writers to identify the hundred books they would include in a "Bibliothèque Idéale." Jean Cocteau's list, which mentioned three hundred and fifty-two titles, included as No. 309 his own *La Difficulté d'être.* No. 316 on his list was André Gide's *L'Immoraliste.* One can imagine the glint in his eyes as Cocteau added at the end of his overburdened list: "Il ne s'agit naturellement pas de *jugment,* mais de ce que j'emporterais en vitesse et au premier coup d'œil." ("Of course, it is not a matter of *judgment,* but of what I would carry away quickly and at first glance.") Queneau, *Pour une bibliothèque idéale* (Paris: Gallimard, 1956), pp. 93–106.

70. Cocteau, *Le Potomak* (Paris: Stock, Delamain et Boutelleau, 1950), p. 313.

71. Letter Cocteau to Gide, undated [March 1914]. Doucet Y547.15.

72. Cocteau, *Le Potomak,* pp. 391–392.

73. Letter Cocteau to Gide, dated 1916. Doucet Y547.14. Cocteau also drew from that wartime Christmas Eve part of the inspiration for his poem *Le Cap de Bonne-Espérance.*

74. Letter Cocteau to mother, undated [Christmas 1915]. Archives Cocteau, Milly-la-Forêt. See Appendix 6.

75. Letter Cocteau to Gide, dated May 24, 1918. Doucet Y547.22.

76. This undated postscript, probably originally part of Cocteau's letter to Gide of January 23, 1923, was later dated by Gide, as were a number of letters in this correspondence. Doucet Y547.75.

77. Cocteau, *Lettre à Jacques Maritain* (1926) (Paris: Stock, 1964), p. 70.

78. Cocteau, "Le Secret professionnel," *Le Rappel à l'ordre,* p. 215.

79. *Ibid.*, pp. 215–216.

80. Private copy of *Jean l'Oiseleur* (Paris: Champion, 1925). Collection Mme Catherine Gide, Paris.

81. Dermit is extremely modest about his film experiences. He makes no pretention to being an accomplished actor, even though, without professional training, he acquitted himself creditably in Cocteau's films.

82. Letter Cocteau to Gide, undated [March 1914]. Doucet Y547.20.

83. Letter Cocteau to Gide, dated January 19, 1918. Doucet Y547.19.

84. Letter Cocteau to Gide, dated October 7, 1921. Doucet Y547.27.

85. Letter Cocteau to Gide, dated July/August [19]22. Doucet Y547.30.

Le Violon d'Ingres was an early title Cocteau considered for the album of his drawings that was published by Stock in 1923 under the title *Dessins.* "Le violon d'Ingres" is an expression used to describe an artist's attempt to work in an art form different from his customary medium.

86. Letter Cocteau to mother, dated July 19, 1922. Archives Cocteau, Milly-la-Forêt.

87. Letter Cocteau to mother, dated October 7, 1922. Archives Cocteau, Milly-la-Forêt.

88. Letter Cocteau to mother, dated October 24, 1922. Archives Cocteau, Milly-la-Forêt.

89. Letter Cocteau to Gide, dated October 28, 1922. Doucet Y547.31. Cocteau's plea to Gide in this letter for a reaction to his *Le Secret professionnel* would seem to contradict the report to his mother three months earlier: "Je rentre il y a 10 minutes de Ste. Maxime et trouve une lettre de Gide qui habite en face de nous, l'île de Porquerolles et me complimente beaucoup sur mon 'passage' des Ecrits Nouveaux (Secret Professionnel)." ("I came in ten minutes ago from Sainte-Maxime and found a letter from Gide, who is living across from us, on the island of Porquerolles, and compliments me highly on my 'passage' in *Ecrits Nouveaux (Secret professionnel).*") Letter Cocteau to mother, undated [July 1922]. Archives Cocteau, Milly-la-Forêt. The explanation for this apparent discrepancy is that Cocteau's letter to his mother refers to the *Ecrits Nouveaux* version of his *Le Secret professionnel,* whereas the letter to Gide refers to the book version, with illustrations by Picasso, which had just been published by Stock.

90. Letter Cocteau to Gide, dated "Eté [19]23." Doucet Y547.39. The "malgré que non erratum" probably refers to a comment by Gide on *Thomas l'Imposteur,* to which Cocteau alludes in his interview with Léon Pierre-Quint. Pierre-Quint, *André Gide* (Paris: Stock, Delamain et Boutelleau, 1952), p. 463.

91. Letter Cocteau to Gide, dated March 1929. Doucet Y547.48. Elsewhere in his work Cocteau contributed unwittingly to his reputation for facile writing by publicly describing how he had written this novel in about fifteen days.

92. Letter Cocteau to Gide, undated [November or December 1936]. Doucet Y547.69.

93. Letter Cocteau to Gide, undated; dated by Gide as June 3, 1917. Doucet Y547.17.

94. Letter Cocteau to Gide, undated [1927]. Doucet Y547.43.

95. Letter Cocteau to Gide, dated January 20, 1919. Doucet Y547.24.

96. Letter Cocteau to Gide, undated [July 1914]. Doucet Y547.13. The quotation beginning "Honnête peuple Suisse!" was taken by Cocteau from Gide's *L'Immoraliste,* Pléiade edition, pp. 457–458. *Le Coup de dés* refers to the Mallarmé work.

97. Letter Cocteau to Gide, dated November 25, 1925. Doucet Y547.41. The Abbaye de Solesmes, near Le Mans, was rumored to be the retreat of Jacques Copeau, and of Cocteau following his "conversion" in 1925 by Jacques Maritain.

98. Letter Cocteau to Gide, dated February 26, 1945. Doucet Y547.54.

99. Letter Gide to Cocteau, dated December 31, 1950. Archives Cocteau, Milly-la-Forêt.

100. Letter Cocteau to Gide, dated January 2, 1951. Doucet Y547.65.

CHAPTER 7:   Invasions, Immunities, Influences

1. Letter Cocteau to Gide, undated; dated by Gide as April 16, 1917. Doucet Y547.16.

2. Letter Gide to Cocteau, dated "Lundi matin" [April 23, 1917]. Archives Cocteau, Milly-la-Forêt.

3. Letter Cocteau to Gide, dated June 3, 1917. Doucet Y547.17.

4. Letter Cocteau to Gide, dated November 25, 1925. Doucet Y547.41.

5. An undated letter from Cocteau to Gide, probably written in early February of 1930, had already urged Gide to attend a rehearsal. Doucet Y547.68.

Cher André,
Que pensait la R[evue] H[ebdomadaire] en publiant cette merveille que la générale X lirait comme on écoute Ch.[arles] du B.[os] chez Maritain? Ce portrait repoussé est un prodige de rire contenu.

> Je vous embrasse.
> Jean

P.S. Tâchez de venir une minute à la répétition.

(Dear André,
What was the R[*evue*] H[*ebdomadaire*] thinking of when it published that marvel—which General X's wife would read the way they listen to Ch[arles] du B[os] at Maritain's? This repoussé portrait is a wonder of restrained laughter.

> Fondest regards.
> Jean

P.S. Try to come to the rehearsal for a minute.)

6. Letter Cocteau to Gide, dated February 11, 1930. Doucet Y547.67.

7. Gide, *Journal, 1889–1939*, Bibliothèque de la Pléiade (Paris: Gallimard, 1951), p. 1105. Entry dated January 20, 1932.

8. *Ibid.*, p. 1267. Entry dated July 12, 1937.

9. Cocteau, "Gide vivant," *Poésie critique, I* (Paris: Gallimard, 1959), p. 221.

10. Letter Cocteau to Gide, dated January 13, 1939. Doucet Y547.53.

11. Claude Mauriac, *Conversations avec André Gide* (Paris: Albin Michel, 1951), p. 270.

12. Letter Cocteau to Manager, Cinéma du Colisée, undated. Doucet Y547.56.

13. Léon Pierre-Quint, *André Gide* (Paris: Stock, Delamain et Boutelleau, 1952), p. 465.

14. Letter Gide to Cocteau, dated July 31, 1946. Archives Cocteau, Milly-la-Forêt.

15. Letter Cocteau to Gide, dated November 29, 1950. Doucet Y547.64.

16. Letter Gide to Cocteau, dated December 2, 1950. Archives Cocteau, Milly-la-Forêt.

17. For a listing of Cocteau's film works consult *Jean Cocteau* by René Gilson, Cinéma d'Aujourd'hui series, No. 27 (Paris: Seghers, 1964), pp. 169–175.

18. Letter Cocteau to Gide, dated "Samedi Soir" [early 1947]. Doucet Y547.55.

19. Cocteau, *Journal d'un inconnu*, Nouvelle Série des Cahiers Verts (Paris: Grasset, 1953), p. 113.

20. Cocteau, "Gide vivant," *Poésie critique, I*, p. 211.

21. Letter Cocteau to Gide, dated July 5, 1949. Doucet Y547.61.

22. Letter Cocteau to Gide, dated August 1949. Doucet Y547.62.

23. Letter Gide to Cocteau, dated August 27, 1949. Archives Cocteau, Milly-la-Forêt.

24. Letter Cocteau to Gide, dated January 15, 1950. Doucet Y547.63. Marc Allégret recently tried to arrange for a version of *Les Caves* to be filmed in Italy, but the authorization was denied.

25. Letter Cocteau to Gide, dated July 19, 1945. Collection Mme Catherine Gide, Paris.

26. Letter Cocteau to Gide, dated July 28, 1946. Doucet Y547.91.

27. Letter Gide to Cocteau, dated July 31, 1946. Archives Cocteau, Milly-la-Forêt.

28. Letter Cocteau to Gide, undated [February or March 1914]. Doucet Y547.6.

29. Postcard Gide to Cocteau, dated January 12, 1914. Archives Cocteau, Milly-la-Forêt.

30. Letter Cocteau to Gide, dated January 20, 1919. Doucet Y547.24. The *NRF's* second postwar issue was scheduled for July 1919.

31. Letter Cocteau to Gide, dated July 28, 1946. Doucet Y547.91. The text Cocteau offered was probably from *La Difficulté d'être*, which he had completed in early July.

32. Cocteau, "Mesure," *L'Arche*, 24 (February 1947), 13–18. This article was later published as part of *La Difficulté d'être* (Paris: Paul Morihien, 1947).

33. Archives Cocteau, Milly-la-Forêt. Payment by Gallimard was in two parts: 1,000 francs for an "Etude sur Rousseau destiné à la Littérature Française," and 500 francs for a "Choix de textes de Rousseau."

34. *Tableau de la littérature française*, préface par André Gide (Paris: Gallimard, 1962), p. 8.

35. An abbreviated version of Cocteau's article appeared serially in the *Revue de Paris* for November-December 1938 and January 1939. A revised version was reprinted in Cocteau's *Poésie critique, I*, pp. 273–332.

36. Claude Mauriac, *Conversations avec André Gide*, p. 69.

37. Claude Mauriac, in his study *Jean Cocteau ou la vérité du mensonge* (Paris: Odette Lieutier, 1945), p. 170, takes the same view: "S'il [Cocteau] aime Rousseau, bien sûr, c'est qu'il s'aime – . . . il parle de son auteur, et à travers lui, de lui-même." ("If he [Cocteau] likes Rousseau, of course, it's that he likes himself– . . . he speaks of his author, and through him, of himself.")

38. Cocteau, "Rousseau," *Tableau de la littérature française*, p. 302.

39. *Ibid.*, p. 207.

40. *Ibid.*, p. 302.

41. *Ibid.*, pp. 282–283.

42. *Ibid.*, pp. 291, 297, 269, 292.

43. Cocteau, "Gide Vivant," *Poésie critique, I*, p. 210.

44. Cocteau, *Journal d'un inconnu*, p. 112.

45. Cocteau, *La Comtesse de Noailles oui et non* (Paris: Perrin, 1963), p. 16. Gide's *Anthologie de la poésie française* included only poets who were already deceased. Jean Denoël, who assisted Gide with this work, explains that this was Gide's way of limiting the number of poets in the anthology, while avoid-

ing criticism for glaring omissions such as Jean Cocteau. However, when the *NRF* published its 1958 anthology of French poets whose work had appeared in the pages of the *NRF*, a selection of Cocteau's poetry was included.

46. Letter Cocteau to Gide, dated April 20, 1912. Doucet Y547.1.

47. Cocteau, *Opium* (Paris: Stock, Delamain et Boutelleau, 1956), pp. 225–226.

48. Letter Cocteau to Gide, undated [summer 1918]. Doucet Y547.21.

49. Letter Cocteau to Gide, dated 3 February 1931. Doucet Y547.51.

50. Cocteau, *La Difficulté d'être*, p. 46.

51. Cocteau, *La Comtesse de Noailles oui et non*, p. 97.

52. Cocteau, "Eloge des Pléiades," *Nouvelle Revue Française*, 245 (February 1, 1934), 194–197.

53. Cocteau, *Le Rappel à l'ordre* (1926) (Paris: Stock, Delamain et Boutelleau, 1948), "Préface 1923," p. 9.

54. Cocteau, *Journal d'un inconnu*, p. 133.

55. Cocteau, *La Difficulté d'être*, p. 46.

56. Cocteau, *Lettre à Jacques Maritain* (1926) (Paris: Stock, Delamain et Boutelleau, 1964), p. 54.

57. Interview with François Mauriac, October 1968, Paris.

58. Pierre-Quint, *André Gide*, p. 463.

59. Cocteau, *La Difficulté d'être*, p. 48.

60. Copy of *Le Potomak* sent to Gide by Cocteau. Collection Mme Catherine Gide, Paris.

61. Letter Cocteau to Blanche, dated October 17, 1919. Collection Georges Mévil-Blanche, Offranville.

62. Draft of open letter Cocteau to Gide, undated [May-June 1919]. Doucet F.D. 1152-3.

63. The name "Eugène," taken from a character in *Le Potomak*, became a derogatory label that Cocteau and his friends applied to people and objects.

64. Cocteau, *Le Potomak* (1919) (Paris: Stock, Delamain et Boutelleau, 1950), p. 50.

65. *Jean Cocteau: Entretiens avec André Fraigneau*, Bibliothèque 10-18 (Paris: Union Générale d'Editions, 1965), p. 7. The interviews in this book were broadcast over the French Radio (RTF) from January 26 to March 28, 1951.

66. Justin O'Brien, *"Paludes* et *Le Potomak," Cahiers André Gide, I* (Paris: Gallimard 1969).

67. Cocteau, *Le Potomak*, p. 262.

68. Frederick Brown, *An Impersonation of Angels: A Biography of Jean Cocteau* (New York: Viking, 1968), p. 201.

69. Draft of letter Cocteau to Gide, dated May 15, 1922. Archives Cocteau, Milly-la-Forêt. The passage referred to above was deleted from the letter by Cocteau before he sent it to Gide. The final letter (Doucet Y547. 89) is in the Doucet library.

70. Cocteau, *Le Potomak*, p. 14.

71. Joseph Campbell, *The Hero with a Thousand Faces* (New York: Bollingen, 1949), p. 36.

72. As Sigmund Freud has pointed out: "The eye corresponds to an erogenous zone in the looking and exhibiting mania." *Three Contributions to the Theory of Sex*, Modern Library (New York: Random House, 1938), p. 57.

73. Cocteau, *Opium,* p. 107.

74. Letter Cocteau to mother, dated July 6, 1922. Archives Cocteau, Milly-la-Forêt.

75. Cocteau, "Préface au passé," *Poésie critique, I,* p. 13.

76. Cocteau, *Journal d'un inconnu,* p. 106.

77. Cocteau, *Le Potomak,* p. 340.

78. Cocteau, *Lettre à Jacques Maritain,* p. 54.

79. Curiously enough, the close ties between *Paludes* and *Le Potomak* were passed over in silence by Cocteau in his *Le Cordon ombilical,* a little book purporting to record the origin of certain of his works.

80. Interview with Jean Marais, Paris, October 1968.

81. Letter Gide to Marc Allégret, dated April 25, 1918. Collection Marc Allégret, Paris. This entire letter, which gives a further dimension to the relation between Gide and Allégret, is reproduced in Appendix 7.

82. Gide, *Journal,* p. 758. Entry dated May 18, 1922.

83. Letter Cocteau to Gide, dated October 28, 1922. Doucet Y547.31.

84. Letter Cocteau to mother, undated [1922]. Archives Cocteau, Milly-la-Forêt.

85. Letter Cocteau to mother, undated [1917]. Archives Cocteau, Milly-la-Forêt. Another, earlier letter written to his mother from Rome on March 16, 1917, while Cocteau was working with Picasso, shows signs of his inner struggle and the influence of Picasso at the time: "quel exemple quotidien de probité sublime, de simplicité laborieuse! Je l'admire [Picasso] et je me dégoûte. J'essaye de m'améliorer, de tuer en moi ce qui dérange, ce qui diminue." ("what a daily example of sublime honesty, of arduous simplicity! I admire him [Picasso] and I disgust myself. I'm trying to improve myself, to kill in me what disturbs, what lessens.")

86. Letter Cocteau to Gide, dated April 7, 1923. Doucet Y547.37.

87. Cocteau, *Lettre aux Américains* (Paris: Grasset, 1949), p. 94.

88. Cocteau, *Le Cordon ombilical* (Paris: Plon, 1962), p. 28.

89. *Ibid.,* pp. 12–13.

90. Cocteau, *La Comtesse de Noailles oui et non,* p. 230.

91. Cocteau, "Démarche d'un poète," *Poésie Critique, II* (Paris: Gallimard, 1960), p. 17.

92. Cocteau, *Portraits-Souvenir* (Paris: Grasset, 1953), pp. 232–233.

93. Cocteau, *Mon Premier Voyage (Tour du monde en 80 jours)* (Paris: Gallimard, 1937), p. 7.

94. Letter Cocteau to Gide, dated August 1924. Doucet Y547.40.

95. Cocteau, *Le Mystère de Jean l'Oiseleur* (Paris: Champion, 1925), p. 26.

96. Gide, "Lettre à J.C. (non-envoyée)." *Nouvelle Revue Française,* 195 (December 1, 1929), 764–765. This letter was later reprinted in *Divers* (Paris: Gallimard, 1931), pp. 201–202.

97. Draft of first in a series of three postcards Gide to Cocteau, dated January 18 [1931]. Collection Mme Catherine Gide, Paris.

98. End of second card in series of three postcards Gide to Cocteau, dated January 18 [1931]. Archives Cocteau, Milly-la-Forêt.

99. End of third card in series of three postcards Gide to Cocteau, dated January 18 [1931]. Collection J.-J. Kihm et J.-J. Poulet-Allamagny, Paris. Six years later Gide repeated this anecdote in his *Journal* entry for December 15, 1937.

100. Gide, *Les Faux-Monnayeurs* (Paris: Gallimard, 1949), p. 41.

101. Letter Cocteau to Gide, dated February 3, 1931. Doucet Y547.51. In this letter Cocteau juxtaposes Gide's *Séquestrée* with the homages and memoirs of Marshals Joffre and Foch, the French military heroes of World War I. Articles on both men had appeared in the issues of *L'Illustration* for January 3, 10, and 23, 1931. The cover of the same magazine for January 31 bore a photograph of comtesse Anna de Noailles, who had been the first French woman to be designated a Commander of the French Legion of Honor.

102. Cocteau, "Gide vivant," *Poésie critique, I*, p. 212.

103. Cocteau, *Poésie critique, II*, p. 11.

104. Cocteau, "Discours d'Oxford," *Poésie critique, II*, p. 179.

105. Pierre-Quint, *André Gide*, pp. 462–463.

106. Cocteau, "Gide vivant," *Poésie critique, I*, pp. 216–217. In his *Journal d'un inconnu* Cocteau explains further what he meant by saying Gide "m'a appris qu'il ne fallait tirer profit de rien." Here he says: "je songe au credo de Gide: 'Je n'admets pas que rien me nuise, je veux que tout me serve, au contraire. J'entends tourner tout à mon profit.' C'est le credo de la visibilité. Pour obtenir le credo de l'invisibilité (le mien), il n'y a qu'à tirer un négatif de ces phrases. . . ." *Journal d'un inconnu*, pp. 85–86. ("I think of Gide's credo: 'I do not admit that anything will harm me, I want everything to be useful to me, on the contrary. I intend to turn everything to my advantage.' This is the credo of visibility. To obtain the credo of invisibility (mine) one only need develop a negative from these sentences. . . .")

107. George Painter, *André Gide* (London: Cox and Wyman, 1968), p. 95. Also Claude Mauriac, *Conversations avec André Gide*, pp. 107–108, and *Correspondance André Gide–Roger Martin du Gard* (Paris: Gallimard, 1968), I (1913–1934), 36.

108. Painter, *André Gide*, p. 129. Jean Cocteau was also a source of inspiration for characters in the works of other French writers, including Proust, Apollinaire, and Aragon.

109. Gide, *Voyage au Congo*, in *Journal, 1939–1949; Souvenirs*, Bibliothèque de la Pléiade (Paris: Gallimard, 1954), p. 802.

110. Gide, *Le Retour du Tchad*, in *Journal, 1939–1949; Souvenirs*, Bibliothèque de la Pléiade (Paris: Gallimard, 1954), p. 954.

CHAPTER 8: Jugements sans Appel

1. Letter Cocteau to Gide, dated April 20, 1912. Doucet Y547.1.

2. Letter Cocteau to Gide, dated "Samedi" [June/early July 1912]. Doucet Y547.3.

3. Letter Cocteau to Gide, dated August 27 [1914]. Doucet Y547.12.

4. Gide, *Journal, 1889–1939*, Bibliothèque de la Pléiade (Paris: Gallimard, 1951); p. 504. Entry dated November [15] 1914.

5. Letter Cocteau to mother, dated August 7, 1917. Archives Cocteau, Milly-la-Forêt.

6. Letter Cocteau to Blanche, dated October 8, 1919. Collection Georges Mévil-Blanche, Offranville.

7. Gide, *Journal*, p. 651. Entry dated April 18, 1918.

8. Letter Cocteau to Gide, dated August 24, 1918. Doucet Y547.23. The "poulain sauvage" is probably Marc Allégret, who had accompanied Gide to

England shortly before. Cocteau's postscript probably refers to the old convent of Saint-Louen, near Chinon, where Blanche and others stayed during the bombardment of Paris by Big Bertha, the famous long-range German artillery piece.

9. Letter Cocteau to mother, dated August 21, 1918. Also letter Cocteau to Blanche, dated August 24, 1918. Both letters are in the Archives Cocteau, Milly-la-Forêt.

10. Marc Allégret, however, recalls that he had already met Cocteau before Gide brought them together.

11. Letter Gide to Allégret, dated January 19, 1919. Collection Marc Allégret, Paris. For this entire letter see Appendix 9.

12. Gide, *Journal*, p. 688. Entry dated January 1, 1921.

13. Cocteau in his 1924 preface to *Visites à Maurice Barrès* later expressed regret at the harshness of his attack on Barrès. Cocteau, *Le Rappel à l'ordre* (1926) (Paris: Stock, Delamain et Boutelleau, 1948), p. 151.

14. An allusion to Cocteau himself, who had written *Le Gendarme incompris* with Raymond Radiguet.

15. Letter Gide to Cocteau, undated [September 1921]. Collection Mme Catherine Gide, Paris.

16. Letter Cocteau to Gide, undated; dated October 7, 1921, by Gide. Doucet Y547.27. Cocteau's comment, "comme le Gendarme éclaire un côté (petit) de l'Ecclésiastique," refers to the *critique-bouffe, Le Gendarme incompris,* which he wrote with Raymond Radiguet. It was based in part on Mallarmé's poem "Ecclésiastique," and was produced at the Théâtre Michel on May 24, 1921.

The text of Cocteau's *Les Mariés de la Tour Eiffel* appeared in *Les Œuvres libres* for March 1923 (No. 21). Cocteau refers to his preface in his letter to Gide dated August 1924, following publication of *Les Mariés* in March 1924 by the *NRF.*

17. Letter Cocteau to Gide, dated September 3, 1922. Collection Mme Catherine Gide, Paris.

18. Gide, *Journal*, p. 743. Entry dated September [10], 1922.

19. *Correspondance André Gide–Roger Martin du Gard* (Paris: Gallimard, 1968), I (1913–1934), 192.

20. Gide, *Journal*, p. 754. Entry dated January 16, 1923.

21. Letter Cocteau to Gide, undated [January 17–18, 1923]. Doucet Y547.34.

22. Copy of letter Gide to Cocteau, originally undated; dated later by Gide "24 juin 23" but probably written January 24, 1923. Doucet Y547.34 (verso).

23. Letter Cocteau to Gide, dated January 29, 1923. Doucet Y547.35.

24. Fragment of letter Cocteau to Gide, dated in Gide's hand "Hiver 1922–1923." Doucet Y547.75.

25. Cocteau, "D'un ordre considéré comme une anarchie," *Poésie critique, I* (Paris: Gallimard, 1959), p. 69.

26. "Quand je lui [Gide] remis *Thomas l'Imposteur,* il me rendit l'ouvrage avec des indications précieuses de sa main, surtout des suppressions de mots décoratifs, sauf les *malgré que,* qu'il a gardés et dont il m'a remercié." ("When I delivered *Thomas l'Imposteur* to him, he returned it with precious notations in his own hand, mostly suppressions of decorative words, except for the

malgré que's which he left in and for which he thanked me.") Léon Pierre-Quint, *André Gide* (Paris: Stock, Delamain et Boutelleau, 1952), p. 463.

27. Gide, *Journal*, p. 758. Entry dated May 18, 1923.

28. Letter Cocteau to Gide, undated [April 1925]. Doucet Y547.33.

29. Gide, *Journal*, p. 942. Entry dated October 11, 1929.

30. Letter Cocteau to Gide, dated February 11, 1930. Doucet Y547.67.

31. Letter Cocteau to Gide, dated July 14, 1930. Doucet Y547.49.

32. Cocteau's article, as well as others written for *Le Figaro* by Cocteau at this period, was later incorporated into his book *Portraits-Souvenir*.

33. *Correspondance André Gide–Roger Martin du Gard*, II, p. 17.

34. Letter Gide to Cocteau, dated February 28, 1935. Archives Cocteau, Milly-la-Forêt. On February 23, Gide had already written Martin du Gard a note of thanks indicating his pleasure with the Cocteau article: "Mille mercis pour la communication du Cocteau – que j'ai lu avec ravissement. . . ." *Correspondance André Gide–Roger Martin du Gard*, II, 19.

35. *Correspondance André Gide–Roger Martin du Gard*, II, 27.

36. *Ibid.*, p. 29.

37. Letter Cocteau to Gide, undated; dated by Gide "1937?" but probably written November or December 1936. Doucet Y547.69.

38. Page 34 of this copy, now in the collection of Mme Catherine Gide, bears an interesting marginal note about Khill in an unknown handwriting: "Mère française, père arabe! Vrai nom: Marcel Kelilou d'où sa beauté – que ce pauvre gosse repose en paix!" ("French mother, Arab father! Real name: Marcel Kelilou, whence his beauty – may this poor youngster rest in peace!")

39. Letter Gide to Cocteau, dated March 30, 1937. Archives Cocteau, Milly-la-Forêt. In his biography of Jean Cocteau, *An Impersonation of Angels* (New York: Viking, 1968), p. 313, Frederick Brown incorrectly dates Gide's letter as March 1932 and relates it to Cocteau's earlier *Le Livre blanc*.

40. Claude Mauriac, *Conversations avec André Gide* (Paris: Albin Michel, 1951), p. 48.

41. This report should be compared to Cocteau's letter to Gide, dated January 13, 1939. See Chapter 7, p. 192, above. Cocteau also said later to Roger Stéphane that the absence of physical incest in *Les Parents terribles* impressed Gide, who urged: "Il *faut appuyer* là-dessus, c'est ce qui est admirable dans votre pièce." ("You must lay stress on this, that's what's admirable in your play.") Roger Stéphane, ed., *Jean Cocteau, entretien avec Roger Stéphane*, Collection Portrait Souvenir (Paris: Jules Tallandier, 1964), p. 175.

42. Mauriac, *Conversations avec André Gide*, pp. 67–68. Gide's play was the one-act farce *Le Treizième Arbre*.

43. This information highlights some nuances of Cocteau's letter of November 25, 1925, congratulating Gide on Valéry's election to the Academy.

44. Mauriac, *Conversations avec André Gide*, p. 68. Mauriac indicated in an interview, Paris, June 1968, that he believes Cocteau's *drame* was in not being wanted as a young writer by either of the chief groups of his era: the Surrealists (Breton was a bitter enemy), and the *NRF* (where Gide was "Pope"). Gide even secured a minor position for Breton at the *NRF* for a short time.

45. This passage appears in the manuscript of Mauriac's journal, but not in the published *Conversations avec André Gide* (p. 69).

46. Mauriac, *Conversations avec André Gide*, p. 70.

47. Roger Stéphane, "Mes Rencontres avec André Gide," *Magazine Littéraire*, 14 (January 1968), 16.

48. Interview with Claude Mauriac, Paris, October 1968. Pierre Georgel, a young friend of Jean Cocteau's, in his dissertation "L'Introspection dans l'œuvre de Jean Cocteau" (Faculté des Lettres de Paris, 1964), agrees with Gide that Cocteau is not responsible for his "mensonges."

49. Claude Mauriac, *Une Amitié contrariée* (Paris: Grasset, 1970), pp. 113, 114.

50. Cocteau, "Le Discours d'Oxford," *Poésie critique, II* (Paris: Gallimard, 1960), p. 189.

51. Letter Cocteau to Claude Mauriac, dated July 1939. Collection Claude Mauriac.

52. Cocteau, "Gide vivant," *Poésie critique, I*, pp. 231–232.

53. The article later appeared as part of *Feuillets d'automne* (p. 180), published in 1949 by *Mercure de France*.

54. Cocteau, "Paul Verlaine, Place du Panthéon," *Poésie critique, I*, p. 205.

55. *Ibid.*, p. 206.

56. *Ibid.*, p. 207.

57. Letter Cocteau to Gide, dated July 28, 1946. Doucet Y547.91.

58. Letter Gide to Cocteau, dated July 31, 1946. Archives Cocteau, Milly-la-Forêt.

59. Cocteau, *Le Sang d'un poète* (Monaco: Editions du Rocher, 1957), p. 13.

60. Cocteau, *La Difficulté d'être* (Paris: Paul Morihien, 1947), p. 39.

61. Letter Cocteau to Gide, dated "Samedi Soir" [1947]. Doucet Y547.55.

62. Letter Cocteau to Gide, dated August 1924. Doucet Y547.40. "Souvent votre réserve me peinait. Mais votre bonté envers Thomas, Roméo, Les Mariés me donnait du courage." ("Your reserve often hurt me. But your kindness toward *Thomas, Roméo, Les Mariés*, gave me courage.")

63. Cocteau, "Gide vivant," *Poésie critique, II*, p. 213.

64. Gide, *Journal*, p. 295. Entry dated April 11, 1948.

65. Cocteau, "On ne peut se permettre," *Hommage à André Gide, Nouvelle Revue Française*, November 1951, p. 91.

66. Cocteau, "Gide vivant," *Poésie critique, I*, pp. 208–209.

67. *Ibid.*, p. 210.

68. *Ibid.*, p. 223.

69. *Ibid.*, p. 212.

70. *Ibid.*, p. 213.

71. *Ibid.*

72. *Ibid.*, p. 218.

73. *Ibid.*, p. 219.

74. Letter Cocteau to Kihm, dated March 22, 1958. Collection J.-J. Kihm, Paris.

75. Cocteau, "Gide vivant," *Poésie critique, I*, p. 219.

76. *Ibid.*

77. *Ibid.*, p. 221. The last sentence no doubt reflects Cocteau's annoyance at the role of Passavant assigned him by Gide in *Les Faux-Monnayeurs*.

78. Cocteau, "Gide vivant," *Poésie critique, I*, p. 224. Gide's own view of his *Journal* as a mirror of his life is reflected in the statement Edouard makes about his journal in *Les Faux-Monnayeurs:* "C'est le miroir qu'avec moi je

promène." Gide's "composition en abîme," his technique of writing a novel about an author writing a novel, is also a multiple mirror effect.

79. Cocteau, "Gide vivant," *Poésie critique, I*, p. 225.

80. *Ibid.*

81. *Ibid.*, p. 226.

82. *Ibid.*, p. 230.

83. Cocteau, "Discours sur la poésie," *Poésie critique, II*, p. 214.

84. Cocteau, "Discours de réception à l'Académie Française," *Poésie critique, II*, p. 167.

85. Cocteau, "Gide vivant," *Poésie critique, I*, p. 233.

86. Letter Cocteau to Mary Hoeck, dated January 10, 1955. Archives Cocteau, Milly-la-Forêt.

87. Cocteau, *Journal d'un inconnu*, Nouvelle Série des Cahiers Verts (Paris: Grasset, 1953), p. 113.

88. *Ibid.*, p. 114.

89. Cocteau here maliciously referred, for example, to "Loeb et Leopold, deux jeunes Américains qui avaient trop lu Gide, deux jeunes adeptes de la gratuité, deux jeunes meurtriers intellectuels." "Discours de recéption à l'Académie Française, *Poésie critique, II*, p. 154. ("Loeb and Leopold, two young Americans who had read too much Gide, two young adepts of the gratuitous, two young intellectual murderers.")

90. Letter Cocteau to mother, dated August 1912. Archives Cocteau, Milly-la-Forêt.

91. Cocteau, *Journal d'un inconnu*, p. 121. Cocteau's chronic dissatisfaction with translations of his work, especially those in English, is shown in his letters to Mary Hoeck, one of his English translators. Monroe Wheeler, friend of Cocteau, now counselor to the Trustees of the Museum of Modern Art in New York, reports that Cocteau persuaded him to translate *Orphée*. Unfortunately the first draft was sent to the Gate Theater in London and was subsequently lost before completion.

92. Collection Justin M. O'Brien, Columbia University Library, New York.

93. Letter Cocteau to Jean Dauven, September 11, 1955. Collection Jean Dauven, Paris.

94. Note Cocteau to Jean Dauven, undated, in margin of Dauven's manuscript. Collection Jean Dauven, Paris.

95. Letter Cocteau to Jean Dauven, dated November 28, 1955. Collection Jean Dauven, Paris.

96. Letter Cocteau to Jean Dauven, dated December 17, 1955. Collection Jean Dauven, Paris.

97. Letter Cocteau to Jean Dauven, undated [December 1955]. Collection Jean Dauven, Paris.

98. André Fraigneau, ed., *Jean Cocteau: Entretiens avec André Fraigneau*, Bibliothèque 10-18 (Paris: Union Générale d'Editions, 1965), p. 3.

CHAPTER 9:   Rivalry — the Root and the Flower

1. Interview with Jean Paulhan, Boissise-la-Bertrand, March 24, 1968. The reader will appreciate that M. Paulhan, and the other colleagues of André Gide and Jean Cocteau interviewed, are not here quoted in full. Only those comments specifically bearing on the origins of the rivalry between the two great authors are cited. The views expressed, being limited

in scope, must not therefore be taken as their comprehensive judgments of Gide and Cocteau as men and artists.

2. Léon Pierre-Quint, *André Gide* (Paris: Stock, Delamain et Boutelleau, 1952), pp. 462–463.

3. The characters in Gide's novels are seldom entirely inspired by real-life acquaintances. Cocteau, Allégret, and Gide himself served only as points of departure for the characters of Passavant, Olivier, and Edouard respectively.

4. Gide, *Les Faux-Monnayeurs* (Paris: Gallimard, 1949), p. 89. The italics are mine.

5. *Ibid.*, p. 411.

6. Interview with Marc Allégret, Paris, October 1968.

7. Interview with Marcel Jouhandeau, Malmaison, April 1968.

8. Interviews with Claude Mauriac, Paris, 1968. Although Gide, like Cocteau, lost favor with young French readers after World War II, his fortunes in recent years have seemed to improve. According to the *Index Translationum* published annually by UNESCO, Gide was the fifteenth most translated French author in 1964, dropped to twenty-second in 1965, and climbed back to fifteenth in 1966. These figures may indicate that André Gide is at last emerging from writer's purgatory.

9. Interview with François Mauriac, Paris, October 1968.

10. François Mauriac, *Nouveaux Mémoires intérieurs* (Paris: Flammarion, 1965), p. 186.

11. Interview with Roger Stéphane, Paris, October 1968.

12. Draft of letter Cocteau to Gide, dated May 15, 1922. Archives Cocteau, Milly-la-Forêt.

13. Cocteau, "Gide vivant," *Poésie critique, I* (Paris: Gallimard, 1959), p. 213.

14. Cocteau, *La Comtesse de Noailles oui et non* (Paris: Perrin, 1963), p. 280.

15. Cocteau, *Journal d'un inconnu,* Nouvelle Série des Cahiers Verts (Paris: Grasset, 1953), p. 39.

16. Jean-Jacques Kihm, Elizabeth Sprigge, and Henri C. Béhar, *Jean Cocteau, l'homme et les miroirs* (Paris: La Table Ronde, 1968), p. 293.

17. Cocteau, *Journal d'un inconnu,* p. 113. In his *Notes sur André Gide* (Paris: Gallimard, 1951), p. 123, Roger Martin du Gard observed that by September 1937 after one of the Pontigny *décades:* "Gide n'a pas tenu sa place, dans cette décade. Les jeunes se détournent de ce vieillard." ("Gide has not held his position in this decade. The young are turning away from this old man.")

18. Cocteau, "Gide vivant," *Poésie critique, I*, pp. 217–218.

19. Cocteau, *Journal d'un inconnu,* pp. 19, 15.

20. Cocteau, *Portraits-Souvenir* (Paris: Grasset, 1935), p. 12.

21. Pierre-Quint, *André Gide*, p. 463.

22. Cocteau, "Discours d'Oxford," *Poésie critique, II* (Paris: Gallimard, 1960), p. 179.

23. Cocteau, "Discours sur la poésie," *Poésie critique, II*, pp. 215–216.

24. Cocteau, *Portraits-Souvenir,* p. 112.

25. Letter Cocteau to Gide, dated March 1929. Doucet Y547.48.

26. Letter Cocteau to Gide, dated January 13, 1939. Doucet Y547.53.

27. Cocteau, *The Difficulty of Being*, trans. Elizabeth Sprigge (New York: Coward-McCann, 1967), p. viii.

28. Cocteau, *Opium, journal d'une désintoxication* (Paris: Stock, Delamain et Boutelleau, 1956), p. 72.

29. Paul Morand, *Monplaisir ...en littérature* (Paris: Gallimard, 1967), p. 246.

30. Letter Cocteau to Gide, dated May 9, 1922. Doucet Y547.86.

31. In a letter to his mother in 1922, before he had won admission to the *NRF*, and with Breton's intransigence toward him at its height, Cocteau wrote in despair of the "cannibales" who surrounded him in Paris, of "les haines qui m'entourent, l'incompréhension, la coalition des vieux *et des jeunes*. Si tu suivais comme moi . . . le mouvement en tête duquel la plus simple justice devrait me mettre, tu n'en reviendrais pas de mon aventure" ("the hates that surround me, the lack of understanding, the coalition of the old *and the young*. If you followed as I do . . . the movement at whose head the simplest justice should place me, you wouldn't get over my adventure"). Archives Cocteau, Milly-la-Forêt.

32. Pierre-Quint, *André Gide*, p. 467.

33. Michel Sanouillet, *Dada à Paris* (Paris: Jean-Jacques Pauvert, 1965), p. 420.

34. Pierre-Quint, *André Gide*, pp. 467–468.

35. Sanouillet, *Dada à Paris*, pp. 192, 540.

36. Gide, "Dada," *Nouvelle Revue Française*, 79 (April 1920), 477–481.

37. Cocteau, *Maalesh* (Paris: Gallimard, 1949), pp. 26–27.

38. Letter Cocteau to Gide, dated May 9, 1922. Doucet Y547.86.

39. Letter Gide to Cocteau, dated May 12, 1922. Archives Cocteau, Milly-la-Forêt.

40. Interview with Gérard Magistry, Paris, 1968.

41. Cocteau, *Journal d'un inconnu*, p. 103.

42. Claude Mauriac, *Conversations avec André Gide* (Paris: Albin Michel, 1951), pp. 94–95.

43. Letter Cocteau to Gide, dated 1947. Doucet Y547.55.

44. Cocteau, *Maalesh*, pp. 26–27.

45. *Les Faux-Monnayeurs* forms an integral part of the cycle of confessional and polemical works by Gide which dealt with the homosexual issue; *Corydon* and *Si le grain ne meurt* were also being written during the period 1917 to 1919. Gide's implied argument in *Les Faux-Monnayeurs* is that there are virile friendships that are salutary, such as that of Edouard and Olivier (Gide-Allégret), and others that corrupt, such as that of Passavant and Olivier (Cocteau-Allégret). Gide had already emphasized this thought in his letters to Allégret of April 25, 1918, and January 19, 1919. (See Appendix 7 and Appendix 9.)

46. Gide, *Et nunc manet in te, suivi de Journal intime* (Paris and Neuchâtel: Ides et Calendes, 1951), p. 111.

47. Gide, *Et nunc manet in te*, pp. 110–111.

48. *Les Faux-Monnayeurs* was published in 1926. Following its appearance there appears to be a lull of nearly two years in the correspondence between Gide and Cocteau.

49. At the time of his trip to England with Gide in June 1918, Marc Allégret, born in Basel, Switzerland, on December 22, 1900, was nearing

his eighteenth birthday. George D. Painter's comment that Allégret was only fifteen at the time is incorrect. Painter, *André Gide* (London: Cox and Wyman, 1968), p. 84.

50. Pierre-Quint, *André Gide,* p. 463.

51. Cocteau, "Gide vivant," *Poésie critique, I,* pp. 210–211.

52. Pierre-Quint, *André Gide,* p. 391.

53. Claude Mauriac, *Conversations avec André Gide,* p. 88. The complete text of the conversation, including proper names, is given here as reported by M. Mauriac in interviews in Paris, October 1968.

54. Claude Mauriac, *Conversations avec André Gide,* pp. 107–108.

55. Gide, *Journal, 1889–1939,* Bibliothèque de la Pléiade (Paris: Gallimard, 1951), p. 626.

56. *Ibid.,* p. 640.

57. *Ibid.,* p. 640.

58. *Ibid.,* p. 645.

59. *Ibid.,* p. 649.

60. *Ibid.,* p. 650. In Gide's letter of April 25, 1918 (Appendix 7), to Marc Allégret he refers to their forthcoming trip together to England: "les vraies conversations n'auront lieu qu'en Angleterre." Collection Marc Allégret, Paris.

61. Gide, *Journal,* p. 651.

62. *Ibid.,* p. 652.

63. *Ibid.*

64. *Ibid.* This visit is also referred to in Gide's letter to Allégret of April 25, 1918. Collection Marc Allégret, Paris.

65. Letter Cocteau to Gide, undated [Summer 1918]. Doucet Y547.21.

66. Schlumberger, *Madeleine et André Gide,* p. 189.

67. Gide, *Journal,* p. 656.

68. Gide, *Les Faux-Monnayeurs,* p. 468. Even as Gide often used real-life acquaintances as "points de départ" for his fictional characters, so he undoubtedly used real-life events and emotions as points of departure for their counterparts in his fiction. For esthetic purposes his treatment of Cocteau in *Les Faux-Monnayeurs* was probably carried to a higher pitch of severity than the real-life attitudes on which it was based.

Both Gide and Cocteau enjoyed puns, as their correspondence shows. The word "Passavant" can be assigned three meanings: "ignorant," "pushy," and "breaking wind."

69. Gide, *Les Faux-Monnayeurs,* p. 123.

70. In this instance Gide's veiled criticism of Cocteau is perhaps itself counterfeit. Art, as he well knew, was also a means to an end for Gide himself, as it was for Cocteau: the means of reestablishing his inner equilibrium. Gide was also well aware that Cocteau's art, like his own, was in part driven by a "secrète exigence de tempérament": homosexuality.

71. Gide, *Les Faux-Monnayeurs,* p. 244.

72. The final part of this passage brings to mind the exchange of private letters (Doucet Y547.34 and Y547.35) between Gide and Cocteau about the patina that conceals a work of art. Cocteau's literary doctrine included the notion that the poet's function is to rub away this patina. Gide's implication here is that if Cocteau's false patina of gold were rubbed off it would reveal not a masterpiece but a piece of glass. A further nuance to Gide's

criticism lies in the fact that crystal was the talisman of the Surrealists. Thus, by extension, not only Cocteau but the Surrealists too may be considered counterfeits.

73. Gide, *Les Faux-Monnayeurs*, p. 46. "Le Balcon" was a poem by Jean Cocteau mentioned in his letter to Gide of January 20, 1919. (Doucet Y547. 24.) The poem appeared in Cocteau's *Poésies, 1917–1920* (Paris: Editions de la Sirène, 1920), p. 52.

74. According to George Painter, this fictitious work has its real counterpart in Cocteau's *Le Grand Ecart*, which was published in 1923. (Painter, *André Gide*, p. 96.)

75. Gide, *Les Faux-Monnayeurs*, p. 98. This comment, and the wry observation, "Passavant défend son livre et l'explique. Cette lettre irrite Edouard plus encore que les articles" (*Les Faux-Monnayeurs*, p. 88) ("Passavant defends his book and explains it. That letter irritates Edouard even more than the articles"), echo Gide's constant urging of Cocteau to let his work speak for itself. Although Gide felt an author should not attempt to justify his own *works*, he nevertheless appears to have considered it legitimate for an author to justify *himself* in his works, for he often attempts to do so.

76. Gide, *Les Faux-Monnayeurs*, p. 98.

77. Cocteau, "Gide vivant," *Poésie critique, I*, p. 232.

78. *Ibid.*, p. 233.

79. Gide, *Les Faux-Monnayeurs*, p. 411.

80. *Ibid.*, p. 274.

81. *Ibid.*, p. 272.

82. *Ibid.*, p. 279.

83. Jean Lambert, *Gide familier* (Paris: René Julliard, 1958), p. 101.

84. In his *Journal des Faux-Monnayeurs* (p. 85), Gide wrote his famous phrase: "Inquiéter, tel est mon rôle." Jean Cocteau was also conscious of his own role as a disturber; in his *Journal d'un inconnu* (pp. 116–117) he observed: "Si j'écris, je dérange. . . . J'ai la faculté de dérangement. . . . Je dérangerai après ma mort. Il faudra que mon œuvre attende l'autre mort lente de cette faculté de dérangement." ("If I write, I disturb. . . . I have the power of disturbing. . . . I will disturb after my death. My work will have to wait for the other slow death of that power to disturb.")

85. Mss. in collection Arthur King Peters, New York, New York.

86. In view of Capote's testimony in *Observations* that Gide and Cocteau last met in Sicily in the spring of 1950, it would appear that either Cocteau's memory for dates has again deceived him here, or that he chose to use the encounters at Melun and the Comédie-Française because they paint a more friendly picture of the final contacts between the two authors.

87. This refers no doubt to Gide's last letter to Cocteau dated "Dernier jour de l'an 1950." Archives Cocteau, Milly-la-Forêt.

Selected Bibliography

I

Books by Jean Cocteau *

Bacchus. Paris: Gallimard, 1952.
La Belle et la Bête, journal d'un film. Monaco: Editions du Rocher, 1958.
Le Cap de Bonne-Espérance. Paris: Editions de la Sirène, 1919.
La Comtesse de Noailles oui et non. Paris: Librairie Académique Perrin, 1963.
Le Coq et l'Arlequin. Paris: Editions de la Sirène, 1918.
Le Cordon ombilical. Paris: Plon, 1962.
La Corrida du 1er mai. Paris: Grasset, 1957.
La Difficulté d'être. Paris: Paul Morihien, 1947.
The Difficulty of Being. Trans. Elizabeth Sprigge. New York: Coward-McCann, 1967.
Les Enfants terribles. Paris: Arthème Fayard, 1951.
Le Grand Ecart. Paris: Stock, Delamain et Boutelleau, 1947.
Journal d'un inconnu. Nouvelle Série des Cahiers Verts. Paris: Grasset, 1953.
Lettre aux Américains. Paris: Grasset, 1949.
Lettres à André Gide avec quelques réponses d'André Gide. Ed. Jean-Jacques Kihm. Paris: La Table Ronde, 1970.
Le Livre blanc. (1928.) Illus. Paris: Editions du Signe, 1930.
Maalesh. Paris: Gallimard, 1949.
La Machine infernale. Paris: Grasset, 1962.
Mon Premier Voyage (Tour du monde en 80 jours). Paris: Gallimard, 1937.
My Contemporaries. Ed., introd., and trans. Margaret Crosland. London: Peter Owen, 1967.
Le Mystère de Jean l'Oiseleur. Paris: Champion, 1925.
Notes sur le testament d'Orphée. Liège: Dynamo, 1960.
Œuvres complètes de Jean Cocteau. 11 vols. Lausanne: Marguerat, 1946–1951.

* Dates given in parentheses following a title are dates of original publication.

Opium, journal d'une désintoxication. Paris: Stock, Delamain et Boutelleau, 1956.

Orphée. (1927.) Paris: Stock, 1965.

Orpheus, Œdipus Rex, The Infernal Machine. Trans. Carl Wildman. London: Oxford University Press, 1962.

Poésie critique, I. Paris: Gallimard, 1959.

Poésie critique, II, monologues. Paris: Gallimard, 1960.

Poésies, 1917–1920. Paris: Editions de la Sirène, 1920.

Portraits-Souvenir. Paris: Grasset, 1953.

Le Potomak. (1919.) Paris: Stock, Delamain et Boutelleau, 1950.

Le Rappel à l'ordre. (1926.) Paris: Stock, Delamain et Boutelleau, 1948.

Le Sang d'un poète. (1948.) Monaco: Editions du Rocher, 1957.

Le Secret professionnel. Paris: Stock, Delamain et Boutelleau, 1922.

Le Testament d'Orphée. Monaco: Editions du Rocher, 1961.

Théâtre. 2 vols. Paris: Gallimard, 1963, 1965.

Thomas l'Imposteur. Collection Soleil. Paris: Gallimard, 1934.

(and Maritain, Jacques.) *Jean Cocteau — Lettre à Jacques Maritain. Jacques Maritain — Réponse à Jean Cocteau.* 2 vols. (1926.) Paris: Stock, Delamain et Boutelleau, 1964.

Periodical Articles by Jean Cocteau

"Le Diable au corps." *Nouvelle Revue Française,* 115 (April 1923), 703–705.

"Eloge des Pléiades." *Nouvelle Revue Française,* 245 (February 1, 1934), 194–197.

"Gide est mort. Vive Gide." *France-Amérique,* March 4, 1951, p. 5.

"Jean-Jacques Rousseau." *Revue de Paris,* November-December 1938, pp. 742–747; and January 1939, pp. 54–79.

"Lettre à André Gide." *Ecrits Nouveaux,* 18–19 (June-July 1919), 153–160.

"Mesure." *L'Arche,* 24 (February 1947), 13–18.

"La Nouvelle Musique en France." *Revue de Genève,* 21 (March 1922), 397–400.

"Le Numéro Barbette." *Nouvelle Revue Française,* 154 (July 1, 1926), 33–38.

"On ne peut se permettre." *Nouvelle Revue Française,* November 1951, pp. 90–92.

"Réponse à André Gide." *Ecrits Nouveaux,* 18–19 (June-July 1919), 153–160.

"Secrets de beauté." *Fontaine.* Edition de Paris, 42 (May 1945), 165–181.

"La Voix de Marcel Proust." *Nouvelle Revue Française,* 112 (January 1923), 90–92.

Unpublished Documents — Cocteau

Letters between Jean Cocteau and Jacques-Emile Blanche. Collection Georges Mévil-Blanche, Offranville.

Letters between Jean Cocteau and Jean Dauven. Collection Jean Dauven, Paris.

Letters between Jean Cocteau and Henri Ghéon. Collection M. and Mme François Corre, Montagne.

Letters between Jean Cocteau and André Gide. Fonds Gide and Fonds Doucet, Bibliothèque Littéraire Jacques Doucet, Paris.

Letter from Jean Cocteau to Marcel Jouhandeau. Fonds Jouhandeau, Bibliothèque Littéraire Jacques Doucet, Paris.

Letters between Jean Cocteau and his mother. Archives Cocteau, Milly-la-Forêt.

Letters between Jean Cocteau and Jacques Rivière. Collection Mme Jacques Rivière, Dourgne; and Bibliothèque Littéraire Jacques Doucet, Paris.

Manuscript of *Le Secret professionnel.* Collection Gérard Magistry, Paris. Now in the Bibliothèque de l'Arsénal, Paris.

Miscellaneous correspondence of Jean Cocteau. Archives Cocteau, Milly-la-Forêt.

Unpublished passages from the journal of Claude Mauriac, Paris.

Books about Jean Cocteau

Jean Cocteau. Catalogue of Galerie Briant-Robert. Paris, 1925.

Jean Cocteau. Catalogue of Musée de Lunéville, by Pierre Chanel. Paris, 1968.

Jean Cocteau et son temps. Catalogue of Musée Jacquemart-André, by Pierre Georgel. Paris, 1965.

Hommage à Jean Cocteau. Catalogue of Musée des Beaux-Arts de Nantes. May 21–June 15, 1964.

Brown, Frederick. *An Impersonation of Angels: A Biography of Jean Cocteau.* New York: Viking, 1968.

Brosse, Jacques. *Cocteau.* Pour une Bibliothèque Idéale. Paris: Gallimard, 1970.

Chanel, Pierre. *Album Cocteau.* Paris: Tchou, 1970.

Colin-Simard, ed. *Gide vivant – Paroles de Jean Cocteau.* Paris: Amiot Dumont, 1952.

Fermigier, André. *Jean Cocteau entre Picasso et Radiguet.* Collection Miroirs de l'Art. Paris: Hermann, 1967.

Fowlie, Wallace. *Jean Cocteau: The History of a Poet's Age.* Bloomington: Indiana University Press, 1966.

———. *The Journals of Jean Cocteau.* Ed. and trans. Wallace Fowlie. Bloomington: Indiana University Press, 1956.

Fraigneau, André. *Cocteau par lui-même.* Ecrivains de Toujours series. Paris: Editions du Seuil, 1965.

———. *Jean Cocteau: Entretiens avec André Fraigneau.* Bibliothèque 10-18. Collection dirigée par Michel-Claude Jalard. Paris: Union Générale d'Editions, 1965.

Georgel, Pierre. "L'Introspection dans l'œuvre de Jean Cocteau." Faculté des Lettres de Paris, 1964. (Unpublished dissertation.)

Gilson, René. *Jean Cocteau.* Cinéma d'Aujourd'hui series, No. 27. Paris: Seghers, 1964.

Kihm, Jean-Jacques. *Cocteau.* Bibliothèque Idéale. Paris: Gallimard, 1960.

———, Sprigge, Elizabeth, and Béhar, Henri C. *Jean Cocteau, l'homme et les miroirs.* Paris: La Table Ronde, 1968. (This is the revised French edition of the earlier English version *Jean Cocteau: The Man and the Mirror.* The French version is the more complete and accurate of the two.)

Lannes, Roger. *Jean Cocteau.* Poètes d'Aujourd'hui series. Paris: Seghers, 1945.

Magnan, Jean-Marie. *Cocteau.* Collection Les Ecrivains devant Dieu. Paris: Desclée de Brouwer, 1968.

Mauriac, Claude. *Une Amitié contrariée.* Paris: Grasset, 1970.

————. *Jean Cocteau ou La Vérité du mensonge.* Paris: Odette Lieutier, 1945.

Oxenhandler, Neal. *Scandal and Parade: The Theater of Jean Cocteau.* New Brunswick: Rutgers University Press, 1957.

Phelps, Robert. *Professional Secrets: An Autobiography of Jean Cocteau.* New York: Farrar, Straus and Giroux, 1970.

Sprigge, Elizabeth, and Kihm, Jean-Jacques. *Jean Cocteau: The Man and the Mirror.* London: Victor Gollancz, 1968.

Steegmuller, Francis. *Cocteau: A Biography.* Boston: Little, Brown, 1970.

Stéphane, Roger, ed. *Jean Cocteau, entretien avec Roger Stéphane.* Collection Portrait Souvenir. Paris: Jules Tallandier, 1964.

Periodical Articles about Jean Cocteau

Autour de Jean Cocteau. La Table Ronde, No. 94 (October 1955).

Memorial Jean Cocteau. *Revue des Belles-Lettres,* Nos. 1, 2 (1969).

Allard, Roger. "*Vocabulaire.*" *Nouvelle Revue Française,* 105 (June 1922), 745–747.

Aragon, Louis. "*Le Coq et l'Arlequin.*" *Littérature,* I (March 1919), 19.

Auric, Georges. "Théâtre des Champs-Elysées." *Nouvelle Revue Française,* 89 (February 1921), 224–227.

Fierens, Paul. "La Rose de François." *Nouvelle Revue Française,* 116 (May 1923), 836.

————. "*Plain Chant.*" *Nouvelle Revue Française,* 120 (September 1923), 350.

Ghéon, Henri. "*La Danse de Sophocle.*" *Nouvelle Revue Française,* September-October 1912, pp. 507–511.

Lacretelle, Jacques de. "*Le Grand Ecart.*" *Nouvelle Revue Française,* 118 (July 1923), 101–103.

Morand, Paul. "Spectacle-Concert." *Nouvelle Revue Française,* 74 (April 1920), 609–610.

Pourrat, Henri. "*Thomas l'Imposteur.*" *Nouvelle Revue Française,* 123 (December 1, 1923), 756–758.

Rivière, Jacques. "*Le Secret professionnel.*" *Nouvelle Revue Française,* 110 (November 1922), 631–633.

II

Books by André Gide

Ainsi soit-il ou Les Jeux sont faits. Paris: Gallimard, 1952.

Anthologie de la poésie française. Bibliothèque de la Pléiade. Paris: Gallimard, 1949.

Anthologie des poètes de la N.R.F. Paris: Gallimard, 1960.

Les Cahiers et les poésies d'André Walter. 14th ed. Paris: Gallimard, 1952.

Les Caves du Vatican (1914). Paris: Gallimard, 1951.

Correspondance André Gide–Roger Martin du Gard. 2 vols. Paris: Gallimard, 1968. Vol. I (1913–1934), with notes by Jean Delay. Vol. II (1935–1951).

Correspondance André Gide–Paul Valéry (1890–1942). Paris: Gallimard, 1955.

Et nunc manet in te, suivi de Journal intime. Paris and Neuchâtel: Ides et Calendes, 1951.

Les Faux-Monnayeurs. Paris: Gallimard, 1949.

Feuillets d'automne. Paris: Mercure de France, 1949.

L'Immoraliste. Paris: Mercure de France, 1951.

Incidences. Paris: Gallimard, 1951.

Journal des Faux-Monnayeurs (1926). Paris: Gallimard, 1967.

Journal, 1889–1939. Bibliothèque de la Pléiade. Paris: Gallimard, 1951.

Journal, 1939–1949; Souvenirs. Bibliothèque de la Pléiade. Paris: Gallimard, 1954.

The Journal of André Gide. Trans. with introd. Justin O'Brien. 4 vols. New York: Knopf, 1951.

In Jean Cocteau, *Lettres à André Gide avec quelques réponses d'André Gide.* Ed. Jean-Jacques Kihm. Paris: La Table Ronde, 1970.

Littérature engagée. Paris: Gallimard, 1950.

Pages de journal. Paris: Charlot, 1944.

Pretexts—Reflections on Literature and Morality. Selected, ed., introd., and partly trans. Justin O'Brien. New York: Delta Book, Dell, 1964.

Romans, récits et soties, œuvres lyriques. Bibliothèque de la Pléiade. Paris: Gallimard, 1958.

Si le grain ne meurt. Paris: Gallimard, 1966.

La Symphonie pastorale. Paris: Robert Léger, 1962.

La Symphonie pastorale. Text established by Claude Martin. Lettres Modernes. Paris: Minard, 1970.

Tableau de la littérature française. Préface par André Gide. Paris: Gallimard, 1962.

Théâtre. Paris: Gallimard, 1951.

Periodical Articles by André Gide

"Dada." *Nouvelle Revue Française,* 79 (April 1920), 477–481.

"Lettre à J.C. (non-envoyée)." *Nouvelle Revue Française,* 195 (December 1, 1929), 764–765.

"Lettre ouverte à Jean Cocteau." *Nouvelle Revue Française,* 63 (June 1919), 125–128.

"La Nouvelle Parade de Jean Cocteau." *Ecrits Nouveaux,* 22 (October 1919), 70–72.

IIe Entretien avec André Gide, ed. Amrouche, Jean. Recording for RTF. Paris: Discothèque de la ORTF, January–April 1949.

Unpublished Documents — Gide

Letters André Gide to Marc Allégret. Collection Marc Allégret, Paris.

Letters between André Gide and Jacques-Emile Blanche. Collection Georges Mévil-Blanche, Offranville, and Bibliothèque Littéraire Jacques Doucet, Paris.

Letters between André Gide and Countess Anna de Noailles. Courtesy of Professor Claude Martin, University of Saint-Etienne, France, and Bibliothèque Littéraire Jacques Doucet, Paris.

Letters between André Gide and Jacques Rivière. Collection Mme Jacques Rivière, Dourgne, and Bibliothèque Littéraire Jacques Doucet, Paris.

Unpublished passages from the journal of Claude Mauriac, Paris.

Books about André Gide

Arland, Marcel, and Mouton, Jean, eds. *Entretiens sur André Gide.* Paris: Mouton, 1967.

Brée, Germaine. *Gide.* New Brunswick: Rutgers University Press, 1965.

Combelle, Lucien. *Je dois à André Gide.* Paris: Frédéric Chambriand, 1951.

Cotnam, Jacques. *Essai de bibliographie chronologique des écrits d'André Gide.* Special printing for the Société des Amis d'André Gide, 1971.

Delay, Jean. *La Jeunesse d'André Gide.* Vocations series. Collection dirigée par Henri Mondor. 2 vols. Paris: Gallimard, 1959, 1963.

Derais, François, and Rambaud, Henri. *L'Envers du Journal de Gide.* Paris: Le Nouveau Portique, 1951.

Fowlie, Wallace. *André Gide: His Life and Art.* New York: Macmillan, 1965.

Guérard, Albert J. *André Gide.* New York: Dutton, 1963.

Herbart, Pierre. *À la recherche d'André Gide.* Paris: Gallimard, 1952.

——. *Souvenirs imaginaires suivis de La Nuit.* Paris: Gallimard, 1968.

——. *La Vie d'André Gide.* Avant-propos et commentaires par Pierre Herbart. Paris: Gallimard, 1955.

Hytier, Jean. *André Gide.* 1938 lectures at the University of Algiers. Garden City, N.Y.: Doubleday, 1962.

Index détaillé des quinze volumes de l'édition Gallimard des Œuvres complètes d'André Gide. Established by Justin O'Brien and his students at Columbia University, 1949.

Lambert, Jean. *Gide familier.* Paris: René Julliard, 1958.

Martin, Claude. *André Gide par lui-même.* Ecrivains de Toujours series. Paris: Editions du Seuil, 1967.

Martin du Gard, Roger. *Notes sur André Gide (1913–1951).* Paris: Gallimard, 1951.

Mauriac, Claude. *Conversations avec André Gide.* Paris: Albin Michel, 1951.

Naville, Arnold. *Bibliographie des écrits d'André Gide.* Paris: Matarasso, 1949.

O'Brien, Justin. *Portrait of André Gide: A Critical Biography.* New York, Knopf, 1953.

Painter, George D. *André Gide.* London: Cox and Wyman, 1968.

Pierre-Quint, Léon. *André Gide.* Paris: Stock, Delamain et Boutelleau, 1952.

Rossi, Vinio. *André Gide: The Evolution of an Aesthetic.* New Brunswick: Rutgers University Press, 1967.

Saint-Clair, M. *Galerie privée.* Paris: Gallimard, 1947.

Schlumberger, Jean. *Madeleine et André Gide.* Paris: Gallimard, 1956.

Stéphane, Roger, and Darbois, Roland. *André Gide.* Portrait Souvenir series. Film for ORTF. Paris: ORTF, 1964.

Periodical Articles about André Gide

Hommage à André Gide. Nouvelle Revue Française, November 1951. Special issue entirely devoted to Gide.

O'Brien, Justin. "*Paludes* et *Le Potomak.*" *Cahiers André Gide, I.* Paris: Gallimard, 1969. Pp. 265–282.

Stéphane, Roger. "Mes Rencontres avec André Gide." *Magazine Littéraire,* 14 (January 1968), 16.

III

General — Books

Arnheim, Rudolf. *Film as Art.* Berkeley and Los Angeles: University of California Press, 1966.

Brée, Germaine, and Guiton, Margaret. *An Age of Fiction.* New Brunswick: Rutgers University Press, 1957.

Breton, André. *Manifestes du Surréalisme.* Paris: Jean-Jacques Pauvert, 1962.

Campbell, Joseph. *The Hero with a Thousand Faces.* New York: Bollingen, 1949.

Capote, Truman. *Observations.* New York: Random House, 1959.

Emié, Louis. *Dialogues avec Max Jacob.* Paris: Corrêa, Buchet et Castel, 1954.

Fäy, Bernard. *Les Précieux.* Paris: Perrin, 1967.

Freud, Sigmund. *Three Contributions to the Theory of Sex.* Modern Library. New York: Random House, 1938.

Gabory, Georges. *Essai sur Marcel Proust.* Paris: Le Livre, 1926.

Jacob, Max. *Correspondance Max Jacob, 1876–1921* Ed. François Garnier. Vol. I. Paris: Editions de Paris, 1953.

Martin du Gard, Maurice. *Les Mémorables.* Paris: Flammarion, 1957.

Martin du Gard, Roger. *Devenir.* Paris: Nouvelle Revue Française, 1922.

Mauriac, François. *Nouveaux Mémoires intérieurs.* Paris: Flammarion, 1965.

Monnier, Adrienne. *Rue de l'Odéon.* Paris: Albin Michel, 1960.

Morand, Paul. *Monplaisir ...en littérature.* Paris: Gallimard, 1967.

Painter, George D. *Proust, the Later Years.* Boston: Little, Brown, 1965.

Peterson, Elmer. *Tristan Tzara: Dada and Surrational Theorist.* New Brunswick: Rutgers University Press, 1971.

Peyre, Henri. *The Contemporary French Novel.* New York: Oxford University Press, 1955.

Proust, Marcel, and Rivière, Jacques. *Correspondance Marcel Proust et Jacques Rivière, 1914–1922.* Ed. Philip Kolb. Paris: Plon, 1955.

Queneau, Raymond. *Pour une bibliothèque idéale.* Paris: Gallimard, 1956.

Sachs, Maurice. *La Décade des illusions.* Paris: Gallimard, 1950.

Sanouillet, Michel. *Dada à Paris.* Paris: Jean-Jacques Pauvert, 1965.

Schlumberger, Jean. *Œuvres.* Vol. IV. Paris: Gallimard, 1959.

―――. *Rencontres.* Paris: Gallimard, 1968.

Waldberg, Patrick. *Chemins du Surréalisme.* Brussels: Editions de la Connaissance, 1965.

General — Periodical Articles

"Avertissement." *Nouvelle Revue Française,* 1 (November 15, 1908), 1.

"Une lettre inédite de Marcel Proust à Jean Cocteau." *Le Figaro Littéraire,* October 19, 1963, p. 7.

Copeau, Jacques. "Un Essai de rénovation dramatique: Le Théâtre du Vieux-Colombier" *Nouvelle Revue Française,* 57 (September 1913), 337–353.

Rivière, Jacques. "De la sincérité envers soi-même." *Nouvelle Revue Française,* 37 (January 1912), 6.

Schlumberger, Jean. "Considérations." *Nouvelle Revue Française,* 1 (February 1909), 5–6.

Index

The text of this book was set in Baskerville Lino-film and printed by offset on RUP Special Book supplied by Lindenmeyr Paper Corporation, Long Island City, N.Y. Composed, printed and bound by Quinn & Boden Company, Inc., Rahway, N.J.